MW01267700

TEACHER'S HANDBOOK
TO THE LONGMAN
LATIN READERS

LONGMAN

Teacher's Handbook to the Longman Latin Readers

Copyright © 1988 by Longman. All rights reserved. No part of this publication may be reproduced, stored in a retrieval system, or transmitted in any form or by any means, electronic, mechanical, photocopying, recording, or otherwise, without prior permission from the publisher.

Longman, 95 Church Street, White Plains, NY 10601

Associated companies:
Longman Group Ltd., London
Longman Cheshire Pty., Melbourne
Longman Paul Pty., Auckland
Copp Clark Pitman, Toronto
Pitman Publishing Inc., New York

Authors: **Professor William S. Anderson,** University of California, Berkeley, California
Andrew C. Aronson, The Sidwell Friends School, Washington, DC
E. J. Barnes, C. W. Jefferys Secondary School, North York, Ontario, Canada
Professor Robert Boughner, Mary Washington College, Fredericksburg, Virginia
Professor Stephen G. Daitz, The City College and the Graduate School, City University of New York, New York, New York
Sally Davis, Wakefield High School, Arlington, Virginia
Mary Purnell Frederick, The Head-Royce School, Oakland, California
Jane Harriman Hall, Mary Washington College, Fredericksburg, Virginia
Professor Gilbert Lawall, University of Massachusetts, Amherst, Massachusetts
Professor Alexander G. McKay, McMaster University, Hamilton, Ontario, Canada
Professor John T. Ramsey, University of Illinois at Chicago, Chicago, Illinois
Professor Betty Nye Quinn, Mount Holyoke College, South Hadley, Massachusetts

Series Editor: **Professor Gilbert Lawall,** University of Massachusetts, Amherst, Massachusetts

Consultants: **Jane Harriman Hall,** Mary Washington College, Fredericksburg, Virginia
Richard A. LaFleur, University of Georgia, Athens, Georgia
Robert E. Morse, Saint Andrew's School, Boca Raton, Florida

Executive editor: Lyn McLean
Production editor: Elsa van Bergen
Text and cover designer: Gayle Jaeger
Production supervisor: Judith Stern

ISBN 0-582-36770-0

4 5 6 - CRC - 0201

Text Credits and Sources

All of the following are reprinted by permission of the publishers and the Loeb Classical Library, Cambridge, Massachusetts: Harvard University Press, unless indicated otherwise.

Pages 24, 24–25: From *Cicero, Letters to Atticus*, translated by E. O. Winstedt, © 1962. Page 25: From *Cicero, The Letters to His Brother Quintus*, translated by W. Glynn Williams, © 1972. Page 25: From *Lucretius, De Rerum Natura*, translated by W. H. D. Rouse and M. F. Smith, © 1975. Pages 25, 26, 27: From *Cicero, De Re Publica, De Legibus*, translated by Clinton Walker Keyes, © 1970. Page 28: From *Appian's Roman History*, translated by Horace White, © 1964. Page 29: From *Livy*, translated by Alfred C. Schlesinger, © 1959. Page 31: From *Cicero, De Senectute, De Amicitia, De Divinatione*, translated by William Armistead Falconer, © 1979. Pages 31–32: Reprinted by permission of Oxford University Press, from *The Dialogues of Plato*, translated by B. Jowett, © 1920. Page 32: From *Cicero, Tuscalan Disputations*, translated by J. E. King, © 1966. Page 32: From *Cicero, De Senectutue, De Amicitia, De Divinatione*, translated by William Armistead Falconer, © 1979. Page 32: From *Cicero, Vol. XIV*, translated by N. H. Watts, © 1979. Page 32: Reprinted by permission of Oxford University Press, from *The Dialogues of Plato*, translated by B. Jowett, © 1920. Page 32: From *Cicero, Tuscalan Disputations*, translated by J. E. King, © 1966. Page 33: From *Cicero, De Senectute, De Amicitia, De Divinatione*, translated by William Armistead Falconer, © 1979. Page 33: From *Cicero, De Natura Deorum, Academica*, translated by H. Rackham, © 1967. Page 33: From *Cicero, Tuscalan Disputations*, translated by J. E. King, © 1966. Page 33: From *Cicero, De Officiis*, translated by Walter Miller, © 1975. Page 34: From *Cicero, De Natura Deorum, Academica*, translated by H. Rackham, © 1967. Page 35: From *Ovid, Metamorphoses*, translated by Frank Justus Miller, © 1956. Page 36: Reprinted by permission of Oxford University Press, from *The Dialogues of Plato*, translated by B. Jowett, © 1920. Page 36: Reprinted by permission of Columbia University Press, from *Macrobius: Commentary on the Dream of Scipio*, translated by William H. Stahl, © 1952. Page 36: From *Aristotle, Vol. XV*, translated by W. S. Hett, © 1970. Pages 36–37: From *Lucian*, translated by A. M. Harmon, © 1953. Page 37: From *Sallust*, translated by J. C. Rolfe, © 1980. Page 37: Reprinted by permission of Oxford University Press, from *The Works of Aristotle*, translated into English under the editorship of W. D. Ross, © 1931. Page 37: From *Juvenal and Persius*, translated by G. G. Ramsay, © 1979. Page 38: Reprinted by permission of Oxford University Press, from *The Dialogues of Plato*, translated by B. Jowett, © 1920. Page 38: From *Cicero, De Re Publica, De Legibus*, translated by Clinton Walker Keyes, © 1970. Page 39: Reprinted by permission of Oxford University Press, from *The Dialogues of Plato*, translated by B. Jowett, © 1920. Page 40: From *Cicero, Tuscalan Disputations*, translated by J. E. King, © 1966. Page 40: Reprinted by permission of Columbia University Press, from *Macrobius: Commentary on the Dream of Scipio*, translated by William H. Stahl, © 1952.

TABLE OF CONTENTS

N.B.   See page 5 (bottom of first column and top of second) for an important note about the asterisks in the bibliographies in this handbook. See page 7, "Vocabulary," for an explanation of the use of asterisks in the vocabularies in the individual readers.

INTRODUCTION TO THE LONGMAN LATIN READERS

THE LITERARY DIMENSION OF THE ECCE ROMANI LATIN PROGRAM

The fundamental purposes of the ECCE ROMANI Latin course are to teach students to read Latin, to introduce them to some basic cultural patterns and structures in the ancient Roman world, and to improve their English language skills through knowledge of Latin and its pervasive influence on English. Throughout the materials assembled to achieve these purposes will be found much Latin literature. In adapting the ECCE ROMANI program for use in American and Canadian schools, the revision editors have attempted to give it a distinct literary orientation. There was already an emphasis on the rhetorical devices of literary style such as asyndeton, anaphora, and parallelism, and there were already passages from ancient authors in English translation to provide background to the discussion of cultural topics. In the revision more passages from ancient authors have been added, some in both Latin and English translation. Many of the **sententiae** come from literary sources. Extracts from the Latin poets have been added: for example, selections from Catullus and Horace (Book 2, page 71) and some of the **versiculī** (for example, number 21 at the end of Book 3 and several in Book 4). The focus on Vergil in the chapters on Roman education (35–37) provides an opportunity for teachers to bring in additional material on Rome's greatest poet and on his Homeric models, the *Iliad* and the *Odyssey*, and suggestions are made in the third teacher's handbook that the pictures on the wall at Cornelius' banquet in Chapter 31 be used as an opportunity for discussion of mythology and a reading of the myths from literary sources. The cultural background readings included at the back of the first four teacher's handbooks are drawn mostly from literary sources and will provide opportunities to introduce stu-dents to a variety of Roman authors of all periods. Teachers who use *The Romans Speak for Themselves I* and *II* as readers to accompany ECCE ROMANI 1–4 will be teaching passages of considerable literary merit from some of the most important Roman authors. Book 5, containing unadapted extracts from a variety of authors, will be found to provide opportunities for discussion of literary as well as cultural, political, and historical matters, especially in the extracts from Petronius, Cicero, Pliny, and Martial. The ECCE ROMANI program thus provides ample opportunity for introducing and discussing Latin literature alongside the basic teaching of reading skills, imparting of cultural awareness, and improvement of English language skills. For many useful suggestions on what, when, and how to teach Latin literature in the Latin program, see the "CAES Latin Teaching Handbook" titled *Literature*.

* * *

THE LONGMAN LATIN READERS

The next stage in the Longman Latin program is a series of six readers to be used after Book 5 or its equivalent in the Longman Latin program or after the basics have been covered with any other textbook series, either in high school or at the college/university level. The titles and editors of the readers are as follows:

1. *Cicero's Somnium Scipionis: The Dream of Scipio,* prepared by Sally Davis and Gilbert Lawall.
2. *Cicero and Sallust: On the Conspiracy of Catiline,* prepared by E. J. Barnes and John T. Ramsey.

3. *The Aulularia of Plautus: The Pot of Gold*, prepared by Gilbert Lawall and Betty Nye Quinn.
4. *Selections from Ovid's Metamorphoses*, prepared by William S. Anderson and Mary Purnell Frederick.
5. *Selections from Vergil's Aeneid Books I, IV, VI: Dido and Aeneas*, prepared by Jane Harriman Hall and Alexander G. McKay.
6. *Catullus and Horace: Selections from Their Lyric Poetry*, prepared by Andrew C. Aronson and Robert Boughner.

These readers are fairly uniform in format and each (with few exceptions) consists of the following:

1. An introduction on the author(s) and work(s) included in the reader.
2. The Latin selections arranged on right-hand pages, with each selection introduced by an English lead-in and accompanied at the bottom of the page by comprehension and study questions.
3. Running vocabulary and grammatical notes and questions on the facing, left-hand pages.
4. Background or comparative readings from other literature (in English translation).
5. Grammar review exercises based on the Latin in the reader.
6. A full Latin–English vocabulary.

The six student's books as described above are supported by this teacher's handbook. In addition to this Introduction, this handbook contains a section on how to teach students to read Latin poetry, a historical outline, and separate sections for each of the readers. The section on reading Latin poetry and the historical outline may be photocopied and shared with students. Each of the sections on the separate readers contains the following:

1. Historical and literary background.
2. Detailed and extensive teaching notes or essays on the material in the reader.
3. A literal translation of all of the Latin in the reader, to show exactly how the editors understand the Latin and to serve as an aid to the teacher.
4. A brief, annotated bibliography of books and articles that will be especially useful to the teacher, arranged alphabetically by title for easy reference to the content of the books and articles (note that we include the words *a* and *the* in the alphabetization and that we include the publisher's name, city, and state to help in ordering books that are in print). Asterisks mark books that are listed in the standard ref-

erence works as being in print at the time of publication of this handbook. Some of the other titles may also still be in print. Otherwise, they can be found in libraries.

While the readers themselves are each self-contained and may be taught in any sequence, we would recommend that they be read in the following order: the "Somnium Scipionis," the "Catiline," Plautus, Ovid, Vergil, and Catullus–Horace.

The "Somnium Scipionis" is an excellent sequel to ECCE ROMANI 5, which has Cicero at its center and introduces Roman political life of the late Republic and early Empire. The "Somnium" immediately captivates students with its vision of Scipio transported to the outer rim of the universe, standing "in a lofty place bathed in clear starlight," and gazing down first on the entire universe and finally onto the tiny planet earth. The instruction he there receives from his adoptive grandfather, the elder Scipio Africanus, seems to compress the entire sweep of ancient cosmological, geographical, political, social, ethical, moral, and philosophical thought into a coherent message of proper conduct for the individual within the context of society, state, and cosmos. There is something for every student in this thrilling, brief description of one of the most suggestive dreams ever dreamed in the ancient world.

The story of the conspiracy of Catiline has for centuries provided the most memorable and instructive introduction to the detailed workings of the Roman political system in the late Republic, and as such it remains unsurpassed. Instead, however, of subjecting our students at this level to the endless pages of Cicero's elaborate and highly rhetorical Catilinarian orations in a vacuum, we have chosen selections from Sallust's account of the conspiracy to serve as a basic framework within which excerpts from Cicero's orations are presented at the occasions on which they were delivered. Above all, the modern student wants the *story*, and "What happened next?" was the main concern of the editors in selecting passages for this book. It is an ideal sequel to the "Somnium Scipionis"; it reveals Cicero in action at the dramatic and gripping high point of his political career and thus balances the view of Cicero the contemplative in the "Somnium."

Next comes poetry. We recommend beginning with Plautus' *Aulularia*, partly because it is earliest chronologically and partly because it will present fewer problems as far as poetic language and word order are concerned. The archaic spellings have been eliminated from this version of the play, and we do not recommend that any attention be paid to the meters of Plautus at this stage in the students' study of Latin. Rather, we wish teachers to stress the *drama* of each scene as it unfolds and to take full advantage of reading the play aloud and acting it out. As with the "Catiline," the emphasis should be on "What happens next?" With that emphasis students will quickly be caught up in the drama of the play, the interaction and intrigue of the characters, and their distinct personalities which are portrayed with broad strokes and enhanced with subtle details. The study questions provided in the student's book and discussion questions provided in the teacher's handbook help teachers and students explore this play as a familial and social drama in which typical Roman values of frugality and self-interest are at first perverted, carried to extremes, and allowed to rend the familial and social fabric but are ultimately rectified so as to permit a happy ending, with wealth being properly used to cement a familial and social contract of marriage.

The selections from Ovid will provide an excellent introduction to the reading of Latin poetry with attention to metrics and all the artifices of style. Again, the primary focus of attention will be on the story, but the study questions for the students and the material in the teacher's handbook will allow the teacher to highlight something of the complexity of Ovid's genius as a narrator and lead students to appreciate his tantalizing blend of humor and seriousness. An ironic humor plays over the seemingly simple account of admirable piety in the story of Baucis and Philemon; Galatea's seemingly simplistic account of the Cyclops Polyphemus' love for her becomes a complex narrative in which she unwittingly reveals much about herself and a whole series of misunderstandings that love generates; and Narcissus and Pentheus are seen to share characteristics and actions that lead to their respective dooms in tales that echo and ironically reinforce one another by their juxtaposition. Themes of love and hate and of piety and impious arrogance weave in and out of these four tales and will provoke much discussion as the episodes are read in the sequence in which they are presented in this book.

There is no better introduction to Vergil's *Aeneid* than the love story of Dido and Aeneas, which may be lifted out of the larger fabric of the poem and enjoyed as a tale complete in itself with its own beginning, middle, and end. This is what has been done in our Vergil reader. Students will immediately recognize and identify with the character types represented by Aeneas and Dido, and the study questions and notes direct students and teachers to a deep appreciation of these two characters as fully rounded, complex human beings acting in and responding to events in the course of

their encounter—events that inevitably precipitate the tragic death of the queen and lead to the empty encounter of Aeneas with the shade of Dido in the underworld. There is opportunity here for lively discussion of the Roman character and Roman values and of parallels and contrasts with the ideals that we hold today. And, thanks to the notes and study questions in the student's book and the wealth of information in the teacher's handbook, discussion of these issues by students using this text will be firmly grounded in the *language* that Vergil uses and in a sensitive awareness of the whole array of literary devices that he employs.

Students coming from their reading of Vergil will be well prepared to continue with the greatest of Rome's lyric poets, Catullus and Horace. Absent is the strong story line of narrative to carry the reader forward, and instead we have short poems that are arresting for their combination of frank disclosure of personal feelings, desires, and reflections with an artistry and technique that create a certain aloofness and distance between the poet and his reader. Students will be attracted by Catullus' great feeling and personal intensity, and also by his lighter, playful moods, his sad memorials, and his invective and coarse ridicule heaped upon friends and enemies. Study of Horace brings us to the inauguration of the Augustan Age and to the concerns and reflections of a poet writing at this momentous transition from Republican to Imperial Rome. If some of the intimacy of Catullian lyric is lost, it is replaced by a fluidity and subtlety of verse unlike anything else in Latin and a philosophical and meditative strain that incorporates the best of the Epicurean philosophy into the Horatian ideal typified by a glass of wine in the company of friends, surrounded by the natural beauty of a simple country estate.

The Longman Latin readers thus range over the highlights of Latin literature from Plautus through the Republic to the Augustan Age. They present a number of different genres and present vivid images of both the men and the women of Roman history and poetic imagination. Of paramount importance is the gripping human interest of these masterworks of Latin literature; there is material here to attract students' immediate interest and to give them food for thought for a lifetime. The political, social, moral, and philosophical ideals of the Romans as presented in these works have since antiquity been touchstones against which successive ages of mankind have tested and measured themselves, and we must not allow the younger generations today to be ignorant of them. For many of our students the appreciation that we give them of the artistry and beauty of these works of ancient literature will be their first sustained encounter with the esthetic beauty of literary and poetic expression and their first full exploration of the unique power that words can have when crafted by the human mind into literary, rhetorical, and poetic form. Above all, our students' minds will be touched by the values embodied in these ancient works. Students will be challenged to think hard and critically about those values and to reflect on their own values and their own relation to others around them, to society, to the world, and to the cosmos within which they live.

* * *

TEACHING THE LONGMAN LATIN READERS

Vocabulary

The Longman Latin readers are designed to be used in the third, fourth, and fifth years of high school Latin and in intermediate Latin classes at the college level. While they contain many features that will be familiar to users of the ECCE ROMANI Latin program, they may be used after completion of any basic Latin program. We have tried to be especially helpful in the matter of vocabulary. We have assumed that students coming from any basic textbook series would be familiar with the words for the first and second years contained in Colby's *Latin Word Lists*. We accordingly do not include these words in the facing running vocabularies that are a special feature of this series. Words from Colby's lists for the first and second years that occur in each reader are, however, available to students in the end-vocabulary that accompanies each reader. Words not included in Colby's list for the first and second years are glossed in the facing vocabularies. If the word occurs more than once in the reader, it is marked in the facing vocabulary at its first occurrence with an asterisk, which indicates that the student should pay particular attention to the word at this time. These words will not be glossed again in the facing vocabularies, but they are available to students in the end-vocabulary, where they are also marked with asterisks. A few very common words, some compound verbs of obvious meaning, and some words that can easily be deduced are not included in the facing vocabularies even though they are not in Colby's lists for the first and second years. Students will, however, find these words in the end-vocabulary. This handling of the vocabulary makes the readers

suitable for use after completion of any basic Latin textbook series, and the readers may be used in any sequence, since the vocabulary is presented with the same assumptions in each reader.

Basic vocabulary entries on the left-hand pages are given in the form familiar from the ECCE ROMANI Latin course, with the principal parts of all verbs that are not completely regular being spelled out in full and the genitive singular of all third-declension nouns also spelled out in full. When a translation of a word or group of words as used in the particular context of the Latin passage is being given, the Latin word or words in boldface are followed by a colon, and the translation is put in quotation marks. This is done to distinguish these entries from regular vocabulary entries. In the end-vocabularies, in order to economize on space, all entries are given in the form in which they appear in the *Oxford Latin Dictionary*.

Grammar

The readers assume that the student is familiar with the basic morphology and syntax of Latin that is generally covered in the first two years of high school study (see, for example, the "Syllabus" of the National Latin Exam). Along with the facing vocabularies will be found notes and questions on grammatical constructions that are generally reserved for the third and fourth years of high school Latin study (see, again, the "Syllabus" of the National Latin Exam). The amount of attention given to grammar will depend largely on the discretion of the teacher; the notes facing the Latin text provide opportunities that teachers may handle as they wish. Some will pay only minimal attention to the details of syntax, while others will want their students to be sure they understand each construction thoroughly and will from time to time review and consolidate selected aspects of morphology and syntax. For these teachers, we provide at the end of four of the readers, and in this teacher's handbook for a fifth, grammar exercises and review materials based on the Latin texts in the individual readers and some sight-reading.

Comprehension, Translation, and Discussion

The method of teaching the Latin in these readers should not differ markedly from the methods used in teaching reading passages at earlier instructional levels. Accordingly, the following recommendations are based on recommendations for teaching reading passages in the ECCE ROMANI Latin program (see the first teacher's handbook, pages 6–7, and the fifth teacher's handbook, pages 4 and 24–25).

Before beginning any reading passage, the teacher should always be sure that the context is clear to the students. This is provided both by the Introduction to each reader and by the English lead-ins that precede each Latin passage. The content of the reading passage should be the focal point of class activities. The teacher should resist the temptation to make the readings exercises in sight translation or descriptive grammar, since this approach will only alienate and frustrate students. In general, the teacher should first guide students toward a comprehensive understanding of the text before requiring a literal translation. The Latin text should be read first in Latin, either by the teacher or by selected students, with careful attention to phrasing and to vocal identification of clauses and "sense units," in order to establish the general shape of the passage. After reading the passage in Latin, students may be asked to explore the text individually or in pairs or small groups, with the teacher circulating about the classroom and serving as a resource person. Or the text may be presented to the class as a whole, perhaps by means of an overhead projector, so that key words and grammatical constructions may be underlined and phrases and clauses bracketed or highlighted in colored markers. If the teacher chooses to explore the text in a "Socratic" question-and-answer fashion, the questions should be phrased so as to guide the students to a progressive understanding of the text. The teacher should avoid bogging the lesson down in grammatical explication during the preliminary reading of the text and should answer questions as directly as possible, without lengthy explanations. Whether general comprehension is arrived at through individual, group, or whole class activities, attention should be given to answering the questions provided beneath each segment of the text. These questions may be used orally or as the basis for written exercises, and they may be handled in class or assigned for homework. After the passage has been read in Latin and studied for general comprehension, then literal translation, oral or written, may be required of the students. Before making this assignment, the teacher may wish to spend some time on formal grammatical analysis, with special attention to the grammatical notes and questions in the notes facing the Latin passage.

Discussion of the subject matter of the text may begin with the questions provided below each passage. These are intended to focus attention on key matters of content and style and to stimulate thinking and sharing of opinions. The teacher should use these questions merely as guidelines and should let the discussion follow the interests of the students, rather than dictating direction or tempo. The teacher might request that students bring to the next class several questions of their own on the passage to pose to their classmates.

Teaching the Individual Readers

The six individual readers in this series are generally uniform in format, and the material for each reader in the teacher's handbook is fairly predictable. The following comments on each set of materials (student's book and teacher's handbook) may, however, prove of use in planning the teaching of the individual readers.

The "Somnium Scipionis"

The primary focus here will be on Cicero and his political thought, with emphasis on his debt to Greek philosophy. Along with many of the segments of the Latin text in the student's book there are passages in English translation from other works of Cicero and from other ancient authors (and one passage from a modern historian) for comparison with the segment of the Latin text. These provide background information and should aid discussion of key themes in the "Somnium." In the notes in the teacher's handbook will be found further useful background information for the teacher, especially on philosophical, astronomical, and geographical matters. Students should become quite familiar with the figures of Pythagoras, Plato, and Aristotle, with the Stoic and Epicurean philosophies, and with ancient conceptions of the cosmos and of terrestrial geography. A series of topics for students' reports is offered at the end of the Introduction to the material in this teacher's handbook on the "Somnium," and references for further reading on these topics are given in the Bibliography. The Passages for Comparison at the end of the student's book are to be read after completion of the Latin text and offer opportunities for comparing the views of Plato, Lucretius, Manilius, and Seneca with those of Cicero, especially on the nature of the soul and on life after death. An additional comparative reading, this one from Vergil, is provided at the end of the teaching notes in this handbook, and it can be read in both Latin and English translation after the students have read the "Somnium" and the translation of Plato's myth of Er. The grammar questions in the notes facing the Latin text in the student's book tend to focus on uses of the subjunctive in subordinate clauses, and these and other features of morphology and syntax are treated in the Exercises at the end of the student's book, which can usefully be tackled after completion of the reading of the "Somnium," as consolidation of key grammatical points. Students are introduced to several key stylistic terms in the notes facing the Latin text, and these are listed at the end of the Introduction to the material on the "Somnium" in this teacher's handbook.

The "Catiline"

The focus here is on political life in the late Republic, with the spotlight on Catiline and Cicero (background material in Introduction to student's book) and on the Sullan legacy and the political and economic conditions within which the conspiracy was hatched (material in Introduction to the teaching notes in this handbook). The selections from Sallust preserve the archaic features of his language. These are fully explained in the facing notes and will cause students no problems; they are catalogued for the teacher at the end of the Introduction to the material on the "Catiline" in this teacher's handbook. The grammatical explanations in the facing notes call particular attention to subordinate constructions and help students understand and visualize the precise relationships between words and clauses. The style of Sallust and that of Cicero are discussed briefly in the Introduction to the student's book, and Sallust's characteristic **brevitās** is discussed at the end of the Introduction to the material on the "Catiline" in this teacher's handbook. Numerous stylistic terms are introduced in the notes facing the text in the student's book, and these are defined and illustrated in a glossary in the student's book. (In all of the readers in the series, stylistic terms are set in italics at their first appearance in the notes.) The student's book also contains brief comments on the structure of Roman speeches, with identification of the parts of all six speeches contained in the volume. The Background Readings at the end of the student's book present the views of four modern historians on the motives of those involved in the conspiracy, the interests of Caesar and Crassus, and the unresolved historical problems. They should be read after completion of the Latin readings and are included as opportunities for further thought and discussion. There are four sets of exercises at the end of the student's book, to be done at intervals throughout the reading of the text; they emphasize subordinate constructions, manipulation of clauses, and prose composition. The teaching notes provide additional information on language, style, and historical background of direct use to the teacher in elucidating and discussing each segment of the text with students in class.

Plautus

Plautus' *Aulularia* provides an introduction to drama, ancient and more recent. It is significant as a work of the earliest Latin author of whom we have complete works extant and as an example of a Roman reworking of Greek material. The language of the play in the version given here has been adapted to eliminate most of the archaisms that students would find bothersome or troubling. Some distinctive features of the language have been left intact and are catalogued in the Introduction to the student's book and mentioned in the notes facing the Latin text. We do not recommend that any attention be paid to scansion and metrics (a very complex matter in Plautus' comedies), and in fact the adaptation of the language has occasionally resulted in loss of the metrical patterns. Rather, we urge that teachers approach the play as a living drama to be performed and acted out scene by scene in class with attention to expressive delivery of lines, staging, and the interaction among the characters. Reference is made to two short adaptations of the play that are suitable for memorization and performance for Latin clubs and on other occasions. The questions below the Latin text in the student's book are designed to pinpoint the basic content of the scenes and to clarify action and character. Additional questions are provided in the notes in the teacher's handbook to help the teacher in discussions of larger issues such as the motivation of the characters, the structure and movement of the drama, and the significance of the scenes and of the play as a whole. The exercises at the back of the student's book consist of sentences to translate from English to Latin and are to be done after the designated segments of the play are read. The sentences are based fairly closely on the text of the play itself, and students should not find them difficult. The Passages for Comparison at the end of the student's book offer extracts from Menander's *Dyskolos*, which presents many similarities to Plautus' *Aulularia*, and from Molière's *L'Avare*, which was based on Plautus' play. In the Introduction to the material on Plautus in this teacher's handbook will be found a fairly detailed outline of Menander's *Dyskolos* to enable the teacher to gain some appreciation of the similarities and differences between the Greek and the Latin plays. We recommend that the Passages for Comparison and detailed discussion of the relationships among the three plays be reserved until students have finished reading the *Aulularia*. Let them savor the full flavor of Plautus' play and make up their minds about it before drawing comparisons with the other plays. Ample time, however, should be budgeted for the latter, since students will enjoy seeing how Menander and Molière handled similar characters and situations. Comparison with Menander will prompt discussion of the larger issue of the relationship between Greek and Latin literature, which is touched on in the introductions to both the student's book and the material on Plautus in this handbook. In reading the *Aulularia*, students will become acutely aware of the pervasive influence of Greece and things Greek on the Romans of Plautus' time (especially notable is the large number of Greek words that Megadorus uses in his tirade against extravagant women). Students who have read the "Somnium Scipionis" will already be familiar with the debt of the Romans to the Greeks, and they will become even more familiar with it in the Ovid, Vergil, and lyric readers to follow. The formative influence of Greece on Rome and the distinctively Roman reworking of Greek models and rethinking of Greek ideas are themes that teachers can use to link together their students' experiences with the readers in this series.

Ovid

Two of the selections from Ovid offer further opportunities to compare Greek and Roman treatments of the same theme. To accompany Ovid's telling of the story of Acis, Galatea, and Polyphemus, we offer for comparison extracts from Homer's *Odyssey* and an *Idyll* of Theocritus, giving two distinctly different Greek views of the Cyclops Polyphemus; to accompany Ovid's telling of the story of Pentheus, we offer an extract from Euripides' *Bacchae*. When the Ovid book is taught, the Passages for Comparison should be read along with or immediately after each of the episodes in Latin is read. The Ovid reader brings us to the Augustan Age, which is the setting for the lives of two other authors in the Longman series, Vergil and Horace. The Augustan setting of Ovid's writing is treated in the introductions to both the student's book and the material on Ovid in this handbook. In the teaching of Ovid, attention should be focused, however, on the stories themselves and on how the author consciously and deliberately shapes them for his own purposes. This is the recurrent issue addressed in the questions that accompany the Latin text in the student's book, and this is the burden of the essays on the individual episodes that are included in the material on Ovid in this teacher's handbook. The teacher should be thoroughly familiar with the interpretations offered in these essays before teaching the episodes. Awareness of Ovid's unique shaping of the individual episodes will also be enhanced by the comparisons with other authors at the back of the student's

book: the Old Testament and Guillaume de Lorris in addition to Homer, Theocritus, and Euripides (mentioned above). The Ovid reader offers an introduction to the style, meter, and grammar of Augustan epic poetry. The material on Ovid in this handbook includes a detailed analysis of the style and meter of a selected passage and a review of Latin grammar as used by Ovid. This latter section may be photocopied and shared with your students.

Vergil

With Vergil we continue the focus on the Augustan Age and also the focus on the story and how the author shapes the action and reveals the nature and motivation of his characters. There are a number of passages for comparison at the back of the student's book, and these should be read carefully and discussed in conjunction with the relevant passages in the Latin text. They reveal Vergil's reshaping of Greek material, particularly from Homer and the Hellenistic epic poet Apollonius of Rhodes. The questions accompanying the Latin text call particular attention to poetic and rhetorical devices and invite students to ask themselves not only *what* is happening or being said but also *how* it is being described or being said. The notes in this teacher's handbook provide additional background and observations on the language and style and on the interpretation of character and motivation, to accompany each segment of the Latin text. The exercises at the back of the student's book are of various sorts and are to be done periodically throughout the reading of the text; they include two sight-reading passages with multiple choice questions similar to those that appear on the Advanced Placement Examination. The Vergil reader will provide teachers with a useful resource in teaching the Advanced Placement syllabus in Vergil.

Catullus–Horace

With the Catullus–Horace reader, students will be continuing their study of poetry (with a variety of new meters), and they will be bridging the Republic and the Augustan Age. They will be continuing to make comparisons between Greek and Latin writings (with the comparative passages presented now in conjunction with particular poems in the student's book instead of being gathered at the end of the book), and they will also be invited to evaluate English translations or adaptations. There is a continuing focus on poetic devices and on the relationship between the meter and the content. The questions in the student's book invite students to think carefully about what they are reading and to articulate their feelings about it—to become aware of many different things that the lyric poets are trying to do and say in their brief but meticulously crafted poems. The notes on the poems in the teacher's handbook offer general appreciations of the individual poems and help with some of the questions in the student's book.

The selections from Catullus and Horace in this Longman Latin reader include more than half of the poems on the Advanced Placement Catullus–Horace syllabus; the remaining poems on the syllabus will be available in a volume with a similar format forthcoming from *NECN* Publications. Taken together, the two volumes will provide an ideal foundation for the Advanced Placement lyric course.

* * *

BIBLIOGRAPHY

A.C.L./N.J.C.L. National Latin Exam: 1978– 1987. Available from ACL/NJCL National Latin Exam, PO Box 95, Mount Vernon, VA 22121. Contains the "Syllabus" on pages 15– 18.

Latin Word Lists: Years One through Four with English Meanings and Instructions in Latin Word Formation, by John K. Colby. Longman Inc., White Plains, NY, 1987. The vocabulary list used in determining what words to gloss in this series of readers.

Literature, by David J. Perry. "CAES Latin Teaching Handbook." The Classical Association of the Empire State, 1985. Available from David J. Perry, 130 Maple Avenue, Rye, NY 10580. Suggestions, sample lessons, and bibliography for the teaching of Latin literature at all levels of the Latin program.

Roman Civilization: Resources for Teaching the Culture of the Classical World, by Robert M. Costa. "CAES Latin Teaching Handbook." The Classical Association of the Empire State, 1987. Available from David J. Perry, 130 Maple Avenue, Rye, NY 10580. Extensive bibliography on Roman civilization for use by teachers and students at all levels of the Latin program.

Teacher's Guide to Advanced Placement Courses in Latin, by Vincent J. Cleary, Margaret Brucia, Sally R. Davis, David H. Porter, and Theodore W. Wells. Advanced Placement Program, The College Board, 1986. Available from Advanced Placement Program, CN6670, Princeton, NJ, 08541-6670. Contains descriptions of the Advanced Placement courses in Vergil and Catullus–Horace, with suggestions for teaching the syllabi. The entire 1987 Advanced Placement Latin Examination and Key may also be ordered from the Princeton address above.

THE PRONUNCIATION AND READING OF CLASSICAL LATIN

INTRODUCTION

This part of the teacher's handbook is based on material supplied by one of the authorities on the pronunciation and reading of classical Latin, Professor Stephen G. Daitz, The City College and the Graduate School, City University of New York. He is the author of a cassette recording and accompanying booklet entitled *The Pronunciation and Reading of Classical Latin: A Practical Guide.* This recording and booklet explain in greater detail and demonstrate the method of reading Latin described below, and teachers interested in learning and applying this method will find it helpful to acquire them (see the Bibliography at the end of this section). This part of the teacher's handbook may be photocopied and distributed to students.

Scholars all agree that the works of classical Latin literature were composed to be read aloud and listened to rather than to be read silently. Latin literature was therefore essentially an *oral* phenomenon. Although Latin is, of course, an ancient language with no surviving native speakers, we are fortunate to possess much information concerning the actual pronunciation of classical Latin.

Our sources of information range from the writings of ancient Roman grammarians and rhetoricians, who often give precise descriptions of various aspects of classical pronunciation, to the research of modern linguists based upon comparative study of other Indo-European languages, including the descendants of Latin, the Romance languages. As a result, linguists all over the world are today in general agreement about the pronunciation of classical Latin (see *Vox Latina: The Pronunciation of Classical Latin*). By applying the results of linguistic research, we can achieve a "restored" pronunciation in our reading of Latin that will give us a good approximation of the sounds of Latin spoken and heard in the first century B.C. and first century A.D. in Rome.

The restored pronunciation of classical Latin is not difficult to learn, and its use can offer several advantages to teachers and students. First, we will have the intellectual satisfaction of knowing that our pronunciation and reading are historically and linguistically correct. Second, we will have the esthetic satisfaction of coming closer to the real sounds of Latin literature. A poem will begin to *sound* like a poem with its unique combination of vowels, consonants, and rhythm, each element falling into place and combining into an artistic whole. Teachers and students will simply derive greater pleasure from the reading of Latin. Third, since form and meaning are entirely interdependent in a work of art, an increased and accurate awareness of the form (including the sounds) of a work of Latin literature will inevitably augment the total understanding of the work.

The most practical way for teachers to use the restored pronunciation is first to practice it until its use becomes comfortable and then to use it consistently in class from the very beginning of Latin instruction. If possible, its introduction should be accompanied by a brief explanation to the students of how we know how classical Latin was pronounced and of why it is important to pronounce and read the Latin in as authentic a manner as possible.

* * *

BASIC PRINCIPLES

Pronunciation

Most consonants are pronounced as in English, but the following differences should be noted:

b before **s** or **t** is pronounced like English *p*: ur<u>b</u>s, o<u>b</u>tineō.
c is always hard and pronounced like English *k*: <u>c</u>ibus.
g is always hard, as in English "get": **gemit**.
gn in the middle of a word is pronounced like the *ngn* in English "hangnail": **ma<u>gn</u>us**.
m at the end of a word is nasalized with lips apart, as in French "ca<u>mp</u>" (phonetically kā): **puella<u>m</u>** (phonetically puellā).
r should be rolled (trilled): <u>r</u>āmus.
s is pronounced as in English "<u>s</u>ing," never as in "ro<u>s</u>es": cīvi<u>s</u>.
v is pronounced like English *w:* <u>v</u>īlla.

Double consonants, such as **mm, ll, pp,** and **tt,** should be held approximately twice as long as the single consonant.

The following approximations are offered for the pronunciation of short and long vowels. Long vowels should be held approximately twice as long as short vowels. The symbol ˘ over a vowel indicates a short vowel, and the symbol ¯ indicates a long vowel. In the texts of this series, when a macron (long mark) is not found over a vowel, the vowel is short. Careful observation of the macrons over the vowels will help with both the pronunciation and the accentuation of Latin words.

SHORT VOWELS
ă = English "t<u>o</u>p" (p<u>a</u>ter)
ĕ = English "p<u>e</u>t" (<u>e</u>go)
ĭ = English "s<u>i</u>p" (<u>i</u>terum)
ŏ = English "b<u>u</u>t" (<u>o</u>mnis)
ŭ = English "f<u>oo</u>t" (<u>u</u>bi)

LONG VOWELS
ā = English "f<u>a</u>ther" (m<u>ā</u>ter)
ē = English "th<u>ey</u>" (v<u>ē</u>rus)
ī = English "mach<u>i</u>ne" (<u>ī</u>ra)
ō = English "h<u>o</u>ly" (c<u>ō</u>nsul)
ū = English "b<u>oo</u>t" (<u>ū</u>nus)

The diphthong **ae** is pronounced like the *y* in English "sk<u>y</u>" (<u>ae</u>quus).
The diphthong **au** is pronounced like the *ow* in English "h<u>ow</u>" (<u>au</u>dit).
The diphthong **ei** is pronounced like the *ay* in English "s<u>ay</u>" (d<u>ei</u>nde).

Classical Latin Accentuation

1. Terminology. In a word of three or more syllables, the last syllable is generally referred to as the *ultima*, the next to the last as the *penult*, and the syllable immediately preceding the penult as the *antepenult*. Thus in the word **cōgitō**, the syllable -tō is the *ultima*, the syllable -gi- is the *penult*, and the syllable cō- is the *antepenult*.
2. If a Latin word has only *two* syllables, the accent is always on the *penult*; e.g., **púer**.
3. In a Latin word of three or more syllables, if the *penult* is a *long* syllable, *it* receives the accent.
4. In a Latin word of three or more syllables, if the *penult* is a *short* syllable, it is the *antepenult* that receives the accent.

Examples of *long* penult (accent on penult):

fortúna, antíquus, cōnsérvō, puélla

Examples of *short* penult (accent on antepenult):

cógĭtō, vídĕō, pátrĭa, ígĭtur

The symbols - and ˅ , which were previously used to designate *vowel* length, are used in the examples above and in the remainder of this material to designate *syllabic* quantity, i.e., to indicate whether a *syllable* is long or short. As we shall see from the rules of syllabic quantity, a short *vowel* does not necessarily mean a short *syllable*. Some scholars prefer the designations "heavy" and "light" to those of "long" and "short" when speaking of syllables. Although the use of the terms "heavy" and "light" does avoid ambiguity by distinguishing between vowel length and syllabic quantity, these two terms nevertheless have for users of American English connotations of stress and lack of stress that could cause confusion in the oral rendition of Latin poetry. Accordingly, the traditional terms "long" and "short" are retained here when we are speaking of syllables, for reasons of greater effectiveness in teaching the reading of Latin poetry aloud.

Rules to Determine Syllabic Quantity

1. A syllable may be classified as long either by *nature* or by *position*.
2. A syllable is classified as long by *nature* if it contains any one of the long vowels or any diphthong. This syllable is said to be long by the *nature* of its vowel or diphthong.
3. A syllable is classified as long by *position* if it contains any one of the *short* vowels that is then followed by at least *two* successive consonants (even if the consonants are in different words). This syllable is said to be long by the *position* of its vowel in front of two or more consonants. Note that the letters **x** and **z** count as double consonants and **qu** as a single consonant, while **h** is not here regarded as a consonant. A syllable containing final, nasalized **m** is also considered long.
4. If a syllable does not qualify as long either by nature or by position, it is classified as short.

Exceptions to the General Rules of Syllabic Quantity

A combination of a plosive consonant (**p, b, c, g, t,** or **d**) plus a liquid consonant (**l** or **r**) may or may not "make position," i.e., the syllable preceding such a combination may theoretically be classified as either long or short. (Such a syllable is indicated by the symbol ⨯ .) Thus we may read the word **patris** either as **pāt-ris** (long penult) or as **pă-tris** (short penult). Note that in **pāt-ris** the penult is a closed syllable (closed by the **t**), while in **pă-tris** the penult is an open syllable with the **t** initiating the following syllable. (A closed syllable ends with a consonant, and an open syllable ends with a vowel.) Latin poetry has examples of the same syllable classified as both long and short in the very same verse; e.g., Vergil, *Aeneid* II.663 **pă-tris, pāt-rem,** and Ovid, *Metamorphoses* XIII.617 **volŭ-crī, volūc-ris**.

* * *

DACTYLIC HEXAMETER

Scansion and Reading of the Dactylic Hexameter

1. A dactyl = one long syllable + two short syllables = - ˅ ˅
2. A spondee = two long syllables = - -
3. A trochee = one long syllable + one short syllable = - ˅
4. A dactylic hexameter with the maximum number of dactyls = five dactyls + one spondee or one trochee =

```
  1     2     3     4     5     6
- ˅ ˅ | - ˅ ˅ | - ˅ ˅ | - ˅ ˅ | - ˅ ˅ | - ⨯
```

Spondees may be substituted for dactyls in the first five feet, but the substitution of a spondee in the fifth foot is rare.

5. The full metrical scheme of the dactylic hexameter, including possible substitutions of spondees for dactyls, is:

   1   2   3   4   5   6
   – ⏑⏑ | – ⏑⏑ | – ⏑⏑ |– ⏑⏑ | – ⏑⏑ | – ⏑

6. Elision. In the reading of Latin poetry, when a word ending in a vowel, diphthong, or **m** was followed by a word beginning with a vowel, diphthong, or **h** within a single verse (e.g., **multum ille**), the final syllable of the first word and the first syllable of the second word were usually so pronounced as to produce one combined syllable rather than two separate syllables. This effect of metrical shortening is generally referred to as *elision*. In the specimen texts it is indicated by the symbol ‿. In the case of elision of short vowels (e.g., **atquĕ‿altae**), the elided vowel was probably not sounded at all (**atqualtae**). In the case of long vowels, diphthongs, and final **m**, there was probably enough of the elided letters sounded to suggest their original identity. Thus:

> **prōmīsī ultōrem > prōmīsyultōrem**
> **Jūnō aeternum > Jūnwaeternum**
> **multum ille > multw̃ille** (w̃: the nasalization with the lips apart starts with the w and carries into the i)

Reading Vergil, *Aeneid* I.1–7 (Dactylic Hexameter)

Here is the passage with no metrical markings:

> Arma virumque canō, Trōiae quī prīmus ab ōrīs
> Ītaliam fātō profugus Lāvīniaque vēnit
> lītora, multum ille et terrīs iactātus et altō
> vī superum, saevae memorem Iūnōnis ob īram,
> multa quoque et bellō passus, dum conderet urbem
> īnferretque deōs Latiō; genus unde Latīnum
> Albānīque patrēs atque altae moenia Rōmae.

Note that **Trō-iae** is pronounced as two syllables and that **Lā-vīn-ia-que** is pronounced as four.

Stage 1. Rhythm *without* words (chanted on la la . . . , keeping stress *equal* on all syllables):

> lā lă lă | lā lă lă | lā lā | lā lā | lā lă lă | lā lā
> etc.

Stage 2. Rhythm *with* words (chanted, keeping stress *equal* on all syllables):

> Ārmă vĭ | rūmquĕ că | nō Trō | iāe quī | prīmŭs ăb | ōrīs

> Ītălĭ | ām fā | tō prŏfŭ | gūs Lā | vīniăquĕ | vēnĭt

> lītŏră | mūltum‿ĭl | le‿ēt tēr | rīs iăc | tātŭs ĕt | āltō

> vī sŭpĕ | rūm sāe | vāe mĕmŏ | rēm Iū | nōnĭs ŏb | īrām

> mūltă quŏ | que‿ēt bēl | lō pās | sŭs dūm | cōndĕrĕt | ūrbēm

> īnfĕr | rētquĕ dĕ | ōs Lătĭ | ō gĕnŭs | ūndĕ Lă | tīnūm

> Ālbā | nīqĕ pă | trēs āt | que‿āltāe | mōenĭă | Rōmāe.

Stage 3. Rhythm + words + accents (chanted; accented syllables stressed):

> Ármă vĭ | rúmquĕ că | nō Tró | iāe quī | prímŭs ăb | órīs

Ītálĭ | ām fắ | tō prŏ́fŭ | gūs Lā | víniǎquě | vénĭt

lítŏră | mūltum_ĭl | le_ēt tér | rīs iāc | tátŭs ět | áltō

vī sŭ́pě | rūm saé | vae mĕ́mŏ | rēm Iū | nónĭs ŏb | íram

múltă quŏ́ | que_ēt bél | lō pás | sūs dūm | cónděrět | úrbēm

īnfēr | rétquě dě́ | ōs Látĭ | ō gĕ́nŭs | úndě Lă | tínūm

Ālbā | níquě pắ | trēs át | que_áltae | móenĭă | Rṓmae.

Stage 4. Rhythm + words + accents (*spoken* tones)

Stage 5. = Stage 4 + phrasing and intonation

N.B. For the sake of simplicity, it is suggested that *all* elided syllables be omitted at stages 2, 3, and 4.

Reading Ovid, *Metamorphoses* I.1–4 (Dactylic Hexameter)

We have used the first seven lines of the *Aeneid* as an example because these lines will be familiar to all Latin teachers; we recommend that these lines be used for teaching the hexameter to students who will be reading the selections from Vergil as their first encounter with the hexameter. Study, discussion, recitation, and memorization of these lines will serve as an excellent introduction to the selections from the *Aeneid* contained in the reader. For those students who will be reading the selections from Ovid's *Metamorphoses* as their first encounter with the hexameter, we recommend using the first four lines of that poem instead:

In nova fert animus mūtātās dīcere fōrmās
corpora: dī, coeptīs—nam vōs mūtāstis et illa—
adspīrāte meīs prīmāque ab orīgine mundī
ad mea perpetuum dēdūcite tempora carmen!

Stage 3. Rhythm + words + accents (chanted; accented syllables stressed):

Ĭn nŏ́vă | fērt ắnĭ | mūs mū | tátās | dícěrě | fṓrmās

cŏ́rpŏră: | dī, cŏ́ep | tīs—nām | vōs mū | tástĭs ět | íllă—

ādspī | rátě mĕ́ | īs prī | máque_ăb ŏ | rígĭně | múndī

ād mĕ́ă | pērpĕ́tŭ | ūm dē | dúcĭtě | témpŏră | cárměn!

(Note that we include the punctuation here, whereas with the first seven lines of the *Aeneid* above the punctuation was omitted for the sake of simplicity in viewing the metrical patterns.)

A caesura (word-end within a metrical foot, sometimes coinciding with a pause in the sense) may occur in the second, third, or fourth foot of the dactylic hexameter line; an effective caesura occurs after the word **coeptīs** in the second line of the passage from Ovid above. An effective diaeresis (word-end between metrical feet, sometimes coinciding with a pause in the sense) occurs after the word **corpora** in the same line.

* * *

OTHER METERS

Once the above method for reading the dactylic hexameter has been acquired, the same method, with the same stages, can be easily applied to the other meters of Latin poetry. Examples are given here of the other meters that students will encounter in the Catullus–Horace reader. The sample verses are taken from the first poem that utilizes the particular meter.

Hendecasyllabic

Metrical scheme:

    – – – ◡ ◡ – ◡ – ◡ – ⏓
    – ◡
    ◡ –

Note the substitutions that are possible at the beginning of the line, and note the choriamb (– ◡ ◡ –). Here and with most of the other lyric meters discussed below we do not divide the lines into feet. For more technical discussion and analysis of lyric meters, see *The Meters of Greek and Latin Poetry*.

Stage 1. Rhythm *without* words (chanted on la la . . .)
Stage 2. Rhythm *with* words (chanted)
Stage 3. Rhythm + words + accents (chanted)

As an example, we give the opening lines of the first poem in the Catullus–Horace reader (Catullus 5.1–6):

Vīvámūs, mĕă Lésbĭa̲ātque̲ămémŭs,

rūmōrésquĕ sénūm sĕvērĭórūm

ómnēs únĭŭs āestĭmémŭs ássĭs!

Sólēs óccĭdĕre̲ēt rĕdírĕ póssūnt;

nóbīs cūm sĕmĕl óccĭdīt brévīs lūx,

nōx ēst pērpétŭa̲ūnă dōrmĭéndă.

Stage 4. Rhythm + words + accents (*spoken* tones)

Stage 5. = Stage 4 + phrasing and interpretation

Again, for the sake of simplicity, it is suggested that *all* elided syllables be omitted at stages 2, 3, and 4.

Choliambic

The choliambic meter is based on the iambic trimeter (three pairs of iambic measures):

    ⏓ – | ◡ – | ⏓ – | ◡ – | ⏓ – | ◡ ⏓

In the choliambic (Greek for "limping iambic") meter, the next to the last syllable is long instead of short, thus producing the limping effect.

Metrical scheme of the choliambic:

ᵛ – | ᵕ – | ᵛ – | ᵕ – | ᵕ – | – ᵛ

Sample (Catullus 8.1–2):

Mísēr | Cătúl l lĕ, dé | sĭnās | ĭnēp | tĭrĕ,

ēt quōd | vĭdēs | pĕrĭs | sĕ pér | dĭtūm | dúcās.

Sapphic Strophe

Metrical scheme:

(three lines)   – ᵕ – – – ‖ ᵕ ᵕ – ᵕ – ᵛ
(one line)   – ᵕ ᵕ – ᵛ

The double vertical lines mark a caesura, which normally falls after the fifth syllable in the first three lines (although it occurs in only one line of the following sample).

Sample (Catullus 51.1–4):

Íllĕ mī pār éssĕ déō vĭdétŭr,

íllĕ, sī fās ēst, ‖ sŭpĕrárĕ dĭvōs,

quī sédēns ādvérsŭs ĭdéntĭdēm tē

spéctăt ĕt aúdĭt

Elegiac Couplet

Metrical scheme:

Hexameter: – ≈ | – ≈ | – ≈ | – ≈ | – ≈ | – ᵛ
Pentameter: – ≈ | – ≈ | – ‖ – ᵕ ᵕ | – ᵕ ᵕ | ᵛ

The elegiac couplet may be described as a dactylic hexameter followed by a dactylic pentameter. The spondee in the fifth foot of the hexameter is rare. In the pentameter, the second half of the third foot and the second half of the sixth foot of a hexameter have been truncated, thus giving two sets of two and a half feet (= five feet or a pentameter). A diaeresis (here frequently coinciding with a pause in the sense) normally occurs after the third foot of the pentameter (marked here with double vertical lines).

Sample (Catullus 70.1–2):

Núllī | sē dí | cīt múlĭ | ēr méă | núbĕrĕ | mállĕ

quăm mĭhĭ, | nōn sī | sē ‖ Iúppĭtĕr | ípsĕ pé | tăt.

Second Asclepiadean

Metrical scheme:

Glyconic: − − − ⏑ − ⏑ ⏓

Asclepiadean: − − − ⏑ ⏑ − ‖ − ⏑ ⏑ − ⏑ ⏓

Note the choriambs (− ⏑ ⏑ −).

Sample (Horace *Odes* I.3.1–2):

     Sīc tē dīvă pŏtēns Cȳprī,

         sīc frátrēs Hélĕnāe, ‖ lúcĭdă sídĕră

Fourth Asclepiadean

Metrical scheme:

Asclepiadean (two lines):   − − − ⏑ ⏑ − ‖ − ⏑ ⏑ − ⏑ ⏓

Pherecratean: − − − ⏑ ⏑ − ⏓

Glyconic: − − − ⏑ ⏑ − ⏑ ⏓

Sample (Horace *Odes* I.5.1–4):

     Quīs múltā grácĭlīs ‖ tē púĕr īn rósā

     pērfúsūs líquĭdīs ‖ úrgĕt ŏdórĭbŭs

         grátō, Pȳrrhă, sŭb ántrō?

            Cuī flávām rélĭgās cómām,

Alcaic Strophe

Metrical scheme:

(two lines)   ⏓ − ⏑ − − ‖ − ⏑ ⏑ − ⏑ ⏓

            ⏓ − ⏑ − − − ⏑ − ⏓

              − ⏑ ⏑ − ⏑ ⏑ − ⏑ − ⏓

Sample (Horace *Odes* I.9.1–4):

     Vídēs ŭt áltā ‖ stēt nívĕ cándĭdūm

     Sóráctĕ, nēc iām ‖ sūstínĕānt ónŭs

         sílvāe lăbōrántēs, gĕlúquĕ

            flúmĭnă cōnstítĕrīnt ăcútō.

Fifth Asclepiadean

A choriamb (− ⏑ ⏑ −) is added to the asclepiadean line as shown in the patterns of the second and fourth asclepiadeans above.

Metrical scheme:

     − − − ⏑ ⏑ − ‖ − ⏑ ⏑ − ‖ − ⏑ ⏑ − ⏑ ⏓

Sample (Horace *Odes* I.11.1):

Tū nē quaēsíěrīs, ‖ scírě néfās, ‖ quēm míhǐ, quēm tíbǐ

First Asclepiadean

Metrical scheme:

− − − ∪ ∪ − ‖ − ∪ ∪ − ∪ ⏓

Sample (Horace *Odes* III.30.1):

Ēxégī mǒnǔméntum‿āerě pěrénnǐǔs

Second Archilochean

Metrical scheme:

− ⏓ │ − ⏓ │ − ⏓ │ − ⏓ │ − ⏓ │ − ⏓
    − ∪ ∪ │ − ∪ ∪ │ ⏓

Note the similarities to the elegiac couplet.

Sample (Horace *Odes* IV.7.1–2):

Dīffū │ gérě nī │ vēs, rédě │ ūnt iām │ grámǐnǎ │ cámpīs

ārbǒrǐ │ búsquě có │ mae

Three Hints for Reading Latin Aloud

1. Try to avoid *lengthening* a short accented syllable. For example, in the words **cánō** and **pátrēs**, keep the accented syllables *short*.
2. Try to avoid *shortening* a long *unaccented* syllable. For example, in the words **mūnītíssimus** and **īnfērrétque**, keep the first two syllables of each word *long*. Likewise, in the words **órīs** and **áltō**, keep the last syllable *long*.
3. Latin prose should be read aloud with the same pronunciation of vowels and consonants, the same accentuation, and the same observation of syllabic quantity as in the reading of poetry. There is no indication from any ancient source that the basic principles for the reading of prose were in any way different from those of poetry.

* * *

BIBLIOGRAPHY

**The Meters of Greek and Latin Poetry*, by J. W. Halporn, M. Ostwald, and T. G. Rosenmeyer. University of Oklahoma Press, Norman, OK, revised ed., 1980.

**The Pronunciation and Reading of Classical Latin: A Practical Guide*, by Stephen G. Daitz. "The Living Voice of Greek and Latin Literature" series. Two cassettes and booklet. Jeffrey Norton Publishers, Inc., Guilford, CT, and London, 1984. Available from Audio Forum, On the Green, Guilford, CT 06437.

**Vox Latina: The Pronunciation of Classical Latin*, by W. Sidney Allen. Cambridge University Press, Cambridge and New York, NY, 2nd ed., 1978. An authoritative discussion of the pronunciation of classical Latin and of the evidence of how it was pronounced.

HISTORICAL OUTLINE

			B.C.	
			1184	Traditional date of the Trojan War
			814	Traditional foundation date for Carthage by Phoenicians
			753	Traditional foundation date for Rome
ca.	750	–	650	Homer; composes the *Iliad* and the *Odyssey*
ca.			700	Hesiod; composes the *Works and Days* and the *Theogony*
ca.			620	Birth of Alcaeus of Lesbos, lyric poet
ca.			612	Birth of Sappho of Lesbos, lyric poet
			509	Founding of the Roman Republic
ca.	485	–	406	Euripides, Greek tragic poet (*Bacchae*)
ca.	460	–	400	Thucydides; writes history of the Peloponnesian War
ca.	450	–	385	Aristophanes; Old Comedy
ca.	429	–	347	Plato, Greek philosopher
	384	–	322	Aristotle, Greek philosopher
ca.	342	–	289	Menander; New Comedy
	341	–	270	Epicurus, founder of the Epicurean school of philosophy
	335	–	263	Zeno, founder of the Stoic school of philosophy
			323	Death of Alexander the Great
ca.	305	–	240	Callimachus, author of the *Aetia* and other poems
ca.	300	–	260	Theocritus, author of pastoral poems
ca.	295	–	?	Apollonius Rhodius, author of the *Argonautica*
	264	–	241	First Punic War: Rome versus Carthage
ca.	254	–	184	**TITUS MACCIUS PLAUTUS**
			240	Livius Andronicus produces play in Rome
	236	–	183	Publius Cornelius Scipio Africanus Major (known as the elder Scipio or Scipio Africanus)
			235	Gnaeus Naevius active as playwright in Rome
	234	–	149	Cato the Elder
	218	–	201	Second Punic War; Hannibalic occupation of Italy (218–203)
			216	Battle of Cannae (Apulia), Rome's worst military disaster
			202	Scipio Africanus defeats Hannibal at Zama (North Africa)
	185	–	129	Publius Cornelius Scipio Aemilianus (Scipio Africanus Minor, the younger Scipio)
	149	–	146	Third Punic War; destruction of Carthage by Scipio Africanus Minor
ca.	138	–	78	Lucius Cornelius Sulla
			133	Tiberius Gracchus tribune; proposes agrarian reform
			129	Setting of "Somnium Scipionis"; death of Scipio Africanus Minor
	123	–	122	Gaius Gracchus, tribune
	106	–	48	Gnaeus Pompey, the Great
	106	–	43	**MARCUS TULLIUS CICERO**
	100	–	44	Gaius Julius Caesar
	94	–	55	Lucretius, author of the *De rerum natura*
ca.	86	–	35	**GAIUS SALLUSTIUS CRISPUS** (Sallust), author of the *Bellum Catilinae*
ca.	84	–	54	**GAIUS VALERIUS CATULLUS**, lyric poet, of Verona

	82	– 79	Sulla's dictatorship and reforms designed to strengthen the power of the Senate
ca.	82	– 30	Marcus Antonius (Mark Antony, the Triumvir)
		70	First consulship of Pompey and Crassus
	70	– 19	**PUBLIUS VERGILIUS MARO** (Vergil; born 15 October)
	67	– 66	Pompey's war with the pirates
	65	– 8	**QUINTUS HORATIUS FLACCUS**, of Venusia
		63	Consulship of Marcus Tullius Cicero; Catilinarian conspiracy; birth of Gaius Octavius, later Augustus (63 B.C.–A.D. 14)
		60	First Triumvirate: Caesar, Pompey, and Crassus
		59	Caesar consul
	58	– 50	Caesar in Gaul and Britain (55, 54)
		58	Cicero's exile in Macedonia
		57	Catullus in Bithynia; Cicero recalled from exile
		55	Second consulship of Pompey and Crassus
	54	– 51	Cicero writes the *De republica* (including the "Somnium Scipionis")
		49	Caesar crosses Rubicon (11 January); civil war; Caesar reaches Rome in April; Vergil leaves Rome for Naples and the Garden (Epicurean School) of Siro
		48	Pompey defeated at Pharsalus (Thessaly), murdered in Egypt
		46	Pompeians defeated in Africa; suicide of Cato at Utica
ca.		46	Horace goes to Athens to study philosophy
	46	– 44	Dictatorship of Julius Caesar
		44	Assassination of Caesar (15 March)
	44	– 35	Sallust writes histories (including the *Bellum Catilinae*)
		43	Birth of **PUBLIUS OVIDIUS NASO** (Ovid; 43 B.C.–A.D. 17)
		43	Formation of the Second Triumvirate: Antony, Lepidus, and Octavian
		42	Battle of Philippi (Macedonia); deaths of Brutus and Cassius
	42	– 37	Vergil composes his ten *Bucolics* (*Eclogues*)
		41	Horace returns to Rome and becomes a quaestor's clerk
	41	– 40	Octavian distributes land to veterans; Vergil and Horace lose their estates
		39	Horace introduced to Maecenas
		37	Treaty of Tarentum (Octavian and Mark Antony); Vergil composes *Eclogue* X and publishes the collection and begins his verse treatise on agriculture (*Georgics*)
	36	– 32	Antony in the East; marries Cleopatra VII
		31	Battle of Actium (September); defeat of Antony and Cleopatra
		30	Octavian in Egypt; suicides of Antony and Cleopatra; Rome annexes Egypt
		29	Vergil publishes the *Georgics* and plans the *Aeneid*; Octavian celebrates triple triumph over Dalmatia (35–34), Actium (31), and Egypt (30)
		27	Octavian receives title of Augustus and reorganizes the Roman state
		23	Establishment of the Augustan Principate; Augustus rules with tribunician power and proconsular **imperium**; Vergil reads *Aeneid* II, IV, and VI to Augustus and his sister Octavia; Horace publishes Books I–III of *Odes*
		19	Vergil leaves for Greece and Asia Minor to refine his epic and to resume his philosophical studies; contracts illness in Greece and dies after landing at Brundisium in Italy (21 September, 19 B.C.); *Aeneid* published posthumously by Varius and Plotius Tucca; Ovid publishes *Amores*
		13	Horace publishes Book IV of *Odes*
ca.	4		Birth of Lucius Annaeus Seneca, the philosopher (ca. 4 B.C.–A.D. 65)
		A.D.	
		8	Ovid's *Metamorphoses* finished; Ovid exiled to Tomi.
		14	Death of the emperor Augustus
	14	– 37	Tiberius emperor
		17	Death of Ovid
	37	– 41	Gaius Caligula emperor
	41	– 54	Claudius emperor
	54	– 68	Nero emperor
		65	Suicide of Seneca

CICERO'S SOMNIUM SCIPIONIS
THE DREAM OF SCIPIO

INTRODUCTION

Historical and Political Background

Cicero began writing the *De republica* in 54 B.C., and it was completed by 51 B.C. It was a particularly difficult task, as Cicero attests in his letters, and it was carried out with considerable sensitivity to the current political situation in Rome (thus, for example, the decision to set the scene of the dialogue in the remote past). The decade prior to publication of the *De republica* was a critical and momentous period for the Roman Republic and for Cicero's political career. The traditional Republican forms of political structure and activity were circumvented and disrupted by ambitious individuals who were seeking power—and ultimately absolute power—for themselves and who were willing to use any means at their disposal—even physical coercion, gangsters, and terror—to achieve it. The Republican "constitution" was subverted, and Cicero, who prided himself on being the savior of the Roman state for his role in exposing and crushing the Catilinarian conspiracy in 63 B.C., now found himself in a series of extremely difficult and embarrassing political situations and unable to restore the old **concordia ordinum** under senatorial control. Eventually, Cicero withdrew from active participation in political life and turned to philosophy and to writing about the ideal orator-statesman, the ideal state, and the laws with which it should be governed. He thus describes in his writings, the *De oratore*, the *De republica*, and the *De legibus* what he despaired of seeing in real life.

Two developments in the decade under consideration were particularly damaging to Republican political life: the formation of the so-called first triumvirate, which consolidated political power in the hands of three men, and the recruitment and deployment of armed gangs for purposes of disruption and coercion. The first triumvirate, a coalition of Pompey, Crassus, and Caesar, formed in 60 B.C. just prior to Caesar's consulship with Bibulus in 59, had as its original aim the securing of measures that Pompey had been unable to secure through normal procedures upon his victorious return in 62 B.C. from his campaigns in the East—namely, ratification of his arrangements for Roman control in the East, provision of land on which to settle his veterans, and better terms for the tax collectors (**pūblicānī**) in the province of Asia. As consul, Caesar quickly got all of these measures adopted, but not without resorting to strong-arm tactics that included use of Pompey's veterans to drive opponents from the Forum and resulted in permanent alienation of his Optimate colleague. With the help of his henchman, the tribune Vatinius, Caesar secured proconsular command of Cisalpine Gaul and Illyricum (instead of Italy as decreed by the Senate), and, with the help of Pompey, Transalpine Gaul was added to his command; Caesar clearly saw his command in Gaul as an opportunity for aggrandizement of his power and prestige, and the five-year term of his command would provide a lengthy immunity from prosecution for illegal acts during his consulship. The alliance of Caesar with Pompey was cemented by Pompey's marriage to Caesar's daughter, Julia, and the triumvirate, in spite of its unpopularity, secured the election of sympathetic consuls for 58 B.C. It was clear that real power in the Roman state now lay in the hands of the coalition. Cicero refused to join it in spite of frequent invitations from Caesar, and Cato saw it as the beginning of the end of the Republican form of government.

The triumvirate regarded Cicero and Cato as the main threats to their power and determined to get rid of them. This they did through the tribune Clodius in 58 B.C. Cato was sent on a special mission to incorporate Cyprus into the empire, and Cicero was frightened out of Rome by passage of a bill that revived with retroactive force the old provision making it illegal to put a Roman citizen to death without appeal to the people—a bill aimed at Cicero for the execution of the Catilinarian conspirators in 63 B.C. Two other bills introduced by Clodius were even more damaging to the stability of the Republic: one provided free distribution of grain to the plebs (replacing sale of grain at subsidized prices), and the other revived the political clubs (collēgia), which could easily be manipulated and used to coerce and terrorize the assemblies, candidates, and officeholders. When Cicero went into exile, his cherished house on the Palatine was burned and his Tusculan villa looted. His despair was so great that in exile in Macedonia he even contemplated suicide. Clodius, however, may have overplayed his hand, and Pompey began to work for Cicero's recall. His and others' efforts were plagued with violence from Clodius' gangs and with rioting that left many dead even in the Forum. Counterforces were organized by Milo and Sestius, and finally a bill was passed for Cicero's recall, with Milo's thugs and senatorial dignitaries overseeing the balloting (57 B.C.). Cicero's restoration, however, did not end the violence, and attacks were made by Clodius' forces on the houses of Cicero, of his brother Quintus, and of Milo, and Cicero himself was attacked on the Sacred Way. In 56 B.C., Clodius as aedile brought suit against Milo, and the result was a shouting and shoving match in the Forum between the supporters of these two demagogues.

With Caesar absent in Gaul, the triumvirate tended to dissolve; Pompey and Crassus were looking after their own interests in Rome and becoming concerned over the rapid rise of Caesar's power from his base in Gaul. In 56 B.C. Caesar arranged a conference with Pompey and Crassus at Luca in Cisalpine Gaul, and the coalition was reaffirmed. It was agreed that Pompey and Crassus would be consuls in 55 B.C., and that Pompey would get Spain and Libya for five years, Crassus would have Syria, and Caesar's command in Gaul would be extended. Pompey and Crassus forcibly secured the consulship in 55 B.C., and the other arrangements were ratified through the efforts of a tribune. It was again clear that the triumvirate was the real center of power in the Roman state.

This situation was not to last long, however. Pompey's wife, Julia, died in childbirth in 54 B.C., loosening Pompey's ties to Caesar, and Crassus was murdered while retreating from his disastrous engagement with the Parthians in 53 B.C. The coalition was over. The elections for 52 B.C. were repeatedly postponed because of mob violence sponsored by the candidates, and early that year Clodius was murdered by Milo's ruffians, the Senate House was burned to the ground as a funeral pyre for Clodius, and ultimately the Senate appealed to Pompey, who was made sole consul with the task of restoring order in the city. Supreme power lay in the hands of one man, Pompey, now reconciled with the senatorial class in their shared fear of Caesar, who was crushing the last revolts of the Gallic tribes (defeat of Vercingetorix, 52 B.C.) and was eager to return to Rome in triumph to seek the consulship at the earliest possible moment. Elaborate maneuvering over the terms of Caesar's return led to his being declared an enemy of the state, his fateful crossing of the Rubicon, and civil war with Pompey and the Senate (49–46 B.C.). With Caesar's victory, the Republic was dead, and Caesar ruled as autocrat and monarch (46–44 B.C.) until his assassination on the Ides of March.

Cicero and the Writing of the *De republica*

The decade prior to publication of the *De republica* was a generally unhappy period for Cicero. During Caesar's consulship in 59 B.C., Cicero, having refused to join the triumvirate and having criticized Caesar openly, removed himself from politics by retiring to Antium and devoted himself to literary pursuits and composition of a book on geography. His exile in Macedonia in 58 B.C. was a crushing blow, and his recall in 57 was bought at the price of agreeing not to criticize the enactments pushed through by Caesar during his consulship. In 56 B.C., however, after appealing for a new concord of the orders and civil peace, Cicero brought up the issue of the Campanian land grants legislated by Caesar in 59. Before the issue could be resolved, the conference of the triumvirs at Luca took place, and the coalition, now reaffirmed, threatened Cicero with a second banishment unless he abided by the terms of his recall in 57. Cicero had no choice but to swallow the bitter pill and submit. This he did. He now supported initiatives of Caesar and was forced in several court cases to defend his former political enemies at the behest of Caesar and Pompey. For Cicero the loss of political freedom was painful indeed:

> But think of the sufferings I undergo when I am taken for a lunatic if I say what I ought about the State, for a slave if I say what expediency dictates, and for a cowed and helpless bondsman if I hold my tongue. (*Ad Att.* IV.6, tr. E. O. Winstedt)

Cicero largely retired from public life. In 55 B.C., he wrote the following to Atticus from Cumae, where he was enjoying the library of Faustus:

> But upon my word the more I am deprived of other enjoyments and pleasures on account of the state of politics, the more support and

recreation do I find in literature. And I would rather be in that niche of yours under Aristotle's statue than in their curule chair, and take a walk with you at home than have the company which I see will be with me on my path. (*Ad Att.* IV.10, tr. E. O. Winstedt)

In 54 B.C., with writing of the *De republica* already well under way, Cicero wrote to his brother in an outburst of despair and anger:

I withdraw myself, it is true, from all public cares, and devote myself to literature; and yet, I will divulge to you what, on my oath, I especially wished to keep hidden from you. It is agony to me, my dearest brother, sheer agony, to think that there is no constitution, no administration of justice, and that during the period of my life when my proper influence in the Senate should have been at its zenith, I am either distracted by my forensic labors, or fortified only by my literary pursuits at home, while that aspiration to which I had been passionately devoted from my very boyhood, "*Far to excel, and alone to be leader of others,*" has completely vanished; that my foes, in some cases, I have left unattacked, in others I have even defended; that not only my inclinations, but my very dislikes are not free; and that in all the world I have found in Caesar the one man to love me as I could wish, or even (as others think) the one man who had any wish to do so. (*Ad Quint. frat.* III.VI.4, tr. W. Glynn Williams)

Such was Cicero's mood when composing the *De republica*.

The *De republica*

The *De republica* begins with arguments in favor of active involvement in public life as opposed to the quiet life of retirement recommended by the Epicureans. While Cicero's contemporary, the Epicurean poet Lucretius, mocked the active life of ambitious politicians who labor "night and day with surpassing toil to mount upon the pinnacle of riches and to lay hold on power" (*De rerum natura* II.12–13, tr. Rouse/Smith), Cicero sees man as essentially a social creature: "Nature has implanted in the human race so great a need of virtue and so great a desire to defend the common safety that the strength thereof has conquered all the allurements of pleasure and ease" (*De republica* I.I.1, tr. C. W. Keyes). When Scipio (see Introduction to the student's book) in the *De republica* is asked to tell "which form of government he considers the best"

(I.XX.33), he begins by defining the nature of the state as an organization based on man's nature as a social creature:

Well, then, a commonwealth is the property of a people. But a people is not any collection of human beings brought together in any sort of way, but an assemblage of people in large numbers associated in an agreement with respect to justice and a partnership for the common good. The first cause of such an association is not so much the weakness of the individual as a certain social spirit which nature has implanted in man. For man is not a solitary or unsocial creature, but born with such a nature that not even under conditions of great prosperity of every sort is he willing to be isolated from his fellow men. (I.XXV.39, tr. C. W. Keyes)

Scipio defines three good forms of government—monarchy, aristocracy, and democracy—but sees dangers of these degenerating respectively into the bad forms of tyranny, oligarchy, and mob rule. To protect against such perversions, Scipio follows in the footsteps of Plato, Aristotle, the Stoic philosophers, and Polybius, the second century B.C. Greek historian of Rome, and recommends a mixed constitution containing elements of all three forms of good government. This "mixed and evenly balanced constitution" will provide stable government and has no perverted form into which it can degenerate; under its governance "every citizen is firmly established in his own station," and there will be no change of the government for the worse "except through great faults in the governing class" (*De republica* I.XLV.69, tr. C. W. Keyes). Rather than describing a fictional ideal state as Plato had done in his *Republic,* Scipio in the second book of the *De republica* traces the history of Rome and the development of its political institutions with their various checks and balances as an actual manifestation of a mixed constitution in evolution and operation. While it is never explicitly stated which Roman political institutions correspond to the three pure forms of good government, it seems likely that the various assemblies of the people would correspond to democracy, the senate and the magistracies (except for the consulship) would correspond to aristocracy, and the consulship to monarchy. The Roman state as it had evolved over centuries of time and as it had been shaped by evolutionary, historical forces and the genius of numerous statesmen thus serves as a pattern of the ideal mixed constitution (*De republica* II.XXXIX.65–66).

At the end of the second book discussion moves from the ideal state to the ideal citizen or statesman, and he is described in the following eloquent passage, which passes quickly from the virtues of the statesman to the harmony he is to bring to the state:

> Of course he should be given almost no other duties than this one (for it comprises most of the others)—of improving and examining himself continually, urging others to imitate him, and furnishing in himself, as it were, a mirror to his fellow-citizens by reason of the supreme excellence of his life and character. For just as in the music of harps and flutes or in the voices of singers a certain harmony of the different tones must be preserved, the interruption or violation of which is intolerable to trained ears, and as this perfect agreement and harmony is produced by the proportionate blending of unlike tones, so also is a State made harmonious by agreement among dissimilar elements, brought about by a fair and reasonable blending together of the upper, middle, and lower classes, just as if they were musical tones. What the musicians call harmony in song is concord in a State, the strongest and best bond of permanent union in any commonwealth; and such concord can never be brought about without the aid of justice. (II.XLII.69, tr. C. W. Keyes)

Book III deals with justice and with refutation of popular views, which had been set forth by Carneades, the founder of the New Academy, based on considerations of expediency and self-interest, that claim that governments can function efficiently only if they are unjust and that individuals are fools if they give justice precedence over self-interest and self-preservation. In Scipio's view, justice is essential to the state because it is a manifestation of a universal, absolute, God-given law, which he praises in the following passage permeated with Stoic pantheism:

> True law is right reason in agreement with nature; it is of universal application, unchanging and everlasting; it summons to duty by its commands, and averts from wrongdoing by its prohibitions. And it does not lay its commands or prohibitions upon good men in vain, though neither have any effect on the wicked. It is a sin to try to alter this law, nor is it allowable to attempt to repeal any part of it, and it is impossible to abolish it entirely. We cannot be freed from its obligations by senate or people, and we need not look outside ourselves for an expounder or interpreter of it. And there will not be different laws at Rome and at Athens,

or different laws now and in the future, but one eternal and unchangeable law will be valid for all nations and all times, and there will be one master and ruler, that is, God, over us all, for he is the author of this law, its promulgator, and its enforcing judge. Whoever is disobedient is fleeing from himself and denying his human nature, and by reason of this very fact he will suffer the worst penalties, even if he escapes what is commonly considered punishment. (III.XXII.33, tr. C. W. Keyes)

Book IV (now mostly lost) deals with education, and Book V (also mostly lost), with customs and laws and with the character and actions of the ideal statesman (with an eye to Plato's philosopher-king). This ideal citizen or statesman is variously termed in the fragments a rēctor rērum pūblicārum, a moderātor reī pūblicae, and a prīnceps cīvitātis. This ideal statesman has been variously thought by scholars (1) to prefigure the emperor Augustus, (2) to suggest Pompey (made sole consul in 52 B.C. for the preservation of law and order in Rome), (3) to embody the role Cicero felt himself especially qualified to play, or (4) to suggest the role that Scipio himself might have played in 129 B.C. at the height of the Gracchan crisis if he had been made dictātor instead of being assassinated. The aims of this ideal statesman are described as follows:

> Just as the aim of the pilot is a successful voyage, of the physician, health, and of the general, victory, so this director of the commonwealth (moderātor reī pūblicae) has as his aim for his fellow-citizens a happy life, fortified by wealth, rich in material resources, great in glory and honored for virtue. I want him to bring to perfection this achievement, which is the greatest and best possible among men. (V.VI.8, tr. C. W. Keyes)

The rewards awaiting such statesmen are described in Scipio's dream at the end of Book VI.

Cicero's Political Thought

Except insofar as the conception of a single rēctor or moderātor or prīnceps may prefigure the dictatorship of Caesar and the autocracy of Augustus, Cicero's political thought in the *De republica* and in the *De legibus*, written to accompany it, looks more to the past than to the future. And, it may be noted that in the *De legibus*, which followed the *De republica*, there is no mention of the rēctor, moderātor, or prīnceps (perhaps Caesar's dictatorship soured Cicero on the Platonic notion of the philosopher-king). The ideal state as Cicero portrays it, with its harmonious balance among the orders in a strictly hierarchical structure and with its ideal of the enlightened statesman *(De republica)* or orator *(De oratore)* dedicated to public service, seems strangely out of step with the political developments in Rome during the decade prior to publication of the *De republica* and was in fact soon to be rendered wholly anachronistic by the civil wars that began with Caesar's crossing of the Rubicon and ended with the Battle of Actium. A new order was indeed to be established, but it owed little to Cicero's desire to see a restoration of the old Republican constitution as it existed before the revolutionary reforms of Tiberius Gracchus. Unable to participate happily in the political world of his own day, Cicero dreams unrealistically of a world of the past that was never to be revived.

Yet, in other ways Cicero's political thought as formulated in the *De republica* and the *De legibus* was to have profound influence on the future. The theory of the mixed constitution was taken up by many later thinkers such as Aquinas, Machiavelli, and Montesquieu, and it influenced British and American political thought and institutions. Perhaps even more important, the Stoic doctrine of natural law, the conception of the equality and brotherhood of all men under this universal law, and the obligation of states to function in harmony with it became cornerstones in the common heritage of Western political thought. The basic Stoic notion here is that man is a part of nature and is subject to nature's laws because man possesses reason and because the soul that animates him is one with the soul that animates nature. Reason as a spark of divinity in man makes him akin to God. In order to fulfill his true potential, man must live in accord with reason, which he shares with other men as well as with God. Man is therefore a social animal, and all men are essentially equal, no matter how different they are in possessions or position in society: "No single thing is so like another, so exactly its counterpart, as all of us are to one another" (*De legibus* I.X.29, tr. C. W. Keyes). All men are subject to one law: "We are born for Justice, and that right is based, not upon men's opinions, but upon Nature" (*De legibus* I.X.28, tr. C. W. Keyes). From this derives "man's fellowship and union with his fellow-men" (*De legibus* I.X.28–29, tr. C. W. Keyes). The state must therefore acknowledge the mutual obligations and recognize the mutual rights that bind its citizens together into a moral community. The authority of the state will be based on the collective power of the people; political power rightfully exercised will be the corporate power of the people; and the state and its law will be subject to a universal, natural law or the law of God. Even if publication of the *De republica* did not spark a revival of the political order that existed in Rome before the Gracchan revolution, nevertheless these Stoic ideas of man, society, nature, and God which Cicero grafts onto his description of the evolution and laws of the ideal Roman state were to have a formative influence on all subsequent political thought, and they retain their power and validity today.

Aids for Teaching the "Somnium Scipionis"

Attention should be paid to the rhetorical quality of Cicero's prose and the rhetorical devices that give it its special quality. Particular attention should be paid to the following devices, which are pointed out for the first time in the notes to the lines of which the numbers are given in parentheses: *syllepsis* (10), *anaphora* (38), *alliteration* (48), *chiasmus* (72), *personification* (100), and *hendiadys* (123).

On the pages of the student's book and in the following teaching notes will be found abundant comparative material to help students and teachers understand the various events, concepts, and ideas contained in the "Somnium Scipionis" within the larger historical, political, and intellectual context of Roman history, Cicero's age, and Cicero's other writings. It is probably safe to say that none of the ideas expressed in the "Somnium" is original with Cicero; nor are they intended to be. Rather, Cicero is here presenting in a strikingly original form and in highly polished, elegant, and memorable prose a coherent summation and consolidation of many traditions of ancient thought, with the rhetorical purpose of convincing the reader of the eternal value of selfless dedication to the welfare of the state. The comparative material assembled in the student's book and the teaching notes is intended to clarify the meaning of the ideas and concepts expressed in the work and to allow students to see them in their distinctive coloring and identity as *Greco-Roman* ideas—as unique expressions of the cultural traditions that flowed together in the first century B.C. to make Cicero and his thought what they were.

The "Somnium Scipionis" offers rich possibilities for students to do research and report to the class on particular topics. The following list gives some of the possibilities, paragraph by paragraph throughout the "Somnium." The Bibliography contains references to specific materials that students may consult in preparing reports.

IX–XI: the Punic Wars and the careers of the two Scipios.
XI–XII: Tiberius Gracchus and the younger Scipio.

XIII: Cicero's conception of the state (rēs pūblica) and the role of the ideal statesman.

XIV: Pythagorean, Orphic, and Platonic views of life and death.

XV: the Stoic conception of the universe, God, the divine fire, the human soul, and the purpose of human life.

XVI–XVII: ancient astronomy, astrology, and the geocentric conception of the universe.

XVIII: the music of the spheres.

XIX–XX: ancient conceptions of the earth's geography.

XXI: floods and conflagrations in ancient views of the history of the world.

XXII: the Great Year.

XXIII: ancient attitudes toward glory and fame.

XXIV–XXVI: ancient conceptions of the immortality of the soul and its life after death.

At the end of the student's book there are passages in English translation from other ancient authors to allow students to see how radically Cicero has altered his model, Plato's myth of Er; to see some of the ancient controversy surrounding Cicero's ideas (comparison with Lucretius, who rejected the idea of the immortality of the soul); and to see some later adaptations in antiquity of the concepts embodied in the "Somnium." Some students may be interested in the influence of the "Somnium" on later literature. The commentary of Macrobius shows how the work was understood in the early Middle Ages; there are echoes of the "Somnium" in Boethius' *Consolation of Philosophy* (II.VII); and of particular interest are lines 127–154 of the twenty-second Canto of Dante's *Paradiso* and Chaucer's *Parliament of Fowls* (or *The Parliament of Birds*); for editions, see the Bibliography.

* * *

TEACHING NOTES

Lines 1–11:

1. Manius Manilius (1) and his colleague L. Marcius Censorinus, consuls in 149 B.C., had command of the Roman forces in the first year of the Third Punic War but made little progress in the struggle. According to Appian (*Punica* X.71) and Valerius Maximus (5.2. ext. 4), Sci-

pio had already come to Masinissa in 151 or 150 B.C. to seek reinforcements and elephants to aid the consul Lucullus, under whom Scipio was serving as military tribune in Spain. Appian records that on that occasion "Masinissa greeted him with the greatest cordiality, having been a friend of his grandfather" (*Punica* X.72, tr. H. White). Cicero, however, makes it appear that the visit he describes as taking place in 149 B.C. was Scipio's first visit to the king. A second visit of Scipio to Masinissa's kingdom is reported to have taken place late in 149 or early in 148, but Masinissa died shortly before his arrival (see Appian, *Punica* XVI.105). It thus seems likely that the visit recorded in the "Somnium" is a fiction based on Scipio's visit to Masinissa in 151 or 150 and located by Cicero at the beginning of Scipio's service in Africa for dramatic effect.

2. **amīcissimum** (3): ties of friendship between families were considered serious and sacred by the ancients, and obligations were passed down regarding these friendships from generation to generation. (For background information on friendship and conventions of hospitality in the Roman world, see *Roman Life*, pp. 183–185.) Masinissa was greatly indebted to the elder Scipio, who had restored him to his kingdom and enlarged his holdings to include much of those of Syphax, a rival Numidian chieftain formerly allied to Carthage. The younger Scipio is portrayed as anxious to renew the bond that his adoptive grandfather had formed so many years before.

3. **Sōl . . . reliquī Caelitēs** (5–6): the sun and the other heavenly bodies are represented as divine later in the "Somnium" (66, 87–88, 94–95). Cicero's allusion here to the Numidians' worship of the heavenly bodies may have been intended as a bit of local color, for the Numidians claimed to be descendants of the Persians (see Sallust, *Bellum Jugurthinum* 18), who worshiped the heavenly bodies, especially the sun.

4. Suggestion for students' project: find out about the conventions of hospitality in the ancient world (*Roman Life*, pp. 183–185, will provide a start). Why was the guest–host relationship (especially between families living in different geographical areas) so important in the ancient world? What practical advantages were realized by this tradition of hospitality?

Lines 12–22:

1. **artior** (16): "deeper," lit., "tighter," reinforcing the notion of sleep "embracing" (**complexus est**, 16) the exhausted Scipio. At the end of

his dream, sleep "releases" him (**somnō solū-tus sum**, 218). In the section that leads up to the dream, Cicero is carefully setting a naturalistic physical and psychological background for the dream. This contrasts strongly with the fairy-tale aspect of Plato's Myth of Er, which is given in the Passages for Comparison at the back of the student's book.

2. **Hīc mihi . . . Āfricānus sē ostendit** (16–19): help students with comprehension of the basic sentence before dealing with the parenthesis.

3. **crēdō . . . loquī** (16–19): as this elaborate parenthesis is explored for comprehension and translation, the attention of students should be called to the artful arrangement of words and phrases. **Ferē** is echoed by **saepissimē**; **cōgitātiōnēs sermōnēsque**, by **cōgitāre et loquī**; **in somnō**, by **vigilāns**. These words and phrases are balanced on either side of the pivotal words **tāle quāle**. The effects and purpose of balance and antithesis such as this should be discussed.

4. 16–19: the notion that our waking thoughts and conversations are the source of the content of our dreams is as old as Herodotus (VII.16): "the visions that wander around in our dreams are the thoughts we have been thinking during the day." See also Cicero, *De divinatione* II.LXII.128, and Lucretius, *De rerum natura* IV.962–972.

5. **Ennius** (18): only fragments of the *Annales* survive. A number of ancient authors refer to Ennius' dream of Homer (e.g., Cicero, *Academica* II.51 and 88; Horace, *Epistles* II.1.50; Lucretius, *De rerum natura* I.120–126; and Persius, *Satires* VI.9–11). Ennius in his dream saw Homer, who told him that he had once been a peacock and that his soul had been transferred from that state into Ennius, according to the law of transmigration expounded by Pythagoras.

6. **ex imāgine** (20): for background information on the Romans' religious beliefs and practices regarding ancestors, see *Roman Life,* pp. 370–373, and *Death and Burial in the Roman World,* pp. 47–48. First the waxen funerary image and then the full figure of Publius Cornelius Scipio Africanus Major dominate the dream of the younger Scipio and contribute to its deeply Roman atmosphere.

7. **memoriae trāde** (22): there are two possible interpretations of this phrase: (1) "imprint these things in your memory" or (2) "hand these things down to your posterity." The former seems more likely in the immediate context, as the elder Scipio seems to be speaking directly to his adoptive grandson about his own life and destiny, but the other meaning may be intended as well.

8. Suggestion for students' project: find out about the Romans' beliefs and practices regarding ancestors (the references in note 6 above will provide a start). How do they give support to the kind of dream experience described here? How do the appearance and manner of the apparition fit with the kind of religious training the younger Scipio might have had concerning his ancestors?

Lines 23–32:

1. **excelsō et plēnō . . . illustrī et clārō** (25): note the balance of the pairs of adjectives.

2. **hōc bienniō . . . ēvertēs** (26–27): for the younger Scipio's career, see *The Oxford Classical Dictionary,* p. 963, and *Scipio Aemilianus,* passim. A summary by Velleius Paterculus of Scipio's last years appears on pages 15 and 17 of the student's book.

3. **cōnsul** (27): Scipio assumed the consulship in 147 B.C. at the age of 39, well before the legal minimum of 42 established by the *Lex Villia Annalis* (180 B.C.). The summary preserved of Livy's Book L describes the election as follows: "Since he was under age to be made consul lawfully, there was a great struggle between the commons, who campaigned for him, and the senators, who for some time resisted him, before he was exempted from the statutes and declared consul" (tr. A. C. Schlesinger). As one of the consuls for 147, Scipio took charge of the war against Carthage, but it was not until the following year (146) and with new consuls in office that the city finally fell to the Roman forces still under Scipio's command. The elder Scipio's statement, **Hanc hōc bienniō cōnsul ēvertēs.** . . . (26–27) is thus not exactly accurate, but it does emphasize the dramatic quality of this part of Scipio's career.

4. **dēligēre iterum cōnsul absēns** (30): this passage is the only evidence that Scipio was chosen consul in absentia. The summary of Book LVI of Livy gives quite a different reason why Scipio's election to a second consulship was exceptional: "Since the Numantine War was dragging along through the fault of the commanders and to the shame of the State, the consulship was offered to Scipio Africanus on the initiative of the senate and the Roman People. He was forbidden to accept this office by a law which ruled that no one should be consul a second time, but as in his first consulship, Scipio was exempted from legal restrictions" (tr. A. C. Schlesinger). Cicero, rather

than mentioning the illegality of Scipio's second consulship, wants only to emphasize its exceptional aspect and so describes Scipio as chosen *in absentia*. Cicero may have chosen the verb **dēligere** instead of the usual **creārī** to suggest that Scipio was the choice of the best qualified candidate rather than of a legally qualified one.

5. **rem pūblicam . . . perturbātam** (32): at this point it will be useful to introduce some discussion of the Gracchi, their program of reform, and the importance that later generations attached to this period as a critical turning point in Roman history. Scipio's brilliant military and political career was brought to a premature end at a moment when he was intensely involved in trying to block and dismantle the Gracchan reforms. Cicero saw these efforts as the pinnacle of Scipio's political activity, but others such as Sallust saw abuses of power on both sides in the struggles over the Gracchan reforms and saw the state irrevocably split into two hostile factions (see the passage of Sallust quoted on page 11 of the student's book; for more of Sallust's views, see all of paragraphs XLI and XLII of the *Bellum Iugurthinum*). Cicero blamed only Tiberius Gracchus for shattering the "stability of the community" (see passage in student's book). The passage from Velleius Paterculus (c.a. 19 B.C.–A.D. 30) on page 13 of the student's book suggests both the popularity of the Gracchan land reforms with the people and the intensity of the opposition of the nobles—an opposition cloaked in patriotic fervor and readily embracing violence and murder in an attempt to roll back the reforms and preserve the status quo (for Publius Cornelius Scipio Nasica Serapio, see *The Oxford Classical Dictionary,* p. 963).

The conclusion of the passage from Velleius should be compared with the passages from Sallust and Cicero on page 11 of the student's book for their recognition of this period of turbulence as a great turning point in Roman history. In Cicero's eyes the younger Scipio Africanus was something of a political martyr in his defense of the state against the forces of reform unleashed by Tiberius Gracchus. Here, in Cicero's eyes, was the ideal statesman who lost his life in the midst of his attempt to restore the old order. We suggest that a more balanced view of the situation be presented to students, with discussion of the varied and conflicting social, economic, and political forces that came to a head in this critical historical period. For full and provocative discussion with a range of viewpoints, see *Tiberius Grac-*

chus: Destroyer or Reformer of the Republic? and *Scipio Aemilianus,* Chapters XV and XVI.

Lines 33–43:

1. **plēnus** (36): the numbers 7 and 8 were considered "full" or perfect for separate reasons. Eight was considered perfect because it was the first cube after 1, because it was equal to 7 (a perfect number) plus 1, and because it was the product of 2 and 4. Seven was considered a sacred or magic number in many cultures. Marcus Terentius Varro (116–27 B.C.), a learned scholar of Cicero's time, treated the importance of the number 7 at great length in his *Hebdomades* or *De imaginibus,* which contained biographies and portraits of 700 famous Greeks and Romans; although the work is lost, many observations from it on the importance of the number 7 are reported by Aulus Gellius (III.X). Number mysticism, by which a certain few numbers were thought of as magically and mystically perfect in themselves, was widespread among the ancients and had its roots in prehistoric times. Plato, much influenced by the Pythagoreans, who based their philosophy on numbers, gave a great impetus to number mysticism (see, for example, Plato, *Timaeus* 39D).

2. **sociī . . . Latīnī** (38–39): i.e., all the inhabitants of Italy who were allies of Rome and who were disturbed by the Gracchan land reforms that threatened their holdings. Scipio responded to their pleas, offered them his support, and obtained deferral of the application of the reforms.

3. **nītātur** (39): the verb suggests a pun on the name Scipio: **scīpiō** = a rod or cane on which one might lean for support (**nītātur**). A similar play on words may be seen in the phrase **in tuum nōmen** (37–38), playing on the proverbial equation **nōmen ōmen**.

4. **effūgeris** (41): the younger Scipio died at the age of 56, as the dream foretold, in 129 B.C., under mysterious circumstances. His sudden death was never explained, but persistent rumors involved his political enemies, the supporters of the Gracchi. The passage from Velleius quoted on pages 15 and 17 of the student's book suggests something of Scipio's uncompromising stance against the Gracchan reforms and his arrogance toward the supporters of those reforms ("men like you, to whom Italy is only a stepmother"). Both Velleius and Cicero (in the passage from *De amicitia* quoted on page 17 of the student's book) see only the "brilliance" of Scipio's career (the passage from Cicero calls to mind the scene of Cicero himself

being escorted home by torchlight after delivery of his fourth oration against Catiline and the execution of the conspirators). The passage from Astin's book on Scipio (quoted on page 17 of the student's book) suggests something of the true complexity of the actual political situation and something of the understandable anger of the Gracchans and their supporters when confronted with Scipio's attempts to repeal the reform legislation (mention of these efforts of Scipio is conspicuously absent from the passages quoted from Velleius and Cicero). It is hard to believe that within these circumstances Scipio's death would have been from natural causes. Various culprits were mentioned: his adoptive sister Cornelia, mother of the Gracchi; his wife, Sempronia, sister of the Gracchi; or one or other of the officers appointed to redistribute the land (Carbo, Fulvius Flaccus, C. Gracchus). Some sources speak of natural death, others of suicide.

5. Suggestion for students' project: the elder Scipio uses the words **fātōrum** (34) and **fātālem** (37) in his revelation of Scipio's destiny. To what Latin verb are these words related? Have students look up the following terms in a large Latin dictionary: **fātum, Fāta, Parca (Parcae), fortūna,** and **Fortūna.** Have them look up "Fate" in *The Oxford Classical Dictionary.* Students may then be asked to address the question to what extent Scipio seems to take the concept of fate seriously.

Lines 44–50:

1. **in caelō . . . locum** (46): the passage from the treatise on astrology by the first-century A.D. poet Marcus Manilius quoted on page 19 of the student's book illustrates this idea that there is a reward in the heavens for those who have served their country. (For Manilius, see *The Oxford Classical Dictionary,* p. 644.)

2. The statement in 48–49 that there is nothing more welcome to the god who rules the universe than **concilia coetūsque hominum iūre sociātī, quae cīvitātēs appellantur** is illuminated by the extract quoted on page 19 of the student's book from the *De republica* that gives Cicero's view of what constitutes a **cīvitās** or a **rēs pūblica,** an institution arising, according to Cicero, from "a certain social spirit which nature has implanted in man," and so under the care of the god who rules the world (47–48). Note how far removed Cicero's ideal of the commonwealth is from the description of the actual state of affairs at the time of Tiberius Gracchus and Scipio given by Sallust in the passage quoted on page 11 of the stu-

dent's book. The two passages should be carefully compared.

3. **hārum . . . revertuntur** (49–50): note the play on sounds in **hārum . . . hinc . . . hūc** and the the paired expressions **rēctōrēs et cōnservātōrēs** and **profectī . . . revertuntur.**

4. **rēctōrēs et cōnservātōrēs** (49): Cicero's conception of the ideal statesman is described in the passage (quoted on page 21 of the student's book) from a letter of his dated 27 February 49 B.C., after Caesar had crossed the Rubicon and shattered any possibility of compromise with the Senatorial faction. This crisis, which occurred not long after Cicero completed writing the *De republica* (ca. 54–51 B.C.) and which could have been foreseen from the time of Crassus' death in 53 B.C., should be compared with the crisis provoked by the Gracchan reforms in the time of the younger Scipio.

Lines 51–57:

1. **ē corporum vinclīs tamquam ē carcere** (54): for the idea of the body as chains or imprisonment of the soul, see Cicero's *De amicitia* IV.14: "If the truth really is that the souls of all good men after death make the easiest escape from what may be termed the imprisonment and fetters of the flesh (**ē custōdiā vinclīsque corporis**), whom can we think of as having had an easier journey to the gods than Scipio [Africanus Minor]?" (tr. W. A. Falconer). Cf. also *De senectute* XXII.81, for similar language used of the soul's release from the chains of the body (**corporis vinculīs**). The conception of death as release of the soul from the shackles of the body goes back to Plato (*Phaedo* 67d 1–5) and the Pythagoreans. Cicero is here beginning to introduce philosophical and religious views that were widely held in his day and had their origins in Greek thought (particularly in Plato). Some of them may seem strange and even bizarre to modern students, and we urge that teachers take special care in elucidating the views Cicero presents and the language and images that he uses to express them.

2. **ēvolāvērunt** (54): for the conception of the soul as winged, see Plato's *Phaedrus,* 246: "Of the nature of the soul, though her true form be ever a theme of large and more than mortal discourse, let me speak briefly, and in a figure. And let the figure be composite—a pair of winged horses and a charioteer. . . . The wing is the corporeal element which is most akin to the divine, and which by nature tends to soar aloft and carry that which gravitates down-

wards into the upper region, which is the habitation of the gods" (tr. B. Jowett). The idea that the soul is winged may go back to Pythagoras.

3. **vestra . . . vīta mors est** (54–55): this notion goes back to Euripides and Plato and beyond them to the Pythagoreans and Orphics. The attraction of this idea for the Christians is shown by the chapter title from St. Augustine quoted on page 23 of the student's book.

The classical literary statement of this theme is in Plato's *Phaedo*, and Cicero summarized the argument in the quotation from his *Pro Scauro* quoted on page 23 of the student's book. According to this view of life and death, the task of the philosopher while alive is to free the soul from the shackles of the body to the greatest extent possible in preparation for death (Plato, *Phaedo* 67). Cicero was intrigued with this idea and adapted the argument from the *Phaedo* as follows:

> For what else do we do when we sequester the soul from pleasure, that is, from the body; from private property, the handmaid and servant of the body; from public interests; from any kind of business; what, I say, do we then do except summon the soul to its own presence, force it to companionship with itself and withdraw it completely from the body? But is severance of the soul from the body anything else than learning how to die? Let us, therefore, make this preparation and dissociation of ourselves from our bodies. This will, both for the time of our sojourn on earth, resemble heavenly life, and when we shall be released from our chains here, the progress of our soul will be less retarded. For they who have always been caught in the shackles of the body, even when they are set free, advance more slowly, like men who have been many years bound with chains. And when we have come yonder, then and not before shall we live; for this life is indeed death (**nam haec quidem vīta mors est**). (*Tusculanae disputationes* I.XXXI.75, adapted from the translation of J. E. King)

Whereas in the passage quoted above from the *Tusculanae disputationes* Cicero takes the idea of life as a preparation for death (or rather for the true life to come) directly from Plato, in the "Somnium" he modifies it and converts it into a truly Roman idea by specifying that it is the souls of patriots and statesmen that will

escape most quickly to their blissful afterlife in the heavens (see lines 209–211 of the "Somnium," on page 55 of the student's book). Plato had, on the contrary, urged the disengagement of the soul during its sojourn on this earth "from public interests; from any kind of business" (see the passage above). It is important to note throughout the "Somnium" how Cicero gives a Roman tone and flavor to Greek philosophical ideas.

Lines 58–70:

1. **Quīn hūc . . . venīre properō?** (60–61): the Pythagoreans and Plato forbade suicide: "Pythagoras bids us stand like faithful sentries and not quit our post until God, our Captain, gives the word" (Cicero, *De senectute* XX.73, tr. W. A. Falconer). "Yet even these teachers [Pythagoras and Plato], though they praise death, forbid us to fly from life, asserting that such conduct is a violation of the compact and law of nature" (Cicero, *Pro Scauro* IV, tr. N. H. Watts). "There is a doctrine whispered in secret that man is a prisoner who has no right to open the door and run away; this is a great mystery which I do not quite understand. Yet I too believe that the gods are our guardians, and that we men are a possession of theirs" (Plato, *Phaedo* 62, tr. B. Jowett). In certain circumstances, however, the human and the divine choice of the right time to depart from life appear to coincide, and suicide is justified:

> Cato departed from life with a feeling of joy in having found a reason for death; for the God who is master within us forbids our departure without his permission; but when God Himself has given a valid reason as He did in the past to Socrates, and in our day to Cato, and often to many others, then of a surety your true wise man will joyfully pass forthwith from the darkness here into the light beyond. All the same he will not break the bonds of his prisonhouse—the laws forbid it—but as if in obedience to a magistrate or some lawful authority, he will pass out at the summons and release of God. (Cicero, *Tusculanae disputationes* I.XXX.74, tr. J. E. King)

2. Special care should be taken with the clauses and phrases in lines 63–67, emphasizing that the sentence consists basically of two coordinate clauses: **Hominēs . . . sunt . . . generātī** and **iīs . . . animus datus est.** It may be useful to sort out and discuss individu-

ally the various ideas that Cicero has compressed into this elaborate sentence.

3. **quī tuērentur illum globum** (64): cf. Cicero, *De senectute*, XXI.77: "But I believe that the immortal gods implanted souls in human bodies so as to have beings who would care for the earth (**quī terrās tuērentur**) and who, while contemplating the celestial order, would imitate it in the moderation and consistency of their lives" (tr. W. A. Falconer). Compare the idea contained in lines 46–50 of the "Somnium" that the god who rules the world is especially pleased with commonwealths of men and those who rule them. Cicero insists upon the responsibility of men to society and the earth on which they live. It was to take care of that earth that they were created.

4. **iīsque animus datus est ex illīs sempiternīs ignibus** (65): Stoic doctrine held that the soul consists of a pure fire that is life-giving and salutary rather than being destructive; this doctrine is explained in the passage from Cicero's *De natura deorum* quoted on page 25 of the student's book. The doctrine may be traced back through Plato to the Pythagoreans who, as Cicero stated in his *De senectute* XXI.78, "never doubted that our souls were emanations of the Universal Divine Mind" (**ex ūniversā mente dīvīnā dēlībātōs animōs habērēmus**) (tr. W. A. Falconer); compare Cicero, *De natura deorum* I.XI.27, "Pythagoras . . . believed that the entire substance of the universe is penetrated and pervaded by a soul of which our souls are fragments" (tr. H. Rackham).

In the *Tusculanae disputationes* I.XIX.43, Cicero describes the ascent of the soul after death as follows (tr. J. E. King):

> If it survives unadulterated and unchanged in substance, it is of necessity carried away so rapidly as to pierce and part asunder all this atmosphere of ours, in which clouds, storms and winds collect because of the moisture and mist produced by evaporation from the earth. When the soul has passed this tract and reaches to and recognizes a substance resembling its own, it stops amongst the fires which are formed of rarefied air and the modified glow of the sun and ceases to make higher ascent. For when it has reached conditions of lightness and heat resembling its own, it becomes quite motionless, as though in a state of equilibrium with its surroundings, and then, and not before, finds its natural home, when it has pierced to conditions resembling its own, and there, with all its needs satisfied, it will be nourished and maintained on the same food which maintains and nourishes the stars.

This doctrine of astral immortality of the soul was widely held in antiquity and tended to replace the older mythological doctrine of an afterlife in an underworld (Hades). See *Lore and Science in Ancient Pythagoreanism*, "Harmony of the Spheres and Astral Immortality," pp. 350–368.

Lines 71–83:
1. **pietātem, . . . magna . . . maxima** (72–73): for gradations of **pietās** or obligations, compare the passage from *De officiis* quoted on page 27 of the student's book. The footnotes to that passage suggest people Cicero may have had in mind as the villains who outraged their fatherland. Cicero repeats the idea of a hierarchy of obligations at the end of the first book of the *De officiis*: "Our first duty is to the immortal gods; our second, to country; our third, to parents; and so on, in a descending scale, to the rest" (I.XLV.160, tr. W. Miller).
2. **illum . . . locum** (74): the Milky Way, sometimes thought of as a pathway to the heavens, sometimes as the abode of immortal souls (see *Lore and Science in Ancient Pythagoreanism*, pp. 366–368).
3. **magnitūdinēs** (78): note how with this word Cicero is leading up to Scipio's realization of how small the earth is (**terra . . . parva**, 81) and how insignificant the Roman empire (**quasi punctum**, 82).
4. **ultima ā caelō, citima ā terrīs** (80): note the parallelism.
5. **Stellārum . . . globī / terrae magnitūdinem** (80–81): note the effect of the parallel arrangement of the words (genitive and its noun / genitive and its noun) and the use of the word **magnitūdinem:** "the spheres of the stars surpassed the magnitude of the earth." Our normal perspective on things is reversed and Cicero ingeniously prepares for the belittling of the earth and the Roman Empire (81–83).

Lines 84–101:
1. **Novem . . . orbibus vel potius globīs cōnexa sunt omnia** (85–86): for introductions to ancient astronomy, see *The Encyclopaedia Britannica*, "Astronomy," Vol. 2, pp. 643–644; *The Oxford Classical Dictionary*, "Astronomy," pp. 134–135; and *A Short His-*

tory of Ancient Astronomy from Earliest Times through the Nineteenth Century, Chapter II, "Greek Astronomy." The universe is here thought of as concentric spheres one inside the other with the sphere of the fixed stars on the outside (**in quō sunt īnfīxī illī quī volvuntur stellārum cursūs sempiternī,** 88–89) and the earth at the center (**medium,** 64). Cicero, in agreement (as Macrobius, I.XIX.2, says) with Archimedes and the Chaldeans, places the elements of the geocentric system in the following order inside the sphere of the fixed stars: (1) Saturn, (2) Jupiter, (3) Mars, (4) the sun, (5) Venus, (6) Mercury, (7) the moon, and (8) the earth (see also Cicero, *De divinatione* II.XLIII.91).

Plato, following the Egyptians (Macrobius, I.XIX.2), and himself followed by Aristotle, gave a different order: (1) Saturn, (2) Jupiter, (3) Mars, (4) Mercury, (5) Venus, (6) the sun, (7) the moon, and (8) the earth (see *Timaeus* 38–39 and *Republic* X.616–617). Ptolemy, an astronomer, mathematician, and geographer of the second century A.D. (see *The Oxford Classical Dictionary,* pp. 897–898), accepted the system as Cicero described it and passed it along to the Middle Ages and the Renaissance.

The alternative heliocentric theory of Aristarchus of Samos and Seleucos of Seleucia, formulated in the third and second centuries B.C. and based on sound mathematical arguments, was overwhelmed by the proponents of the geocentric view and remained a minority opinion until Copernicus (A.D. 1473–1543) revolutionized astronomical theory.

2. The passage from Cicero's *De natura deorum* quoted on page 29 of the student's book is included to provide a sense of the awe that Cicero felt in contemplating the heavens and his resulting belief in a divine power that rules the world.

3. For the belief that the heavenly bodies are, in fact, gods, see Cicero, *De natura deorum* II.XXI.54: "This regularity therefore in the stars, this exact punctuality throughout all eternity notwithstanding the great variety of their courses, is to me incomprehensible without rational intelligence and purpose. And if we observe these attributes in the planets, we cannot fail to enroll even them among the number of the gods" (tr. H. Rackham).

In the "Somnium," Cicero emphasizes two aspects of divinity in the heavens: the outer sphere in which the fixed stars revolve (88–89) and which he describes as **summus ipse deus arcēns et continēns cēterōs** [deōs, i.e., the other planets] (87–88); and the sun,

described in human terms as **dux et prīnceps et moderātor lūminum reliquōrum, mēns mundī et temperātiō** (94–95). For the divinity of the fixed stars, see Cicero, *De natura deorum* II.XXI.55: "Now the continual and unceasing revolutions of these stars, marvellously and incredibly regular as they are, clearly show that these are endowed with divine power and intelligence; so that anyone who cannot perceive that they themselves possess divinity would seem to be incapable of understanding anything at all" (tr. H. Rackham).

Cicero in the *Academica* points to the Stoic antecedents of these views: "Zeno and almost all the other Stoics think the aether [the substance of the upper heavens] a supreme deity, endowed with a mind whereby the universe is ruled; Cleanthes, the Stoic of the older families as it were, who was a disciple of Zeno, holds that the sun is lord and master of the world" (II.XLI.126, tr. H. Rackham).

Cicero clearly regards all of the celestial bodies as gods (87–88), and in the case of Jupiter and Mars he mentions the effects that these divinities have on earthly life: **hominum generī prosperus et salūtāris** (91, of Jupiter) and **horribilis . . . terrīs** (92, of Mars). In the *De natura deorum* II.XLVI.119, Cicero comments more extensively on the effects of the celestial bodies: "Saturn has a cooling influence, the middle planet, that of Mars, imparts heat, the one between them, that of Jove, gives light and a moderate warmth, while the two beneath Mars obey the sun [**sōlī oboediant:** cf. "Somnium" 96–97, **Hunc ut comitēs cōnsequuntur Veneris alter, alter Mercuriī cursus**], and the sun itself fills all the world with light [**suā lūce compleat:** cf. "Somnium" 96 **suā lūce lūstret et compleat**], and also illuminates the moon, which is the source of conception and birth and of growth and maturity" (tr. H. Rackham).

While insisting on the divinity and effective power of the planets, Cicero spurned the popular and widespread belief in Chaldean astrology and its attempt to predict the fortunes of individuals by study of the configuration of the heavens at the moment of the person's birth. For the history of astrology in the ancient world, see *The Encyclopaedia Britannica,* "Astrology," Vol. 2, pp. 640–641B, and *The Oxford Classical Dictionary,* "Astrology," pp. 133–134. For Cicero's rejection of astrology, which he terms "incredible madness" (**dēlīrātiōnem incrēdibilem**), see *De divinatione* II.XLII.89ff.

4. **contrāriō mōtū atque caelum** (89–90): the spheres of the planets were thought to rotate from west to east while the sky turns from east to west. See Ovid, *Metamorphoses* II.70–73, Phaethon addressing his son: "Furthermore, the vault of heaven spins round in constant motion, drawing along the lofty stars which it whirls at dizzy speed. I make my way against this, nor does the swift motion which overcomes all else overcome me; but I drive clear contrary to the swift circuit of the universe" (tr. Frank Justus Miller).

5. **mediam . . . regiōnem Sōl obtinet** (94): one important consequence of Cicero's adoption of the Chaldean rather than the Egyptian (Platonic) arrangement of the celestial bodies (see note 1 above) is that it places the sun in the middle with three rotating bodies to either side: Saturn, Jupiter, Mars, THE SUN, Venus, Mercury, the moon. The central position of the sun is a function of its crucial role in the planetary system as **dux et prīnceps et moderātor lūminum reliquōrum, mēns mundī et temperātiō** (94–95). All of these terms have political overtones and suggest a comparison between the universe as here described and a well-organized commonwealth governed by a **prīnceps**. (Compare the passages from *De republica* II.XLII.69 and V.VI.8 quoted in the Introduction to these teaching notes.) Some of these terms may also recall Pythagorean musical theory, with the sun occupying a position and performing a function parallel to the position and function of the middle string of the seven-stringed lyre. The lyre and the commonwealth would thus be microcosms of the rational order and harmony of the universe.

6. **Īnfrā** (98): the doctrine that everything below the level of the moon is perishable while the moon and everything above it are immortal may go back to Pythagorean origins.

Lines 102–116:

1. **sonus** (103): the idea that each of the planets, as it whirls in its sphere, makes a certain sound and that together all of them make beautiful and harmonious music is often attributed (rightly or wrongly) to Pythagoras, who made many discoveries in mathematics and music and was thought to have applied those discoveries to the motions of the heavenly bodies. (See the passage from Quintilian quoted on page 33 of the student's book; for discussion of the evidence for attributing these views to Pythagoras, see *Lore and Science in Ancient Pythagoreanism*, pp. 350–356.) The notion that the movement of the heavenly spheres produces music has intrigued men ever since. In fact, as late as the seventeenth century the celebrated German astronomer Johannes Kepler wrote a treatise examining the mathematical relationships of the orbits of the planets to determine whether the intervals were "harmonious." The "music of the spheres" is often mentioned by English poets: e.g., Shakespeare (*Merchant of Venice* V.1):

> There's not the smallest orb which thou beholdest,
> But in his motion like an Angel sings.

and Milton (*Paradise Lost* V.177–179):

> And ye five other wandering fires that move
> In mystic dance, not without song, resound
> His praise, who out of darkness call'd up light.

For information on Pythagoras and Greek music, see *The Oxford Classical Dictionary*, "Pythagoras," pp. 903–904, and "Music and the Philosophers," pp. 705–706.

2. **intervallīs . . . distinctīs** (104–105): the sound produced by the movements of the heavenly bodies or their spheres may be analyzed as individual sounds at unequal but rationally proportioned intervals, like the sounds in a musical scale. Be sure that students recognize that **imparibus** and **distinctīs** both modify **intervallīs**. Attention should be called to the unusually effective interplay of sounds in the Latin here: <u>in</u>terval<u>līs</u> . . . <u>im</u>par<u>ibus</u>; <u>dis</u>iunctus . . . <u>dis</u>tinctīs; <u>prō</u> . . . <u>par</u>te; and <u>rat</u>ā . . . <u>rat</u>iōne.

3. **impulsū et mōtū** (105): different sounds are produced by the different speeds at which the celestial bodies travel.

4. **acūta cum gravibus temperāns** (105–106): the music of the spheres "harmonizes the high with the low." Compare the role of the sun as described in lines 94–95, as the controlling, moderating, harmonizing force in the system of heavenly bodies. Control and the harmony that results from it are key themes here.

5. **summus . . . īnfimus** (108–110): note the careful arrangement of words between these two extremes.

6. **concitātior** (109): it is differences in the velocity of the celestial bodies or spheres that produce the different tones that make up the harmonious music.

7. **octō cursūs** (112): i.e., the spheres of the fixed stars and of Saturn, Jupiter, Mars, the sun, Venus, Mercury, and the moon. The system boxes itself into a corner here, and it is not possible to tell how Cicero thought he was extricating himself. If we were only counting Saturn, Jupiter, Mars, THE SUN, Venus, Mercury, and the moon, there would be no problem, since the notes would correspond to the seven strings of the lyre, with the sun as a median point in the scale (see note 5 to lines 84–101 above). The inclusion of the sphere of the fixed stars (108–110), however, adds an eighth element, hence **Illī . . . octō cursūs** (112).

Plato had simply said, "The eight together form one harmony" (*Republic* X [617], tr. B. Jowett). Cicero attempts to give an explanation by stating that two of the eight spheres or circuits produce the same sound (**in quibus eadem vīs est duōrum**, 112), so that the eight spheres produce only seven sounds (**septem efficiunt distinctōs intervallīs sonōs**, 112–113). Which two spheres produce the same sound? Macrobius (II.IV.9) attempts to explain: "Mercury and Venus accompany the sun at the same rate of speed and follow its course like satellites" (tr. W. H. Stahl); cf. the description in the "Somnium" of Venus and Mercury as **comitēs** "companions" or "satellites" of the sun (96).

Another possibility is that the sounds of the sphere of the moon and that of the fixed stars (i.e., the lowest and the highest) are pitched at the octave of one another and are therefore, according to Aristotle, "at one and the same time the same and different" (*Problems* XIX.17, tr. W. S. Hett). This may have been a Pythagorean view of the matter; Cicero might have been content with thinking that Mercury and Venus moved at the same speed and therefore produced the same sound. For further discussion, see *Lore and Science in Ancient Pythagoreanism*, "Harmony of the Spheres and Astral Immortality," pp. 350–368.

8. **doctī hominēs . . . imitātī . . . coluērunt** (114–116): the idea that the order and harmony of the universe are based on number and that men may imitate these through music and so prepare their souls for a return to their celestial home is Pythagorean. Cicero seems to be opening a similar possibility to people such as philosophers or astronomers (who are not necessarily musicians) in lines 115–116 (**aliī quī praestantibus ingeniīs. . . .**); cf. Plato, *Phaedrus* 248. Earlier the elder Scipio had stated that it is true statesmen who are assured a place in heaven

(44–46) and had recommended cultivation of **iūstitia** and **pietās**, especially in the context of the state (71–72). Here (114–116) the men who prepare their journeys to the heavens are musicians and philosophers or astronomers (**quī . . . dīvīna studia coluērunt**, 115–116). There is no contradiction here, for Plato had already stressed the need for inner, spiritual harmony as a prerequisite to the performance of just actions in the context of the city state (*Republic* 443). The harmony of the spheres is a macrocosm of the harmony that should exist within the individual, as well as of the harmony that should exist within the state, the **cīvitās** or **rēs pūblica**; see also Plato, *Timaeus* 47.

Lines 117–124:

1. **Nīlus** (118): Pliny, *Naturalis historia* VI.181, also speaks of a cataract of the Nile that falls with such noise that the inhabitants of the region are deaf.

2. Students may wish to analyze and discuss the logic of the explanations being put forward here (117–123) of why men do not hear the music of the spheres. How convincing are they? Such explanations did not convince Aristotle, as is shown by the passage quoted on page 35 of the student's book.

Lines 125–133:

1. **spectātō . . . contemnitō** (127): the future imperative (a form which may be new to students) has a solemn ring to it and was often used in formulations of general rules of conduct and in formal legal documents.

The quotations from Plato and Seneca on pages 37 and 39 of the student's book illustrate the themes of philosophical detachment, aspiration to higher things, and disdain of things human or earthly. The passage from Seneca uses the theme of the ascent to heaven as preparation for learning to despise gold, wealth, ostentation, and earthly pursuits of seafaring, warfare, and statecraft.

In a satirical work by the second-century A.D. Greek author Lucian of Samosata, the Cynic philosopher Menippus is represented as donning wings (in the manner of Daedalus and Icarus) and soaring into the heavens, from which vantage point he is able to observe the pettiness of human life: "As a matter of fact, since the whole of Greece as it looked to me then from on high was no bigger than four fingers, on that scale surely Attica was infinitesimal. I thought, therefore, how little there was for our friends the rich to be proud of; for it seemed to me that the widest-acred of them all had but a single Epicurean atom under cultivation" (*Icaromenippus* 18, tr. A. M. Harmon).

Cicero takes this commonplace theme of the ascent into the heavens as a means of gaining perspective on the pettiness of human aspirations and pretentions and focuses it on the particular theme of scorning earthly fame or glory. This latter theme may contain lessons for any statesman, even for the younger Scipio. The final message of the "Somnium" is that a true statesman should be concerned with the health of the fatherland (**dē salūte patriae**, 209–210) and not with his own personal glory or fame, since the latter are transient and limited and the former is in keeping with the ultimate purposes of men's existence on this earth (**quī tuērentur illum globum** 64) and the favor of the god who rules the world (46–49).

The exhortation to despise the pursuit of human glory and to put the interests of the state first may, however, be thought of as directed more to the ambitious actors on the stage of Roman politics in Cicero's own day than to the younger Scipio Africanus. The real target of the exhortation contained in the "Somnium" may have been Pompey and Caesar, each jockeying for supreme power in a rivalry that was soon to precipitate civil warfare more devastating than any Rome had ever known. **Haec caelestia semper spectātō, illa hūmāna contemnitō**; would Pompey or Caesar heed the message? (Compare the passage from Cicero's letter of 27 February 49 B.C., on page 21 of the student's book.)

Cicero's contemporary, Sallust, had much to say about the pursuit of glory. In the olden days it was a good thing for the Roman state: "Their hardest struggle for glory was with one another; each man strove to be first to strike down the foe, to scale a wall, to be seen of all while doing such a deed. This they considered riches, this fair fame and high nobility. It was praise they coveted. . . ." (*Bellum Catilinum* VII.6, tr. J. C. Rolfe). This noble quest for glory came to be replaced, Sallust contends, by "lust for money first, then for power" (X.3); "Avarice destroyed honor, integrity, and all other noble qualities. . . . Ambition drove men to become false. . . ." (X.4–5). Glory was now sought by those who, "destitute of noble qualities, rely upon craft and deception" (XI.2). An outstanding exception in the days of Sallust and Cicero was the younger Cato, who "preferred to be, rather than to seem, virtuous," so that "the less he sought fame (**glōria**), the more it pur-

sued him" (*Bellum Catilinum* LIV.6, tr. J. C. Rolfe).

2. **Vidēs . . . potestis** (129–133): for the science of geography in the ancient world, see the *Encyclopaedia Britannica*, Vol. 10, pp. 151–152, and *The Oxford Classical Dictionary*, p. 463. In early Greek poetry the earth was thought of as a flat disc surrounded by the stream of Ocean; Pythagoras revolutionized thinking by hypothesizing that the earth was a globe, and this view prevailed in antiquity.

Lines 134–143:

1. **angustāta verticibus, lateribus lātior** (141): Herodotus had posited that the inhabited area of the world was broader from east to west than it was from north to south; Aristotle explains that view (which came to be widely accepted) in the passage quoted on page 39 of the student's book.

2. **Ōceanum** (142): when the earth was regarded in early times as being flat, Ocean was thought of as a stream encircling the inhabited world. See *The Oxford Classical Dictionary*, "Oceanus (mythological)," pp. 744–745. When the earth came to be thought of as a globe, the conception of Ocean changed; see *The Oxford Classical Dictionary*, "Oceanus (geographical)," p. 745. The pseudo-Aristotelian treatise *De mundo* (perhaps written as late as the second century A.D.) states: "It is probable that there are many other continents separated from ours by a sea that we must cross to reach them, some larger and others smaller than it, but all, save our own, invisible to us. For as our islands are in relation to our seas, so is the inhabited world in relation to the Atlantic, and so are many other continents in relation to the whole sea; for they are as it were immense islands surrounded by immense seas" (392b.20–25, tr. E. S. Forster).

Lines 144–149:

1. **Caucasum . . . Gangēn** (145–146): commonly cited landmarks of the eastern limits of the habitable world known to the ancients; cf. Juvenal X.1–2: "In all the lands that stretch from Gades to the Ganges and the Morn. . . ." (tr. G. G. Ramsay). The map on page 40 of the student's book shows the world as it was thought of in the time of Eratosthenes (third century B.C.). It shows the Ganges; teachers should have students locate the Caucasus Mountains, not named on the map but located between the Euxine and the Caspian Sea.

2. Be sure students carefully distinguish the ablative plural case endings in **reliquīs, ul-**

timīs, and **partibus** (146–147) from the genitive singular case endings in **orientis, obeuntis, sōlis, aquilōnis,** and **austrī** (146–147).
3. This paragraph provides good examples of rhetorical questions, to which no immediate answer is expected. There are three, introduced by **num** (144), **Quis** (146), and **quam . . . diū** (149). A fourth rhetorical question is presented indirectly in **quantīs . . . velit** (148).
4. Students' attention should be called to the emphasis achieved by separating **diū** from its modifier **quam** and by placing it last in the sentence (149). This is the rhetorical figure known as hyperbaton ("transposition"), and it throws special emphasis on the transposed element (here **diū**).

Lines 150–158:
1. The concept of periodic floods and conflagrations will interest students, who will be familiar with the Biblical flood. Plato, *Timaeus* 22, spoke of conflagrations that occur at great intervals of time and of deluges sent by the gods to purge the earth. The Stoics incorporated predictions of periodic floods and conflagrations into their view of the history and future of the cosmos. The passage from Cicero's *De natura deorum* on page 43 of the student's book attempts to explain the periodic occurrence of conflagrations in terms of the physics and dynamics involved in the interchange among the four elements: earth, air, fire, and water. Seneca, in the passage quoted on page 43 of the student's book, is less certain about what causes the periodic flooding, but he has no doubt that floods occur and destroy the human race. Lucretius, of the Epicurean school of thought, is equally certain about periodic conflagrations and floods caused by the triumph of one element over the other in the eternal warfare of the elements (*De rerum natura* V.373–415). The myth of Phaethon (Ovid, *Metamorphoses* I.748–II.405) recorded one such conflagration, and the flood sent by Jupiter to punish and obliterate the human race recorded one such deluge (Ovid, *Metamorphoses* I.253–261).
   Cicero is here using the concept of periodic floods and conflagrations to show that no one's glory or fame will extend very long because of the periodic catastrophes. He was undoubtedly thinking of a passage in Plato's *Timaeus* where it is explained that Egypt, because of its peculiar geography, has escaped destruction from conflagrations and floods and so preserves a long and unbroken historical record. Plato ex-

plains: "Whereas just when you [Greeks] and other nations are beginning to be provided with letters and the other requisites of civilized life, after the usual interval, the stream from heaven, like a pestilence, comes pouring down, and leaves only those of you who are destitute of letters and education; and so you have to begin all over again like children, and know nothing of what happened in ancient times, either among us [Egyptians] or among yourselves" (*Timaeus* 23, tr. B. Jowett). Thus, as Cicero says, **nōn modo nōn aeternam, sed nē diūturnam quidem glōriam adsequī possumus** (153–154).
2. **certē meliōrēs** (156): the notion that men of earlier generations were superior to men of the present age was a commonplace of popular moralizing.
3. **ūnīus annī** (157): as is clear from the ensuing discussion (159–168), Scipio refers to the "great," cosmic, or cyclic year. Before that becomes clear, the statement here will seem paradoxical.

Lines 159–168:
1. **cūncta astra redierint** (161): this will be the "great" or cosmic year, a concept deeply rooted in ancient astronomical speculation from the time of Pythagoras. Plato commented: "The perfect number of time fulfils the perfect year when all the eight revolutions, having their relative degrees of swiftness, are accomplished together and attain their completion at the same time. . . ." (*Timaeus* 39, tr. B. Jowett), and he set the length of this "cyclic year" at 10,000 of our years. Cicero in his lost *Hortensius* gave the length as 12,954 of our years (see Tacitus, *Dialogus* 16.7); Macrobius (II.XI.11) gave it as 15,000 years.
2. **Rōmulī animus** (164): Romulus' death is described as follows by Cicero in *De republica* II.X.17: "After Romulus had reigned thirty-seven years, and established those two excellent foundations of our commonwealth, the auspices and the senate, his great achievements led to the belief that, when he disappeared during a sudden darkening of the sun, he had been added to the number of the gods" (tr. C. W. Keyes).
3. **vīcēsimam partem** (168): Romulus died (according to tradition) in 716 B.C. Five hundred and sixty-seven years have thus elapsed between then and the time of Scipio's dream: 567 x 20 = 11,340 years. See note 1 above for the number 12,954; since Cicero writes **nōndum** in line 167, there is no disagreement between these two estimates.

Lines 169–178:

1. **neque tē sermōnibus vulgī dē- dideris... sed loquentur tamen** (172–175): after the previous paragraphs with their general descriptions of the universe and general philosophizing and exhortations, the elder Scipio seems to be returning to the actual political circumstances within which the younger Scipio was to become involved, culminating in his death amidst the turbulence over the Gracchan reforms.

2. The remarkable chiastic arrangement of all the words in **obruitur . . . extinguitur** (177–178) should be carefully analyzed and the effect of the arrangement discussed. This rhetorical flourish caps off the elder Scipio's exhortation to despise human fame and glory.

Lines 179–189:

1. Note that in lines 183–185 the elder Scipio is elucidating an abstract philosophical or psychological concept (the essence of the self) by using concrete nouns and pronouns, since classical Latin did not have terms for such ideas as "essence," "being," "individual," and "the self." Note in particular the italicized words: **nec enim *tū* is es quem *fōrma ista* dēclārat, sed *mēns cuiusque* is est *quisque*, nōn *ea fīgūra* quae *digitō* dēmōnstrārī potest**, (very literally translated) "for you are not that one (is) whom that shape of yours (ista) declares, but each person (quisque) is that one (is), namely, the mind of each one (mēns cuiusque), not that figure that can be pointed to with a finger." This conception of human identity is Pythagorean in origin. Cicero, in the passage from the *Tusculanae disputationes* given on page 49 of the student's book, illustrates the concept with the saying of the Delphic oracle, "Know thyself," which was inscribed in the temple of Apollo at Delphi. Cicero took this demonstration of the concept of the individual directly from Plato's *First Alcibiades* 130.

   In the same passage from the *Tusculanae disputationes* in the student's book, Cicero uses the word **animus** for "soul," corresponding to the word *psychē* in Plato's *First Alcibiades,* whereas in line 184 of the "Somnium" he uses the word *mēns* (**mēns cuiusque is est quisque**). In discussing the spiritual aspect of man, Plato distinguished between *nous* (= Latin **mēns**) and *psychē* (= Latin **animus**). The former term, *nous/mēns,* represents the intelligence of the world and the rational part of the human soul (*psychē/animus*). Thus, Cicero referred to the sun as the **mēns mundī**

(95), which rules the world. Aristotle, following Plato, also distinguished the *nous* as the immortal part of the soul, and the Stoics equated the soul of the world with *nous,* the rational intelligence that penetrates the universe and supplies men with the rational part of their soul. Cicero here (184) uses **mēns** rather than the more general term **animus** because he is leading up to the comparison in 186–189 of the human soul that rules the body and the divine intelligence that rules the world. That divine intelligence that rules the world is the **mēns mundī** already identified with the sun (95). (The words **moderātur** and **prīnceps**, 186–187, further recall the description of the sun as **prīnceps et moderātor**, 94–95, tightening the analogy between the role of the sun in the universe and that of the rational part of the soul within the individual.) However, when Cicero actually draws this comparison in 186–189, he uses the word **animus** rather than **mēns**, because Plato, in the passage from the *Phaedrus* which Cicero translates in the next paragraph, used the word *psychē* and not *nous,* because in that passage he was describing the human soul in general and not the ruling intelligence of the universe.

2. **Deum tē igitur scītō esse** (185): this is a striking statement, but a logical deduction from the premises that the soul is divine and that individuals are to be equated with their souls. The passage from the *Tusculanae disputationes* quoted on page 48 of the student's book elaborates upon this idea and upon the powers of the soul that indicated its divinity to the ancients.

3. **et ut mundum . . . animus sempiternus movet** (188–189): cf. Plato, *Laws* X (896): "As the soul orders and inhabits all things that move, however moving, must we not say that she orders also the heavens?" (tr. B. Jowett).

4. The carefully developed parallel and chiastic arrangements of words in lines 188–189 should be carefully explored and perhaps diagrammed with students' help.

Lines 190–202:

1. Cicero's Latin should be carefully compared with the English translation of the passage from Plato that Cicero is here faithfully translating. Some discussion may be elicited of why Cicero chose to translate this passage rather than developing the argument himself and of the propriety of this sort of borrowing (without explicit acknowledgment) from an earlier author. It may be noted that Cicero inserts this

same translation of Plato in the *Tusculanae disputationes* but prefaces it there with an acknowledgment of his debt to Plato: "This thought gave rise to Plato's well-known argument, developed by Socrates in the *Phaedrus* and placed by me in the sixth book of my work *On the State*" (I.XXII.53, tr. J. E. King). Cicero rehearses these and other arguments of Plato for the immortality of the soul in *De senectute* XXI.78.

2. To judge from Macrobius' commentary, Plato's attempt to prove the immortality of the soul, which Cicero translates here, was not only famous but also frequently paraphrased and reduced to simple, syllogistic form. One version, which Macrobius quotes, goes as follows: "The soul is self-moved; that which is self-moved is the beginning of motion; that which is the beginning of motion has no birth; that which has no birth is immortal; therefore the soul is immortal" (II.XIII.12, tr. W. H. Stahl).

3. How does the tone of this passage differ from the rest of the "Somnium"? Cicero seems to want the elder Scipio to sound here more like an inspired philosopher or prophet than a Roman statesman or loving uncle. Here he is made to speak exclusively in the hierophantic tones of high philosophical discourse. It might be interesting at this point to have students skim the earlier paragraphs to find phrases that are "conversational" and that create a warmer and more human mode of discourse, such as **ut scītis** (2), **crēdō equidem** (16), **Ades . . . animō** (21), **nē multa** (39–40), **St! Quaesō** (42), **sīc habētō** (44–45), **Immō vērō** (53), **Quīn tū aspicis** (55), **Nōnne aspicis** (85), and **Quīn etiam** (150).

4. This is a good section in which to look at the words Cicero uses to connect the separate parts of his argument—useful and necessary elements of any logical discussion: **nam, autem, quandō, igitur, quia, quīn, nec, enim, quodsī, sīquidem,** and **vel.**

5. **semper** (190): this word translates the Greek text as Cicero had it, but not as Plato wrote it. A papyrus shows that Plato wrote *autokinēton* "self-moving"; this was changed before Cicero's time to *aeikinēton*, "always moving," which Cicero translated with **semper.**

6. **orīgō . . . oriuntur** (195): attention may be called to the play on words from the same root.

Lines 209–218:

1. **pervolābit** (211): for the flight of the soul, see note to line 54, **ēvolāvērunt.**

2. In describing the flight of the soul, Cicero is thinking of the passage from Plato's *Phaedrus* 246–248 (partially quoted in the note to line 54, **ēvolāvērunt**). In this final paragraph he was also thinking of the passages quoted from the *Phaedo* on page 56 of the student's book, in which the fate of the souls—good and evil—are contrasted. The passages repay careful study and comparison with Cicero. What is it in Plato that results in the good soul's reaching the company of the gods? How does Cicero incorporate this into his passage? What does Cicero say about the training of the good soul that is totally absent from Plato? [Answer: that the state, the **patria**, is its proper grounds for activity and exercise and that souls properly exercised there will fly more quickly to their true home in the heavens; note that this has been Cicero's point all along—astral immortality is above all for those who have "served, aided, and expanded the **patria**" (45).] What for both Plato and Cicero constitutes the chief reason for the failure of the souls of some to reach heaven quickly? [Answer: devotion to bodily pleasures.] Note that Cicero goes beyond Plato in adding that such souls "violate the laws of gods and men" (215–216). That is, Cicero is, again, interested in the political or social aspects of men's lives, whereas Plato concentrates exclusively on the autonomous individual. It should also be noted that the evil souls in Plato end their wanderings through reincarnation or imprisonment in other bodies with natures as evil as in their former lives whereas the souls in Cicero after years of punishment finally return to their origin in the heavens.

* * *

FURTHER PASSAGE FOR COMPARISON

When students have finished reading the "Somnium," they should be directed to the Passages for Comparison in the student's book and should read and discuss them carefully. The teacher may also wish to bring in the passages from Boethius, Dante, and Chaucer mentioned at the end of the Introduction to these teaching notes on the "Somnium." A final exercise and one that would bring students back to the Latin would be to have them read the following passage from Vergil's

Aeneid (VI.724–751) and to compare it with ideas in the "Somnium" and in Plato (particularly in the myth of Er). Anchises is explaining to Aeneas in the underworld why it is that spirits are hovering in great throngs in a wooded area along the banks of the river Lethe. In words that are reminiscent of both Cicero's "Somnium Scipionis" and Plato's myth of Er, Anchises explains that these souls are waiting to be reincarnated. His explanation begins from the very beginning of all things:

"Prīncipiō caelum ac terrās campōsque liquentīs
lūcentemque globum lūnae Tītāniaque astra
spīritus intus alit, tōtamque īnfūsa per artūs
mēns agitat mōlem et magnō sē corpore miscet.
Inde hominum pecudumque genus vītaeque volan-
   tum
et quae marmoreō fert mōnstra sub aequore pon-
   tus.
Igneus est ollīs vigor et caelestis orīgō
sēminibus, quantum nōn noxia corpora tardant
terrēnīque hebetant artūs moribundaque membra.
Hinc metuunt cupiuntque, dolent gaudentque,
   neque aurās
dispiciunt clausae tenebrīs et carcere caecō.
Quīn et suprēmō cum lūmine vīta relīquit,
nōn tamen omne malum miserīs nec funditus omnēs
corporeae excēdunt pestēs, penitusque necesse est
multa diū concrēta modīs inolēscere mīrīs.
Ergō exercentur poenīs veterumque malōrum
supplicia expendunt: aliae panduntur inānēs
suspēnsae ad ventōs, aliīs sub gurgite vastō
īnfectum ēluitur scelus aut exūritur ignī
(quisque suōs patimur manīs; exinde per amplum
mittimur Ēlysium et paucī laeta arva tenēmus),
dōnec longa diēs perfectō temporis orbe
concrētam exēmit lābem, pūrumque relinquit
aetherium sēnsum atque aurāī simplicis ignem.
hās omnīs, ubi mīlle rotam voluēre per annōs,
Lēthaeum ad fluvium deus ēvocat agmine magnō,
scīlicet immemorēs supera ut convexa revīsant
rūrsus, et incipiant in corpora velle revertī."

Translation:
"First, a spirit within nourishes the heavens and lands and the watery fields and the shining globe of the moon and the Titan stars [i.e., the sun, called Titan, and the other stars]; a mind infused through the parts moves the whole mass and mingles itself in the great body.

"From here [from this spirit or mind], [arises] the race of men and beasts and the lives of flying creatures and the marvels that the sea bears under its marble-like surface.

"These original seeds of things possess a fiery vigor and a heavenly origin so far as harmful bod-ies do not impede them, nor earthly limbs and mortal parts weaken them.

"From here [i.e., from their earthly bodies] they feel fear, desire, sorrow, and joy, and they do not clearly see the upper air, [since they are] closed in by darkness and a blind prison.

"Indeed, not even when, on the last day, life departs, does every evil or all the plagues of the body leave the wretched ones completely, and it is necessary that the many accretions built up within over a long time grow deeply in amazing ways.

"Therefore, they [these souls with bodily taint] are disciplined by penalties, and they pay the pun-ishments of their old misdeeds: some are hung stretched out to empty winds; for others the stain is washed away beneath an enormous flood, or it is burned out by a flame. Each one of us suffers his own shade.

"Next, we are sent through wide Elysium, and we few possess the happy fields, until, after the circle of time has been fulfilled, the long-awaited day removes the intermingled stain and leaves the ethereal sense and the fire of pure air unsullied.

"All these, when they have rolled the wheel [of time] through a thousand years, the god summons in a great column to the River Lethe, so that they, not remembering, may see again the sky above and begin again to want to return into bodies."

* * *

TRANSLATION

IX. When I arrived in Africa as military tri-bune for the fourth legion, as you know, serving under the command of Manius Manilius, nothing was more important to me than meeting Masinissa, a king who was, for good reasons, a very dear friend of my family. When I came to him, the old man embraced me and wept copiously; then a little while afterwards he looked upwards to the heavens and said, "O supreme Sun, and all you other Dwellers of the Heavens! I give you thanks that, before I depart this life, I see in my kingdom and under my roof Publius Cornelius Scipio, by whose very name I am rejuvenated; and so never for a moment does the memory of that excellent and invincible hero depart from my mind." And then we asked each other questions—I, about his kingdom, he, about our republic; we passed the entire day exchanging many words back and forth.

X. After I had been received with regal splendor, we prolonged our conversation late into the night, while the old king spoke of nothing but Africanus. He recounted not only all his deeds but even his words. Then, when we parted to go to bed, a deeper slumber than usual took hold of me, since I was exhausted from traveling and I had stayed up to such a late hour. At this point, in the form which was more familiar to me from his image than from his actual person, Scipio Africanus appeared to me [in a dream] (I think this was a result of what we had been talking about; for it regularly happens that our thoughts and conversations give rise to something in a dream: just as Ennius wrote concerning Homer, whom he, of course, used to think about and talk about very often in his waking hours). When I recognized him, indeed I shuddered in fear, but he said, "Pay attention and put away your fear, Scipio, and entrust what I am going to say to your memory.

XI. "Do you see that city there, forced by me into submission to the Roman people, which is now renewing those former hostilities and cannot remain quiet?"—(and from a lofty place full of stars and bright with clear starlight he pointed out Carthage)—"the city which you now come to attack, with the rank of almost a simple soldier? Within two years, as consul you will overthrow this city, and through your own efforts you will earn for yourself the cognomen, which you have had up to this point as an inheritance from me. Moreover, when you have destroyed Carthage, celebrated your triumph, become censor, and gone on embassies to Egypt, Syria, Asia, and Greece, you will be elected consul again, in absentia; you will bring a great war to a close, and you will destroy Numantia. But, when you are carried to the Capitol in your triumphal chariot, you will come up against a government disturbed by the plans of my grandson.

XII. "At this point, Africanus, it will be necessary for you to hold forth to your country the light of your mind, your genius, and your wisdom. But I see a path branching in two directions as if [it were] the path of the fates of this time [of your life]. For when your lifetime has completed seven times eight returning circuits of the sun, and when both of those two numbers (each of which is considered perfect for its own reason) will in their natural course have fulfilled for you your fated total—then, to you alone, and to your name, the entire country will turn; the Senate, all good citizens, allies, and the people of Italy will look to you for guidance. You will be the one person on whom the salvation of the state depends; to be brief, you must, as dictator, restore order to the republic—if you escape the wicked hands of your kinsmen." At this point when Laelius cried out and the others groaned

quite vehemently, Scipio, smiling gently, said, "Sh! Please don't wake me from my dream; listen a little longer to the rest."

XIII. "But, Africanus, understand this, so that you may be even more ready to come to the defense of the republic: a place in heaven has been marked off for all those who have served, aided, and expanded their country, where these blessed ones may enjoy eternal life. For there is nothing that happens on this earth that is more pleasing to that supreme deity who rules the entire universe than the meetings and gatherings of men, joined lawfully, which are called states. The rulers and protectors of these states come from this [heavenly] place and return here."

XIV. At this point, although I was thoroughly terrified (not so much by the fear of death as by the treachery of my kinsmen), I nevertheless asked Scipio whether he himself and my father Paulus, and those others whom we considered dead, were actually living. He said, "Indeed, they are living, those who have flown out of the chains of the body as if from a prison; and in fact, what is called life by you, is death. Why don't you look at your father Paulus coming toward you?" And as I saw him, I, for my part, wept an abundance of tears. He embraced me, and as he kissed me he told me to stop weeping.

XV. As soon as I was able to speak, my weeping controlled, I said to him: "I beg you, most revered and excellent father, since *this* is life, as I hear Africanus say, why am I tarrying on earth? Why do I not hurry to come to you here?" "That is not how it is," he said. "For unless that deity, whose domain is everything you see, has freed you from the confinement of your body, entrance to this place cannot be opened to you. For men have been brought forth according to this law: that they watch over that sphere which is called 'earth,' which you see in the middle of the universe; and to each of them has been given a soul, made from the eternal fires that you call stars and planets, which, being round and globular and animated by divine spirits, complete their circular orbits with amazing swiftness. Wherefore, Publius, the soul is to be kept in the custody of the body by you and all good men; nor must you depart from the life of men except by the order of the one by whom this soul was entrusted to you, lest you seem to have shirked the human duty assigned to you by god.

XVI. "But you, Scipio, as your grandfather here, and as I who bore you, cultivate justice and a sense of responsibility—which is great in the case of parents and kinsmen, but greatest of all in the case of your country. That life is the way to heaven and to this gathering of those who have now finished living and, released from their bodies, inhabit that place that you see (there was a circle shining forth among the stars with a most splendid brightness), which you call the 'Milky Way' (the term that you have learned from the Greeks)." From that point, all the other things seemed marvelous and extremely bright to me as I beheld them. Moreover, there were the stars that we never see from this place [on earth], and the magnitude of all these was such as we had never expected. Among these, the smallest one, farthest from heaven and closest to earth, was shining with a borrowed light. The spheres of the stars, however, easily surpassed the magnitude of the earth. Indeed, the earth itself now seemed so small to me that I felt sorry for our empire, by which we touch [only] a tiny point, as it were, of it.

XVII. Since I was gazing even more intently at the earth, Africanus said: "How long, I ask, will your mind be fixed on the ground? Don't you see into what heavenly regions you have come? All [parts of the universe] are joined together by these nine circles, or rather spheres. One of these, the outermost, is [the circle] of heaven, which embraces all the rest; it is the supreme divinity himself, enclosing and containing the others; in this sphere have been fixed those eternal paths, which roll themselves along, of the stars. Placed under this sphere are seven [spheres], which revolve backwards with a motion opposite to that of the sphere of the heavens; one of these spheres is held by that [planet] that on earth they call Saturn. Next comes that splendor favorable and beneficial to the race of mankind, which is said to be of Jupiter; then the one that you call Mars, red and inspiring horror on earth; next, below this, the Sun occupies a region almost in the middle—ruler, chief, and guide of all the other lights, the mind and guiding principle of the universe, and of such great size that he illuminates and fills everything with his radiance. Next, as companions [of the Sun] follow the courses of first Venus and then Mercury; and in the lowest orbit, the Moon whirls around, ablaze with the rays of the Sun. But beneath [the Moon], there is nothing but what is mortal and perishable, except the souls given to the race of men as a gift of the gods; above the Moon, all things are eternal. And the Earth, which is at the center and ninth in order, does not move and is the lowest of all; and all masses are drawn toward it by their own gravitational pull."

XVIII. When I was gazing at these things in astonishment, I said, as I recovered myself, "What? What is the sound, so loud and beautiful, that fills my ears?" "This is," he said, "that [music] that is produced by the impulse and motion of the spheres themselves, [a music] distinguished by intervals that are unequal but nevertheless fixed rationally according to a certain proportion; this brings about diverse balanced harmonies, tempering the high-pitched [tones] with the low ones. For movements of such magnitude cannot be set in motion in silence, and nature ordains that at one extreme [the movements] make low-pitched sounds and at the other, high-pitched sounds. For this reason, the highest and star-bearing sphere of the heavens, the revolution of which is swifter, moves with a high-pitched, strong sound; but the lowest, that of the moon, moves with the lowest-pitched tone. For the ninth sphere, that of the earth, remains motionless and always clings to its abode, embracing its place in the center of the universe. But the other eight spheres, of which the velocities of two are the same, produce seven sounds at distinct intervals—a number by which almost all things are tied together. Learned men, imitating this [musical harmony] on the strings of their instruments and in their songs, have opened for themselves a return to this place, just as have others who, with outstanding ability, have pursued during their human lives divine studies. Filled with this sound, the ears of men have become deaf [to it]; for there is no weaker sense in you [than your hearing]. This is just as when the Nile rushes down from very lofty mountains at the place that is called Catadupa; the people who inhabit that area are lacking their sense of hearing because of the magnitude of the sound. But this sound is so mighty because of the extremely swift revolution of the entire universe that the ears of men cannot perceive it, just as you cannot look directly at the sun, and [if you do] your sense of sight is overpowered by its radiance." As I admired these things, I nevertheless kept returning my eyes to the earth again and again.

XIX. Then Africanus said, "I see that you even now are still gazing at the dwelling place and home of men; if it seems small to you, as it is, keep your gaze always on these heavenly things and scorn the human ones. For what fame resulting from the talk of men or what glory worth seeking can you actually achieve? You see that the earth is inhabited in sparse and narrow places, and between those little 'spots' where it is inhabited, vast empty spaces have been cast. You also see that those who inhabit the earth are not only separated in this way so that nothing can flow between them from one to another, but that they stand partly oblique, partly transverse, and partly even opposite in relation to you. From these people surely you can expect no fame.

XX. "Moreover, you see the same earth encircled and surrounded by certain zones, of which the two that are most widely separated and are supported at the top and bottom by the very poles of heaven are frozen with frost; the central zone, on the other hand, which is the broadest, is scorched by the fire of the sun. There are two habitable zones: of these, the southern one (in which the people who set foot imprint their footsteps opposite to yours) has no connection to your race [of men]. This other northern [temperate zone], which you inhabit: observe how small a part of it belongs to you. For the whole land that is inhabited by you is like a little island, narrower from north to south, wider from east to west, surrounded by that sea which on earth you call the Atlantic, the Great Sea, or Ocean. Although it has such a great name, you see how small it really is. From these very lands, inhabited and familiar, could your name or that of any one of us climb over the Caucasus Mountains, which you see, or swim across that Ganges River? Who in those remaining distant regions of the rising or setting sun or in the regions of the north or the south wind will hear your name? Once these have been eliminated, you can see immediately in what narrow regions your fame is eager to be spread. Moreover, those who do talk about us—how long will they do so?

XXI. "Indeed, even if those generations of men to come should wish to pass on the praises of each one of us, which they [will have] received from their fathers, to those who come afterwards, nevertheless, because of worldly floods and conflagrations, which necessarily happen at fixed times, we cannot achieve an eternal, or even a long-lasting, fame. Moreover, what does it matter that there will be talk about you by those who will be born after you, since there was none by those who were born before you, [XXII.] who were no fewer and were certainly better men [than you]; especially since among those very [men] by whom our names *can* be heard, not one can encompass the recollection of a single year? For men commonly measure a year by the return of only the sun, that is, of one heavenly body; in fact, however, when *all* the heavenly bodies return at once to the same place from which they started, and, at long intervals, bring back the original configuration of the entire sky, then that can be truly called a revolving year; in which I hardly dare to say how many generations of men are contained. For just as once, long ago, the sun seemed to men to suffer eclipse and be extinguished, when the spirit of Romulus entered into these very regions, whenever the sun will again be eclipsed at the same point and at the same time, then when all the constellations and heavenly bodies are summoned back to the same starting point you may consider a year to have been fulfilled. Understand that not even a twentieth part of this year has been completed.

XXIII. "Wherefore, if you despair of returning to this place, in which are all [the rewards] for great and outstanding men, of what value, finally, is that fame of men, which can barely last for a small part of a single year? Therefore, if you wish to look aloft and gaze upon this dwelling place and eternal home, do not give yourself over to the talk of the common crowd nor place hope of your fortunes in human rewards. Virtue herself must draw you by her own attractions to true glory. What others may say about you, let them see to it themselves; they will say it, regardless. But all that talk is limited by these narrow bands of the regions that you see; nor has talk about any man been everlasting; it is obliterated by the deaths of men and snuffed out in the forgetfulness of posterity."

XXIV. After he had said these things, I said, "Truly, Africanus, if indeed a sort of pathway to the entrance of heaven lies open to those who have served their country well, I shall strive all the more vigilantly now, since such a great reward has been shown to me, although from childhood I have followed in my father's footsteps and yours and I have not failed to measure up to your glory." And he said, "Truly, strive on, and understand this: that *you* are not mortal, but only this body; and you are not that which this shape of yours outlines; but the mind of each one of us is each one [i.e., the real self], not that form that can be pointed out with the finger. Know that you are a divine being, if indeed it is divinity that thrives, perceives, remembers, and foresees and that so guides, regulates, and moves the body that has been placed at its command just as that supreme divinity [guides, regulates, and moves] the universe; and just as that eternal divinity itself moves the universe, which is partly mortal, so an everlasting spirit moves the frail body.

XXV. "For what is always in motion is eternal; however, that which brings motion to another thing and is itself put in motion by another must necessarily come to the end of its life when that motion comes to an end. Therefore only that which moves itself, because it is never deserted by itself, never ceases to be in motion; nay, rather, this is the source, the first cause of movement for all other things that move. But there is no beginning of the first cause; for all things arise from the first cause, which itself cannot be born from any other thing. For that which was brought forth from another source would not be a *first* cause; and if it never has a beginning, then indeed, neither does it perish. For the first cause, if extinguished, will not by itself be brought to life again by any other thing, nor will it create something else from itself, if indeed it is necessary that all things arise from a first cause. Thus it happens that the beginning of motion has its existence from that which itself moves by itself. Moreover, this [first cause] can neither be born nor die, or else, by necessity, the entire heavens and all of nature would collapse; nor would she [nature] find any force by which she could again be impelled and set in motion. [XXVI.] Since it is obvious, therefore, that what moves by itself is eternal, who is there who would deny that this property has been given to spirits? For anything that is set in motion by an outside impulse is without spirit, but that which is with spirit is put in motion from within by its own impetus; for this is the proper nature and power of the soul; which if it is the one thing of all things that itself moves itself, surely it has not been subject to birth and it is eternal.

"Exercise your soul in the best pursuits! The best concerns are for the safety of your country, and your soul, if it is engaged and trained in these things, will fly more swiftly to this, its own resting place and home. And it will do this even more quickly if already then, when it is enclosed in the body, it projects itself outward, and, contemplating those things that are outside, draws itself out of the body as much as possible. For the souls of those who have given themselves over to the pleasures of the body and have put themselves forth as servants of those [pleasures], and of those who have violated the laws of gods and men at the instigation of those pleasure-serving desires—[the souls of these men,] after slipping out of their bodies, fly around the earth itself and do not return to this place except after being tortured for many generations."

He departed; sleep released my limbs.

*   *   *

ANSWERS FOR EXERCISES

Exercise I: Verbs
1. **vīveret(ne)**, indirect question. 2. **tuērentur**, relative clause of purpose. 3. **lūstret . . . compleat**, result clause. 4. **possit**, relative clause of characteristic. 5. **videant**, jussive. 6. **vigilāvissem**, causal clause. 7. **videāminī**, negative purpose clause. 8. **moveātur**, relative clause in indirect statement. **neget**, relative clause of characteristic. 9. **possint**, result clause.

Exercise II: Dative or Ablative Case?
1. "yours," dative of possession. 2. "to your country," dative indirect object. 3. "eternal life," ablative with special verb. 4. "to that god," dative with adjective. 5. "by fear," ablative of cause (or means). 6. "from these confinements," ablative of separation. 7. "according to this law," ablative of specification. 8. "with marvelous speed," ablative of manner. 9. "by you," dative of agent. 10. "to me as I watched," dative indirect object. 11. "by the light of another," ablative of means. 12. "to the race," dative with adjective. 13. "by their own inclination," ablative of means. 14. "in silence," ablative of manner. 15. "for themselves," dative indirect object. 16. "the sense," ablative of separation. 17. "by the heat," ablative of means. 18. "at a fixed time," ablative of time when. 19. "by the return," ablative of means. 20. "your glory," dative with compound verb.

Exercise III: Grammatical Forms
1. F. 2. C. 3. E. 4. B. 5. J. 6. G. 7. I. 8. A. 9. H. 10. D.

Exercise IV: Pronouns and Adjectives
1. intensive, ablative, plural, "very." 2. indefinite, genitive, singular, "of anyone." 3. personal, genitive, plural, "of us." 4. demonstrative, accusative, singular, "this." 5. relative, accusative, singular, "which." 6. demonstrative, accusative, singular, "that." 7. interrogative, nominative, singular, "Who?" 8. linking **quī**, ablative, plural, "And . . . they/these." 9. interrogative (used in an exclamation), ablative, plural, "what." 10. reflexive, accusative, singular, "itself." 11. intensive, nominative, plural, "Those (very ones)." 12. relative, nominative, plural, "who." 13. personal, ablative, plural, "us."

Exercise V: Translation into Latin
Hominēs enim sunt hāc lēge generātī, quī tuērentur illum globum quem in hōc templō medium vidēs, quae terra dīcitur, iīsque animus datus est ex illīs sempiternīs ignibus quae sīdera et stellās vocātis, quae globōsae et rotundae, dīvīnīs animātae mentibus, circulōs suōs orbēsque cōnficiunt celeritāte mīrābilī. (lines 63–67)

Exercise VI: Principal Parts
1. **patēre, patuī**, to stand open. 2. **nancīscor, nactus sum**, to obtain. 3. **căreō, cărēre, caritum**, to be without. 4. **attingō, attingere, attigī**, to come in contact with. 5. **possum, posse, potuī**. 6. **parere, peperī, partum**, to bear, give birth. 7. **dīlātō, dīlātāvī, dīlātātum**, to stretch, extend. 8. **mālō, mālle**, to prefer. 9. **nītor, nītī**, to strive. 10. **orior, orīrī, ortus sum**.

11. praebēre, praebuī, praebitum, to offer.
12. percontor, percontātus sum, to question, investigate.

* * *

BIBLIOGRAPHY

Cicero's *De republica* and the "Somnium Scipionis"

(The Latin text presented in this edition and the teaching notes owe much to the following editions, commentaries, and studies—listed in chronological order.)

M. Tulli Ciceronis Tusculanarum Disputationum Liber Primus et Somnium Scipionis: Edited, with Introduction and Notes, by Frank E. Rockwood. "College Series of Latin Authors." University of Oklahoma Press, Norman, OK, 1966 (reprint of 1903 edition).

Études sur le songe de Scipion (Essais d'histoire et de psychologie religieuses), by Pierre Boyancé. Feret & Fils, Editeurs, Bordeaux, Paris, 1936.

Cicerone: Somnium Scipionis: Introduzione e Commento, by Alessandro Ronconi. Felice le Monnier, Florence, 1961.

De re publica librorum sex quae manserunt, by K. Ziegler. "Teubner" edition. Teubner, Leipzig, 1964.

Somnium Scipionis: Quellen, Gestalt, Sinn, by Karl Büchner. "Hermes Einzelschriften," 36. Franz Steiner Verlag, Wiesbaden, 1976.

Cicéron: La République Tome II—Livres II–VI, by Esther Bréguet. "Budé" edition. Société d'Edition "Les belles lettres," Paris, 1980.

Macrobius' Commentary

Macrobius: Commentary on the Dream of Scipio, Translated with an Introduction and Notes, by William H. Stahl. "Records of Civilization, Sources and Studies," No. XLVIII. Columbia University Press, New York, NY, 1952.

Cicero

(The Introduction to the teaching notes owes much to the works by Boak, Sabine, Rawson, Lacey, and Sabine and Smith in the following sections of this bibliography.)

A History of Rome to 565 A.D., by Arthur E. R. Boak. The Macmillan Company, New York, NY, 1985. Pp. 204–240.

*"Cicero," *The Oxford Classical Dictionary.* 2nd edition, Oxford University Press, Oxford and New York, NY, 1970. Pp. 234–238.

Cicero and the Roman Republic, by F. R. Cowell. Chanticleer Press, New York, NY, 1948.

Reference Works for Special Projects on Sections of the "Somnium Scipionis"

IX–XI: The Punic Wars and the Careers of the Two Scipios:

Scipio Aemilianus, by A. E. Astin. Oxford University Press, Oxford and New York, NY, 1967.

Scipio Africanus: Soldier and Politician, by H. H. Scullard. "Aspects of Greek and Roman Life" series. Cornell University Press, Ithaca, NY, 1970.

**The Oxford Classical Dictionary,* "Punic Wars," pp. 900–901.

**The Oxford Classical Dictionary,* "Scipio Africanus Major," p. 962, and "Scipio Aemilianus Africanus Numantinus," p. 963.

XI–XII: Tiberius Gracchus and the Younger Scipio:

**The Gracchi,* by David Stockton. Oxford University Press, Oxford and New York, NY, 1979.

**The Oxford Classical Dictionary,* "Gracchus, Tiberius Sempronius," p. 473.

Tiberius Gracchus: Destroyer or Reformer of the Republic? "Problems in European Civilization" series. D. C. Heath and Company, Lexington, MA, 1970.

XIII: Cicero's Conception of the State and the Role of the Ideal Statesman:

**A History of Political Theory,* by George H. Sabine. Chapter IX, "Cicero and the Roman Lawyers," pp. 159–173. Henry Holt and Company, New York, NY, 4th ed., 1973.

**Cicero: A Portrait,* by Elizabeth Rawson. Chapter 9, "Cicero on the Republic 56–52 B.C.," pp. 146–163. Cornell University Press, Ithaca, NY, 1983.

Cicero and the End of the Roman Republic, by W. K. Lacey. Chapter 5, "Political Eclipse and Political Treatises," pp. 78–95. Harper & Row, New York, NY, 1978.

**On the Commonwealth: Marcus Tullius Cicero,* by George H. Sabine and Stanley B. Smith. "The Library of Liberal Arts." The Bobbs-Merrill

Company, Inc., Indianapolis, IN, and New York, NY, reprint of 1929 edition.

Res Publica: Roman Politics and Society according to Cicero, by W. K. Lacey and B.W.J.G. Wilson. Oxford University Press, Oxford and New York, NY, 1970. Selections from Cicero on various aspects of the Roman Republic.

XIV: Pythagorean, Orphic, and Platonic Views of Life and Death:

Ancient Western Philosophy: The Hellenic Emergence, by George F. McLean and Patrick J. Aspell. Appleton-Century-Crofts, New York, NY, 1971.

*Encyclopaedia Britannica, Vol. 17, "Philosophy, History of: I. Ancient Philosophy," pp. 869–873.

*The Oxford Classical Dictionary, "Pythagoras," pp. 903–904; "Orpheus," p. 758; "Orphism," pp. 759–760; "Plato," pp. 839–842.

*The Presocratic Philosophers: A Critical History with a Selection of Texts, by G. S. Kirk and J. E. Raven. Chapters VII–IX. Cambridge University Press, Cambridge and New York, NY, 2nd ed., 1984. A scholarly presentation of the ancient evidence in the original Greek and in English translation.

XV: The Stoic Conception of the Universe, God, the Divine Fire, the Human Soul, and the Purpose of Human Life:

*Encyclopaedia Britannica, Vol. 21, "Stoics," pp. 265–269.

*The Meaning of Stoicism, by Ludwig Edelstein. "Martin Classical Lectures," Volume XXI. Harvard University Press, Cambridge, MA, 1966.

*The Oxford Classical Dictionary, "Stoa," pp. 1015–1016.

XVI–XVII: Ancient Astronomy, Astrology, and the Geocentric Conception of the Universe:

*A Short History of Astronomy: From Earliest Times through the Nineteenth Century, by Arthur Berry. Chapter II, "Greek Astronomy," pp. 21–75. Dover Publications, New York, NY, 1961, reprint of 1898 edition.

*Encyclopaedia Britannica, Vol. 2, "Astronomy: A. Ancient Astronomy," pp. 643–644, and "Astrology: Astrology in the West," pp. 640–641B.

*The Oxford Classical Dictionary, "Astronomy," pp. 134–135, and "Astrology," pp. 133–134.

XIX–XX: Ancient Conceptions of the Earth's Geography:

*Encyclopaedia Britannica, Vol. 10, "Geography: A. Mediterranean Region," pp. 145–146.

*The Oxford Classical Dictionary, "Geography," p. 463, and "Maps," p. 645.

XXI: Floods and Conflagrations in Ancient Views of the History of the World:

Lucretius, *De rerum natura* V.373–415.

XXIII: Ancient Attitudes toward Glory and Fame:

Cicero, *Ad familiares* V.12: Cicero's desire for fame and glory here may be compared with the disparaging of fame and glory in the "Somnium."

Cicero, *Pro Gnaeo Plancio* 63–66: Cicero's disappointment that his reputation as quaestor in Sicily had not spread beyond the province.

Horace, Odes III.30: Horace's confident claim to eternal fame.

XXIV–XXVI: Ancient Conceptions of the Immortality of the Soul and Its Life after Death:

See references for paragraph XIV above.
Plato, *Phaedo.*
Lucretius, *De rerum natura* III.

The "Somnium Scipionis" in Later Literature

**Boethius, *The Consolation of Philosophy*: Translated with Introduction and Notes by Richard Green. The Liberal Arts Press, Inc. (Bobbs-Merril Co.), New York, NY, 1962.

Chaucer, *The Parliament of Birds*, in *The Complete Poetical Works of Geoffrey Chaucer: Now First Put into Modern English*, by John S. P. Tatlock and Percy MacKaye. Pages 341–353. The Macmillan Company, New York, NY, 1943.

**Dante, *The Divine Comedy*, tr. by Thomas Bergin. "Crofts Classics Series." Harlan Davidson, Inc., Arlington Heights, IL, 1955.

General

Death and Burial in the Roman World, by J. M. C. Toynbee. Cornell University Press, Ithaca, NY, 1971.

*Roman Life, by Mary Johnston. Scott, Foresman and Company, Glenview, IL, 1957.

CICERO AND SALLUST ON THE CONSPIRACY OF CATILINE

INTRODUCTION

The Roman Army and the Sullan Civil War

The Catilinarian conspiracy of 63 B.C. fell in a period that was still very much influenced by the reforms and memory of the dictator Lucius Cornelius Sulla (ca. 138–78 B.C.). Sallust specifically states that the tyranny of Sulla fired the ambition of Catiline (lines 12–14) and Lentulus, one of his chief associates (lines 238–240). We are also told (Sall. *Cat.* 28.4) that Catiline's forces drew recruits from the **Sullānī mīlitēs** (Sulla's veterans), who had been settled on allotments of land in Italy twenty years earlier. Some of these veterans were apparently eager to renew the days of pillage and bloodshed in order to restore their sagging fortunes. Cicero in his *Second Catilinarian* (20) states that the plight of these former soldiers who rallied to Catiline was so desperate that nothing short of recalling Sulla from the grave could set them on their feet again. Sulla had once plunged Italy into a bloody civil war when he returned in 83 B.C. from a war against Mithridates in Asia. Twenty years later, Gnaeus Pompey (106–48 B.C.), one of Sulla's military commanders in the civil war, was bringing a continuation of the war against Mithridates to a conclusion. Those living at the time must have wondered whether Pompey would follow the example of Sulla and make himself absolute master of the state upon his return. The memory of Sulla, therefore, could inspire hope in some, fear in others, that history might repeat itself. All Romans, furthermore, for better or worse, were living under a form of government that had been overhauled by Sulla during his dictatorship (82–79 B.C.). In order to set the Catilinarian conspiracy in a proper historical perspective, it is necessary to review some of the conditions that brought Sulla to power and to consider how the dictatorship of Sulla influenced Roman politics in the succeeding decades.

Sulla, when consul in 88 B.C., had been the first Roman general to use an army to crush his political opponents in Rome. Previous political rivalries had sometimes led to bloodshed when citizens clashed with citizens in the streets and in the assemblies, but never before had Roman legions been employed by an individual commander to reverse the vote in a popular assembly and to butcher his opponents. Sulla's action was made possible by a fundamental change in the way Roman armies were recruited in the late Republic. Down to 108 B.C. Roman soldiers had been drawn from the citizen body as a whole, and only those who possessed a minimum property qualification were eligible for service. When this property qualification was suspended and the consul Gaius Marius in 107 B.C. accepted volunteers from all classes of citizens for his African campaign against Jugurtha, the Roman army was radically altered for the future. Increasingly Rome's soldiers were drawn from the poor and the unemployed. These recruits tended to make a career of soldiering, and they looked to their commander to secure for them the cash bounties and allotments of land that were typically granted to soldiers upon being discharged. Since there was no regular mechanism for awarding these benefits to discharged soldiers, it fell to the individual commanders themselves to ensure that the necessary enabling legislation was passed each time in the assembly. Armies, therefore, tended in time to become personally loyal to their commanders, and Sulla was the first to reveal that a ruthless and ambitious general might override governmental decisions by turning his troops loose on his political opponents.

Not once but twice did Sulla teach Rome this lesson. During his absence from Italy from late 88 B.C. to the spring of 83, while he was engaged in conducting a war against Mithridates in Greece and Asia, Sulla's political foes gained control of the government. His arch enemy, Lucius Cornelius

Cinna, held a string of consulships from 87 to 84, and this government executed or caused to go into exile many of Sulla's supporters. (This Cinna and Sulla are the two Cornelii mentioned in the prophecy that is said to have caused the conspirator Publius Cornelius Lentulus to hope to be the third Cornelius to hold absolute power in Rome [lines 238–240].) The Cinnan government also tried to relieve Sulla of his command by sending out a replacement, but once again the general was able to flaunt the civilian authorities because he could count upon the personal loyalty of his troops. The resulting standoff led ultimately to civil war when Sulla returned with his army to Italy in 83 and negotiations failed to produce a peaceful settlement.

The government, which remained in the hands of Sulla's enemies, fielded armies under commanders of its own, but these newly raised troops proved no match for the seasoned veterans who fought for Sulla. By the end of 82 B.C. Sulla was master of Italy. Only pockets of resistance remained. The two consuls who had been directing the war against Sulla were hunted down and killed by Sulla's forces. A blood bath known as the Sullan proscriptions followed the military victory. Partly to raise money to reward his followers and partly to purge the state of his enemies, Sulla caused the leading figures of the losing side to be seized and executed. The names of these men were posted publicly and cash bounties were offered for their murder. The property of the victims of this purge was confiscated and sold at auction, and many of Sulla's followers were the beneficiaries of these forced sales. Even a citizen who had managed to keep clear of politics sometimes found his name included on the list of the proscribed if his wealth excited the greed of one of Sulla's henchmen. Furthermore, whole districts of Italy suffered in the aftermath of the civil war. Those areas that had supported the losing side were singled out to provide land for Sulla's discharged soldiers—a total of 120,000 individual allotments according to one source. The district of Etruria to the north of Rome was one of the regions where these colonies of Sullan veterans were planted in great numbers. It is not surprising, therefore, to find Catiline's associate, Gaius Manlius, an ex-centurion in Sulla's army, carrying on recruitment in this area nearly two decades later in 64–63 B.C. (lines 88–90). As early as 78 B.C., when one of the consuls, Marcus Lepidus, broke with the government and attempted to raise a rebellion, he selected Etruria as the base of his operations because this area had been so disrupted by the civil war. Many communities and former landowners had been reduced to desperate straits as a result

of having had land taken from them to reward Sulla's soldiers. Then too, as time went on and some of the Sullan colonists exhausted their new-found prosperity through poor management, they might be tempted to answer a call to arms if, under Catiline or a similar leader, they saw a chance to renew civil strife and profit from the turmoil.

The Sullan Constitution

Not only were the conditions in Italy that favored Catiline's revolution largely the product of the Sullan age, but the government itself which was forced to cope with this crisis owed many of its features to Sulla's constitutional reforms. By an act of the assembly in 82 B.C., Sulla was granted the title "Dictator" and given authority to establish laws and reconstitute the state. Most of Sulla's legislation was designed to restore power to the Roman Senate. He filled vacancies in this body (caused by the civil war) with his supporters, and he doubled the size of the Senate from 300 members to 600. Many of the 300 new members of the Sullan Senate were drawn from the equestrian order, those citizens who were among the wealthiest but had never held political office. To curtail the power of the tribunate, Sulla restricted the right of the ten plebeian tribunes to initiate legislation and employ their veto. To discourage ambitious politicians from holding this office, he barred those who were elected to the tribunate from holding any further political office. Sulla reconstituted the standing criminal courts—establishing at least seven of these—and transferred the right to serve on the juries in these courts from the equestrian to the senatorial order. Those who wished to hold the consulship were required first to hold the praetorship and prior to that the quaestorship. For each of these political offices in the so-called **cursus honōrum** a minimum age requirement was established (30 for the quaestorship, 39 for the praetorship, and 42 for the consulship), and an interval of at least two years had to elapse between offices (ten years for the repetition of the same office). The number of annually elected quaestors was increased to twenty, and ex-quaestors were henceforth granted a permanent seat in the Senate. This innovation took an important power out of the hands of the censors, who had previously been charged with filling vacancies in the Senate when a census was held normally every five years. The number of praetors was increased to eight, partly to provide a sufficient number of magistrates to preside over trials in the criminal courts, and partly to produce a sufficient number of ex-magistrates each year to serve as governors of Rome's overseas provinces. Traditionally in this period Roman provinces were governed by ex-consuls and ex-praetors. Under the Sullan scheme there were ten provinces (the two Spains, two Gauls, Sicily, Sardinia and Corsica, Africa, Macedonia, Asia, and Cilicia) and an equal number of ex-magistrates, so that theoretically each year new administrators could be sent out. In this way it was hoped that no one individual could easily follow in Sulla's own footsteps and win the personal loyalty of his troops in the field by serving for a lengthy tenure. Finally, to help the Senate maintain control over its provincial commanders, Sulla toughened the legislation regulating the powers of provincial governors.

The bulk of these Sullan reforms remained in place until another dictator, Julius Caesar, set about reshaping the government along monarchal lines. Cracks in the façade, however, became visible almost as soon as Sulla relinquished power and retired into private life in 79 B.C. Within a year of his death in 78 B.C., the proconsul Marcus Lepidus attempted to raise a revolt in Italy to undo Sulla's reforms. Although this uprising was crushed by the government, there were ominous signs that the Senate lacked the necessary leadership and military commanders loyal to its policies to play the role Sulla had intended for it. In addition to the revolt of Lepidus, war dragged on in Spain for nearly a decade against Sertorius, an ex-praetor in the Cinnan government and a brilliant military commander, who had fled from Italy when resistance to Sulla collapsed. In Asia war was renewed with Mithridates in 74 B.C. and continued as a drain on Roman resources for more than a decade. On the high seas piracy had become so rampant that Italy itself was subjected to raids. The Senate's attempt to crush these brigands by charging one of the praetors in 74 with a special command led to defeat and humiliation two or three years later when the Roman commander was forced to agree to a treaty with the marauders. At about the same time the two consuls of 72 B.C. experienced another humiliating defeat for Roman arms in Italy at the hands of Spartacus, who had sparked a rebellion of slaves.

One figure in particular emerged as Rome's savior in each of these crises but at the same time rose to a position of eminence so great that he threatened the very basis of Sulla's constitution. This figure was Gnaeus Pompey. In 83 B.C., as a young man of only 23, Pompey had raised troops from among his father's (consul 89 B.C.) veterans and performed valuable service in Sulla's cause. He grew so rapidly in power in comparison with his years that even Sulla was forced grudgingly to recognize the cognomen Magnus that Pompey took to himself (in emulation of Alexander the Great)

and to permit Pompey to celebrate a military triumph for his victories in the civil war, although he was not yet old enough to be a senator. In dealing with the revolt of Lepidus and the war with Sertorius, the Senate found it expedient to employ the services of Pompey. In recognition of the considerable power Pompey enjoyed as a result of his past military successes, the Senate named him first propraetor in the war with Lepidus and then proconsul in the war against Sertorius. When at the conclusion of the war in Spain Pompey returned to Italy in 71 and demanded to be a candidate for the consulship, although he was under age and had held none of the prerequisite lower offices, the Senate was forced to allow his candidacy. This former supporter of Sulla, who even in Sulla's lifetime enjoyed an anomalous position of power, revealed the fundamental weakness of the Sullan government. Despite all of Sulla's reforms, the Senate could still be placed at the mercy of a commander who controlled an army personally loyal to himself.

The year 70 B.C., in which Pompey held the consulship with Marcus Licinius Crassus (ca. 112–53 B.C.), another of Sulla's former adherents, witnessed some significant changes in the Sullan settlement that were to have a profound effect on politics in the next two decades. Senatorial juries, which had earned a reputation for corruption in the criminal courts, were diluted by the addition of an equal number of jurors drawn from each of two nonsenatorial classes (the equestrians and the **tribūnī aerāriī**). Henceforth, defendants, who were most often senators themselves, could no longer use their influence in the senatorial class to win a favorable verdict from a majority of the jurors. The full powers of the tribunate to initiate legislation and to exercise a veto were restored, and this reversal of Sulla's policy was soon turned to Pompey's personal advantage. In 67, and later in 66, over the Senate's strenuous objections, tribunician legislation granted Pompey an extended command and vast military resources, first to clear the Mediterranean of pirates and then to conclude the war against Mithridates in Asia.

Finally, it was also in the year 70 B.C. that the first census of the Roman people was held since before the dictatorship of Sulla. One consequence of this census was the removal of 64 senators from the Senate on the grounds of misconduct. Among those who suffered this disgrace were Gaius Antonius (later elected consul with Cicero for 63), Publius Lentulus (consul in 71 and, as praetor in 63, a supporter of Catiline), and Quintus Curius (an informer recruited by Cicero among Catiline's followers). Clearly many who lost the rank of senator in the census of 70 used all possible means, both fair and foul, in the subsequent decade to recover their standing by holding public office again. Antonius and Lentulus, just mentioned, provide examples of political figures who were thrust back into politics and swelled the number of candidates in the 60's who were competing for the same limited number of offices at the top of the political hierarchy.

In the next place, it can be surmised that as a result of the census in 70 many new voters were added to the rolls. Nearly two decades before (in 90–89 B.C.) Rome had been forced by a rebellion of her Italian allies to extend Roman citizenship to all of the communities south of the Po River. In the meantime, however, the vast majority of these potential new voters had been in effect disfranchised by the failure of the government to conclude a full-scale census and enroll the new citizens in the tribes and centuries that made up the voting units in the assemblies. The opportunity for many of these previously unregistered voters to become part of the electoral process after the census in 70 had a potentially unsettling effect on politics in the following decade. Since a candidate in a Roman election ran as an individual and not as the nominee of a political party—there were no political parties as we know them—each candidate had to rely upon his own network of supporters. Those who were likely to have such a political network were persons who belonged to a family that had played an active role in political affairs for generations. Such individuals enjoyed immediate name-recognition among the voters, thanks to the accomplishments of their ancestors. Such persons as well could build upon the political connections and alliances that their families had established both in the Senate and among the important families in the rural districts. These were the families that comprised the ruling oligarchy—the so-called nō-bilēs (lit., "those who are well known"). Yet once the number of potential voters had been increased dramatically by the census in 70, it must have challenged the ingenuity of the members of the nobility to continue to deliver a sufficient number of votes through their existing networks of political connections.

Political and Economic Conditions in the 60's B.C.

One sign that the ruling oligarchy was no longer able to control elections as effectively as it had once been able to do is provided by the increase in corruption and violence attending Roman elections in the 60's. In 67 B.C. the consuls, one of whom, Gaius Piso, was reported to have used bribery to buy his election, were instructed by the Senate to pass tough new legislation against **ambitus** ("electoral corruption"). A year later the two candidates elected to the consulship for 65 were successfully prosecuted for corrupt electioneering—not without first having tried to disrupt at least one of their trials by violence—, and a supplementary election had to be held late in 66 to fill the resulting vacancies for 65. In both 64 and 63, when Catiline was a candidate for the consulship, violence and bribery led to renewed calls for stiffening the penalties against corrupt canvassing. In 64 a tribune friendly to Catiline staved off new legislation by means of his veto, but in 63 Cicero succeeded in putting through a law that tightened the restrictions on what a candidate could and could not do to influence the voters. The need that was felt in this period for stricter laws regulating the conduct of elections shows that the system was no longer functioning smoothly.

This corrupt and disturbed age is the one in which Catiline operated. He and his supporters were driven on, we are told, also by the condition of widespread debt in this period. Many in the countryside of Italy were still reeling from the disruption caused by the civil war with Sulla and the confiscation of land that had occurred after the war to settle his veterans. The economy had also been shaken by the drain placed upon the Roman treasury by the wars in Spain against Sertorius and in Asia against Mithridates. Closer to home, southern Italy had recently been subjected to upheaval by the slave revolt led by Spartacus. During this same period overseas investments must have been disrupted by the raids conducted by pirates on shipping and by the warfare in Asia against Mithridates, which drastically curtailed revenues from this formerly lucrative province. By the mid-60's, conditions were beginning to improve, and this improvement in turn was likely to have encouraged creditors in Italy to call in some outstanding loans for reinvestment of their capital in more attractive ventures abroad. Pompey's whirlwind campaign of 67 had cleared the Mediterranean of piracy, and within the next two or three years Mithridates had been driven a safe distance from Asia. One sign indicating that expectations for the recovery of Asia were running high is the size of the contract awarded by the government to one of the private firms of tax farmers (pūblicānī) who regularly collected the revenues from this province. Apparently the company that had entered into this contract had bid too high relative to the actual value of the revenues that were realized. By the end of the decade, the company asked to renegotiate its contract and ultimately gained, through the consul Julius Caesar in 59, a remission of one-third of its obligation. Another sign that investors were increasingly eager to demand payment of debts in Italy in order to raise capital for overseas investments is provided by a decree of the Senate in 63 that restricted the amount of gold and silver that could leave Italy. It is not surprising, therefore, that both Sallust and Cicero stress the prevalence of debt both in Italy and in the provinces as one of the factors that encouraged Catiline to foment a rebellion.

These, then, were some of the conditions that favored the formation of Catiline's conspiracy. Catiline himself had been a former henchman of Sulla and had taken an active roll in the Sullan proscriptions. Had he been elected consul in 64 instead of Cicero, he probably would have been content to play a modest roll in support of debt reform and other proposals in 63 and then to go off to reap the profits to be made from governing a province as ex-consul in 62. When this candidacy failed and he made a second bid in 63, he tried to compensate for his loss of powerful backers such as Crassus, who appears to have abandoned him, by advocating more radical measures designed to appeal to the masses. When he suffered his second rejection by the voters in 63, all hope of achieving the consulship by election vanished.

Under these circumstances, Catiline, a proud and haughty nobleman, chose to risk all his fortunes on the desperate chance of civil war. Later, another patrician, Julius Caesar, would resort to war in 49 B.C. in defense of his **dignitās** as Catiline had done in 63. Sallust notes, however, that in the case of Catiline it is doubtful whether his revolution could have succeeded even if he had held his own militarily at the beginning of the uprising. Other more powerful figures were waiting on the sidelines and were more likely than Catiline to emerge as masters of the state. If the rebellion had not been stamped out at the Battle of Pistoria in January 62 B.C., a ready-made pretext would have been provided for recalling Pompey and investing him with extraordinary powers to crush the revolutionaries. A tribune friendly to Pompey's interests had already taken steps early in 62 to pass such a proposal. The news of Catiline's defeat, however, reached Rome in time for this legislation to be shelved. To judge from Pompey's cool reception of Cicero's glowing report of how he had crushed Catiline without plunging Italy into a state of war, Pompey was none too pleased by the turn of events.

The success of Cicero and the government in dealing with Catiline deprived Pompey of yet another opportunity to strengthen his own hand by stepping in to rescue the state as he had done in the 70's. Moreover, the boldness inspired in the Senate by the way in which this crisis had been met helps to explain the intransigence displayed by the Senate in failing to take its lead from Pompey during the next few years. After Pompey returned to Italy in late 62 and discharged his army, he was unable to bend the Senate to his will. The stalemate that developed between Pompey and his opponents in the Senate finally drove him to enter into a political alliance with Crassus and Caesar in late 60 B.C. With the formation of this so-called first triumvirate, power inevitably shifted away from the Senate and into the hands of the three dynasts. The triumph of Cicero and the Senate over Catiline was ultimately not able to be translated into lasting power and influence.

Orthography

As was noted in the Introduction to the student's book, Sallust sought to write in a style reminiscent of the fifth-century Greek historian Thucydides (ca. 460/55–400 B.C.). In order to capture in Latin the antique and almost poetical quality that was felt to be present in Thucydides' prose, Sallust turned to the writings of the Elder Cato (234–149 B.C.), who had been the first to compose a history of Rome in Latin. One result of this borrowing is that Sallust apparently revived the older spellings of many Latin words in preference to the standard orthography of his age. Ancient critics make mention of this fact, and we find traces of older forms and spellings in the medieval manuscripts of Sallust. In preparing this book of selections from Sallust and Cicero, the editors decided to retain some of the peculiarities of orthography that by common consent on the part of modern scholars were favored by Sallust. Some modern editors (e.g., Alfons Kurfess in the Teubner text edition, Leipzig, 1957) go still further and print such forms as **quom** for the conjunction **cum**, and **quoius** and **quoi** for **cuius** and **cui**. The aim of the present edition has been to strike a reasonable balance between, on the one hand, an overabundance of archaic forms and, on the other, a regularizing of the spelling to conform with classical usage.

Several words in the first few sections may be singled out to illustrate forms or spellings that are typical of Sallust. The students' attention should be directed, for instance, to the following:

1. -issumus for -issimus: in the superlative, *u* replaces *i* both in regular superlatives such as **vērissumē** (1) and in irregular superlatives, e.g., **maxuma** (12) and **pulcherrumum** (30).
2. -und- for -end-: both the gerundive and gerund of 3rd conjugation verbs are spelled with -und- rather than the familiar classical -end-: e.g., **capiundae** (13) = **capiendae** and **vīsundī** (444) = **vīsendī**.

3. -ēre for -ērunt: for the 3rd person plural of the perfect active indicative, Sallust preferred the more poetical and archaic spelling -ēre to -ērunt, which had become the standard prose form. The first example of such a perfect in the reader is fuēre (7). In the complete text of Sallust's Catiline, there are only four instances of the spelling with -ērunt, two of which appropriately occur in the speech that Sallust attributes to Julius Caesar, while a third is put into the mouth of Catiline himself (46).

4. The archaism of u for i is seen in such words as exīstumō (2) = exīstimō; lubet (9) = libet; and lubīdō (12) = libīdō.

5. After v (consonantal u) there had been a tendency in old Latin to write o rather than u, and Sallust reverted to this practice: e.g., volgus (38) = vulgus; novos (68) = novus; and voltū (166) = vultū.

6. The same tendency to write o after v may be seen in the following, where e had come to be used in standard orthography: dīvorsa (18) = dīversa and vostra (26) = vestra.

7. In a few instances, the substitution involves a consonant rather than a vowel: e.g., honōs (40) (still current in this period) = honor (masculine nominative singular) and relicuōs (226) = reliquōs.

8. Prepositional prefixes of compound verbs and nouns are generally not assimilated: e.g., inmoderāta (11) = immoderāta; adsequerētur (13) = assequerētur; and inpūnitātem (220) = impūnitātem.

9. -īs for -ēs: one spelling that is common to both Sallust and Cicero and may be unfamiliar to students is -īs for -ēs (which became the standard spelling in imperial times) in the accusative plural of 3rd declension adjectives that have -ium in the genitive plural and of i-stem nouns: e.g. omnīs (19), fortīs (29), montīs (61), and hostīs (187). The length of the i in the last syllable clearly distinguishes these accusative plurals from the genitive (and, in some words, the nominative) singular.

An attempt has been made in the notes to comment on most of these peculiarities when each is encountered in the text for the first time. It will be well, however, for the teacher to draw attention to some of these forms in later passages so that students may gain familiarity with Sallust's orthography.

Sallustian *Brevitās*

Brevity is one of the qualities aimed at by Sallust in fashioning a new prose style; in characterizing his style, ancient critics frequently employ the terms brevitās and vēlōcitās. To achieve this sense of rapidity and terseness, Sallust tends to write relatively short sentences strung together in parataxis as opposed to the hypotaxis of a complex period of the Ciceronian type in which the thought is developed in an elaborate series of subordinate clauses. Other features that contribute to this sense of brevity are the frequent use of the historical infinitive (often in a series extending at times to as many as ten members, e.g., lines 91–94), asyndeton (the omission of conjunctions), and ellipsis (the omission of a word or words needed to complete the sense of a sentence).

Examples of asyndeton are found, for instance, in the series inediae, algōris, vigiliae (8) and in the contrasting members satis ēloquentiae, sapientiae parum (10–11) where chiasmus (A B answered by B A) is employed in lieu of an adversative conjunction. In rapid enumeration of points, frequently no particles (such as enim, igitur, or autem—ordinarily so common in Latin) are used to show the logical connection between sentences (e.g., lines 9–11). Finally, as examples of ellipsis one can point to the omission of the verb erat with the subjects corpus (8) and animus (9); the need to supply eī erat with satis ēloquentiae, sapientiae parum (10–11); and the omission of the direct object of incitābant (17), which must be understood from the words animus ferōx (15) in the preceding sentence.

* * *

TEACHING NOTES

The Arabic numbers in boldface affixed to the Latin text identify the source of the selections by chapter number for Sallust's *Bellum Catilinae* and by section number for Cicero's *Catilinarians*. The notes in this handbook are keyed to the text by line number.

2 facinus: this noun, related to the verb faciō, is normally pejorative; it may, however, be given a positive coloring, as in line 31 by means of an adjective, whereas here Sallust possibly revives its former neutral sense of simply "a deed."

5 nōbilī genere: the last Sergius known to have held the consulship was Gnaeus Sergius Fidenas Coxo in 380 B.C. Families such as Catiline's, which could point to consular forebears but had not produced consuls for many generations, did not belong to the inner circle of the nobility, which tended to elect its members to the consul-

ship generation after generation. Catiline, there-fore, did not enjoy the easy and rapid advance-ment to the higher political offices, which tended to be the prerogative of the ruling aristocracy. Two other old patrician families that, after a long pe-riod of decline, had enjoyed a revival of importance in this period and must have served as an inspiration to Catiline were those of Lucius Cor-nelius Sulla (consul 88, dictator 82–79) and Gaius Julius Caesar (consul 59, dictator 49–44). In fact, like the Julii of Caesar's family, who claimed de-scent from the goddess Venus through the Trojan prince Aeneas and his son Ascanius (also known as Julus), the Sergii also traced their ancestry back to Trojan antecedents and claimed as the founder of their family a follower of Aeneas, one Sergestus, who is mentioned in Vergil's *Aeneid* (V.121).

6 caedēs: the dictator Sulla, following his vic-tory in the civil war of 83–82, carried out a purge of his political enemies as well as many innocent citizens, whose confiscated property was used to reward Sulla's soldiers and supporters. Catiline, as a partisan of Sulla, took a hand in these execu-tions. Cicero in his *Oratio in toga candida*, deliv-ered in 64 shortly before the elections, names four of Catiline's victims, one an ex-praetor and another possibly Catiline's own brother-in-law.

8 Corpus. . . . Animus (9). . . . : these two sentences expand upon and flesh out the phrase **vī et animī et corporis** (5); the second of these two genitives is taken up first, thus pro-ducing chiasmus.

inediae, algōris, vigiliae: these objective genitives with the participial adjective **patiēns** denote a lasting or permanent condition ("capable of enduring"); if **patiēns** were construed with the accusative, the description would be restricted to a particular point in time, present relative to the main verb ("enduring"). Cicero (*Cat.* 1.26; cf. 3.16) gives a very similar account of Catiline's reputation for physical endurance, but in place of the rare and archaic **inedia** and **algor**, he writes **famēs** and **frīgus.**

cuiquam: the indefinite pronoun **quisquam** is employed here because of the implied negative: "no one would believe the extent of his endurance."

10 aliēnī . . . suī profūsus: the neuter substantives **aliēnī** and **suī** are objective geni-tives, this being the normal construction with **ad-petēns** and hence extended by analogy to the neighboring adjective **profūsus**, which otherwise would not be expected to govern a genitive.

11 sapientiae: partitive genitive with **parum.**

18 dīvorsa inter sē: the two corrupting in-fluences mentioned are "mutually opposed" in the sense that **lūxuria** involves the squandering of wealth, while **avāritia** drives one to strive for more riches.

19 aes aliēnum: according to Cicero, the problem of personal debt reached crisis proportions in the year of his consulship. Both the upper and lower classes found debt a burden, and property values were depressed because of unstable finan-cial and political conditions. A tribune brought forward a measure to cancel debts in early 63, but this proposal was defeated. In retrospect, Cicero viewed the rescue of the creditor class and the restoration of public credit as one of the chief ac-complishments of his consulship.

26 spectāta . . . forent: the condition starts out as a simple contrary to fact condition in past time but then changes to a mixed condition. After the first two verbs in the apodosis, **cecidis-set** (27) and **fuissent** (28), Sallust switches from the pluperfect to the imperfect subjunctive **cap-tārem** (29) to denote present time relative to Catiline's speech.

27 opportūna: to be taken as a predicate adjective after **cecidisset**; in the next clause, the adverb **frūstrā** supplies the predicate of **fuis-sent** (28), a colloquial usage and here providing a little extra emphasis by the alliteration of the *f*'s. Pairs of alliterative words and phrases abound throughout the speech and serve to heighten the emotional appeal to the audience (e.g., **multīs . . . magnīs**, 29; **fortīs fīdōs**, 29–30; **cum cōnsiderō quae condiciō**, 34).

35 vindicāmus in lībertātem: vindicō (from **vim + dīcō**), lit., "to lay claim to (an object or person)," as in a legal action in which posses-sion or ownership is the point of dispute; hence with **in lībertātem**, "to place a person in a free condition." These words became a slogan and catch phrase of a class of politicians—the so-called **populārēs**—who opposed the dominance of the Roman Senate and claimed to be champions of the power that theoretically belonged to the popular assemblies.

36 paucōrum potentium: the faction that had the greatest influence in the Senate and stood for the status quo styled themselves and their supporters the **optimātēs** (lit., "the best class of citizens"). Sallust eschews this term and prefers instead to call them simply the **paucī**, occasion-ally the **bonī**, or, as here, in the mouth of Catiline, the **paucī potentēs.**

37 populī, nātiōnēs: here these words des-ignate the Roman provinces and territories—**nātiōnēs** for loosely organized societies such as those in Spain and North Africa; **populī** for states such as those found in the provinces of Sicily, Asia, and Macedonia. A contrast is drawn between the rulers of foreign nations (**rēgēs** and **tetrarchae**) who paid a kind of "indirect tax" (**vectīgal**) in the form of bribes to powerful figures in the Senate to ensure the recognition of their status as rulers and friends of the Roman people, and, on the other hand, the provincials, the majority of whom paid a fixed annual land tax (**stīpendium**) based upon a calculation of the average annual produce of the land.

41 perīcula, iūdicia: among those of the senatorial class who, according to Sallust (17.3), attended the meeting at which this speech was delivered, two at least, P. Autronius and L. Vargunteius, had recently been stripped of their senatorial rank as a result of criminal prosecutions. Catiline himself had been prevented from being a candidate for the consulship in the previous year (65 B.C.) because he was under indictment for extortion at the time, and he was soon to face prosecution again shortly after the elections in 64 B.C.

46–47 Tantum modo inceptō: this bold assertion is reminiscent of a more modest proverbial expression (attested as early as Plato in the fourth century B.C.) to the effect that a good beginning amounts to the completion of half a task.

48–49 lībertās . . . dīvitiae, d e c u s, glōria: Catiline's specific proposals are set out by Sallust in greater detail in Chapter 21. Catiline is made to promise the cancellation of debts, proscription of the wealthy, public and priestly appointments for his supporters, and the plunder of open warfare (21.2). This passage helps to supplement the answer that can be drawn from inference to study question 3 on this section. These proposals attributed to Catiline by Sallust before the elections in 64 are also relevant to a consideration of the second half of study question 5.

50–51 bellī spolia magnifica: the reader should bear in mind that this speech has been composed by Sallust and need not accurately represent Catiline's true aims and political program in 64. Sallust views Catiline as a renegade and revolutionary from the very beginning of his career, and the speech put into his mouth has been shaped by this notion on Sallust's part. While Catiline might have been a willing supporter of radical legislative proposals in 63 had he been elected consul for that year, he was far from being so reckless as to advocate armed revolution so long as his hopes of achieving the consulship by election with the backing of powerful supporters in 64 remained high.

51 Vel imperātōre vel mīlite: in the final battle in which Catiline perished fighting against the legions of the Roman government, he is said by Sallust (lines 424–425) to have discharged the duties of both a brave soldier and a good commander. The words **animus** and **corpus** (52) are aptly chosen by Sallust to convey the role of commander and soldier, and they recall a theme developed in the opening chapters of the monograph where Sallust asserts that men are set apart from other beasts by the **animus**. Of men he writes (1.2): **animī imperiō corporis servitiō magis ūtimur** ("we employ the rule of the mind, more the service of the body"). It is, of course, **imperium cōnsulāre**, the supreme executive authority of the consulship, that Catiline hoped soon to possess as a result of election. Hence we find this underlying theme brought out once again in the final line of the speech (54) with the verb **imperāre**.

72 Catilīnae furor: a further setback to Catiline after his defeat in the consular elections of 64 was a prosecution on charges arising from his participation in the Sullan proscriptions nearly two decades earlier. Cicero mentions this impending trial in his *Oratio in toga candida* delivered in the Senate shortly before the elections in 64. The future dictator Julius Caesar, as ex-aedile, presided over this court and may have had a hand in helping Catiline to secure an acquittal.

74 Faesulās: the region of Etruria to the north of Rome had been a stronghold of Sulla's enemies and was punished accordingly after Sulla's victory in the civil war. Land was confiscated from the losing side, and Sulla's veterans were settled on allotments situated in regions that had opposed Sulla. As many as 120,000 Sullan supporters received land and cash bounties, and many of Sulla's ex-soldiers had been settled in Etruria. As early as 78 B.C., the consul Lepidus had attempted to exploit the discontent of the dispossessed round about the town of Faesulae and throughout Etruria to foment a counterrevolution to Sulla's reforms after his death. These additional facts about conditions in Etruria can be brought out in the answer to study question 4 on this section of the text.

82 pactiōne prōvinciae: Cicero let it be known as early as 1 January 63 B.C. that he might decline his allotted province (Macedonia) for the following year. He completed the exchange of provinces with his colleague Antonius in the first half of 63, since by the date of the summer elections Cicero had taken the further step of relinquishing to one of the praetors Cisalpine Gaul, which had originally been allotted to Antonius. This additional piece of information may be brought out to supplement the answer to study question 5.

85 petītiō: in Cicero's *Pro Murena* (51; cf. Plut. *Cic.* 14.3–4), we learn something of Catiline's candidacy in 63 and the events leading up to the election. On the day before the elections were to have been held, the Senate voted a postponement so that an investigation could be made into certain inflammatory remarks that Catiline was alleged to have made to his supporters. The revolutionary flavor of this **contiō domestica** ("private assembly"), as Cicero styles it, agrees in some respects with the rhetoric and program presented by Sallust as part of Catiline's campaign in 64. When on the day originally set for the elections the Senate met to investigate Catiline's conduct of his campaign, no firm measures were adopted. It was, according to Cicero, at a session of the Senate a few days prior to this one that Catiline had uttered the threat to bring about general destruction (**ruīna**) in response to the attacks made against him by his political enemies, a threat transferred by Sallust to the meeting in November (lines 173–174). The elections in 63 were doubtless viewed by Catiline as his last chance to further his political career by legitimate means. Rarely did a candidate experience three defeats for the consulship and later succeed in holding this office. Quintus Lutatius Catulus (consul in 102) is one of the few politicians known to have overcome this disadvantage, and in a sense this was Catiline's third try for the consulship, although admittedly his intended (first) candidacy in 66 was not permitted to progress beyond the declaration of his intention to stand for office. Given Catiline's two previous setbacks (in 66 and 64) and his apparent lack of powerful backers in 63, we can understand, in answer to study question 6, why his defeat in 63 drove him to desperate measures.

85 **cōnsulibus**: more often than not, Catiline is said to have aimed solely at the assassination of only one of the consuls, namely Cicero (e.g., 79, 176, 181). The plural here and below (91), making not only Cicero but also his colleague Antonius the objects of an assassination plot, appears at first glance contradictory. In fact, just above (77–78) Antonius was described as a potential ally of Catiline should he gain election. Nevertheless, if we keep in mind the timing and effect of the agreement Cicero had reached with his colleague to secure his cooperation (see note above on line 82), it is possible to imagine that Catiline was prepared on occasion to work for the destruction of both consuls, while all the time his chief concern was to bring about the removal of Cicero.

88 **C. Mānlium Faesulās**: Manlius, who was earlier reported to be at Faesulae (line 74), had come to Rome with a band of supporters to work for Catiline's election in 63.

92 **incendia**: Sallust states explicitly (48.2, a passage not included in this reader) that the common people turned against the conspirators and sided enthusiastically with Cicero and the government when it became known that the revolutionaries had planned to set fires in Rome. The scale of this intended arson may be judged from the fact that twelve places, according to Sallust (43.2; the number 12 is inflated to 100 by Plutarch, *Cic.* 18.2), were designated for initiating the fires. Plutarch (loc. cit.) adds the details that various members of the conspiracy were assigned the tasks of blocking up the aqueducts and killing any persons who ran to put out the blazes. As we can see from later times, most notably the Neronian fire of A.D. 64, Rome with its narrow streets and timbered buildings was particularly vulnerable to the spread of fires over vast districts. In Republican times, there was no organized fire brigade, and the poor most of all would have suffered from the loss of their modest lodgings in Rome's tenements, since unlike the well-to-do the poor could not seek shelter on estates lying outside the city. These points may be used to flesh out the answer to study question 2 on this section.

95 **Quibus rēbus**: in the chapters immediately preceding this section, Sallust reports some of the following circumstances to which these words allude: on or about October 21, the Senate passed the **senātūs cōnsultum ultimum** instructing the consuls to take whatever steps were necessary to preserve the safety of the state; on about the first or second of November, news reached the Senate that Manlius had taken up arms at Faesulae on 27 October; a variety of rumors and portents gained currency; the Senate pressed into service two ex-consuls and two praetors to secure various parts of Italy; rewards were offered to anyone who would betray information about the conspiracy; gladiators were removed from Rome to prevent the use of these trained professional fighters in an uprising; and watches were posted throughout the city.

97 **cuiquam**: the use of **quisquam** for **ūllus** is common with nouns denoting persons; this usage is extended here to the noun **locō** by its being paired with **hominī**.

103 **timēns**: most recently Catiline had attempted to arrange the assassination of Cicero at his home on the morning of the day before this meeting of the Senate. The details were worked out at a meeting of the conspirators at the house of a senator, Marcus Porcius Laeca, in the Street of the Scythe-makers on the night of 6/7 November. Two of the conspirators volunteered to gain entrance to Cicero's house early the next morning on the pretext of paying a social call and to kill the consul. The informant Curius passed along a warning of the plot through Fulvia in time for Ci-

cero to deny entrance to the would-be assassins. In response to study question 4, it would be useful to bring out some of this background information giving a real basis for one of the motives assigned to Cicero by Sallust.

105 scrīptam: this is a key word in framing an answer to study question 5. Cicero's speech was available to Sallust's readers in published form. It would have been pointless, therefore, for the historian to compose his own version, and the addition of such a speech would have further swelled the size of the monograph and served to divert attention from the villain Catiline.

108 nocturnum . . . vigiliae: see note on line 95; some of the information supplied there can be used to supplement the answer to study question 1.

110 hōrum ōra vultūsque: as further signs of the fear and disapproval of Catiline expressed by the conduct of his fellow senators at this meeting, Cicero (*Cat.* 1.16, 2.12) mentions the fact that Catiline's entrance into the meeting was greeted with stony silence and the consulars vacated the benches near him so that he was forced to sit in isolation.

110–111 Patēre tua cōnsilia: elsewhere in this speech (in passages not included in this reader), Cicero mentions several of Catiline's schemes that miscarried because information was learned of them in advance. A plot to massacre many leading figures in Rome on 28 October was frustrated; some of the intended victims absented themselves from Rome; those who remained behind were shielded by guards supplied by Cicero (Cic. *Cat.* 1.7). On 1 November, Catiline had hoped to seize the town of Praeneste (23 miles southeast of Rome), but he had been prevented from doing so by a garrison stationed in the town by Cicero (Cat. 1.8).

123 orbem terrae: according to standard usage, **orbis terrārum** is ordinarily used to designate the Roman world, while **orbis terrae** is used of the world as a whole. Here the latter phrase may be seen as standing for the former by a rhetorical exaggeration.

128 senātūs cōnsultum . . . vehemēns: in framing an answer to the second part of study question 3, it is important to realize that conditions in 63 were quite different from those on the other occasions when these emergency powers had been granted to the chief magistrates by the **senātūs cōnsultum ultimum.** Always in the past there had existed a clear and evident threat to the state. In previous instances either riots and bloodshed had already occurred or rebel forces had taken the field and were being directed against the state by an avowed revolutionary. In 63, by con-

trast, the threat was not totally out in the open, and there was no concrete evidence to prove Catiline's involvement in a plot until he joined the rebel forces under Manlius—only rumors and hearsay. Cicero (e.g., *Cat.* 1.30; *Mur.* 51) constantly complains of the reluctance on the part of many in the Senate to believe in Catiline's guilt.

133 imperātōrem ducemque: at the time Cicero made this claim, there was no means of proving that Catiline was directing the activities of Manlius at Faesulae. About a week before this meeting of the Senate, word had reached Rome that Manlius had taken up arms on 27 October (Sall. *Cat.* 30.1). The Senate responded by sending the ex-consul Quintus Marcius Rex to Faesulae (Sall. *Cat.* 30.3), and Sallust (*Cat.* 32.3–34.1) reports on negotiations conducted between Marcius Rex and envoys of Manlius who aired their grievances together with a disclaimer of any intention to harm their country. Catiline was able to remain clear of any involvement in these activities of open rebellion by remaining in Rome, where he could direct the activities of his associates against Cicero and members of the government. As a senator, Catiline also enjoyed the advantage of being able to keep abreast of the government's countermeasures so long as he remained in Rome and continued to profess his innocence of any involvement in a plot to destroy the state. The Senate moved swiftly soon after Catiline's departure from Rome to declare both Catiline and Manlius enemies of the state (line 187) once Catiline was known to have joined Manlius at Faesulae. These are some of the points (cf. note on line 128) that may usefully be brought out in response to study question 4.

141–142 perge . . . patent portae; proficīscere: alliteration is used here effectively by Cicero to emphasize his point and convey impatience.

150 perīclitanda: the gerundive is the only form of a deponent verb that is always passive in meaning as well as form; occasionally the perfect participle of some deponents is treated as passive.

160 Iuppiter: once again (compare line 147) Cicero singles out the god Jupiter because the Senate was meeting on this occasion in one of his temples. Furthermore, Jupiter, who was worshiped under the title **Iuppiter Optimus Maximus** in his temple on the Capitoline Hill, was viewed by the Romans as the god who especially watched over the safety of the city.

165–174 Catilīna . . . restinguam: Cicero (*Cat.* 2.13; *Orat.* 129) gives the impression that Catiline made no speech in his defense on this occasion. While it may be true that Catiline did not attempt to answer point by point the charges leveled against him by Cicero, there is nothing to prevent us from supposing that he offered a general defense of his conduct after the fashion of the words attributed to him by Sallust.

165 parātus ad dissimulanda omnia: Sallust (line 9) in his sketch of Catiline's character, specifically attributed this trait to him.

169 maiōrum . . . beneficia: the only ancestor of Catiline known to have performed distinguished service for the state in relatively recent times was his great-grandfather, Marcus Sergius Silus, a hero in the Second Punic War (218–201 B.C.) against Hannibal (Pliny, *HN* VII.104–106).

173 Quōniam quidem: see note on line 85 for the actual occasion on which Catiline is reported by Cicero to have uttered this sinister threat.

179 intempestā: the adjective **intempestus** with **nox** came to designate the dead of night either because these hours were regarded as "timeless" in the sense of lacking clear divisions into units of time, or because this period was viewed as "untimely" in the sense of **intempestīvus**, i.e., not appropriate for conducting affairs.

180–182 mandat . . . parent: to emphasize the jussive nature of these instructions, the verbs **cōnfīrment**, **mātūrent** (181), and **parent** (182) are put in the present subjunctive, while the verb in the subordinate clause (**possent**, 181) is imperfect. This mixture of tenses is made possible by the fact that the main verb **mandat** is in the historical present (grammatically primary, yet reporting an act that occurred in past time).

182–183 cum magnō exercitū . . . accessūrum: the statement made here supplies part of the answer to study question 3. Catiline's plans called for his agents in Rome to set fires in designated places throughout the city and to begin the slaughter of their enemies as soon as he had brought his rebel army within striking distance of the city. The fullest description of this two-pronged plan of attack is provided by Sallust in Chapter 43.1–2 (cf. 44.6; Cic. *Cat.* 3.8).

185 fascibus: consuls and promagistrates of consular rank were entitled to be accompanied by twelve attendants, known as lictors, each of whom carried the **fascēs** as a symbol of the magistrate's authority. The words **aliīs imperī īnsignibus** presumably refer to the curule chair and military cloak (**palūdāmentum**), further trappings of power illegally adopted by Catiline, who behaved as though he had been invested with promagisterial **imperium**. These points may be brought out in answer to study question 4.

188 multitūdinī diem statuit: earlier in this month of November, the Senate had offered

substantial cash rewards to anyone, either slave or freeborn, who was willing to come forward with evidence about the conspiracy (Sall. *Cat.* 30.6). Yet, according to Sallust (*Cat.* 36.5), neither the Senate's offer of rewards nor this later offer of amnesty mentioned here led anyone to betray the conspiracy or to desert Catiline's army. Sallust points to this fact as evidence of how deeply divided the state had become. Others who today believe that Cicero exaggerated the scope of Catiline's plot might argue that the failure of anyone to take advantage of the terms offered by the Senate shows how limited was the number of those actively involved in the plot. This issue may be explored in connection with the answer to study question 6.

190–191 habeant . . . mātūret: primary sequence is employed for the sake of vividness after the historical present **dēcernit** (189), whereas secondary sequence is adopted above in the subordinate clause (188 **licēret**) after **statuit**, which is also best viewed as a historical present (compare **possent**, line 181).

192 ut comperī: shortly after the Allobroges were first approached by the conspirators, they consulted Quintus Fabius Sanga, a Roman who took an interest in affairs in the province of Gaul, and through Sanga, the ambassadors passed along to Cicero information about the plans and activities of Catiline's associates still in Rome (Sall. *Cat.* 41.4–5).

194 cum litterīs mandātīsque: the word order would lead one to conclude that the letters and instructions were to be conveyed by the Allobroges to Catiline. This assumption, however, is contradicted by Cicero's more detailed account later in the speech (*Cat.* 3.8–9). In the fuller version, he mentions again that Volturcius had been entrusted with **litterae** as well as **mandāta** for delivery to Catiline, and he summarizes the content of these messages. He does not, however, state that the Allobroges were carrying any documents to Catiline; rather he says that Lentulus, Cethegus, and Statilius had given a written **iūs iūrandum** (oath of alliance) and **litterae** to the Allobroges for delivery to their countrymen. Perhaps Cicero was being deliberately misleading in the passage before us so as to suggest closer ties between Catiline and the Gauls. It is equally possible, however, that Cicero chose to insert **cum . . . mandātīsque** after **eōdemque itinere** so as to avoid the accumulation of three prepositional phrases in succession and the collocation of **mandātīsque eōdemque**. A better balance is achieved by distributing the four phrases in pairs. Strictly speaking, however, **cum . . . mandātīsque** should be translated in conjunction with **ad suōs cīvīs** rather than with **ad Catilīnam**, the latter phrase being merely intended to describe the meeting that the Allobroges were to have had with Catiline at Faesulae.

195 T. Volturcium: Lentulus had sent Titus Volturcius with the ambassadors to facilitate the meeting that the Allobroges were to have had with Catiline on their journey home (Sall. *Cat.* 44.3). In his testimony before the Senate after his arrest, Volturcius claimed to have only limited knowledge about the conspiracy because he had been recruited as an associate of the conspirators only a few days before (lines 233–236). One modern theory would make Volturcius an agent of Cicero and view him as a spy planted among the conspirators by the consul.

195–196 huic . . . litterās: for the text of this letter, see Sallust, *Cat.* 44.5 and Cicero, *Cat.* 3.12. The version preserved by Sallust shows signs of being slightly more polished than that given by Cicero, who appears to quote verbatim as follows: **Quis sim sciēs ex eō quem ad tē mīsī. Cūrā ut vir sīs et cōgitā quem in locum sīs prōgressus. Vidē ecquid tibi iam sit necesse et cūrā ut omnium tibi auxilia adiungās, etiam īnfimōrum.** ("You will know who I am from the man whom I have sent to you. See to it that you are a real man and consider the position in which you have placed yourself. Consider your needs and see that you join to yourself the aid of all, even that of the lowest.") The implication of the words **etiam īnfimōrum** is clear enough. Lentulus was urging Catiline to abandon his policy of turning away the slaves who wished to join his cause (Sall. *Cat.* 56.5). Catiline did so because he did not want to compromise the standing of himself and his followers by seeming to throw in his lot with runaway slaves. In a message that Volturcius was to deliver orally, Lentulus expressed more openly his view that Catiline should avail himself of the support that was to be had from slaves (Sall. *Cat.* 44.6; Cic. *Cat.* 3.8).

197–198 tōta rēs . . . dēprehenderētur: in answer to study question 2, it is important to bring out Cicero's pressing need at this time to secure concrete evidence of the guilt of Catiline's associates in Rome. Time after time Cicero (e.g., *Cat.* 2.4; *Mur.* 79) mentions the fear caused in him not so much by Catiline and his army as by those whom Catiline left behind in Rome to further the aims of the conspiracy. One of these Catilinarians was the praetor Lentulus, and another was the senator Cethegus; Sallust (*Cat.* 17.3) lists the names of other senators and a like number of equitēs (*Cat.* 17.4) who participated in the plot. The social and political standing of these promi-

nent Roman citizens shielded them from arrest in the absence of any positive proof of their involvement in the plot. Catiline too, of course, enjoyed the same immunity from arrest and detention so long as he remained in Rome and put on a front of innocence (see note on line 133).

206 praefectūrā Reātīnā: Cicero enjoyed close ties with the members of this community as a result of acting as the town's **patrōnus** in Rome and looking out for the interests of its citizens (Cic. *Pro Scauro* 27). In the year of his consulship, Cicero was repaid for his services by the young men from Reate who played an active role as Cicero's personal bodyguard.

212 sōlīs: Cicero gives no indication that the Gauls had been betraying the plans of the conspirators to him. In fact, he goes out of his way in this passage to state that the arrest on the Mulvian Bridge took the Allobroges by surprise.

214 integrīs signīs: letters were commonly tied with string (**līnum**), and wax seals were affixed to the knot to prevent tampering with the contents. The sender of the letter made an impression in the wax, while it was still warm, with his signet ring. When the letters of the conspirators were brought before the Senate on the day following their seizure, Cicero showed the unbroken seals to each of the conspirators and asked them to acknowledge their individual seals before the letters were opened and the contents read out (Cic. *Cat.* 3.10).

219 tantīs cīvibus dēprehēnsīs: although this phrase is most easily understood as an ablative absolute, it could also be taken closely with **factō** (220) as either ablative or dative, the expressions **aliquō facere** ("to do with someone") and **alicui facere** ("to do to someone") being common (e.g., Sall. *Cat.* 52.25, 55.2).

226 aedem Concordiae: the place chosen for the meeting of the Senate on this occasion was symbolically appropriate. Built originally in 367 to mark the resolution of the long-standing struggle between the plebeians and patricians, and refurbished in 121 after the death of Gaius Gracchus and his supporters to announce the restoration of harmony and order after the political upheavals of more than a decade, this temple was associated with the re-establishment of the state's authority after crisis. As a further positive omen, Cicero arranged to have erected on this same day the new statue of Jupiter that had been commissioned two years previously (see note on line 242). The statue of this god, who was regarded as the city's protector, was set up on the Capitoline and made to face east so that the god's gaze would symbolically be directed toward the Forum (Cic. *Cat.* 3.19–21; *Div.* 2.46).

227 senātum advocat: in response to study question 5, it should be pointed out that Cicero felt the need at this stage, and two days later when the fate of the conspirators under arrest was decided, to bolster the authority granted to him under the terms of the **senātūs cōnsultum ultimum**. In past instances, the s.c.u. had permitted magistrates to proceed against citizens in open revolt who were armed and engaged in public demonstrations of force against the state. The situation was somewhat different in 63. Although the written documents seized in the arrest of the Allobroges implicated Lentulus and his associates in a plot to overthrow the government, it could be argued that after the conspirators had been placed under house arrest, they no longer posed any immediate danger to the state and, therefore, as Roman citizens should be granted the right to a trial. Cicero's position was that the conspirators had forfeited their right to be considered citzens by their act of taking up arms against their country. Cicero also felt, and quite rightly, as it appears from Sallust's account (lines 392–395), that the swift and summary execution of the conspirators who had been caught would demoralize those who sided with Catiline and would discourage further recruits to his cause. In an attempt, however, to shield himself from the charge at some future date of having exceeded his authority, Cicero chose to take no steps against Lentulus and the others without first receiving the Senate's authorization. Cicero would later claim (*Phil.* 2.18) that the responsibility for the arrest of the members of the plot was his, while their punishment was decided by the Senate. In fact, the Senate had no authority to decide matters of capital punishment. At most, it could merely advise a magistrate to adopt a given course of action. It was, therefore, possible for Cicero's political enemy Publius Clodius to bring about Cicero's exile five years later in 58 on the grounds that as consul he had put Roman citizens to death without due process of law.

frequentiā: from other passages where attendance figures are given (e.g., Cic. *Att.* 1.14.5), we gather that this description was applied to a meeting of the Senate (here, eius ōrdinis) at which as many as perhaps 400 out of the 600 members of this body were present.

230 Volturcius interrogātus: students may discuss the apparent cynicism and expediency of political policy at Rome. The inquiry's setting may figure in their discussion. There was no official record of Senate proceedings. Cicero had a record kept on this occasion, to forestall errors of memory and the possibility of later tampering with the evidence, and to let all citizens know what the witnesses had said. He made similar arrangements for the Senate meetings of 4 and 5 December.

237 Eadem Gallī fatentur: in guiding students toward an answer to study question 5, help them to see the directness with which the Gallī spoke in contrast with Volturcius' manner and the lack of indication that their testimony had to be drawn out of them.

238 librīs Sibyllīnīs: during the reign of Tarquin, last of Rome's kings, the Sibyl of Cumae is said to have approached the king during a crisis with the claim that nine books in her possession could reveal advice from the gods; she would sell him the volumes. He rejected her price. She withdrew, burnt three of the books, and returned, asking the same price. Again he refused, and she burnt another three. Finally, she asked the original price for the remaining three. Tarquin, desperate, capitulated. The books were kept in the Temple of Jupiter on the Capitoline Hill. In a crisis, the Senate would ask the **quindecimvirī sacrīs faciundīs** to search in them for a parallel to guide magistrates. The original volumes perished in the great fire of 83 B.C. and were replaced.

239 tribus Cornēliīs: the **gēns Cornēlia** was eminent among the **nōbilēs** (families showing at least one consulship). On Sulla's career, see *The Magistrates of the Roman Republic.* Lentulus is attempting to reverse the decline of his branch of the family.

240 Capitōliō: a temple to Jupiter occupied the southern summit of the **Capitōlium** from the beginning of the republic. A fire on 6 July 83 B.C. destroyed it. The temple built to replace it was dedicated in 69 B.C. The rebuilding was begun by Sulla and completed after Sulla's death by Q. Lutatius Catulus (consul 78 B.C.). It was reached by means of a stone-paved, inclined road (**clīvus Capitōlīnus**) up the east face.

241 haruspicēs: these were professional practitioners of the ancient Etruscan art of foretelling the future by means of interpreting lightning or preternatural events of various sorts or by means of inspecting the entrails of animals that had been sacrificed (**haruspex** means "gutgazer"). An illustrated account is given in *The Etruscans: A New Investigation,* pp. 91–101. Romans seem to have been somewhat skeptical about **haruspicīna** (cf. Cicero's *De divinatione*). Haruspicēs were consulted at irregular times, by private citizens (e.g., at a wedding) or by magistrates.

242 bellō cīvīlī: the "civil war" was an intermittent armed struggle (marked by countless assassinations) that flared up repeatedly from as early as the murder of Tiberius Gracchus and his supporters by senators in 133 B.C. until Octavian finally secured the public peace in 30 B.C. The phrase **bellum cīvīle** and others like it occur in many authors. Cicero elsewhere uses it of just such a reckless attack on the state by a single treacherous citizen as Catiline is making. Sallust's use here may be generalized, "through civil warfare." Lentulus' **haruspicēs** could hardly have picked a year in which there would not be some act of civil war. Consulted in 65 when shrines and statues on the Capitoline had been struck by lightning, they announced that there would be civil war unless the gods were appeased. Special games were held in 65, and a new statue of Jupiter was decreed, though not erected until 3 December 63 B.C. (see above on line 226).

244 **abdicātō magistrātū**: misdemeanor by a magistrate could be pursued only upon the expiration of his term or upon his resignation. The ablative absolute **abdicātō magistrātū** may be translated "upon resigning his office." The normal idiom is **abdicāre sē magistrātū**. Occasionally in works of historians **abdicāre** takes an accusative of the office instead, making possible the passive used here.

244–245 **līberīs custōdiīs**: **custōdia** imposes a heavy liability, requiring the **custōs** to restore the property concerned intact. The **custōs** had to produce the prisoner in court for trial. **Lībera custōdia** here means "confinement in a private house."

245 **P. Lentulō Spinthērī**: he was curule aedile. Q. Cornificius (246) had competed with Cicero for the consulship of 63. Gnaeus Terentius (247), a senator this year, is otherwise unknown. Senators may have considered Caesar and Crassus to be uninvolved or may have thought that they might be induced, by playing this role, into tipping their hand.

In Chapters 48 and 49 (not given here), Sallust relates that the commons swung to Cicero's side against Catiline, especially after they learned of the conspirators' intention to set fire to the city. On the next day (4 December), Lucius Tarquinius (of whom we know nothing else) corroborated Volturcius' evidence, even implicating Crassus. Mention of Crassus' name provoked his fellow senators to incredulity or obsequious propitiation; some, of course, owed Crassus everything. In a vote, Tarquinius was discredited. Two optimates accused Caesar but could not enlist Cicero in their attack on Caesar.

250 **praemia**: these had been offered to informers by a decree of the Senate in November (Sall. *Cat.* 30.6) when it was learned that Manlius had taken the field with the army at Faesulae on 27 October. Cicero (*Cat.* 4.5) called the **praemia** "amplissima." A freeman such as Volturcius received 200,000 sesterces, while a slave received freedom and 100,000 sesterces. (At this time 100,000 sesterces was the minimum property requirement to qualify for enrolment in the first census class.)

251 **clientibus**: from early times, free persons of humble means allied themselves to prominent families to obtain their protection. These **clientēs**, though free in law, were half-servile to their **patrōnī**, and their social **auctōritās** and **dignitās** remained inferior. Clients were expected to help the patron and his family in time of need (even, originally, to ransom him should he be captured in war). Under the law, freed slaves became perforce **clientēs** of their former master. A **lībertus** showed **obsequium** and **reverentia**, holding his patron honorable and sacred; his son had to do the same. Patron and freedman bore reciprocal obligations. In this instance, Lentulus may have had some claim on his **clientēs**, if it was assumed that his imprisonment was in any way irregular. Use this information to help students answer study questions 1 and 2.

To prevent violence from intimidating or injuring senators, Cicero had the Senate's deliberations of 5 December protected by armed **equitēs** (**dispositīs praesidiīs**, line 256).

The **senātūs cōnsultum ultimum** of 21 October laid on Cicero and Antonius the ill-defined need to provide for the safety of the state. Evidence of involved witnesses linked the prisoners to Catiline irrevocably, and Catiline and Manlius had already been declared **hostēs**, since they were at large and a state of war existed against them (187). The Senate had just declared treasonous the conduct of Catiline's confederates (lines 258–259), probably on 4 December.

257 **convocātō senātū**: on 5 December, as on the previous day, the Senate was convened in the Temple of Concord on the east shoulder of the Capitol.

259 **Decimus Iūnius Silānus**: elected consul for 62 with L. Licinius Murena, praetor in 65. As consul designate, Silanus correctly was asked to express his **sententia** first.

261 **L. Cassiō [Longīnō]**: Cicero relates elsewhere that this man negotiated with the Allobrogian envoys and was eager to supervise arrangements for the setting of fires throughout Rome. Publius Furius is identified by Cicero (*Cat.* 3.14) as one of the **colōnī** settled by Sulla at Faesulae twenty years earlier. Furius assisted in the negotiations with the Allobroges. Cicero confirms Sallust's statement (Chapter 40) that P. Umbrenus, a freedman, opened negotiations with the Allobroges on behalf of the conspirators. Quintus Annius Chilo participated also. On 3 December,

the Senate had called for his arrest, and at this meeting he was condemned to death in absentia.

Before Caesar spoke, the Senate heard the opinions of the two consuls designate and fourteen ex-consuls, all of whom called for the death penalty. Following Caesar and the other praetors-elect came all ex-praetors; and so on down the lists of aediles, tribunes of the plebs, and quaestors. Cato would be heard near the end of the debate as **tribūnus plēbis dēsignātus** for 62 (which office he assumed on 10 December). Caesar's speech softened Silanus' resolve. Silanus later changed his mind and supported Tiberius Claudius Nero, who moved adjournment so that the Senate could clear their heads of confusion (though he may really have meant just to temporize). Sallust is not reproducing Caesar's speech verbatim. Some sentiments and views that he puts in Caesar's mouth, however, find corroboration in Cicero's *Fourth Catilinarian*.

Sulla's overthrow of the Roman government and his proscriptions of 82 B.C. made senators such as Crassus wonder what the return of Pompey from the East held for them. Caesar was bound to Crassus through enormous election debts of his own. Rumor put Caesar and Crassus in Catiline's service during a failed coup d'état to murder the consuls in 65. In 64, Caesar, as chairman of the **quaestiō dē sīcāriīs** (court trying murders by violence), was particularly severe with others of Sulla's executioners, yet Catiline was acquitted by this same court. Finally, it was clearly the nobles who stood to gain most from Catiline's cry for **novae tabulae**. Yet while Caesar owed Crassus much, surely both Crassus and Caesar saw Catiline's scheme as desperate: nothing Catiline had yet tried in his schemes for power had netted himself or anyone else any profit, and he had always been only a minor figure. Crassus did not even attend the Senate on 5 December to debate the fate of the arrested conspirators; yet he would have been bound to speak up for the rights of Catiline's supporters if Catiline had been able to claim **amīcitia** with him.

That Caesar may have been party to Catiline's scheme was darkly hinted at by Cato even during his speech on 5 December (lines 360–362).

263–267 Caesar's opening argument is that, in a debate where certainty is impossible, emotion must be suppressed in the interest of rational analysis. The Senate is being appealed to here as the intelligent mind of Rome, that calm rational center in the irrational hurricane of political life. As students answer the study questions, help them pick out the ways in which Caesar works out this conflict between emotion and reason in the excerpts given here (lines 263–296).

276–277 **mortem aerumnārum requiem**: it was a philosophical commonplace that death was a release from the sufferings of this world. Cicero (lines 305–308) shows that Caesar was attempting to weaken the appeal of the death penalty. On death as a release into nothingness (Epicurean doctrine), see Lucretius, III.978–1010.

280 **lēx Porcia**: three **lēgēs Porciae** can be distinguished: (1) that of M. Porcius Cato ("The Censor"), praetor 198 B.C., consul 195 B.C., granted citizens **prōvocātiō** against flogging; (2) that of P. Porcius Laeca, tribune of the plebs 199 B.C., extended **prōvocātiō** to citizens in Italy and the provinces; and (3) that of L. Porcius Licinus, consul 184 when M. Cato was censor (or of some other Porcius in the years following the Censor's death in 149), gave soldiers **prōvocātiō** against an officer's capital sentence.

Prōvocātiō was the right of citizens to appeal a magistrate's judgment to the assembly. Ironically here Caesar cites a law passed possibly by the great-grandfather of the Cato who is soon to rise and demand, **mōre maiōrum**, the deaths of citizens (366–370).

281 **aliae lēgēs**: "other laws" permitting exile are mentioned twice in Sallust (51.22 = lines 280–282 of our text, and 51.40). Polybius says "the Romans had a practice" of permitting exile so that a citizen might escape the death sentence. An exile lost civil rights and property under the **aquae et ignis interdictiō**, that is, his life was forfeit within Italy. At *Cat.* 4.10, Cicero refers to a **lēx Semprōnia** that safeguarded Roman citizens, but he stated that "one who is a **hostis** of the state can in no way be a **cīvis**." Catiline had gone to the limit of Roman territory (that farther edge of Etruria). Yet armies already moved on him: he was **hostis** and no longer **exul**.

293 **pecūniās**: Sallust means not just money but property generally.

ipsōs in vinculīs habendōs: this expression is probably metaphorical (i.e., the confinement will be to certain towns in Italy), perhaps based on Cicero's **vincula vērō et ea sempiterna . . . inventa sunt** (lines 308–309) and [Caesar] **nōn dubitat P. Lentulum aeternīs tenebrīs vinculīsque mandāre** (*Cat.* 4.10). This was more than usual imprisonment in the accepted Roman sense, for it was to last to the end of their days (**sempiterna, aeternīs**) with no right of appeal.

The purpose of Cicero's *Fourth Catilinarian* was to crystalize opinion and to indicate Cicero's willingness to pursue whatever course the Senate should decide. He also took the opportunity to suggest strongly which course he would prefer to follow.

Caesar's view was winning; Silanus withdrew his own opening **sententia**. The senators obviously were weighing the force of precedent, as Caesar had warned. But Cicero wanted a decision now: Catiline threatened in the north, Antonius and other commanders had already taken the field against him, and at any time Pompey might return to Rome. A decisive, forceful act now would send a message to Catiline's army that the jig was up: the rebels would be forced to abandon any thought of pardon once they realized that the Senate was prepared to execute members of its own order.

The role of the consul was broad. A good discussion may be found in *Greek and Roman Voting and Elections*, pp. 227–228.

A **senātūs cōnsultum** was a decision, arrived at after debate, that provided the presiding magistrate, at his request (the verb is **cōnsulere**), with senators' opinions and reasoning on a question. The magistrate would incorporate this weight of opinion into a magisterial edict that was binding, where the Senate's **cōnsultum** was not.

304 hoc genus poenae: Roman citizens had been put to death by magistrates armed with the **senātūs cōnsultum ultimum** on four previous occasions in the preceding sixty years against: (1) C. Gracchus in 121 B.C.; (2) Saturninus, a tribune, and Glaucia, a praetor, in 100 B.C.; (3) Sulla, proconsul in Asia, in 83 B.C. (branded **hostis** in absentia); and (4) the proconsul M. Aemilius Lepidus in 77. These were the several precedents presumably invoked by Silanus; yet despite the claim of frequency (**saepe**), only in (1) and (2) had **hoc genus poenae** been imposed (**ūsurpātum**, 305). At least seven later occurrences of the **s.c.u.** can be cited until Octavian effectively made it a dead letter by virtue of the power vested in the Roman emperors.

311 ista rēs: Caesar's proposal would put an onus on unnamed Italian **mūnicipia** (1) to provide and pay for the maintenance of the five captives for life, and (2) to suffer a penalty (lines 314–315) if any of the prisoners succeeded in escaping. Against Caesar's proposal, Cicero later urges several considerations: (1) Silanus' proposal has the support of precedent (see note above on line 304); (2) the punishment proposed by Caesar is **singulāris** (309, "unique," "unparalleled") even though Caesar himself criticized Silanus' **sententia** for being **aliēna ā rē pūblicā nostrā** (272); (3) Caesar's proposal involves **inīquitās** (311)—Cicero may have in mind that it imposes a one-sided burden on the **mūnicipia**, without right of appeal and without taking into consideration the cost, of which Rome pays nothing; no parallel enactment exists imposing such obligations on

mūnicipia, for Rome's relationships with these towns were regularly implemented through **lēgēs** passed by the assembly, not by **senātūs cōnsulta**; and (4) Caesar's proposal presents **difficultās** (311), for it means treating friendly towns in the one-sided manner (314–316) customarily used against conquered enemies.

318 cōntiōnem: this was an informal meeting with the populace (**verba facere ad populum**) on an important event, to proclaim an edict or to inform them of matters to be presented later for vote. During a **cōntiō** the magistrate might be questioned. No **auspicia** were taken.

319–320 facile . . . fuisse: Cicero sides with Silanus' original opinion that the conspirators should be executed, as lines 320–322 suggest. In mid-November the Senate had empowered Cicero's colleague Antonius to lead an army against Catiline. What benefit, it may be asked, could Cicero hope to achieve through the prisoners' execution? He might have hoped to stop the flow of adherents to Catiline's army. He had informed the Senate of Fulvia's evidence; challenged Catiline with it; seen the **s.c.u.** passed; put the gladiatorial schools under surveillance; had armies raised; heard that Manlius' army had taken the field; reported on the meeting at Laeca's house; missed assassination in his own home at least once; seen Catiline threaten the Senate; reported Lentulus' moves to the populace; had the Senate declare Manlius and Catiline public enemies; seen his colleague head north with his army; presented the Allobrogian envoys and five conspirators to the Senate; found caches of arms throughout Rome; delivered another inflammatory speech to the people; and stemmed gang warfare. The Senate was bound by inertia. *Nobody had yet had to pay.* This Cato recognized; his strenuous speech championing Silanus' original view swung the Senate. Cicero had his support; the five conspirators were executed. Immediately Catiline's army began to melt away. A month later Catiline had only one-fourth of his original strength. The watershed was indeed the execution of Lentulus and his four associates.

326–332 prō imperiō . . . dīligentiā: Cicero lists advantages he has foregone. The lure of **imperium** led many promagistrates to pursue military glory through conquest. Many enriched themselves at the provincials' expense; in fact, Rome had a standing court to deal with such extortionists. On the **triumphus** (327), a solemn return into Rome of a victorious magistrate with **imperium**, consult *The Oxford Classical Dictionary*, p. 1095.

334–338 Quodsī . . . mēmineritis: Cicero makes it very clear, in the last few lines of his speech, that he alone, and not the Senate, will bear any blame accruing to whatever action he takes. As he alone has the **imperium** to act, so his alone is the responsibility.

Cato's material addition to the debate is to insist that the five prisoners represent only the present and most acute aspect of a much larger, though distant and far more threatening peril: the growing army of Catiline and Manlius in Etruria (363).

Cicero later admitted to his friend Atticus that it was Cato's speech that won the day. Thus it was Cato's authority too that triumphed, and he only a former quaestor and tribune designate. In the face of the menace embodied in the magnates, Crassus and Pompey, and in the adventuresomeness of Caesar, the optimates saw in Cato, not in Cicero, the leader they desperately needed. He spoke of the duties their rank entailed, of the old virtues that gave them **dignitās et glōria**, and of the true temper of the Roman genius. The Senate was swayed by Cato's political connections among the **nōbilēs** and their own peril amid faction and distrust. They admired his stubbornness, moral courage, and *savoir-faire*, and they wanted the power of his **clientēlae** behind them.

M. Porcius Cato, called **Catō Minor** ("Cato the Younger") or **Catō Uticēnsis**, was great-grandson of the Elder Cato (**Catō Maior**, also known as "Cato the Censor," consul 195 and censor in 184). In 63 B.C. the younger Cato was 32. Military tribune in 67–66 and quaestor perhaps in 64, in 63 he had won a tribunate, which he would take up on 10 December for 62. From 58 to 56 he served as quaestor **prō praetōre** in Cyprus and Byzantium, praetor and president of the **quaestiō repetundārum** in 54, and propraetor in Sicily and Greece in 49–48 and in Africa in 47–46. From before 64 B.C. to 46 B.C., he served as **quīndecimvir sacrīs faciundīs**. He became a relentless champion for the conservative optimate faction, constantly frustrating Pompey, who in retaliation formed the "first triumvirate" with Caesar and Crassus. In 52 he crossed over to Pompey against Caesar. He strove to resist the bloodshed of Roman citizens during this phase of the civil war. In Africa he was able to reconcile the dead Pompey's quarreling adherents. He governed Utica wisely. After the Battle of Thapsus in 46, he committed suicide, and to posterity he was known and honored as **Uticēnsis**. See *The Legend of Cato Uticensis*.

345 Longē mihi alia: Cato begins by expressing his strong antipathy to some opinions that had just been expressed: those of Caesar, of Silanus (in retraction of his opening remarks), and of the numerous senators who thereupon leaped to the side of caution. Critics are not sure whether

Cicero spoke before the ex-praetor Nero (see above, page 62) or vice-versa. Cato followed both of them.

361–362 sī in tantō . . . timēre: on the theory that Caesar may have been party to Catiline's conspiracy, and that Cato is here broadly insinuating this, see above, page 62. We have no means of judging whether Cato's taunt is fair. Certainly Cato's is an emotional speech full of alarm and urgency; there was an accepted view of Caesar as demogogue; and Cato suspects all moves by **populārēs** whether Pompey, Caesar, or Crassus. He could see that a line led straight from Marius, Sulla, Cinna, and Pompey to monarchy. (See *Party Politics in the Age of Caesar*, pp. 17–18). Catiline's cry in 63 for **novae tabulae** was a popularist cry; to that extent at least Caesar and Catiline, as far as Cato was concerned, were on the same side.

365 sī paululum . . . aderunt: Cato's remark to the temporizing Senate is a fine bit of prophecy (see lines 386–388). From the moment that the army of Catiline in Etruria heard that the Senate had actually executed two of its own (Lentulus and Cethegus) through the consul's **imperium**, on the urging of a tribune (Cato), and without benefit of **prōvocātiō** (appeal), that army's resolve (**animus**, 364) did in fact crumble (**īnfirmior erit**) and the army melted away: of the 10,000 men with whom Catiline expected to face Antonius, perhaps only 2,500 or 3,000 men remained.

As the class reads and discusses lines 366–370, have them measure the truth of each detail to see whether Cato accurately and fairly summarizes the evidence for the guilt of the five prisoners. You may also have the class comment on the anaphora **cōnfessī** (368) . . . **cōnfessīs** (369).

371 senātus . . . discessit: the simplest form of expressing a **sententia** in the Senate was to signify in a few words agreement with one or another of the **sententiae** already expressed; one need not even rise from one's seat. Alternatively, senators might go to stand near the man with whose **sententia** they wished to agree. When the presiding magistrate put to a vote the **sententia** that appeared to express the opinion of the majority, he sometimes asked the senators to divide into two blocs, those assenting and those dissenting. This act was called **discessiō**, "division." Junior senators, realizing that a **discessiō** might be called before they had had a chance to speak, voted "with their feet" (as **pedāriī**), joining the senator whose **sententia** they wished to endorse.

373 tresvirōs: the **trēsvirī capitālēs** were three of a total of twenty-six minor magistrates in Rome. They carried out a police role (arresting suspects, running the prison, administering punishment to thieves and slaves, and supervising executions). They collected fines and bonds. Their election took place in the **comitia tribūta**.

375 **in carcere**: the **carcer**, or Mamertine Prison, was on one's left as one headed northward out of the forum up the **Vīcus Lautumiārum** (also known by the name **Clīvus Argentārius**, first attested in the late imperial age) between the **Arx** and the **Cūria** (see plan of the Roman Forum in the student's book, page 6). Originally the Forum had been much lower, swampy ground. The Romans drained this bog, covered the creek flowing through it (creating the **Cloāca Maxima**, or Grand Sewer), and leveled the land over it. A public well was dug where the **carcer** now is; over it was raised a vault (the **Tulliānum**), the lower half of which was carved down into the tufa. Later the top of the **Tulliānum** was sliced away, and the **carcer** proper built over it. The **carcer** is a great hemispherical dome of larger diameter, about 25 feet across the inside. One could get down into the **Tulliānum** from the **carcer** (cf. **dēmissus est**, 379) through an opening in the floor (labeled **A** on the plan in the student's book, page 55). The **Tulliānum** is thought to be about the oldest building in the city. The **carcer** served as a jail for the detention of prisoners awaiting trial, sentencing, or execution. Executions were carried out in the lower chamber.

385 **duās legiōnēs**: Catiline's force would have numbered no more than 12,000. Dio Cassius believed that Catiline's entire force numbered only 3,000 in the final engagement, with no survivors. Thus Sallust was right (lines 392–395) when he said that most of Catiline's army melted away on hearing of the executions in Rome. Metellus had 15,000 to 18,000 men (three legions); Antonius, even more. Use this information to help with study question 2. For the organization of a legion, see *The Roman Army*; but notice that much of the information in such books dates from the imperial period.

Polybius (in *Roman Civilization*, Volume I, Section 164) gives a picture of how an army was constituted in his day (mid-second century B.C.). Following the reforms of Gaius Marius (consul 107, 104–100, and 86 B.C.), the cohort (each comprising three units known as maniples, which were in turn divided into two subunits known as centuries of roughly 60 men each) replaced the maniple as the tactical unit; the division of each legion into three lines continued, but the troops were no longer differentiated by experience and weapons (on the Polybian model); and the soldiers tended to be career veterans. The division of each legion into ten cohorts arranged in checkerboard fashion in three lines was the norm in Caesar's army, and we may

presume that this is how Antonius' army and the forces of Metellus were marshalled. In addition to the common soldiers and their officers (centurions and military tribunes), other members of the force were the **aquilifer**, who carried the **aquila** (the standard identifying each legion), and **signiferī**, who carried each cohort's or maniple's **signum**. There were as well contingents of **funditōrēs** (slingers), **mūnītōrēs** (sappers), and **sagittāriī** (bowmen, who often served as snipers). Finally, there were bands of engineers, wheelwrights, smiths, armorers, carpenters, doctors, cooks, musicians, orderlies, servants, and muleteers.

387 **castra**: Sallust (*Cat.* 30.1, 3, etc.) and Cicero (line 131, **in Etrūriae faucibus conlocāta**, describing the camp as "established in a pass giving access to Etruria") indicate that Manlius' camp lay near Faesulae. In the winter mud Catiline's light armament was an advantage. (See *Geographical Background of Greek and Roman History*, p. 112.) The proconsul Marcius Rex, who had been dispatched to Faesulae in early November (Sall. *Cat.* 30.3) and to whom Manlius had sent a message outlining his aims (Sall. *Cat.* 32.3–34.1), had held his position and not attacked. Rome was safe in spite of Lentulus and his incendiaries: the proconsul Metellus Creticus had gone out to Apulia to raise a force there (Sall. *Cat.* 30.3), and the praetor Pompeius Rufus (30.5) occupied Capua; other proconsulars were available in Rome if needed (L. Licinius Lucullus, L. Manlius Torquatus, and L. Licinius Murena from Gaul). In Transalpine Gaul, C. Licinius Murena was keeping Catilinarian agents in hand (Sall. *Cat.* 42.3).

395–397 **relicuōs . . . Trānsalpīnam**: Sallust (56.4) had written, "After Antonius and his army began to draw near, Catiline marched through the mountains, moving his camp now towards the City and now towards Gaul; he gave the enemy no chance to fight." Catiline was dodging back and forth through the hills above the Arnus, moving faster than Antonius' army. Sallust does not say that the battle was fought at or near Pistoria. He says only that Pistoria was the region into which Catiline withdrew to dodge Antonius. This would let him escape into Gaul, but in carrying out this plan he was cut off by Celer.

398 **agrō Pīcēnō**: Celer's station in Picenum and the **Ager Gallicus** found him at Ariminum (see map in the student's book, page 3) at the junction of the **Via Flāminia** and the **Via Aemilia**; this route was the most common way of getting from Rome to Cisalpine Gaul and on to Transalpine Gaul. (Caesar four years later called it "the shortest route," *B.G.* I.10.3–5.) Only by marching north to the **Via Aemilia** could Catiline

move in accordance with Sallust's hints: he should have reached Bononia before Celer did. But we see him now in this situation: Celer's three legions standing at Bononia and blocking his advance to the north, Antonius' army behind (58.6), and the perilous uplands to either side: in fact, a perfect box (line 404). He would find neither in the mountains nor on the coast road to Genua enough rations to feed his army (a factor mentioned in Catiline's speech to his army: Sall. *Cat.* 58.6 frūmentī . . . egestās); only the lush Po basin produced that. Thus, while sitting trapped somewhere between Bononia and Pistoria, Catiline, we may assume, made the deliberate choice of coming southward out of the hills to attack Antonius' larger force. Catiline spent weeks planning his moves, first at Arretium (lines 184–185) and later in his camp near Faesulae: he would have canvassed the very best of local opinion on good choices of route. Indeed the shadowy "man from Faesulae," who commanded the left wing of Catiline's army in the field battle (Sall. *Cat.* 59.3; see also text, line 429), may well have been a local veteran who knew the difficult upland passes.

406 statuit . . . cōnflīgere: why did Catiline decide to fight it out with Antonius' consular army rather than with Celer's three legions? Maybe Catiline hoped that his former amīcus would let him win, and maybe Antonius' gout (411) was an attack of guilt. If Catiline won, nothing stood between him and Rome, and his soldiers could plunder for food on the way thither. Or else, in the event he lost, Catiline might have expected more leniency from Antonius than from Celer. It was Rome that Catiline had wanted to seize from the first. Celer was sitting in the plain by Bononia waiting for Catiline to come down onto land where Celer would wipe him out; and if Catiline won against Celer, he would have access to food for his men, but Antonius' army would still lie between him and Rome. Catiline expected (Sall. *Cat.* 58.20) that the mountains would reduce the effectiveness of Antonius' army; this indeed the outcome shows to have happened (lines 442–444).

The date of the battle is unknown. On 3 January a tribune tried to pass a bill recalling Pompey from the East to defeat Catiline's army, so that by that date news of any defeat had not reached Rome. By the middle of the month, Catiline's head was brought into Rome to prove his death. Winter travel from Faesulae to Rome, well over two hundred Roman miles, would have been comparatively slow. Perhaps a date of 5–7 January is as reasonable as any.

In Chapter 58 Catiline speaks to his depleted army before the battle. He explains why he waited so long while dodging Antonius' army (expecting reinforcements from Rome); the nature of his followers' difficulty; why they should choose courage over cowardice and exile; why he feels confidence in them; why the terrain favors them. The narrative resumes at line 407. Sallust (59.3) adds that Catiline had kept the silver eagle that had been used by Marius as his emblem in 101 B.C.; and his **aquilifer** carried it in this, Catiline's last battle.

412 M. Petrēiō lēgātō: Cicero elsewhere praises Petreius for his service on this occasion. Sallust (59.6) lists a thirty-year career (from 92 to 62). After defeat in the Battle of Thapsus against Caesar in 46 B.C., Petreius and his ally Juba, King of Numidia, carried out a mutual suicide pact at Zama.

417 tubā: the straight **tuba,** a four-foot long natural horn with cylindrical bore, was made of bronze (sometimes iron); it produced a shrill tone. The **tubicen** might produce as many as eleven harmonics. The bronze **cornū** had a conical bore and curved into more than a half-circle. It was carried rising over the shoulder of the **cornicen,** its bell facing forward. A bronze **lituus** now in the Vatican is almost five feet (1.4 meters) long. It is J-shaped, is tuned in G, and produces six notes. The **tuba** sounded moving out and attack, encouragement during battle, retreat, the signal to halt or make camp, and posting sentries. The more frail call of the **būcina** signaled the beginning of each **vigilia.** The **cornū** was sounded to call the relief for sentries and give battle signals; later it replaced the **būcina.** The **cornicinēs** usually kept close to the standards. The frieze of Trajan's column in Rome shows most instruments used by the military. See further: *The History of Musical Instruments* and *Ancient and Oriental Music.*

420 cum īnfestīs signīs: it is possible that the standard borne by the **signifer** had a totemic and holy significance. Frequently the figure of an animal surmounted the pole (students will be able to cite similar associations prompted by the names of favorite sports teams today). Soldiers could see their own elevated **signum** and from it gain the confidence of knowing they were secure amid their group. The **signum,** much like a flag in modern times, was to be fought for; when it fell, morale might disappear. To move cohort or maniples, the commander had the tribune order the **signum** to move; with it went its men. Thus the **signa** were a kind of semaphore. In the *The Oxford Classical Dictionary*, see articles under "Signa Militaria" (p. 988) and "Standards, Cult of" (p. 1011), and in the *Oxford Latin Dictionary*, see the entries under **corōna, phalerae,** and **vexillum** (pp. 447, 1372, and 2052).

The two armies had attacked on the run (line 420) and, probably because of the terrain and difficulty in securing a balanced stance, had thrown down their heavy **pīla**. Petreius placed his **veterānī** as the vanguard (412–414), just as Catiline had removed the centurions and re-enlisted veterans from his reserve and put them in his front rank (Sall. *Cat.* 59.3). Seasoned, heavy-armed, veteran professionals, maybe struggling uphill, won out in the end over less-experienced, light-armed desperadoes falling down onto them. It is clear, however, that Petreius' army found their victory costly, and this may well have been partly due to the difficult terrain. Catiline had chosen his ground wisely.

445 **spoliandī grātiā**: stripping the dead was one of many processes that ensued after battle. First it would be necessary to find and rescue survivors. Next, the victors would search for their own dead and gather them aside. Enemy dead would be picked over for any valuables before being left; their kin or survivors, or inconvenienced local gentry, were free to bury or cremate their bodies unhindered. The corpse was bathed, dressed in clothing, laid on a couch, and lamented. Burial (with or without cremation) followed as soon as convenient; grave-gifts were bestowed if possible. A funeral was held by the grieving family even if the body could not be found.

* * *

TRANSLATION

References to the Latin text are by line number.

Sallust's *Bellum Catilinae*

(1–4) I shall give an account of the conspiracy of Catiline as truthfully as I am [lit., will be] able; for this deed I consider especially noteworthy because of the novelty of the crime and danger. I must make clear a few points concerning Catiline's character before I commence my account.

(5–14) Lucius Catiline, a nobleman by birth, was a man of great mental and physical power, but his character was wicked and depraved. From an early age, he took pleasure in civil wars, massacres, lootings, and civil dissension, and in these activities he spent his youth. His body was capable of enduring hunger, cold, and wakefulness beyond the limits that anyone would believe. His spirit was bold, crafty, versatile, capable of any pretense or concealment, covetous of what did not belong to him and profligate of his own assets. He was passionate in his cravings and possessed sufficient eloquence but too little prudence. His insatiable spirit always yearned for those things that were extravagant, surpassing belief, and excessively lofty. After the despotism of Lucius Sulla, a very great passion for seizing control of the state had come over Catiline, nor did he consider by what methods he achieved this end a matter of importance as long as he gained absolute power for himself.

(15–18) More and more each day his fierce spirit was driven on by his lack of financial means and his sense of guilt at his crimes, both of which circumstances he had made more pressing by those practices that I mentioned above. He was driven on, moreover, by the decadent condition of the morality of the state, which was being corrupted by luxury as well as greed, two very ruinous and mutually opposed evils.

(19–25) Both because debt was widespread throughout the Roman world and because many of Sulla's veterans were longing for civil war since they had squandered their resources and recalled the by-gone days of plundering and victory, Catiline formed the plan of crushing the state. There was no army in Italy; Gnaeus Pompey was waging war in distant lands; as a candidate for the consulship, Catiline had high hope; the Senate was decidedly not vigilant; conditions were on the whole secure and untroubled; but these factors were thoroughly favorable to Catiline.

(26–32) "If your courage and trustworthiness had not been adequately observed by me, this favorable set of circumstances would have been presented to no purpose; high hope and tyranny within our grasp would have been in vain, nor with the backing of cowardly and unreliable supporters would I be pursuing a risky course of action in place of taking no chances. But because in many critical situations I have learned that you are brave and loyal to me, for this reason my spirit has dared to embark upon a very momentous and glorious enterprise, and at the same time because I have perceived that you and I share in common the view of good and evil—for to desire the same things and to be opposed to the same things [i.e., to have the same likes and dislikes], that indeed is secure friendship.

(33–47) "All of you have separately heard on previous occasions the projects that I have been meditating. But increasingly each day my spirit is inflamed when I consider what the circumstances of our lives will be unless we set ourselves free. For after the state lapsed into the jurisdiction and control of a few powerful figures, to those individuals kings and petty monarchs were tributary, for their advantage nations and peoples paid taxes. All the rest of us, although energetic and righteous, nobles as well as those who lack distinguished ancestors, were a mere rabble without regard and without influence, subservient to those who would stand in awe of us if the state were in a healthy condition. Accordingly, all influence, power, political office, and riches are in their hands or in the hands of persons whom those men favor; they leave for us defeat in politics, the risks of prosecution, trials, and poverty. How long, I ask you, my very brave men, shall we endure this state of affairs? Is it not preferable to die courageously than to lose shamefully a wretched and inglorious life of the sort in which you have been an object of contempt to another's haughtiness? But in very truth, victory is in our grasp. Youth is in our favor, our spirits are keen; by contrast our opponents have all grown feeble thanks to their years and their wealth. There is need only for a beginning of the enterprise; prevailing conditions will put the rest in order.

(48-54) "Therefore, why not rouse yourselves? Behold, that liberty, that liberty that you have often yearned for, moreover wealth, honor, and glory are placed before your eyes; fortune has established all these [things] as prizes for the victors. Conditions, the occasion, threats of prosecution, poverty, and the glorious spoils of war encourage you more than my speech. Employ me either as your leader or as a common soldier; neither my spirit nor my physical energies will be lacking to you. I shall carry out with you these very projects, I hope, as consul, unless perchance my wits deceive me, and you are more ready to be slaves than to be masters."

(55-69) One of the members of this conspiracy was Quintus Curius, born of a by no means lowly station but sullied with disgraces and crimes, a man whom the censors had removed from the Senate on the grounds of his disgraceful conduct. There existed in this man as much folly as boldness; neither did he keep confidential that which he had heard nor did he conceal his own crimes; in short he had no compunction about what he said or did. He had been carrying on a long-standing love affair with Fulvia, a woman of noble birth, but when he was less pleasing to her because he was less able to make lavish presents on account of his lack of means, all at once boasting, he began to promise heaven and earth; at times, he made physical threats if Fulvia was not obedient to him; finally, he behaved more overbearingly than he had been accustomed to do in the past. But Fulvia, having found out the cause of Curius' arrogance, did not keep secret such dan-

ger to the state, but suppressing her source, she related to very many the things that she had heard about Catiline's conspiracy and how she had heard them. This circumstance especially stirred support among the voters to entrust the consulship to Cicero. For previously, the nobility generally seethed with jealousy and believed that the consulship was, as it were, sullied, if a new man, however outstandng, obtained it. But when the danger materialized, envy and haughtiness were put aside.

(70-75) Therefore, when the election was held, Cicero and Gaius Antonius were announced the victors, and this outcome at first had shaken the members of the conspiracy. Nevertheless, Catiline's frenzy was not lessened, but he set more projects in motion daily; he arranged for weapons throughout Italy in favorable places; he conveyed money borrowed on his own credit and that of his friends to a certain fellow Manlius at Faesulae, who was the first to raise the standard of war.

(76-87) Despite making ready these preparations [for revolt], Catiline none the less sought election to the consulship for the following year since he hoped that if he should be elected he would easily employ Antonius according to his wishes. Meanwhile he did not remain inactive but laid traps for Cicero in every way. Yet Cicero did not lack craft or cunning for taking precautions. From the beginning of his consulship, by making grand promises, he had arranged through Fulvia for Curius, concerning whom I made mention just a little above, to reveal to him the plans of Catiline. In additon to this, by means of an agreement concerning the assignment of provinces, he had forced his colleague not to side against the government, and he secretly kept himself constantly surrounded with a bodyguard of friends and retainers. After the day of the election had come, and neither the candidacy of Catiline nor the plots which he had laid against the consuls on the Campus Martius had resulted in success, Catiline decided to make war and to adopt radical measures inasmuch as those things that he had tried in secret had turned out adverse and disastrous.

(88-94) Therefore, he sent off Gaius Manlius to Faesulae and into that part of Etruria, a certain Septimius of Camerinum into the territory of Picenum, and Gaius Julius to Apulia; besides he sent various associates to various places wherever he believed anyone would be advantageous to him.

Meanwhile, at Rome he undertook many projects at the same time: he laid plots against the consuls; he caused armed men to occupy favorable places; he armed himself with a weapon and bid the others to do likewise; he urged his men to be always alert and at the ready; he made haste day and night, went without sleep, and was worn out neither by the lack of sleep nor by effort.

(95-105) The state had been agitated by these preparations, and the outward appearance of the city had been altered. In place of unbounded joy and wantonness, which had been brought into being by a long-lasting calm, suddenly sadness came over everyone: people rushed around, quaked with fear, had little reliance in any person or place, were not in a full state of war yet lacked peace, and each measured the dangers according to his own fear.

But Catiline's cruel spirit continued to further those same projects despite the fact that armed guards were being established [to protect the state] and despite the fact that he himself had been indicted by Lucius Paulus under the lēx Plautia [covering acts of violence]. Finally, he came into the Senate either for the sake of concealing his guilt or to justify himself as though he had been provoked by abuse [from his political enemies]. On that occasion, the consul Cicero, whether fearing Catiline's presence or moved by anger, delivered a brilliant speech and one beneficial to the state, which he afterwards circulated in a published version.

Cicero's *Oratio in L. Catilinam I*

(106-114) "To what extent I ask you, Catiline, will you take advantage of our patience? How long will that madness of yours mock us? To what limit will that unbridled boldness of yours swagger? Have you not been moved at all by the garrison of the Palatine by night, by the city's sentinels, by the people's fear, by the flocking together of all patriots, by this most fortified place for holding a meeting of the Senate, by the looks and facial expressions of all these [senators]? Do you not perceive that your plans are exposed? Do you not see that your conspiracy is held in check by the knowledge of all these persons? What one of us do you think is unaware of what you did last night and the night before, where you were, whom you called together, and what plan you adopted?

(115-120) "Oh the times, oh the conduct of men! The Senate knows these things, the consul sees [them], yet this fellow is still alive. Alive? But on the contrary, he even comes into the Senate, he becomes a participant in governmental counsels, he marks and picks out for slaughter with his eyes each of us. Yet we, brave men [that we are], seem to fulfill our obligation to the state if we should go on avoiding the frenzy and daggers of this fellow. Long ago, Catiline, you ought to have been led to execution by order of the consul; the

destruction that you are devising against us ought to have been inflicted upon you.

(121-130) "But [is it the case that] we consuls shall put up with Catiline, who is craving to lay waste the world with slaughter and fire, while the pontifex maximus, the illustrious Publius Scipio, though he was holding no public office at the time, killed Tiberius Gracchus, who was to a degree weakening the condition of the state? For I leave out of account those instances from remote antiquity, the fact that Gaius Servilius Ahala with his own hand killed Spurius Maelius, who was stirring up a revolution. There existed, there once existed in the state that well-known excellence [of which you have heard] so that courageous men repressed a ruinous citizen with harsher punishments than the bitterest foreign foe. We have a stern and serious resolution of the Senate against you, Catiline. The state is not without the counsel or the leadership of this body. We, we the consuls, I declare openly, are found wanting.

(131-140) "A camp has been established in Italy against the Roman people in a pass giving access to Etruria; the number of the enemy increases each successive day; moreover, we see the commander-in-chief of this camp and the leader of the enemy within our city walls and even in the Senate as he sets in motion daily some internal ruin for the state. If I order you now, Catiline, to be arrested and put to death, I shall have to fear, I suppose, not so much that all patriots will say that this has been done by me too late but rather that someone will say that it has been done too cruelly. But for a definite reason I am not yet led to do this thing that ought to have been over and done with long ago. Then finally you will be put to death, when no one will be able to be found so wicked, so abandoned, so like you as to [lit., who] admit that your execution has not been rightly performed.

(141-156) "Since this is the situation, Catiline, proceed as you have begun; go forth now at last from the city. The gates stand open; set out. For too long that camp of Manlius misses you as its commander. Lead out with you all your men, or at least as many as possible; cleanse the city. You will free me from great fear provided a wall exists between you and me. You are not able any longer to dwell with us; I shall not endure it, I shall not put up with it, I shall not allow it. We must feel grateful to the immortal gods and to this god Jupiter Stator himself, guardian of old of this city, because we have now so often escaped this scourge so abominable, so dreadful, and so dangerous to the state. The supreme safety of the state ought not to be exposed to danger too often through the actions of one man [lit., in one man].

As long as you intrigued against me while consul-elect, I defended myself not by means of a bodyguard furnished by the state but by means of vigilance on my own part. When at the recent consular elections you wished to kill me, the consul, and the candidates competing with you on the Campus Martius, I checked your wicked attempts with a bodyguard and forces composed of my friends, without raising any open disturbance. Finally, as often as you made an attack against me, I opposed you on my own, although I saw that my destruction had been linked with great disaster to the state.

(157–164) "With these omens, Catiline, go forth to that unholy and wicked war to [lit., with] the complete salvation of the state, to your own ruin and destruction, and to the destruction of those who have joined themselves with you by means of every crime and act of murder. You, Jupiter, will [assuredly] ward off this [enemy of the state] and his associates from your own temples and the temples of the other gods, from the buildings and ramparts of the city, and from the lives and property of Roman citizens. You will punish with everlasting torments both in this life and after death those men [who are] enemies of right-minded citizens, traitors to their country, brigands of Italy, and united among themselves by a league in [lit., of] crimes and a wicked alliance."

Resumption of Sallust's *Bellum Catilinae*

(165–174) But when Cicero took his seat, Catiline, as he was ready to conceal all, with a humble expression on his face and a pleading voice began to ask the senators not to believe anything rashly concerning him; [he asserted] that, born of such a family, he had so ordered his life from youth that he counted upon nothing but good things; they were not to think that he, a patrician, whose good deeds and those of his ancestors had benefited the Roman common people so many times, had need for the destruction of the state, while Marcus Tullius, who was nothing short of a naturalized citizen, was preserving the state. When to this slur he was adding other insults, all the senators began to raise a din and call him a public enemy and murderer. Then in his rage, Catiline said: "Inasmuch as I have been indeed hemmed in by my enemies and am driven headlong, I shall quench the flames that engulf me with radical measures."

(175–183) Then he dashed out of the meeting to his house. There he reflected on many things in private, and because his plots against Cicero were not succeeding, and he realized that the city was fortified with watches against fire, he

believed the best course of action was to increase the size of his army and to anticipate his opponents by making ready the many things of the sort that would be useful in war before the government could enroll its legions. Therefore he set out for Manlius' camp with a few associates in the dead of night. He commissioned Cethegus, Lentulus, and the rest in whom he knew to exist ready boldness, to strengthen the resources of their association by whatever means they could, to hasten along the plot against Cicero, and to prepare slaughter, arson, and other deeds of war; [he assured them] that very soon he would draw near to the city with a large army.

(184–191) Catiline stayed a few days at the house of Gaius Flaminius in the region of Arretium while he equipped with weapons this region that had previously been incited to rebellion, and he then assumed the fasces and other trappings of authority and pressed on to the camp to join Manlius. When these activities were found out at Rome, the Senate declared Catiline and Manlius public enemies and set a date for the remaining mass of individuals [involved in the plot]—except for those condemned of capital crimes—before which they might lay down their arms with impunity. Furthermore, the Senate decreed that the consuls should hold a levy of troops, that Antonius should hasten to pursue Catiline, and that Cicero should look after the protection of the city.

Cicero's *Oratio in L. Catilinam III*

(192–215) "Accordingly, when I found out that the ambassadors of the Allobroges had been tampered with by Lentulus for the purpose of stirring up a war in Transalpine Gaul and an uprising of Gauls on Italy's northern frontier, and that they had been dispatched with letters and instructions to their fellow citizens in Gaul and to Catiline on the same journey, and that Titus Volturcius had been attached to them as a companion and a letter had been given to Volturcius for Catiline, I felt that an opportunity had been presented to me to have the whole affair detected clearly not only by me but also by you and the Senate, an outcome that was very difficult to achieve and one that I had always prayed for from the immortal gods.

"Consequently, yesterday I summoned to my presence the brave and patriotic praetors Lucius Flaccus and Gaius Pomptinus. I revealed the situation and showed them the course of action that I had decided to take. Those praetors, since their feelings toward the state were entirely loyal and exemplary, undertook the task without reluctance and without delay. When evening was approaching, they secretly reached the Mulvian

Bridge, and there they took up a position in two divisions in the neighboring houses so that the Tiber River and bridge lay between them. Moreover to that same spot both the praetors themselves had led, without anyone's suspicion, many brave men, and I myself had sent with arms a good many young men picked from the praefecture of Reate, whose services I continuously use in the defense of the state.

"Meanwhile, close to the end of the third watch, when the ambassadors of the Allobroges with a large escort together with Volturcius were beginning to set foot on the Mulvian Bridge, an attack was made upon them. Swords were drawn both by the Gauls and our men. Only the praetors were fully aware of what was taking place; the rest were in the dark. Then by the intervention of Pomptinus and Flaccus, the fight that had broken out was brought to a stop. Whatever letters were in the hands of that escort were handed over, with the seals intact, to the praetors. The men themselves were placed under arrest and brought before me when it was growing light."

Resumption of Sallust's *Bellum Catilinae*

(216–229) Following the completion of this operation, the consul was speedily informed through messengers about everything. But Cicero experienced at the same time great concern as well as gladness. For he rejoiced knowing that the state had been snatched from dangers by the revelation of the conspiracy; yet, on the other hand, he was troubled and uncertain about what should be done given the fact that such important citizens had been implicated in a very serious crime; he believed that their punishment would mean trouble for him, yet to let them off would contribute to the destruction of the state. Accordingly, having strengthened his resolve, Cicero ordered to be summoned to him Lentulus, Cethegus, Statilius, Gabinius, and likewise Caeparius of Terracina, who was preparing to set out for Apulia to arouse the servile class. The others came without delay, [but] Caeparius, having left his house a little before and having learned of the disclosure [of the plot], had fled from the city. The consul himself led Lentulus by the hand before the Senate because he was a praetor; he ordered the rest to come with their guards into the Temple of Concord. Cicero summoned the Senate to this temple and introduced at a well-attended meeting of the Senate Volturcius and the ambassadors; he ordered the praetor Flaccus to bring to the same place the case with the letters which he had taken from the legates.

(230–236) Volturcius was questioned about the journey and the letters, and finally about the nature of his plan and his motive. At first he began to invent another story and to lie about the conspiracy. Later, when told to speak under a governmental pledge of immunity, he revealed everything as it had been done. He gave information that he had been admitted as a confederate [in the plot] a few days earlier by Gabinius and Caeparius: that he knew no more than did the envoys, but that he was merely accustomed to hearing from Gabinius that Publius Autronius, Servius Sulla, Lucius Vargunteius, and many besides were part of the conspiracy.

(237–242) The Gauls made the same confession, and when Lentulus tried to cover his guilt they refuted him not just with the letters but with things he had been accustomed to say: that according to the Sibylline Books despotic rule over [lit., of] Rome was foretold for three Cornelii; that previously [there had been] Cinna and Sulla, and now he was the third, for whom it was fated to be in charge of the City; and finally that this was the twentieth year since the burning of the Capitol, a year which the soothsayers, reading the omens, had often revealed would be bloody with civil warfare.

(243–248) And so the letters were read from beginning to end. (All signatories had already acknowledged their signets in the wax.) The Senate [then] voted that Lentulus, upon resigning his magistracy, should be held with the others under house arrest. Consequently Lentulus was given into the charge of Publius Lentulus Spinther, who was currently an aedile, Cethegus to Quintus Cornificius, Statilius to Gaius Caesar, Gabinius to Marcus Crassus, and Caeparius (who a little earlier had been caught running away) to Gnaeus Terentius, a senator.

(249–255) While this was going on in the Senate, and rewards were being voted to the Allobrogian envoys and to Titus Volturcius because their evidence had been proved reliable, the freedmen of Lentulus and some of his clients, following a variety of routes, were trying to round up laborers and slaves in the streets to free Lentulus from custody. Others were scouting for ringleaders who for a price often organized public mischief. Besides this, Cethegus was sending messengers to his slaves and freedmen (a select bunch trained for the purpose) to embolden them to insurrection, to form up their brigade, and to break in to release him with arms.

(256–262) The consul got wind of these goings-on. He stationed guards as the circumstance and the time dictated and called a meeting of the Senate. He asked what they wished to be done concerning the men who had been put under arrest. (A little while earlier a full meeting of the Senate had decided that these men had acted as enemies of the state.) Then Decimus Junius Silanus, currently the consul-elect and so the first to have been asked his opinion, had proposed that punishment should be exacted from those held under arrest, as well as from Lucius Cassius, Publius Furius, Publius Umbrenus, and Quintus Annius in case they should be caught.

(263–267) "All men, Fathers of the Senate, who ponder difficult questions, should be uninfluenced by considerations of hatred or friendship, anger or pity. When these emotions get in the way, the mind finds it hard to make out the truth, and no single person has ever obeyed his impulses at the same time as his self-interest. Whenever you apply close attention, your attention wins out; if the impulses gain possession, they seize hold, and the mind's power fails.

(268–273) "I know for sure that Decimus Silanus, a brave and energetic man, said what he did say because of his concern for the state, and that he was exercising neither favoritism nor antagonism in a matter of such importance. I know that such is the character, such the moderateness of the man. However, his opinion seems to me, not cruel—for in the case of such men [i.e., the conspirators under arrest] what cruelty could be perpetrated?—but foreign to the spirit of our land. For surely, Silanus, either dread or a sense of injury drove you, on the eve of taking up your consulship, to opt for a novel sort of punishment.

(274–278) "Regarding fear it would be pointless to debate, especially since through the devotion to duty of our eminent consul we see such substantial armed support about us. As regards the punishment, I myself can affirm (and this is what the present issue involves) that amid human grief and sorrows death is a rest from suffering, it is not punishment; it releases all the ills of humankind, and after death there is occasion for neither sorrow nor joy.

(279–285) "But, by the gods who never die, why did you not add onto your opinion that they should be punished with a flogging first? Because the Porcian Law forbids it? Yet there are other laws that provide in like manner that citizens who have been found guilty are not to be executed but rather should be allowed to go into exile! Or was it because being flogged is a more severe punishment than being executed? But what punishment is harsh or too severe for men found guilty of such a horrid crime? But if [you did not ask for flogging] because it is the less onerous punishment, how is it consistent to respect the law in the less impor-

tant instance, even though you have disregarded it in the greater?

(286–291) "But [you say] who will criticize a decree passed against men who are destroyers of their country? Time will do so, and day passing day, and so will Fortune, whose whim rules the nations of humankind. Whatever comes about for these prisoners will happen deservedly; but you, Fathers of the Senate, must consider what precedent you are establishing for other criminals. All bad precedents have risen out of decent concerns. But whenever the power of government has fallen to those who do not comprehend it or are not so virtuous, then that precedent passes on from those who deserve and are worthy [of such punishment] to those who do not deserve it and are innocent.

(292–296) "Do I suggest, therefore, that the prisoners be let go and the size of Catiline's army be increased? Not in the least. But I do make these proposals: that their financial holdings should become state property, and that the men themselves should be held under restraint in the towns that can most easily afford the expense; that no one hereafter is to bring their case before the Senate or argue it before the assembly of the people; and that the Senate should regard that anyone who acts contrary to these proposals will be acting against the state and the security of its citizens."

Cicero's *Oratio in L. Catilinam IV*

(297–310) "I perceive two expressions of opinion. One is that of Decimus Silanus, who proposes that the men who tried to destroy this state should be punished with death. The other is that of Gaius Caesar, who suspends the death penalty and embraces all the bitterness of the alternative forms of punishment. Both speakers are observing the highest degree of strictness in accordance with both the respect in which we hold them and the importance of the situation. The one thinks it not right that men who have tried to deprive us all of life, to destroy lawful authority, and to snuff out the name of the people of Rome, should for even an instant benefit from life and from this air we all breathe; and he remembers that the kind of penalty he proposes has often been applied to violent citizens in this very state. The other speaker understands that death was instituted by the undying gods not to function as a punishment, but rather as a requirement of nature and even a rest from toil and misery. And so wise men have never gone to meet death unwillingly, and the brave often even with eagerness. But, in fact, chains have been hit upon (and chains for life) certainly to serve as an unparalleled punishment for this wicked crime. He orders [the prisoners] to be distributed among the towns of Italy.

(311–316) "Such a provision as that seems to involve unfairness if you choose to impose it or awkwardness if you choose to request it. Still, vote for his opinion if that is your pleasure. For I myself shall undertake and, as I hope, shall find those who will not think that to refuse what you have decreed for the sake of the common safety is in keeping with their own honor. Caesar adds a burdensome penalty onto the townships, in case anyone should break the prisoners' chains: he throws around them dreadful garrisons that are worthy of the crimes of wicked men.

(317–325) "Therefore, if you adopt Caesar's proposal, you will provide me with a colleague dear and pleasing to the people when I inform them about the action taken by the Senate. On the other hand, if you prefer to follow Silanus' proposal, the Roman people will easily release you and me from the blame of cruelty, and I shall show his view to have been by far the gentler of the two. Still, Fathers of the Senate, what cruelty can there be in punishing the monstrousness of such a crime? Of course I am judging according to my own feelings. So may I reap the fruits of a safe commonwealth along with you, as I am moved—[I say this] because in this deliberation I am unusually earnest—not by savage intent (for who is a gentler man than I?) but by some special sense of humanity and pity.

(326–338) "Given this state of affairs, in place of military power, in place of an army command, in place of the governorship of a province that I have turned down, in place of celebrating a triumph and displaying the rest of the emblems of glory that I have refused in order to guard the safety of you and your city, in place of the ties of clientship and hospitality with provincials (which, nevertheless, I strive just as energetically to maintain as I do to acquire them by means of resources available to me in the city), in place of all these advantages, and in exchange for my own special care for you and for this perseverance of mine, which is plain to you all, in protecting our republic, I ask nothing from you except that you remember this moment and all of my year as consul: as long as this shall remain rooted in your minds, I shall consider myself to be hedged round by the securest rampart. But if the violence of criminals deceives and crushes my hope, I entrust to you my little son. Surely he will have enough protection not only for his security but for his honor as well, if you remember that this is the son of the man who preserved your whole way of life by putting himself alone in danger.

(339–344) "Therefore take careful and courageous deliberation, as you have begun, over the supreme safety of yourselves and the people of Rome, over our wives and children, over our altars and hearths, our shrines and temples, over the homes and buildings of our entire city, over our empire and our freedom, over the safety of all Italy, over our worldwide commonwealth. You have as your consul a man who will not hesitate to obey the expression of your will and, as long as he has life, will be able to defend your decisions and to guarantee on his own to carry them out."

Resumption of Sallust's *Bellum Catilinae*

(345–351) "My opinion, Fathers of the Senate, is far different when I think of the dangerous situation we are in and when I examine the stated opinions of several of you. To me these men seem to have been giving us philosophical lectures about the punishment of those who have plotted war against their own homeland, their parents, their altars and their hearths; the situation, however, warns us to beware of the conspirators rather than to argue back and forth what we should decide to do to them. Other wicked deeds one may punish after they have been committed. Unless one use foresight to head off this [crime of treason], once it has occurred one would appeal to the law-courts in vain: when a city has been captured, there is nothing left over for those who lose.

(352–359) "In this assembly a short while ago Gaius Caesar gave a fine, elegant dissertation on life and death. He was of the belief, I suppose, that stories of the underworld are deceptions, [stories to the effect] that the wicked [taking] a different path from [that of] good people occupy gloomy regions, desolate, loathesome, horrible. So he recommended that the prisoners' financial resources be confiscated by the state, and that they themselves should be kept under arrest in the townships; he is doubtless afraid that, if they were to remain in Rome, they may be rescued by adherents of the plot or by a hired mob: as if there were traitors and crooks only in Rome and not anywhere else in Italy, or as if a daring raid would not have more chance of succeeding where resources to repel it are fewer.

(360–365) "So this proposal of his really is quite worthless, if he is afraid of danger from the prisoners. If he alone amid such widespread fear has no fear at all, all the more important is it for me to be afraid for me and for you. Therefore, when you make your decision about Publius Lentulus and the rest, you must be absolutely certain that you are deciding as well about Catiline's army and everyone in the conspiracy. The more deliberate the action that you take now, the shakier will be their resolve. If they notice even the slightest weakness in your behavior, they'll be down upon our necks in a sudden horde.

(366–370) "Therefore my proposal is this: since by an ungodly conspiracy of criminal citizens our state has reached the edge of the direst peril, and since these men have been proved guilty by the evidence of Titus Volturcius and the Allobrogian envoys, and have confessed that they schemed to commit assassination, incendiarism, and other foul and savage crimes against fellow-citizens and their homeland, the self-confessed criminals should be punished according to the practice of our ancestors, as if they had been caught redhanded in capital offences."

(371–374) After the Senate voted its approval of Cato's proposal, the consul thought it best to act in advance of the night coming on so as to prevent any new attempt from being made during that interval. He instructed the three Commissioners of Executions to make the preparations that the execution of the sentence demanded; posting armed guards, he himself escorted Lentulus down into the prison; the praetors did likewise with the other conspirators.

(375–383) Within the prison is a place called the Tullianum. (You get there by going up a little towards the left.) It is about twelve feet deep in the ground. Walls strengthen it on all sides; on top of it is a vault formed from stone arches. Its appearance is ghastly and terrifying because of neglect, gloom, stench. Into this place Lentulus was lowered, and there executioners assigned to the task garroted him. And so this patrician from the most illustrious family of the Cornelii, who had held consular **imperium** at Rome, found an end to his life that befitted his character and the things he had done. The same punishment was visited on Cethegus, Statilius, Gabinius, and Caeparius.

(384–391) While this was going on in Rome, Catiline organized two legions out of the collected forces that he himself had brought and that Manlius already had with him; he filled the cohorts with as many men as he had. Then he distributed out to them equally each volunteer or co-conspirator who arrived at his camp later. It did not take long before he had brought his legions up to full numerical strength, even though at first he hadn't more than two thousand men under his command. But of all this host no more than one man in four was equipped with regulation weapons; the rest carried what fortune put in their hands: hunters' javelins, pikes, some even sharpened stakes.

(392–406) But after the news reached the camp that in Rome the conspiracy had been ex-

posed and that Lentulus, Cethegus, and the others whom I mentioned earlier had been executed, more than half of those that the expectation of loot or the eagerness for an overthrow of the existing order had attracted to an armed uprising melted away. Catiline pulled his remaining fighters back over the rugged hills by forced marches into the region around Pistoria, with the idea thereby of escaping secretly into Transalpine Gaul over the upland trails. However, Quintus Metellus Celer with three legions was encamped at the ready in the district of Picenum; he formed the opinion, as a result of his enemy's awkward situation, that Catiline was intending to do exactly what he did. Consequently, learning of Catiline's route from deserters, he quickly moved camp, digging his army in at the foot of the very mountains where lay the route of Catiline's hurried descent into Gaul. Nor in addition was Antonius far away, considering the fact that with his bulky army he pursued over easier terrain the retreat of this lightly armed foe. But Catiline saw that he was boxed in between the mountains and his enemies' forces, and that, with matters in Rome running against him, it was pointless to attempt flight or to wait for reinforcements. He decided that the best thing to do in this impossible situation was to risk battle. As soon as possible he resolved to join battle with Antonius.

(407–410) Catiline paused briefly. He then ordered the signals to sound, drawing his men into battle formation, and led them down onto level ground. Next he had all the horses removed so that, with the risk evened out for everyone, he would increase his soldiers' courage. As an infantryman himself, he marshaled his army by fitting his numbers to the nature of the terrain.

(411–416) On the other side Gaius Antonius was suffering from gout, and so it was impossible for him to be present at the battle in person. He put his army under the command of his lieutenant-general, Marcus Petreius. Petreius, who had called up veterans because of the uprising, placed them as his vanguard; the rest of the army he held behind them in reserve. He rode about on horseback, addressing each man by name, encouraging them, calling on them to remember that they were contending with highway robbers who weren't even armed, and this in the name of their homeland, their children, their altars and homes.

(417–420) When Petreius, after a full reconnoitre of his situation, had the trumpet sound the attack, he instructed his cohorts to press forward little by little. Catiline's army did the same. After they reached a point where the fighting could be started by skirmishers, the opposing forces ran at each other with deafening shouts. Dropping their spears, they got at it with swords.

(421–425) Petreius' veterans, reliving their old-time courage, pressed ahead keenly at close quarters; their enemies offered resistance you could not call cowardly, and the struggle raged violently. Meanwhile Catiline was hot at it with his light-armed troops in the front lines, running to help any caught in difficulty, summoning fresh reinforcements to relieve the wounded, calculating every need, fighting hard himself, striking down many a foe; he kept carrying out to the letter his duties as a fervent soldier and a loyal commander.

(426–432) Petreius saw Catiline putting up a bigger struggle than he had anticipated. So he drove his commander's guard into the enemy's center. His men threw them into confusion and killed those who resisted, some in some places, others elsewhere, finally attacking the remainder on left and right. Manlius and the man from Fiesole fell fighting in the front lines. Catiline saw that his forces were strewn and that he was left with only a handful of survivors. He remembered his birth and former prestige. Dashing into the thickest of his foes he was run through [again and again] as he fought.

(433–439) When the battle was over, then indeed one could perceive how great were the daring and determination of Catiline's army. Almost everyone in dying was covering with his corpse the same spot he had seized to fight on when alive. A few, however, in the center, who had been scattered by the commander's guard, lay a little farther off, but all nonetheless had fallen with their wounds in front. Catiline in fact was discovered far from his own men, surrounded by the bodies of his foes; he was even perceptibly breathing, and his face still showed the same ferocious spirit it had shown when he was alive.

(440–448) Finally, of the entire [rebel] army, no freeborn citizen was captured either during the fighting or in flight: to such an extent did they value their own lives no more highly than their enemies'. But the army of the Roman people, on the other hand, did not achieve a joyous and bloodless victory: for all its most energetic warriors either fell fighting or left the field badly wounded. There were many as well who had come out from the camp either to survey the scene or to pillage the dead. As they rolled over the enemy corpses, some uncovered a friend, others a former guest or kinsman. There were likewise some who recognized personal enemies. And so a range of emotions flickered across the army: exultation and tears, mourning and gladness.

* * *

ANSWERS TO EXERCISES

Note: students should be allowed to use a standard Latin/English, English/Latin dictionary when doing these exercises.

Lines 1–130

1. coniūrātiōnibus, perīculīs, vultibus, vī, rēbus, modō, lūxuriīs, discordiā, quibus, hāc.
2. Students practice subordination by means of the absolute construction.
   a. Comitiīs habitīs, cōnsulēs dēclārātī sunt M. Tullius et C. Antōnius. *When the election was held, Marcus Tullius and Gaius Antonius were proclaimed consuls.*
   b. Maximō facinore inceptō, lībertātem pulcherrimam tandem habēbimus. *Having undertaken this vast action, we will at last have the most beautiful freedom.*
   c. Armīs in Etrūriā dēpositīs, Antōnius tuīs mīlitibus parcet. *Once you have laid down arms in Etruria, Antonius will spare your soldiers.*
3. variā, variam, variae, variōrum, variīs; audāx, audācī, audācem, audācium, audācī.
4. a. If Pompey were not fighting war in most distant lands, Catiline would not be attempting a revolution. (present contrary to fact condition)
   b. If you believe in me enough, things will work out for us. (future more vivid)
   c. If Fulvia had loved Quintus, she would not have reported Catiline's plans to Cicero. (past contrary to fact)
   d. If Catiline had not hidden armaments in the city, the people would be on his side. (mixed condition: past/present contrary to fact)
   e. If Curius wants to warn Cicero about danger, he sends a message through Fulvia. (general condition, present time)
5. Forming direct commands is the focus here, while indirect commands are handled in 13 in the second group of exercises.
   a. Semper este, omnēs, intentī parātīque. *All of you, be always eager and ready.*
   b. Nōlī, Antōnī, contrā rem pūblicam sentīre. *Antonius, don't turn against your state.*
   c. Comitia ad cōnsulēs dēclārandōs habeāmus. *Let's hold an assembly to elect consuls.*
   d. Nōlī arbitrārī nōs nihil scīre. *Do not think that we know nothing.*

LONGMAN LATIN READERS

6. Students must pay attention here to the dependency of the relative pronoun on its antecedent.
   a. Catilīna cōnscientiam scelerum artibus auxerat, quās suprā memorāvī. *Catiline had increased his consciousness of crimes by means of those practices that I have mentioned earlier.*
   b. Omnēs vōs ea quae mente agitāvī iam audīvistis. *All of you have already heard what I have been considering.*
   c. Ēn illa lībertās quam saepe optāvistis! *There's that renowned freedom that you have often hoped for!*
   d. Cicerō effēcerat ut Q. Cūrius, dē quō paulō ante scrīpsī, cōnsilia sibi prōderet. *Cicero had caused Quintus Curius, about whom I wrote a little earlier, to reveal the plans to him.*
   e. Catilīna rem pūblicam, cuius salūtem omnēs bonī dēfendere dēbēbant, dēlēre cōnātus est. *Catiline tried to destroy the state, whose safety/security all patriots ought to have defended.*
7. Catilīna, senātor Rōmānus cuius animus nimium (nimis alta) semper spērābat (cupiēbat), dominātiōnem reī pūblicae capere cōnstituit. Circiter Kalendās Iūniās, amīcīs et clientibus convocātīs cōnsilium aperuit quod capere ausus erat. "Cotīdiē animī vestrī cupīditāte lībertātis ardeant! Nōsmet ipsī in lībertātem vindicēmus!" Proximō autem annō fēmina quaedam, Fulvia nōmine, Marcum Tullium cōnsulem dē coniūrātiōne certiōrem tandem fēcit. Postquam Catilīna Gāium Mānlium ad exercitum cōnscrībendum (quī exercitum cōnscrīberet) Faesulās mīsit, Cicerō ōrātiōnem apud patrēs habuit. "Quōusque Catilīna patientiā nostrā abutētur? Rēs novās, patrēs cōnscrīptī, mōlītur (Rēbus novīs . . . studet). Dē eō supplicium sūmite meritum."

Lines 131–229
8. hostis, mihi, faciērum, metibus, mūrī, custōdibus, hominum, calamitātī, cōpiae, praesidiīs.
9. a. Cum advesperāsceret. . . . *When it was growing dark, armed men arrived at the Mulvian Bridge with the magistrates.*
   b. Quae cum ita sint (Cum haec ita sint). . . . *Since that is how things are (Given this state of affairs), take away all your people with you to Manlius' camp.*
   c. Cum cōnsul assēdisset. . . . *When the consul had sat down, Catiline began to*

plead with the senators with the intention of deceiving them.
10. Students will suggest different questions in each instance. Possible alternatives are proposed only for the first.
    a. Quā dē causā (Quārē, Quōmodo) hanc tam īnfestam pestem effūgimus? *For what reason (Why, How) have we escaped such a wicked destruction as this?* Iove urbem custōdiente, quid effūgimus? *Thanks to Jupiter's protection of the city, what have we escaped?* Quis, Iove urbem custōdiente, hanc tam īnfestam pestem effūgit? *Who, thanks to Jupiter's protection of the city, has escaped such a wicked destruction as this?*
    b. Quis hāc nocte ad pontem Mulvium perveniet? *Who will reach the Mulvian Bridge tonight?*
    c. Quem convēnērunt lēgātī Allobrogum coniūrātiōnis patefaciendae causā? *Whom did the ambassadors of the Allobroges meet to reveal the conspiracy?*
11. a. Īnsidiae prope Tiberim flūmen collocātae extrā urbem sunt. *The ambush, set up near the Tiber River, is outside the city.*
    b. Catilīna ab inimīcīs circumventus praeceps agitur. *Catiline, surrounded by enemies, is being chased headlong.*
    c. Litterae lēgātīs Allobrogum ad suōs cīvīs redientibus mandātae ad Catilīnam mittēbantur. *Letters entrusted to the Allobrogian ambassadors, who were returning to their own people, were being sent to Catiline.*
12. These sentences contain indirect questions; rules of sequence of tense apply.
    a. The consul pointed out (indicated) to all brave men (people, persons) what he wished done (to be done).
    b. The Allobroges do not understand whether Cicero believes them or not.
    c. Catiline had wondered whatever might be the reason that the letters had been handed over to the praetors with the seals intact.
13. a. Praetor adulēscentīs ex praefectūrā Reātīnā dēlēctōs hortābātur ut impetum in Volturcium facerent. *The praetor was urging (kept urging, began to urge) the youths, who had been picked from the prefecture of Reate, to attack Volturcius.*
    b. Catilīna, antequam ad castra profectus est, Lentulō cēterīsque mandāverat ut opēs factiōnis cōnfirmārent. *Before Catiline left for the camp, he had instructed*

Lentulus and the others to strengthen the resources of the movement.

c. Lēgātī Allobrogum cōnsulem rogant nē Lentulō cōnfīdat. *The ambassadors of the Allobroges are asking the consul not to trust Lentulus.*

14. Numerus cīvium malōrum quī ad castra Mānliāna concurrēbant ut sē Catilīnae exercituī adiungerent in diēs crēscēbat. Cōnsul mīrātus est cūr anteā Catilīnam nōn interfēcisset ut rem pūblicam ab hōc lūctū servāret. Ille ipse deinde Rōmā discessit ut sē cum Mānliō coniungeret. Tandem ēvēnit (accidit) ut lēgātī Allobrogum, populī Gallicī quī trāns Alpēs incolit, ad cōnsulem vēnerint. Quī sēcum litterās tulērunt ab nōnnūllīs senātōribus Rōmānīs signātās, quās illī rogāverant ut in Etrūriam ad Mānlium ferrent. Cicerō īnsidiās ad pontem Mulvium collocāvit, lēgātōsque et litterās integrīs signīs cēpit, et Rōmam ad senātum tulit. Gaudēbat sē coniūrātiōnem patefacere posse, senātōrēsque sibi tandem crēditūrōs esse.

Lines 230–338

15. These insertions express place or space.
Rōmam ad senātum; apud quōsdam senātōrēs; Rōmae; Rōmā; ad suōs.

16. Remind students that the subject of an indirect statement is accusative, the verb is in the infinitive mood, reflexive pronouns and adjectives refer to the subject of the main or governing verb, and subordinate clauses are in the subjunctive mood.

a. Frequēns senātus paulō ante iūdicāvit illōs hominēs contrā rem pūblicam fēcisse. *A full meeting of the Senate a bit earlier resolved that those men had acted against the state.*

b. Sīlānus cēnset coniūrātōs poenās dare dēbēre. *Silanus is of the opinion that the conspirators should pay the penalty.*

c. Lentulus sermōnibus adfirmāre solitus erat sē tertium esse cui librī Sibyllīnī rēgnum praedicāvissent. *Lentulus in conversations had been in the habit of claiming that he was the third for whom the Sibylline Books had foretold royal power.*

17. The student must provide a main clause for the subjunctive purpose clause to depend on. Only present and imperfect subjunctives occur.

a. Decimus Sīlānus dīxit quae dīxerat ut reī pūblicae studium ostenderet. *Decimus*

Silanus said what he did to show his devotion to the state.

b. Cōnsul virīs armātīs senātum circumdedit ut praesidiō senātuī essent. *The consul threw armed men around the Senate to protect them.*

c. Patrēs quid in aliōs parricīdās statuerent cōnsīderāre dēbuērunt nē malum exemplum orīrētur (orerētur). *The senators ought to have thought deeply about what they were deciding as regards other murderers so that a bad precedent would not arise.*

18. The participles are all deponent.

a. fassō. *The Senate willingly spared Volturcius after he admitted what had happened.*

b. solitum. *They asked the senator about the journey, when (because) he was used to hearing from Gabinius that many men were involved in this conspiracy.*

c. cōnātīs. *Accordingly Cicero will reinforce the garrison since Lentulus and Cethegus tried to rouse their freedmen to desperate acts.*

d. orta. *Fear bad precedents, consul, that have (when they have) arisen out of good intentions/pretexts.*

19. These sentences contain an assortment of expressions of purpose other than the purpose clause.

a. To convince the senators, Caesar spoke well and eloquently on the subject of life and death.

b. Catiline entered the Senate for the purpose of hiding his true motive or of exonerating himself.

c. Caesar had hurried into the Senate to put up resistance against Cicero.

20. Volturciō, quippe quī senātuī omnia quae scīvit aperuisset, praemia data sunt. Prōlātae litterae coniūrātōrum ad Catilīnam quī erat apud Faesulās lēctae sunt; lēgātīs autem Allobrogum grātiae āctae sunt quī Rōmānīs auxiliō fuissent. Cum paucī ex coniūrātīs comprehēnsīs effugere cōnātī sint, cōnsul, occāsiōnem nactus, senātum convocāvit ut rogāret quid dē illīs agendum esset. Aliīs alia hortantibus, Cicerō, pollicitus sē quid senātuī plācuisset factūrum esse, tantum ā senātōribus postulāvit ut, sī coniūrātī vīcissent, memorēs essent fīlī suī et eum custōdīrent.

Lines 339–448

21. The normal sequence of tenses is not so important in result clauses as is the natural sense; the conjunction is always **ut**.
    a. Catō tam disertē loquitur ut facile senātōribus persuādeat. *Cato talks so eloquently that he will easily convince the members of the Senate.*
    b. Catilīna tanta scelera ausus est ut senātus eum patriae hostem iūdicāverit. *Catiline dared such great crimes that the Senate declared him an enemy of his country.*
    c. Tot armātī ā cōpiīs dīlāpsī sunt ut Catilīna satis mīlitum nōn habeat ad Metellī exercitum superandum. *So many men under arms have slipped away from his force that Catiline does not have enough soldiers for overpowering Metellus' army.*

22. These sentences review features of the deliberative question and optatives (wishes).
    a. ... quid Catilīna faciat?
    b. Utinam ... comprehendisset ...!
    c. Nē ... redeant!

23. a. duōs annōs (accusative of duration of time). *Catiline has been trying to win the consulship now for two years.*
    b. Nōnīs Decembribus (ablative of time when). *Lentulus and the other guilty conspirators met their end in the Tullianum on December the fifth.*

24. In setting up these clauses of fearing, pay attention to sequence of tenses.
    a. (primary) Timor est (erit, fuit = has been, etc.) nē senātōrēs ... nōn dēcernant / ut ... dēcernant. (secondary) Timor erat (fuit = was, fuerat, etc.) nē senātōrēs ... nōn dēcernerent / ut ... dēcernerent.
    b. (primary) Timor est (etc.) nē senātus ... discesserit. (secondary) Timor erat (etc.) nē senātus ... discessisset.

25. This exercise requires students to reason about cause and effect as well as to manipulate subjunctives.
    a. Cum Caesar misericordiam prōpōnat, patrēs, familiārum et urbis memorēs, Catōnis sententiam probāvērunt. *Although Caesar is suggesting clemency, the senators, remembering their families and city, have approved Cato's opinion.*
    b. Cicerō cum Lentulum et cēterōs coniūrātōs ante comitia dūcere dēbēret, in carcerem ad gulās frangendās statim mīsit. *Although Cicero should have taken Lentulus and the other conspirators before the assembly, he sent them straight to the prison to be strangled.*
    c. Cum Catilīna suīs labōrantibus succurreret, omnia prōvidēret, et multum ipse pugnāret, nē ūnus quidem cīvis ingenuus ex cōpiīs Catilīnae superfuit vel vīvus captus est. *Since Catiline was rushing help to men in trouble, anticipating all needs, and doing a good deal of fighting himself, not a single freeborn citizen out of his host survived or was taken alive.*

26. This passage requires a high degree of sophistication in dealing with indirect discourse, indirect statement, indirect commands, indirect questions, pronouns, and sequence of tenses. Notice that the first paragraph is cast in secondary sequence (after **hortātus est**; then **dīxit** understood) and that the second is in primary sequence (after **affirmat**).

    Catō senātōrēs hortātus est ut vītae timērent, familiae, tēctīs, reī pūblicae Rōmānae; sē enim mīrārī num intellegerent illum exercitum āctūrum esse ex Catilīnae amīcōrum dēcrētīs.

    Sallustius autem affirmat magnum numerum ex Catilīnae cōpiīs in Etrūriā dīlābī coepisse; eum intellēxisse exercitum suum montibus et cōpiīs hostium clausum esse; proeliō cōnfectō, omnīs mīrātōs esse quanta fuerit vīs animī in exercitū Catilīnae.

    Itaque exercitus latrōnum inermium, quōrum aliī novās tabulās spērābant, cupiēbant aliī potentiam senātūs minuere, maiōris lībertātis grātiā duōbus exercitibus ā rē pūblicā in sē missīs resistere ausus est. Quem ad modum nōs eōs exīstimēmus?

* * *

BIBLIOGRAPHY

Annotated Editions of Cicero and Sallust

C. Sallustius Crispus, Bellum Catilinae, by P. McGushin. Brill, Leiden, 1977. The most detailed and up-to-date commentary in English.

*Cicero, First and Second Speeches against Catiline, by H. E. Gould and J. L. Whiteley. St. Martin's, New York, NY, 1943. Reprint, Bristol Classical Press, Bristol, 1982.

*Gaii Sallusti Crispi Catilina, by C. Merivale. Macmillan, London, 1870. St. Martin's, New

York, NY, 1964. Reprint, Caratzas Brothers, New Rochelle, NY.

*Sallust, Bellum Catilinae, by P. McGushin. Bristol Classical Press, Bristol, 1980. School edition; notes mainly historical.

*Sallust's Bellum Catilinae, by J. T. Ramsey. Scholars Press, Atlanta, GA, 1984. Latin text with commentary intended primarily for the college level.

Biographies of Important Figures at the Time of the Conspiracy

*Caesar: Politician and Statesman, by M. Gelzer. Harvard University Press, Cambridge, MA, 1968. Still probably the best and most authoritative account in English.

Cicero: The Ascending Years, by T. N. Mitchell. Yale University Press, New Haven, CT, 1979. Chapters 3 and 4 on the period in which Cicero opposed Catiline.

*Crassus: A Political Biography, by B. A. Marshall. A. M. Hakkert, Amsterdam, 1976.

*Marcus Crassus and the Late Roman Republic, by A. M. Ward. University of Missouri Press, Columbia, MO, 1977. Chapter 7 covers the Catilinarian conspiracy.

*Pompey: A Political Biography, by R. Seager. University of California Press, Berkeley, CA, 1979. Brief, reliable; Chapters 6 and 7 treat events in the late 60's as they were influenced by Pompey.

*Pompey: The Roman Alexander, by P. Greenhalgh. University of Missouri Press, Columbia, MO, 1981. Events in the life of Pompey from youth through 59 B.C.

General Histories

*A History of Rome, by M. Cary and H. H. Scullard. 3rd revised ed. St. Martin's, New York, NY, 1975. Chapter 24 on the uprisings of the 70's (Lepidus and Spartacus) and Catiline's conspiracy in the 60's.

*From the Gracchi to Nero: A History of Rome from 133 B.C. to A.D. 68, by H. H. Scullard. 5th revised ed. Methuen, London, 1982. Chapters 5 and 6 on the 70's and 60's and the repercussions of the events of these years in the next decade.

*History of Rome, by M. Grant. Scribner's, New York, NY, 1978.

Primary Sources in Translation

*Fall of the Roman Republic (Six Roman Lives), by Plutarch. Translated by Rex Warner; Introduction and notes by Robin Seager. Penguin Books, New York, NY, 1972. Includes the lives of Marius, Sulla, Crassus, Pompey, Caesar, and Cicero.

*Handbook of Electioneering, by [Quintus Cicero]. Translated by M. Henderson, in Volume 4 of Cicero, Letters to his Friends. "Loeb Classical Library." Harvard University Press, Cambridge, MA, 1972. Recommends to Cicero the appropriate strategies for defeating his two chief rivals for the consulship, Catiline and Antonius.

*Jugurthine War: Conspiracy of Catiline, by Sallust. Translated by S. A. Handford. Penguin Books, New York, NY, 1963.

*Roman History, Volume 3, Civil Wars, by Appian. Translated by Horace White. "Loeb Classical Library." Harvard University Press, Cambridge, MA, 1913.

*Roman History, vol. 3, by Dio Cassius. Translated by Earnest Cary. "Loeb Classical Library." Harvard University Press, Cambridge, MA, 1914.

*Selected Political Speeches, by Cicero. Translated by Michael Grant. Penguin Books, New York, NY, 1977. Includes the four speeches against Catiline.

*The Twelve Caesars, by Suetonius. Translated by Robert Graves; revised with introduction by Michael Grant. Penguin Books, New York, NY, 1979. The life of Julius Caesar reports some of the rumors and accusations made as to his involvement with Catiline.

Books and Articles

A Companion to Latin Studies, by J. E. Sandys. 3rd edition. Hafner Publishing Co., New York, NY, 1968. Highly informative handbook on all aspects of Roman public, military, and private life.

*Ancient and Oriental Music, Vol. I of The New Oxford History of Music. Oxford University Press, Oxford and New York, NY, 1960.

"Caesar, Cicero, and the Problem of Debt," by M. W. Frederiksen. Journal of Roman Studies 56 (1966) 128–141.

"Catiline and the Concordia Ordinum," by E. D. Eagle. Phoenix 3 (1949) 15–30. Examines the influence of social and economic factors on the events of 63 B.C.

"Catiline: Court Cases and Consular Candidature," by B. A. Marshall. Scripta Classica Israelica 3 (1976–1977) 127–137. A good discussion of Catiline's trial in 64 B.C. on the charge of having participated in the Sullan proscriptions.

"Catiline's Conspiracy," by E. J. Phillips. *Historia* 25 (1976) 441–448. Opposing Waters ("Cicero, Sallust, and Caesar") and Seager ("*Iusta Catilinae*"), argues that Catiline was indeed the dedicated organizer of a conspiracy.

"Cicero and Sallust on Crassus and Catiline," by B. A. Marshall. *Latomus* 33 (1974) 804–813.

"Cicero and the *senatus consultum ultimum*," by T. N. Mitchell. *Historia* 20 (1971) 47–61.

"Cicero, Sallust, and Caesar," by K. H. Waters. *Historia* 19 (1970) 195–215. Suggests that Catiline was driven by Cicero's fervent opposition to adopt a revolutionary course of action that was not part of his original intentions.

"Debt in Sallust," by B. D. Shaw. *Latomus* 34 (1975) 187–196.

Everyman's Classical Dictionary, by J. Warrington. 3rd edition, revised. Biblio Distribution Center, Totowa, NJ, 1970. Compact and kept up to date.

Geographical Background of Greek and Roman History, by M. Cary. Oxford University Press, Oxford and New York, NY, 1949.

Greek and Roman Voting and Elections, by E. S. Staveley. Cornell University Press, Ithaca, NY, 1972.

"In Defense of Catiline," by W. Allen. *The Classical Journal* 34 (1938) 70–85. Seeks to demonstrate that Catiline and his supporters worked for a political program of reform in which they truly believed.

"*Iusta Catilinae*," by R. Seager. *Historia* 22 (1973), 240–248. Presents the evidence suggesting that Cicero's propaganda drove Catiline to throw in his lot with an independent band of revolutionaries assembled in Etruria by Manlius.

Party Politics in the Age of Caesar, by L. R. Taylor. University of California Press, Berkeley, CA, 1949, 1971. Now somewhat out-of-date in its treatment of Roman politics along party lines, but still a valuable contribution.

"Quo usque tandem patiemini?" by D. C. Innes. *Classical Quarterly* 27 (1977) 468.

Roman Civilization: Sourcebook I: The Republic, ed. by Naphtali Lewis and Meyer Reinhold (1951). Reprint, Harper and Row, New York, NY, 1966.

Sallust, by R. Syme. University of California Press, Berkeley, CA, 1964. Still the best and most complete treatment in English of Sallust and his writings.

"Sallust's *Catiline*: Date and Purpose," by L. A. MacKay. *Phoenix* 16 (1962) 181-194.

"Sallust's Political Career," by W. Allen. *Studies in Philology* 51 (1954) 1–14.

"The Catilinarian Conspiracy in Its Context," by E. G. Hardy. *Journal of Roman Studies* 7 (1917) 153–228. A now somewhat outdated but still interesting attempt to view Catiline's activities as part of a chain of events stretching back into the previous decade.

"The Conspiracy of Catilina," by P. A. Brunt. *History Today* 13 (1963) 14–21. A good discussion of social conditions prevailing at the time of the conspiracy and how Catiline attempted to exploit discontent.

"The Early Career of Sallust," by D. C. Earl. *Historia* 15 (1966) 302–311.

The Etruscans: A New Investigation, by M. Cristofani. Orbis, London, 1979.

"The Failure of Catiline's Conspiracy," by Z. Yavetz. *Historia* 12 (1963) 485–499. Seeks to explain why the urban proletariat abandoned Catiline when their support was most needed.

The History of Musical Instruments, by Curt Sachs. Norton, New York, NY, 1940.

The Last Generation of the Roman Republic, by E. S. Gruen. University of California Press, Berkeley, CA, 1974. A good account of political alliances, trials, and the increasing incidence of violence.

"The Last Journey of L. Sergius Catilina," by G. V. Sumner. *Classical Philology* 58 (1963) 215–219. An excellent discussion of the movements of Catiline's army leading up to the final battle and of contemporary events in Rome.

The Legend of Cato Uticensis from the First Century B.C. to the Fifth Century A.D.: With an Apppendix on Dante and Cato, by Robert J. Goar. "Collection Latomus," Vol. 197. Latomus, Revue des Études Latines, Bruxelles, 1987.

The Magistrates of the Roman Republic, by T. R. S. Broughton. 2 Volumes. 1951–1952; Supplement, 1960. Reprint, Scholars Press, Atlanta, GA, 1974. Vol. 3 Supplement, Scholars Press, 1986.

The Oxford Classical Dictionary, ed. by N. G. L. Hammond and H. H. Scullard. 2nd ed. Oxford University Press, Oxford and New York, NY, 1970.

The Roman Army, by Peter Hodge. Longman, White Plains, NY, 1977.

"The Tullianum and Sallust's *Catiline*," by Tenney Frank. *The Classical Journal* 19 (1923–1924) 496–498.

"Was Sallust Fair to Cicero?" by T. R. S. Broughton. *Transactions of the American Philological Association* 67 (1936) 34–46. Concludes that Sallust in his monograph did not deliberately denigrate Cicero.

THE AULULARIA OF PLAUTUS
THE POT OF GOLD

INTRODUCTION

New Comedy and Menander

The dramatic form known as New Comedy was the end product of an evolution from the Old Comedy of Aristophanes, who lived from the mid fifth century to about 385 B.C. The evolution had taken place over a number of decades through a transitional period known as Middle Comedy (about 404 to 321 B.C., of which Aristophanes' late plays, *Ecclesiazusae*, 392 B.C., and *Plutus*, 388 B.C., are considered early examples). The major writer of Greek New Comedy was Menander (342/41–293/89 B.C.), who produced his first play in 321 B.C., shortly after the death of Alexander the Great (323 B.C.), whose conquest of Greece and the East transformed the ancient world and paved the way for the new Greek dynasties all around the eastern Mediterranean in what came to be known as the Hellenistic world. The old days of the autonomous Greek city state that had culminated in the glories of fifth-century Athens were gone forever.

While the action of the comedies of Menander is normally set in Athens or some area of Attica, the plays avoid the hard-hitting social and political satire and personal lampoons that filled Old Comedy in the heyday of the city state. Rather, the plots of the plays unfold in the domestic scene of family relationships and deal largely with romantic interests of characters that are easily recognizable as types drawn from the life of the period. In structure as well, the plays are more realistic than their predecessors in the Old Comedy. The element of high poetry contained in the lyrical choral odes of Old Comedy is gone, along with the chorus itself; the language and meters employed in New Comedy are restrained and naturalistic—almost conversational. The action of the plays is divided neatly into acts, with musical entertainment unrelated to the plot of the play being provided between the acts.

The manuscript tradition of the plays of Menander did not survive the Dark Ages, and for centuries only brief quotations of Menander found in other ancient authors were known. Fortunately, in the twentieth century the sands of Egypt have yielded ancient copies of Menander's plays on papyrus, attesting to the wide popularity of his plays throughout the Hellenistic East. The papyri are generally fragmentary, but one play is nearly complete. This is the *Dyskolos (The Grouch)*, preserved in a papyrus copy from Egypt now in Geneva (the Bodmer Papyrus) and published by scholars in 1959. It is doubly fortunate that this play of Menander bears striking similarities to the *Aulularia* of Plautus. A comparison of the plays will reveal both the distinctive genius of Menander, writing at the culmination of the Greek comic tradition, and the originality with which Plautus, writing near the beginning of the Roman comic tradition, adapted Greek originals to fit his own purposes and the demands of the Roman comic stage.

Menander's *Dyskolos*

The teacher should be familiar at least with the outlines of Menander's *Dyskolos* before beginning to teach Plautus' *Aulularia*. After reading the *Aulularia*, students will find it interesting to compare its characters and plot with those of the *Dyskolos*. The selections from the *Dyskolos* in the Passages for Comparison in the student's book provide some basic comparative material, but, if possible, the entire play of Menander should be read (for an available translation, see the Bibliography). An outline of the play is provided here as basic background for Plautus' play and as a resource for teachers who are not able to have their students read the play in its entirety.

PROLOGUE (quoted in full in the Passages for Comparison in the student's book). The god Pan describes the setting (the old man Knemon's farm in Phyle in Attica), a nearby cave and shrine of the Nymphs, and Knemon's character as a misanthrope. Pan also provides the background information that Knemon had married a widow who had a son, Gorgias, by her previous marriage. Although Knemon constantly quarreled with his wife, they had a daughter, but when the marriage became intolerable, Knemon's wife left him and went to live with her son, now the poor owner of a neighboring farm. Knemon now lives a lonely life of hard labor on his farm, struggling to eke out a meager subsistence from the recalcitrant Attic soil. His daughter, Myrrhine, lives with him, sheltered and pure of heart, and is particularly devoted to worship of the Nymphs, Pan's companions in the nearby cave and shrine (compare the attentions paid by Euclio's daughter to the Lar in the *Aulularia*, lines 23–25). The plot of the play is precipitated by the fact that a young man, raised in the city (although the son of a rich farmer), happened to see Knemon's daughter when out hunting with a friend and, at the instigation of Pan, fell in love with her.

ACT I. Act I introduces the main characters. Sostratos, the young man who has fallen in love with Knemon's daughter, has sent his slave Pyrrhias ahead to pay a visit to the girl's father and now comes on stage himself with his parasite Chaireas to find out what has happened. They are met by Pyrrhias rushing frantically from the fields where he encountered Knemon, who, resenting the intrusion, beat Pyrrhias and chased him out of his fields much as Euclio beats and chases Staphyla out of the house in the opening scene of the *Aulularia*. While Sostratos and Pyrrhias are wondering what to do, the raging Knemon appears on the scene; Sostratos, deserted by his two helpers, is left to confront Knemon himself but does not have the courage to broach the issue of his love for Knemon's daughter, and the old man, after a few rude comments to Sostratos, exits into his house. Sostratos decides to seek help from his father's slave, Geta, but at this moment Knemon's daughter comes out of the house to fetch water from the grotto of the Nymphs, since her old nurse Simiche dropped the bucket down their well. This is an ecstatic moment for Sostratos, who gallantly fetches the water for Myrrhine. Sostratos then leaves to fetch Geta, without knowing that he and Myrrhine were observed by Daos, the old slave of Gorgias, Knemon's stepson, who lives next door. Daos is worried about Sostratos' attentions to Myrrhine and about her unprotected and vulnerable situation and goes off to warn his master, Gorgias. The stage is left empty for the first musical interlude.

ACT II. Daos returns with Gorgias, the latter full of familial concern for his stepsister and worried over the young man who has visited her.

Along comes Sostratos in city dress that immediately arouses suspicions on the part of the poor farmer Gorgias. Sostratos could not find Geta, who was reported to be off helping Sostratos' mother with some sacrifice, and has decided to approach the girl's father himself. Before Sostratos can knock on Knemon's door, Gorgias approaches him and berates him for apparently trying to take advantage of Knemon's daughter, lecturing him in the process on how the rich should not look down on and take advantage of the poor. Sostratos explains his honorable intentions, including his willingness to marry the girl even without a dowry, and he quickly wins Gorgias over as a helper. The latter explains about the poor, antisocial Knemon, who talks only with his daughter and is determined that she marry only someone like himself. Gorgias and Daos propose that the best way for Sostratos to meet Knemon would be to go with them to the fields and dig with them near where Knemon usually goes to dig, accompanied by his daughter. Knemon, it is explained, would more readily accept a proposal from a hardworking farmer than from a fancily dressed urbanite. Sostratos agrees to try this tactic and goes off to the fields to dig with Gorgias. As he departs, he praises the simple homespun virtues of a girl like Myrrhine, who has been raised in isolation from the corrupting influence of society (comments that could be compared to Megadorus' wish to marry the simple daughter of Euclio rather than a wealthy and spoiled woman with a large dowry).

The stage is empty for only a moment before Sikon the cook and Geta appear, dragging a sheep and bringing other provisions for a sacrifice at the shrine of the Nymphs and Pan. The sacrifice (the very one referred to earlier in this Act) was ordered by Sostratos' mother to ward off the effects of a dream she had in which she saw her son shackled by Pan (symbolizing his being made by Pan to fall in love with Knemon's daughter) and put to work in the fields with hoe and wearing the leather jacket of a peasant. The banter of the cook and the slave here as they bring the sheep for sacrifice may be compared to the entrance of the cooks in the *Aulularia* as they bring in two sheep and other provisions for the wedding feast (280–370).

ACT III. Knemon enters from his house, ordering Simiche to lock the door and not let anyone in until he returns from working in the fields (cf. *Aulularia* 89–104, where Euclio orders Staphyla to lock the house in his absence). Before Knemon gets very far, he sees Sostratos' mother and daughter arriving for the sacrifice at the shrine; he is annoyed at the crowd of (in his opinion) insincere sacrificers (they give the most undesirable parts of the animal to the gods) and even refers to them as thieves (compare Euclio's attitude toward the cooks in the *Aulularia*). He decides not to leave home after all. After thus revealing his suspicions of normal people's motives, Knemon continues to reveal his stingy and anti-social character in confrontations with first Geta and then Sikon, who come to his door and try to borrow a kettle (the first of these passages is given in the Passages for Comparison in the student's book). Knemon claims that he has no cooking utensils or condiments or anything else and that he has forbidden everyone to come to his door (compare Euclio's prohibiting Staphyla to loan anything in the *Aulularia*, 90–100).

After a brief empty stage, a new scene begins with Sostratos returning from his stint at hoeing in the fields; stiff and exhausted, he is also disappointed in not having seen either Knemon or his daughter (we have just seen that Knemon was prevented from going to the fields by the arrival of the sacrificers). Sostratos meets Geta coming out of the shrine, and Geta explains about the sacrifice. Sostratos thinks this is a marvelous opportunity to cement his friendship with Gorgias by inviting him and his slave Daos to share in the sacrificial meal and party. When he goes to fetch Gorgias, Simiche appears from Knemon's house complaining that she has now dropped the hoe down the well in an attempt to get the bucket up. Knemon follows, threatening her and chasing her back into the house, saying he will have to go down the well himself to fetch the articles, and at the same time refusing Geta's offer of a piece of rope to help him negotiate the task. Sostratos enters with Gorgias and Daos; Geta highlights the division of social classes by scorning Gorgias and Daos as mere peasants, and Gorgias himself comes to the party only under considerable pressure from Sostratos, who repeatedly insists that he is Gorgias' friend. The warmth of the friendship of the wealthy young Sostratos with the lower-class farmer Gorgias contrasts sharply with the totally negative attitude of the poor old man Knemon toward the wealthy sacrificers in the first part of this Act. One may compare the relationship between the wealthy Megadorus and the ostensibly impoverished Euclio in the *Aulularia;* both plays deal extensively with themes of strained relationships between the social classes.

ACT IV. Simiche rushes out of Knemon's house to seek help for Knemon, who has fallen down the well in his attempt to retrieve the bucket and hoe. The cook Sikon is delighted and sees the accident as a stroke of divine retribution, but Gorgias and Sostratos, thinking differently, rush in and rescue Knemon. When Sostratos reappears, he delivers a kind of messenger's speech in which he tells how the rescue was effected and how he helped by pulling on the rope while at the same time gazing in rapture at his beloved Myrrhine. Knemon is brought out, in sorry shape, probably lying on a pallet, almost as if it were his death bed. His narrow escape with his life and his rescue at the hands of those whom he earlier scorned have brought about a profound change in Knemon, and he summons his estranged wife to hear his thoughts along with Myrrhine and Gorgias. In his great speech, which is given in the Passages for Comparison in the student's book, he explains the origin of his misanthropy and his cynical attitude toward other people's motives, and he admits that he now realizes that he made a mistake in believing that he could survive and live in nearly total isolation and independence. The generous action of Gorgias has proven Knemon's cynical views to be false, and he now adopts him as his son and entrusts to him both his daughter and his farm, the latter to use partly as a dowry and partly as support for the entire family. He still possesses enough of his old cynicism to realize that he himself could not choose a husband for his daughter because no one would suit him, and he still possesses enough of his old idealism to dream of a world in which everyone lived as he did—as isolated as possible from his fellow men, with the result that there would be no social problems, no law courts, no prisons, and no wars. Gorgias, however, does not allow Knemon to unload his responsibilities as Myrrhine's father completely onto himself; he elicits Knemon's consent to Sostratos' marriage to Myrrhine by presenting Sostratos as the kind of sunburnt farmer that Knemon could approve of (Sostratos' stint in the fields pays off here). Knemon's final wish in this scene, however, after he has ordered that there be a proper dowry and wedding, is to be carried back inside into the isolation of his house. The shock of falling into the well and the realization of man's dependence on others for survival have moved Knemon toward reconciliation with family and society, but he refuses to take the final steps and withdraws into his house.

Sostratos now proposes that Gorgias marry his sister, but the poor and diffident Gorgias does not jump at the prospect. Instead, he formally betrothes Myrrhine to Sostratos and praises Sostratos' honesty and his willingness to cross the social and economic barriers and dig in the fields alongside a poor farmer in order to gain the girl he loved. Sostratos' father, Kallippides, now arrives on the scene, having come somewhat late to the sacrifice, and the social and economic barriers are again crossed at the moment when Gorgias recognizes Sostratos' father as both a rich man *and* an outstanding farmer. This paves the way for Gorgias' acceptance of marriage to Sostratos' sister in Act V.

ACT V. While the wealthy Kallippides agrees to allow his son to marry the daughter of a poor man, he balks at the idea of his daughter wedding with the poor Gorgias—one poor in-law is enough! Sostratos, however, persuades him that a true friend is worth more than money stored away or buried in the garden (cf. Euclio's refusal to use his gold as a dowry), and he soon gives in. Gorgias, however, is just as uncomfortable with the idea of having a wife of higher social and economic standing as Kallippides was with the idea of having a son-in-law of lower social and economic standing, but Kallippides, impressed with Gorgias' honesty, joins his son in urging the marriage and Gorgias quickly gives in. The reciprocal marriages across the social and economic barriers are both agreed upon with appropriate dowries stipulated (the wealthy man will give three talents, the poor man one), and the families of Kallippides and Gorgias are brought together in the shrine of the Nymphs. Even Simiche comes to the shrine. The only holdout in this reconciliation of the social orders is old Knemon, whom Sostratos twice urges Gorgias to bring to the shrine but who refuses to come and stays isolated in his own house.

Whereas at the beginning of Act V Kallippides quickly gave in to his son's wishes and Gorgias quickly gave in to Sostratos with the result that the two marriages were harmoniously arranged, Knemon is not so easy to persuade. Geta takes the initiative, both out of an apparently genuine concern for the welfare of the old man and out of a desire to get back at Knemon for his rude treatment of him in Act III. With the help of Sikon the cook, who had also been maltreated by Knemon, Geta brings the ailing old man out of the house on his pallet, and he and Sikon torment him by repeatedly banging on the door and asking to borrow cooking utensils. Simiche joins the fray and lectures Knemon on his continuing bad temper. All Knemon wants is to be left alone. This the three do not allow but urge rather that Knemon join the festivities, the drinking, and the dancing in the shrine. Although holding out to the very end, Knemon is finally overpowered and forced to agree that it would be better to dance with those in the shrine than continue to be tormented in the open, and as the play ends he is garlanded and carried into the shrine with a wedding torch placed in his hand.

Hellenistic Greek Theater and the Beginnings of Roman Literature

The new dramatic form perfected by Menander and his fellow writers of Athenian New Comedy became popular all over the Greek-speaking world. The popularity of theatrical productions in the Hellenistic period is attested by the remains of numerous stone theater buildings of this period at many places in the Mediterranean world. Theater was both internationalized and professionalized, with guilds of artists established, consisting of actors, musicians, and writers of comedy and tragedy, who traveled widely to perform at musical and dramatic festivals. They offered a standard repertoire of plays, consisting of the New Comedy of Menander and his fellow playwrights and of tragedies, primarily those of Sophocles and Euripides.

Latin literature was born in the context of this cosmopolitan Hellenistic Greek culture that spread from the great cities of the Greek kingdoms in the East westward to Sicily and Italy. About twenty years after Menander's death, Andronicus was brought to Rome as a prisoner of war from the Greek-speaking city of Tarentum in the heel of Italy. He must have been well educated and bilingual, for he translated Homer's *Odyssey* into Latin saturnian verse, perhaps as a textbook for his captor's children. In 240 B.C., Andronicus, having by now been freed and having adopted the name of his captor, Livius, and thus known as Livius Andronicus, performed a play, no doubt at the instigation of Roman officials, at a festival celebrating the end of the First Punic War (264–241 B.C.). This play was probably a tragedy translated into Latin from a Greek original. It set a popular precedent, and Latin drama based on Greek originals quickly established itself in Rome, gaining public recognition with the Temple of Minerva on the Aventine set aside as a place for writers and actors to meet. Andronicus wrote both tragedies and comedies, only meager fragments of which remain, but his claim to fame as the originator of Latin literature is secure.

Within five years of Andronicus' first play, we hear of another poet active on the Roman stage (235 B.C.). This was Gnaeus Naevius, of Italic background but from the area of Capua, where Greek influences were strong. He had fought in the First Punic War, and when active as a poet in Rome he offended the powerful political family of the Metelli and was imprisoned for a time and may have been exiled. His productions for the stage included both tragedies and comedies, again modeled on Greek originals. Perhaps in keeping with his involvement with public affairs in Rome, he also wrote patriotic plays on Roman historical themes that would have had no Greek models. These were called "plays in Roman dress" (fābulae praetextae) to distinguish them from the "plays in Greek dress" (fābulae palliātae) derived from Greek originals. Naevius' patriotism and originality are also evident in his *Bellum Poenicum,* an epic poem in saturnian verse on the First Punic War, written in his old age. Only fragments of Naevius' works remain.

The Originality of Roman Comedy

Titus Maccius Plautus (254–184 B.C.) was about twenty years old when Naevius was active on the stage, and to judge from what can be gleaned from the fragments of Naevius, Plautus learned much from him. From his two predecessors Plautus inherited a manner of adapting Greek plays that turned the relatively restrained productions of the Greeks into exuberant musical comedies. As was noted above, the New Comedy of Menander dispensed with the chorus and the elaborate, highly lyrical choral odes of the Old Comedy of Aristophanes; its language and meters were restrained and fairly pedestrian in an attempt to produce an effect of credible realism. The lyrical choral odes that had divided the dramatic scenes of Old Comedy were in effect replaced by impromptu musical interludes between the acts of the play. Fifth-century Greek tragedy had also employed the chorus, which sang elaborate lyrical odes. In fact, of course, choral singing and dancing had constituted the primitive core of both Greek tragedy and comedy. When Andronicus and Naevius adapted Greek tragedies for production in Rome, where there was no native tradition of staged choral performances as there had been in early Greece, they apparently dispensed with the chorus but retained the element of elaborate lyrical song. This they transferred to the characters themselves, who at particularly intense moments of the drama would break into lyrical songs or monodies. When the early Latin playwrights turned to adapting New Comedy, which no longer had any lyrical songs, they likewise gave lyrical songs to the characters. Thus, while Greek New Comedy was written in restrained meters that were alternately spoken and recited, the Latin comedies of Andronicus, Naevius, and Plautus contain elaborate lyrical dialogues or monodies that would have been sung to musical accompaniment.

Other fairly radical changes as well were made by Plautus and his predecessors on the Roman stage as they adapted Greek models to entertain a Roman audience. While Menander was careful to locate the scene of his plays in Athens or some area of Attica (such as Phyle in the *Dyskolos*) and was careful to maintain the appropriate local color throughout the play, Plautus' plays, though nominally set in a particular Greek city (such as Athens in the *Aulularia*), could as easily be set in any of the cosmopolitan cities of the Greco-Roman world and show an amalgam of Greco-Roman cultural allusions. There are many references to distinctly Roman customs, laws, civic institutions, societal problems, and individual traits of character. Thus, in the *Aulularia* the social distinctions between the rich and generous Megadorus and the impoverished and miserly Euclio are presented with distinctly Roman coloring and flavor. Yet, a certain distance from the Roman audience is maintained by the nominal setting of the play in Athens and the Greek costumes and names of the characters.

In constructing his plots, Plautus took liberties with his meticulously coherent and realistic Greek models and did not hesitate to modify, distort, and amplify in order to enhance the element of farce. Something of this may be seen in the *Aulularia* in the prominence of the farcical, slapstick scenes involving the cooks. In the *Aulularia* it appears also that Plautus has deliberately subordinated the romantic plot of Lyconides' desire to marry Euclio's daughter and has brought to the forefront of the play the character of the miserly Euclio. The miser's character is explored not primarily as a block to the marriage of Lyconides and Phaedria but rather in terms of his relationship to Megadorus and in terms of the nearly unbridgeable gulf separating the social orders of the rich and the poor.

In portraying his characters, Plautus deliberately broadens the subtle and psychologically sensitive portrayal of individuals that the authors of Greek New Comedy had brought to the limited variety of types of characters that appeared in their plays (e.g., old man, young lover, courtesan, pimp, shrewish wife, braggart soldier). In Plautus, characterization is broadened and simplified, and the types are reminiscent of the stock characters of the native Italic Atellan farce, in which Plautus may have acted before beginning to adapt plays from the Greek. In his broadened and exaggerated characterizations, Plautus appears to be blending the character types of New Comedy with native Italic traditions. In the *Aulularia* this process may be seen especially clearly by contrasting the simplified and exaggerated characterization of Euclio as a psychopathic miser whose one character trait seems to control all of his actions with the far more subtle characterization of Knemon in the *Dyskolos,* whose motives and philosophy of life are explored and revealed in considerable depth both by those who know him and encounter him and by the man himself.

In contrast to the restrained and naturalistic diction of Menander's comedies, Plautus' plays are characterized by a rich, colorful, and resonant diction that seems to draw on all the resources of the Latin language and revels in puns, double entendres (sometimes with sexual and even homosexual implications), alliteration, and assonance. There is a liberal admixture of Greek, especially in Megadorus' tirade in the *Aulularia* about the luxuries in which rich women indulge.

In all of these departures from the subtlety, economy, and elegance of Greek New Comedy, Plautus is clearly playing to his Roman audience (even the admixture of Greek in the *Aulularia* panders to the newly acquired tastes of the Romans for the exotic luxuries of the East). In one other significant way he brings the play right into the laps of the audience by frequently having his characters break the dramatic illusion of the play and address the audience directly. This is especially frequent with Euclio in the *Aulularia*, and particularly in his distraught lament over the theft of his pot of gold (713–720). Plautus was a master of the stage; he knew his audience; he knew that Greek New Comedy was what the Roman audience wanted at this particular moment in Roman history and in the development of Roman society; and he knew what he had to do to bring Greek New Comedy to that audience as a living form of entertainment. His purpose was to entertain, and the immense popularity that his plays enjoyed with their audiences reveals his success.

Molière's *L'Avare*

Jean Baptiste Poquelin (1622–1673), who took the stage-name Molière, was one of France's greatest writers. A man of the theater, he organized, acted in, and wrote for a troupe called the Illustre Theatre, which was not successful in Paris and so took to a circuit of the provinces that lasted thirteen years. When he did return to Paris, his troupe so pleased the court that it was extended the patronage of Monsieur, the king's brother, and then of Louis XIV himself. Molière's troupe performed at the Palais Royale and is now thought of as the ancestor of the Comédie Française. Molière is most famous for his comedies that satirize and ridicule perversities or eccentricities of character by presenting them in memorable caricatures: the religious hypocrite (*Tartuffe*), the anti-social man (*Le Misanthrope*), the parvenu (*Le Bourgeois gentilhomme*), the hypochondriac (*Le Malade imaginaire*), and, of course, the miser (*L'Avare*). In *L'Avare* (1668), he pushes the character of the miser, Harpagon, to extremes of mania that result in inhumane and sometimes nasty and cruel actions. To the very end, his pathological character remains unregenerate. If anything he seems to sink deeper and deeper into insanity as the play proceeds and as he is cleverly outwitted both by those of the younger generation who surround him and by chance and fortune. The plot of Molière's play is far more complex than that of the *Aulularia*, but Molière adapts many scenes from the Latin play, and we provide translations of some of these in the Passages for Comparison at the end of the student's book. These should provide some basis for comparison of the dramatic and comic spirits of the French and the Latin writers; students' attention should be directed in particular to the contrast between Euclio, who is likely to appear quite understandable and even likable, and the pathological caricature that is Harpagon—so insensate and cruel in his treatment of his children and everyone else around him that he fails to gain even a modicum of the audience's sympathy or pity. If time permits, the entire play of Molière should be read in contrast with Menander's *Dyskolos* and Plautus' *Aulularia*, and we recommend that a French teacher or professor be invited to provide further background to the French play and to participate in discussion and comparison of it with the Greek and Latin plays.

Teaching the Play

The facing vocabularies and notes in the student's book along with the basic content questions at the bottom of the right-hand pages will help students comprehend the Latin and follow the action of the play. Encourage reading for comprehension as a prelude to more exacting translation. In the notes in the teacher's handbook we have provided questions (set in italics) of a more probing sort (often accompanied by suggested answers) to be used after each segment of the text has been comprehended and translated. We strongly urge that the play be taught as a living drama. Have students read aloud and act out each segment of the Latin text. Stage mini-performances of each segment of the text in front of the class; the performances can be repeated with different students playing the roles. Have students discuss how the lines should be read and how the scenes should be staged in order to produce the most dramatic effects. Develop a sense of the relationship between word and action. Bring the play alive!

As was noted in the Introduction to the student's book, we have eliminated most of the archaic spellings and forms and presented a text with forms and spellings that will be familiar to the students. We did not want the archaic language to be a barrier to ease of reading and full enjoyment of the play itself. It is with a similar purpose in mind that we do not recommend teaching of metrics and scansion. The rules of Plautine metrics are extremely complex, and to learn to read Plautine Latin with proper attention to the metrics is a time-consuming task. We would rather see the time devoted to comprehension, translation, discussion, and performance of the text, with the text read aloud expressively and accented as if it were prose. Occasionally, in fact, the elimination of archaic forms and spellings has produced lines that no longer scan. This is unlikely to bother students at this stage in their study. Concentrate their attention on the characters, the rich and fascinating language of the play, and the development of the plot.

Considerable discussion should be devoted to how the play might have ended, and comparisons should be made with Menander's *Dyskolos* and Molière's *L'Avare*. See in particular the article by E. L. Minar, "The Lost Ending of Plautus' *Aulularia;* see the Bibliography.

The short adaptations of the play mentioned at the end of the Introduction to the student's book are suitable for production for other Latin classes or for Classics Day. These adaptations, titled *Plautus' Aulularia: The Pot of Gold: An Adaptation for Production by High School Latin Students* and *The Pot of Gold (adapted from Plautus' comedy for use in first year Latin)* are available from *NECN* Publications (see the Bibliography). The pictures on pages 6, 7, and 58 of the student's book are based on photographs of a production of the *Aulularia* using the first of the adaptations mentioned above. This production was staged by students from the University of Massachusetts at Amherst and local high schools under the direction of Professor Gilbert Lawall in 1982 for the annual Classics Day of the Pioneer Valley Classical Association. The pictures show the use of simple stage sets consisting essentially of house doors and of simple costumes. The sheep were rolled in on their wheels to the great amusement of the audience.

* * *

TEACHING NOTES AND DISCUSSION QUESTIONS

N.B. The questions printed in italics in these notes may be used in discussion of the relevant passages after students have read and translated the Latin using the more general content questions in the student's book. Sometimes possible answers or hints at answers to the discussion questions are given.

Lines 1–22

2: The Lar, originally a guardian of the family's land and worshiped out of doors, became the guardian of the family and the home and was worshiped in a shrine (**larārium**) in the main room of the house (**ātrium**). The Lar was an integral part of the family's life and well-being. His jovial feast, known as the Laralia, was celebrated soon after the winter solstice on a date decided by the **pater familiās**. Prayers were offered to him every morning (cf. lines 23–25) and also at the **cēna**, the chief meal of the day. Special prayers were offered and a wreath placed on the hearth every month on the Kalends, Nones, and Ides, as well as on general holidays.

When a boy celebrated his coming-of-age, he dedicated his locket (**bulla**) and his bordered toga (**toga praetexta**) to the Lar. Likewise in the evening before her wedding day a young woman dedicated her **bulla** and toys to the Lar, and on her wedding day she presented a coin to her new husband's Lar.

In later times there were two **Larēs familiārēs** as can be seen on a shrine in the House of the Vettii in Pompeii. Here the Genius of the family (the guardian spirit) is flanked by Lares with drinking horns (*Roman Life*, p. 400, and p. 439 for description).

1–14: *From the Lar's tone in lines 1–14, what do you think was the household god's opinion of Euclio's grandfather? Back up your answer with references to the Latin.*

1–22: *From the Lar's introduction, do you think that the fault of being miserly will play an important role in this play?*

15–20: *Why did the household god never reveal the presence of the gold to Euclio's father?*

Lines 23–39

23–25: *Why is what Euclio's daughter does for the Lar important?*

23–36: *What do you think is the household god's opinion of the young man who violated Euclio's daughter? Is the Lar more interested in Euclio's daughter or in the young man? Whom is he basically trying to help?*

27: **quō . . . facilius nūptum . . . daret:** when giving a daughter in marriage, the bride's family customarily provided a dowry, which became part of the couple's assets but with a portion set aside for the wife's use (cf. Plautus, *Miles*

Gloriosus, 1274–1278). Obviously a young woman without a dowry had a poor chance of making a suitable marriage, although occasionally, as in this play, a man was willing to forego the monetary arrangements (cf. Plautus, *Trinummus*, 374–379 and 505–511).

30: neque compressam . . . pater (scit): Euclio's ignorance of his daughter's condition is a necessary detail for the plot and may be attributed to his lack of attention to his daughter because of his preoccupation with his treasure and also to the nature of women's apparel. Long, loose-flowing garments would conceal the figure.

36: Cereris vigiliīs: since young women in Athens and Rome were carefully chaperoned and unlikely to be abroad at night in any case, the only credible time for a seduction was a nocturnal religious festival celebrated by women.

There may also have been a connection between the festivals mentioned in the play and the festival for which the play was originally commissioned or purchased. There were two festivals of Ceres: the **lūdī Ceriālēs**, celebrated from 12 to 19 April, and another festival, celebrated in August, which had to be postponed in 216 B.C. because of the public and private mourning following the news of the tragic Roman defeat at Cannae (Livy, XXII.56 and XXXIV.6). Since these festivals were Greek in inspiration, so much so that priestesses were imported from Magna Graecia and the rites were performed in the Greek manner largely influenced by cults in Sicily, it seems more than likely that there were nocturnal assemblies, as was the case for the Athenian Thesmophoria, an all-night festival of Demeter. Nocturnal rites were certainly a feature of Italian Bacchanals and of the Bona Dea celebration, notorious later for the scandal involving Caesar's wife. In the early empire dramatic performances were featured during four days of the Cerealia, and some scholars think that **lūdī scaenicī** were included from the festival's inception in the late third century. If such was the case, the *Aulularia* may present a neat dovetailing of dramatic fiction with actuality. Ravished at the **Cereris vigiliae** in August, Phaedria gives birth in April (not quite **decimō mēnse**, 798) at the time of the Cerealia, when the play was, perhaps, being presented for the first time.

1–36: *From the information given in the speech by the Lar, what does the audience expect the plot to be?*

Students may be asked at this point to write brief outlines of how they expect the plot to unfold. As they continue reading the play, they should repeatedly be asked to compare what they thought would happen with the plot as it actually unfolds.

Here at the beginning students may well be puzzled as to how having the old man next door ask for Phaedria's hand in marriage will make it easier for the young man who violated her to marry her (31–33). Some students may wonder whether it will be of any importance in the plot that the old man is the young man's uncle (34–36).

Actually, Plautus, through the Lar, gives little indication of the details of the plot and in some ways he is deliberately misleading. Although the god has revealed the location of the treasure in order to ensure Phaedria's marriage with a dowry, Megadorus will not ask for a dowry and Lyconides does not enter to plead his own suit until some three quarters of the (extant) play has been enacted. From the prologue the students might expect a careful working out of an involved romantic plot. In actuality, however, the bulk of the play is concerned with the miserly character of Euclio, his concern for his treasure, and his anguish over its theft. The emphasis will be on farce rather than romance.

1–39: *What are the powers, functions, and attitudes of the Lar as he reveals them in the prologue? How has he and how will he safeguard the welfare of the family? What does the presence of the Lar as the prologue speaker tell us about the main focus of the play to come?*

The domestic focus on the character of the family members and on the health and welfare of the family should be noted. Equally important are the relationships between the family and society through marriage connections. The Lar has controlled the history of the family in the past and is determined to see that there is a happy outcome in the future.

What do we learn about Euclio's character, personality, and sense of responsibility from the Lar? Has heredity influenced his character? Is he miserly by nature? How do you think discovery of the pot of gold is likely to influence him? for the better or for the worse? Apart from the pot of gold, what is Euclio's financial situation likely to have been? Like that of his father (11–14)?

Lines 40–54

40: hercle: Hercules, frequently invoked by the exclamation **hercle** or **mehercle**, was a popular god, among the first of foreign deities to play an important role in Roman religion. In the course of one of his labors, that of procuring the cattle of Geryon of Cadiz, Hercules had stopped at the future site of Rome and freed the Greek settlers there from the menace of a fire-breathing monster, Cacus (Vergil, *Aeneid* VIII.184–279). In gratitude, Evander, leader of the inhabitants of the future site of Rome, set up the Ara Maxima in the Forum Boarium close to the Tiber where the festival of Hercules Invictus came to be celebrated on 12 August. Tithes were dedicated to him by victorious generals and prosperous merchants.

40–54: *What is the effect of this opening scene? How is Euclio characterized in it? How is Staphyla characterized?*

What impression do these lines give you of how slaves were treated in the Roman world? With whom will the audience sympathize, Euclio or Staphyla? Does Plautus' use of the maltreated slave-woman to help characterize negative aspects of Euclio tell us anything about how Plautus may have felt that slaves should have been treated?

What humorous touches has Plautus included in these lines?

Lines 55-84

67: mecastor: the oaths **mecastor, pol,** and **edepol** reveal the place which the twins Castor and Pollux held in popular culture. The brothers of Helen of Troy, they were alleged to be the sons of Zeus rather than of Tyndareus, king of Sparta and husband of Leda, and as such were known as the Dioscuri (sons of Zeus). At the end of the fifth century they appeared to help the Romans win the battle of Lake Regillus against a combined force of Latins, and they appeared at Rome to announce the victory (Dionysius of Halicarnassus, *Roman Antiquities* VI.13.1–5). Their temple in the Forum near the Palatine was built on the site where they were seen; the three columns still standing date from 7 B.C. The Dioscuri became the constellation Gemini and, as guardians of sailors, were identified as St. Elmo's fire.

55–84: *In what ways does Plautus begin to reveal Euclio's character as a miser and his obsession with his new-found pot of gold? (60–64, 65–66, 67–73, 79–80)*

What do we learn about the general financial condition of Euclio's household? (82–84)

Lines 85–119

86: *What do the references to Philip and Darius tell us about the level of education or sophistication of Plautus' audience?*

90–100: *What particular form has Euclio's paranoia over his hidden treasure taken?* Note that he wants the house shut off from the outside world. He does not want anyone to come to ask for anything or to come to borrow anything. He wants the fire of the hearth put out (yet the hearth-fire is a symbol of the life and vitality of the household itself and of the city), and he wants it to be said that the water supply has run out (water is also a symbol of the welfare of both city and home). All of this emphasizes Euclio's anti-social feelings (see *Roman Comedy*, p. 36). He is unwilling to lend kitchen utensils (symbols perhaps of the essential nourishing function of the household), and he wants it said that thieves have cleaned them out (thieves = anti-social creatures; but in this case it is Euclio who is anti-social).

To what extent was Euclio anti-social all along and to what extent has his discovery of the gold and his paranoia over it contributed to his anti-social feelings and behavior?

How does Euclio's rejection even of Bona Fortuna (100) show how twisted and perverted his thinking has become?

Why is it that the discovery of the gold did not improve Euclio's life? Need sudden riches necessarily produce anti-social characteristics and behavior? To what extent is Euclio's development typical of human nature, and to what extent is it peculiar to Euclio as an individual?

103–104: *Does it seem to be the usual procedure for the doors to be locked up during the day?*

105–106: *How has Euclio's good fortune brought him extreme unhappiness?* It forces him to stay home all the time and makes it agonizing for him to have to leave and venture out into society for any reason whatsoever—even to collect a donation of money.

107: magister cūriae: Euclio's reluctant departure to receive his share of money being distributed by the **magister cūriae,** the director of his "ward," is sometimes seen as a Plautine importation of a practice of Athenian political life. The phrase **magister cūriae** is not found elsewhere except in first-century A.D. inscriptions. It must, however, have meant something to the audience or Plautus would have invented another excuse to remove Euclio from the stage; certainly his audience could not be expected to recognize a literal translation of some Athenian official's title. Plautus' phrase here may be taken as evidence for the existence of officials with this title in contemporary Roman society. It may be postulated that the money to be distributed represents one of the repayments to citizens of that extraordinary tax exacted during the Hannibalic War—the last repayment of which was made in 197 B.C. from the magnificent spoils gained in a campaign against the Galati in Asia Minor (Livy, XXXIX.7.1–2 and XXXIX.7.5). The headquarters of the **cūriae** were located on the northeast corner of the Palatine.

113–117: *Is it likely that Euclio's acquaintances have changed their attitude toward him? Or is he only imagining things? What evidence is there so far in the play that others have noticed a change in him? (See lines 67–73.)*

Lines 120–150

120: The role and character of Eunomia illustrate the stature of the Roman **māter familiās**. Although in some plays the matron is depicted as a nagging wife, here as the sister of Megadorus and (widowed?) mother of Lyconides, presumably his uncle's heir, she wields great influence over her brother, first convincing him to get married and later interceding with him on her son's behalf to break his engagement. The Roman matron was highly respected, the mistress of her house and the slaves therein, responsible for her children's early training and education, hostess at her husband's parties, free to walk abroad, testify in court, and even manage her own property. The Roman Matronalia, celebrated on the first of March, was somewhat analogous to our Mother's Day.

120–134: *What are the topics of Eunomia's discourse before she gets to the specific topic of her business?* She speaks of proper family relationships (120–122), the loquacity of women (123–126), the closeness of brother and sister (127–128), and the need to give and receive counsel and advice in family matters (129–134).

Eunomia's politeness and her emphasis on shared familial concerns involving faithfulness or trust (**fidēs**, 121, is a key word) and propriety (**aequum est**, 122) all contrast sharply with the portrayal of Euclio and his relationship to Staphyla and society in the previous scenes.

123–141: Students will want to discuss the stereotype of the loquacious woman (123–126) and the notion that all women have faults (135–141). *What do these passages tell us about sexual stereotyping in ancient society?*

144–147: *How would you characterize the relationship between Eunomia and Megadorus? Does Megadorus appear to respect Eunomia and her feelings and views? Does Megadorus show an initial willingness to listen to Eunomia?*

147–148: *What is Eunomia's view of the purpose of the proposed marriage or of marriage in general?*

Lines 151–177

154–157: *What is Megadorus' opinion of marriage?*

158: *How does Eunomia attempt to counter Megadorus' aversion to marriage?* By holding out the carrot of a "very large dowry."

165–169: *For what two reasons is Megadorus content with his bachelor's lot?* He is wealthy enough without a dowered wife. He does not like the trouble and expense involved in maintaining well-dowered wives.

Megadorus objects strenuously both to well-dowered wives and to their extravagances. He sees these extravagances as reducing husbands to servitude. Megadorus' complaints here and in lines 505–535 may allude to feelings provoked in Rome by passage and then repeal of the Lex Oppia. Passed in 215 B.C. during the crisis of the war with Hannibal, this law forbade women to possess more than half an ounce of gold, to wear different-colored garments, or to ride in a carriage in the city or neighboring towns except on religious holidays (see *The Oxford Classical Dictionary*, "Oppius [1]," p. 753). The law was repealed in 195 B.C. amid great controversy recorded by Livy (XXXIV.1–4). Megadorus' complaints against women may thus have been seen by the original audience as more than stereotyped male chauvinism. Apart from such topical allusions, Megadorus' complaints serve to fix his character as a type within the limited range of characters inside the play itself: Euclio is anti-social because of his poverty and his paranoia over the treasure; Eunomia shows a normal concern for traditional familial values and relationships; Megadorus, in contrast to both, shows concern only for his own well-being. Whereas Eunomia's name fits her character perfectly, Megadorus is just the opposite of his name, "Great Giver" or "Mr. Generosity."

Does Megadorus seem to be responding to the true familial concerns expressed by Eunomia, or does he want to base his life solely on personal ease and advantage?

170: *What does Eunomia's reaction to Megadorus' negative comments indicate about their relationship?*

171–174: *Is it credible that Megadorus should so quickly change his mind about marriage? Has he really been against marriage all along, or against marriage to a well-dowered, overbearing woman? Are lines 155–157 merely a stock male response to a matchmaker's proposal?*

Has Megadorus perhaps had the girl next door on his mind for some time? (He does know her—that she is poor—and says that she pleases him, line 174.)

Or are we to understand that his abrupt change of mind and willingness to marry have been brought about by the Lar, as promised in lines 31–32?

Why does Megadorus want to marry Euclio's daughter? What does he mean by **haec pauper placet** *(174)?*

What does his choice for a wife indicate about what he feels would make a happy marital relationship? If money is not a consideration in his willingness to marry, what is? What is it about Euclio's daughter that would make her "pleasing"

(174) to Megadorus? To help with the last question, the teacher may direct attention to how Euclio's daughter has been portrayed to the audience by the Lar in the prologue, as respectful, pious, obedient, and familial. Does Megadorus see her as a perfect "subservient" wife?

170–176: *Does Eunomia's behavior toward Megadorus change after he refuses her choice for his wife?* It becomes colder, merely polite, even brusk.

175: *What is the state of the relationship between Eunomia and Megadorus when they part? How do you think Eunomia feels about the mission she undertook in approaching Megadorus? How is she likely to feel about the prospect of Megadorus' marriage with Euclio's daughter?*

Lines 178–203

182–185: *Why does Megadorus greet Euclio with special cordiality on this occasion? How does Euclio misinterpret his motives?* (There is, of course, no reason why Euclio should have any idea of Megadorus' real intentions—to lead up to asking for the hand of Euclio's daughter.)

186–203: *How does Euclio subsequently misinterpret each of Megadorus' statements? (187–189, 193–198, and 199–202)*

How does Euclio's misinterpretation of Megadorus' intentions intensify as this scene continues and how does it lead to Euclio's darting into his house to check on his money? (203) Note the climactic misinterpretation that forces Euclio to rush into the house: Megadorus speaks of a matter of mutual concern to himself and Euclio (200), thinking of marriage to Euclio's daughter; Euclio thinks he is going to talk about a deal involving the treasure (200–202). Note the irony of the scene, with Euclio insisting that his daughter is unmarriageable because she has no dowry (191), Megadorus promising that he can help with that (193), and Euclio rushing in to check on his gold at the very moment that Megadorus is about to ask for his daughter's hand, probably even without dowry (199–200). On stage neither man understands the motives of the other, but the audience can relish to the full its awareness of their mutual misunderstandings.

187: *How is Megadorus' remark here typical of a man who has always been wealthy?* One may contrast the remark here with the Lar's comment about the life of Euclio's father with a small parcel of land living wretchedly with great labor or suffering (13–14). The smug attitude on Megadorus' part shows no comprehension of the suffering of the poor.

190: Note that to excuse his aside, Euclio replies that he was complaining of his poverty—

not as easy to bear as Megadorus was blithely assuming. All of this emphasizes the differences between the social and economic orders that separate the two men.

193: Megadorus' generosity proferred here would be in keeping with his name, but in fact he does not "give" anything at all.

Lines 204–235

211: *Why does Euclio reply indirectly and in an aside to Megadorus' question in line 210? Is it because Megadorus' question is vague or because Euclio is cautious? How far does Euclio trust Megadorus?*

212–214: *Why do you think Megadorus leads into asking for the hand of Euclio's daughter with so many questions about himself? Is he simply conceited, or is he trying to reassure Euclio and overcome his distrust?*

What do you think of Megadorus' qualifications as a prospective son-in-law? Do they correspond to the Roman sense of values?

214: *Why do you think Euclio drops a comment about Megadorus' money in line 214 (item ut pecūniam)? Is he envious? suspicious? obsessed with the subject? What do you think Euclio's opinion would be of rich men in general?*

220–222: *Why does Euclio think Megadorus is ridiculing him by asking for his daughter's hand? How does he try to draw sympathy from Megadorus? What Latin words might have this effect? Is all of this just a ploy on Euclio's part to avoid having to offer a dowry or is it to make his refusal to give one seem reasonable?*

226–235: *How valid or convincing is Euclio's comparison of the proposed marriage to a yoking of a donkey with a bull? How does the comparison comment on his relationship to Megadorus? What does it tell us about Roman society?*

Students may be asked to compare modern ideas about marriage between members of disparate social classes.

Lines 236–264

236–237: *How does Megadorus think that poor men should relate themselves to the rich? How does this serve as a reply to Euclio's comments about yoking donkeys with bulls?* Note that it is **amīcitia** (246) that Megadorus wishes to establish with Euclio, a kind of political alliance entered upon for the mutual benefit of both parties (see *The Oxford Classical Dictionary*, "Amicitia," p. 52).

238: *How many times does Euclio refer to the fact that there will be no dowry? (238, 255–256, 257–258, and 263 **Istuc**)*

239: *What does Megadorus mean by* **mōrāta rēctē?** *Does he mean simply subservient? Where else does he suggest what a good character for a wife might be?* (See lines 167–169, where he lists what he would *not* want.)

240: Note that Euclio here openly jokes about having discovered a treasure. With his treasure on his mind, he becomes worried when in the next line he hears a noise of digging.

The *Aulularia* offers a particularly active and noisy performance. Euclio runs on and off stage frequently, chasing people out of his house (40, 414–415), leaving abruptly in the middle of a conversation (203, 242), and later trying to hide his treasure. In other plays the noise of creaking doors is regularly referred to, but here an assortment of sounds are to be heard: of an argument in Euclio's house (37), of tools and digging here (241–243), and later in connection with the cooks and the theft of the pot of gold.

246–249: Discuss the relationship between the rich and the poor as revealed in these lines. *Why is the poor man afraid? Why does his fear cause him to act badly? What does he want later? Why can he not have it later?*

250–251: *How is the tone of Euclio's words to Staphyla different from that of his conversation with Megadorus?*

252–253: Note that Megadorus phrases his complaint not in terms of relations between the rich and the poor (as in 246–249 to himself) but in terms of Euclio's making fun of an *old* man. Note his tactfulness in choosing to make his complaint in these terms. (Megadorus is now claiming that Euclio is making fun of him, whereas in 220–222 Euclio had complained that Megadorus was making fun of him.)

256: Spondeō: for this formal language of Roman contracts, see the following note. There were no legal procedures required for a Roman marriage other than the consent of both parties or their guardians.

259–260: Note Euclio's return to the rich man/poor man dichotomy with the charge that "you" (i.e., "you rich men") capriciously treat agreements according to mere whim. It may be asked whether this is a fair charge to level against Megadorus. For the importance of solemn verbal agreements in Roman social and economic life, agreements confirmed by words such as **spondeō** and **fīat** rather than by signatures on paper, see *The Oxford Classical Dictionary,* "Contract, Roman Law of," p. 287, and "Stipulatio," pp. 1014–1015. It is a tribute to Megadorus' patience and determination to secure the hand of Euclio's daughter that he does not become incensed at this insult to his social class.

236–264: *What does Euclio seem to care more about in this whole scene, his money or the fate of his daughter?*

264: macellum: just as the Roman audience could picture Euclio's walk to the northeast corner of the Palatine to receive his money from the **magister cūriae,** so here they could locate Megadorus, setting out for the **macellum,** walking to an area near the Senate House and into the market complex, which spread southward to the farthest edge of the Forum.

Lines 265–279
274–277: *What do the feelings Staphyla expresses here tell us about her relationship with Phaedria?*

Lines 280–294
280–282: Note that only a few lines have elapsed since Strobilus' departure for the Forum with Megadorus to buy provisions for the wedding feast, yet Strobilus now returns with cooks, assistants, flute girls, and provisions. Surely more time must have elapsed, but Plautus does not seem to be concerned with the resulting lack of verisimilitude. Probably no one in the original audience would have noticed.

280–294: In these and the following lines, invite students to sort out the relations among Strobilus, Anthrax, and Congrio and to try to fix the characterization of each of them with reference to the Latin text. *How do Anthrax and Congrio play off each other's humor? Does Strobilus seem to keep up with their word-play?*

Lines 294–326
294–295: Anthrax naturally finds it surprising that Euclio is not footing the bill for his own daughter's wedding. Note how the question as to why Euclio is not footing the bill himself leads to the extended comic repartee over Euclio's miserliness.

309–310: Anthrax's suggestion that the cooks ask Euclio to help them buy their freedom is of course facetious and simply another jab at Euclio's stinginess.

315–320: *Although Euclio refers to himself as* **pauper,** *what is his general reputation according to Strobilus, i.e., in the town?* (Not "poor," but "stingy," "miserly," "mean-spirited.")

Are Strobilus' tales about Euclio to be taken seriously or are they exaggerations? If they are exaggerations, to what extent are we to think of them as being based on some fact? The terms *caricature* and *comic butt* may be useful in answering this question.

322, 326: Themes of the "thief" and of "theft" are here introduced in association with the cooks; these themes anticipate Euclio's fears later about the thievery of cooks and motivate his removal of the pot of gold from the house so that the cooks will not steal it.

What, if anything, do the names of the cooks tell us about their character? Anthrax: Greek word for charcoal. Congrio: from **conger, congrī** (*m*), a conger-eel (from Greek word for same).

326: Note the punning in the words **fūr, trifurcifer,** the latter of which has nothing to do etymologically with the former.

321–326: *What sort of impression do the cooks make with their arguing, insulting, and complaining? How is the tone of this scene different from that of preceding scenes? How does Plautus vary the tone of his scenes? What kind of rhythm is produced as the action moves forward?*

Lines 330–349

339–341: *How valid are Strobilus' arguments that Euclio's house is the better place to cook?*

339–349: *Does Strobilus trust the cooks? Why or why not?*

349: *What has been the purpose of this lengthy scene involving the cooks? Comic interlude? Sheer buffoonery and slapstick?* In retrospect the scene will be seen to have been very important to the plot. In introducing the cooks and the theme of thievery, it motivates Euclio's removal of the pot of gold from the house. Without this, the pot would never have been stolen by the slave of Lyconides, and Euclio would not have been reduced to despair. He would not have come to realize the folly of his self-isolation and would not have undergone a change of mind or character (as he presumably does in the missing part of the play) or have bestowed the gold as dowry, having learned the importance of trust and confidence in the familial and societal framework. The slapstick scene with the cooks is thus essential to the plot, although it also provides comic relief.

Lines 350–370

350: *Why is the door of Euclio's house closed?* Note that Stapyhyla opens the door only after Strobilus identifies himself and says that he is bringing things for the wedding (not coming to borrow anything); cf. 274 and 89–100.

354–356: *What does the fact that Staphyla notices that there is no wine say about her character?* Old women are often portrayed as winebibbers in Plautus.

359: Volcānō studēs: note the elevated expression for the simple idea that the cooks use fire in their occupation.

363–370: Note the development of the theme of thievery. If even Strobilus is concerned over the possibility that the cooks may steal from Megadorus, what are we to expect when Euclio returns and finds cooks in his house? Note that even the best plan that Strobilus can concoct for keeping the thieves from stealing (i.e., having them cook at the bottom of the well) is futile because they would end up eating all the food down there and leaving those above hungry. The moral is that cooks will steal no matter what you do with them. Strobilus' parting line (370) emphasizes his concern over the cooks' thievery.

Lines 371–397

371: Euclio and Megadorus have both been at the market (**macellum**) seeking provisions, but, as is typical of Plautus, they have not seen each other there. Seldom does any action or encounter of principals take place off stage.

371–387: *How do Euclio's actions in the market confirm the opinion of him held by Strobilus?*

Do you think Euclio really intended to buy anything in the market to begin with?

Which lines in Euclio's description of his shopping trip generally summarize his philosophy? (379–381)

385–387: *What does Euclio's purchase of incense and a wreath of flowers tell us about his character? Is he as unfamilial and disrespectful of the Lar as his father had been? Does he have a basic core of goodness in his character?*

Compare Euclio's daughter's offering to the Lar (23–25).

Since the conclusion of the play has been lost, it is dangerous to speculate about it, but hints such as this of a basic core of goodness in Euclio suggest the possibility of regeneration and integration into a happy familial and societal circle with the bestowal of the gold as dowry at the end of the play.

Compare **fortūnātās . . . nūptiās** here (387)—Euclio's real wishes for his daughter at a moment of calm reflection—with his command that not even **Bona Fortūna** be allowed to enter the house (100), expressed in a fit of paranoia over the pot of gold.

388–391: *What two things (388–389) lead Euclio to think his house is being pillaged? How has the audience been prepared for the idea of the cooks as thieves or potential thieves? What third thing (390–391) convinces Euclio that his gold is being stolen?*

394–396: An altar may have been a regular feature of the stage. Certainly altars are specifically referred to in other plays (e.g., *Mostellaria*, 1094, and *Rudens*, 455). Apollo was generally worshiped as the god of prophecy, music, and medicine, and later of the sun. His invocation for help in punishing a thief may have been inspired by the well-known story told in the Homeric *Hymn to Hermes*, 4, "When his cattle were stolen by the infant Hermes (Mercury), he discovered the culprit and forgave him when the boy gave him the lyre which he had just invented."

What dramatic purpose is served by having Euclio not rush into the house at line 393? What is the purpose of the scene at the altar and the invocation of Apollo? The scene highlights the theme of thievery or suspected thievery—the suspicion of which motivates the next stage in the plot (i.e., Euclio's removal of the gold from the house).

Lines 398–405

398–405: *What dramatic purpose does this brief scene serve?* It merely fills time while Euclio is inside chasing Congrio out.

401: gallum: mention of a rooster (**gallus**) five times in the play (401, 465, 469, 470, and 472) has suggested an obvious pun on the Gauls (**Gallī**), in particular the Boii, against whom the Romans campaigned in northern Italy (Cisalpine Gaul) from 196 to 191 B.C., until they were defeated and half of their territory taken for Roman colonies.

Lines 406–424

406: *Whom does Congrio actually address here?* The audience.

408: bacchānāl: Dionysus-Bacchus was worshiped at Rome in a temple of Ceres, Liber, and Libera built in the early fifth century at the foot of the Aventine near the Tiber, where grain ships docked. These deities were Demeter, Dionysus, and Persephone in a Latin form. The wild orgiastic rites of the original Thracian worship of Dionysus were utterly foreign to the ordered discipline of Roman religion and, when they were introduced to Italy and Rome in the early second century the accompanying drunkenness and license were shocking. The nocturnal rites, especially aimed at attracting young people, were considered dangerous by the state, which in 186 B.C. acted to curtail the celebrations. This censorship was undertaken by the government instead of by religious authorities since the rites were regarded as a conspiracy against the welfare of the state. Hence the references in several Plautine plays (*Amphitryon*, 703–705, *Bacchides*, 53, and *Miles Gloriosus*, 855–857) to the Bacchantes as disrupters of law, order, and property rights rather than as religious heretics.

Just as the Bacchantes beat Pentheus, so Congrio has been beaten by Euclio. There may be parody of tragic laments in lines 410 (first half) and 411.

409: Scenes of beating were stock fare in the pre-Plautine Italic farces.

413–414: ligna . . . praebērī and **onustōs fūstibus:** these metaphorical expressions may require further explanations than those given in the vocabulary.

416: trēsvirōs: for more on these officials, see *The Oxford Classical Dictionary*, "Police," p. 851.

Lines 425–448

425–448: When Euclio discovered his door open and heard noise from within (388–389), he suspected thieves were at work, prayed to Apollo for help, and rushed into the house. As he drove Congrio out (406–424), he complained that Congrio had a knife and threatened to denounce him to the authorities for that. Now he asks what business Congrio had in his house (427–428). By line 434 Euclio seems to accept the idea that Congrio is not a thief who has come to steal.

435: Congrio begins afresh: "Why is it, then, that you don't allow us to cook dinner here?" Euclio's answer is that the cooks have taken over the whole house; if they had stuck to their business at the hearth, he would not have bothered them (439–440). Yet, it is at the hearth itself that the gold is buried.

441–444: Euclio goes into the house either to check on the safety of his gold as he has done in the past or to remove the gold from the house. If the latter is his intention, it may be because he now realizes (1) that the gold is buried at the very hearth where the cooks have been and will continue to be working and (2) that since there are so many cooks filling the whole house it would not be safe to hide the gold elsewhere inside.

Congrio, of course, has no idea why Euclio suddenly goes back into the house (444), thinks Euclio intends to keep the cooking utensils that he brought (445–446), and threatens him accordingly (446).

Lines 449–474

449–459: *Why is it that Euclio can now tell Congrio to bring in even a whole flock of slaves (452)?*

460–464: Note the theme again of rich and poor. It is a bold undertaking for a poor man to have dealings with a rich man (460–461). *How does this thought help explain Euclio's reluctance* earlier to become involved with Megadorus? It is a bold undertaking because rich men cannot be trusted, as in the present instance in which Megadorus appears to Euclio to be making all sorts of advances against him, including sending the cooks to steal his gold (462–464). Euclio apparently still regards the whole marriage proposal as a plot to steal his money. Why else, he may think, would Megadorus be willing to take his daughter without a dowry?

465–472: Euclio's paranoia extends even to Staphyla's poultry cock that Euclio seizes upon as an accomplice in the cooks' search for the gold (470–471). So Euclio kills it to deprive the cooks of their helper. If Euclio did not go into the house with the decision already made to remove the gold, the cock's digging around the place where the gold was hidden would surely have given him the idea.

466: pecūliāris: the word is derived from **pecūlium**, which was a technical term for property owned or controlled by a slave or other person who could not have legal rights of ownership. Although all assets of the family and household were legally the property of the **pater familiās**, individuals were allowed to accumulate goods which by custom were considered their own. Slaves through their skills might accumulate enough to buy their freedom. Euclio, well within his legal rights, deprives Staphyla of one of her few possessions.

Lines 475–504

475–495: Megadorus' defense of his willingness to marry a poor man's daughter without dowry and his suggestion that other rich men should follow his example offer many opportunities for discussion. Megadorus mentions four advantages that would result if others adopted his course of action (481–484): there would be more civic harmony, there would be less ill-will against the wealthy, wives would fear punishment more than they do (i.e., would be more subservient to their husbands), and husbands would not have to spend so much money on their wives. Each of these points should be examined and discussed.

479: Note the juxtaposition of **opulentiōrēs** and **pauperiōrum**, highlighting the theme of the rich and the poor.

485–488: Note that Megadorus thinks that only a small minority of extremely greedy men would object to his proposal.

492: *What does Megadorus mean by* **mōrēs meliōrēs***? Mere subservience?*

494–495: Note that Megadorus' speech ends on the theme of purely monetary concerns—husbands would no longer have to pay for expensive mules for their wives.

475–495: *How seriously are we to take Megadorus' proposal? How would various elements in the audience respond to it? Is this a serious blueprint for social reform and a new order of society? Or is it a rich bachelor's plan to ensure his personal comfort, by being allowed the luxury of having a subservient wife who would not make demands upon his purse? How does it fit in with the theme of the dowry in the play?*

498–502: Megadorus continues his argument: women could not use the fact that they have provided their husbands with large dowries to persuade them to spend money on luxuries. *How does Megadorus use alliteration to mock the luxuries listed in lines 501–502?*

503–504: Euclio's comment shows that he realizes the real thrust of Megadorus' proposal—namely, to keep women in their place. Megadorus would make an ideal supervisor of women's character.

Lines 505–535

505–522: *What does the list of merchants tell us about the life of upper class-Romans of this time?* This long list of tradesmen and artisans shows the influx of Greek luxuries into hitherto parochial Roman life as a result of Roman military successes in the East. Such extravagances, made possible by the increase of money available through war, profiteering, or spoils, offended conservative Roman isolationists, like Cato, who resisted Greek importations and Roman interventions in eastern affairs.

523–524: Note that Euclio wants to let Megadorus continue not because he is interested in hearing more about Megadorus' proposal as a plan to reform society but because he wants to hear him continue his description of the character of women and his mocking of their extravagant spending. Euclio enjoys Megadorus' comments because of his miserliness and general niggardliness; he does not really understand Megadorus' proposal or the reasons why he is putting it forth—not out of miserliness, niggardliness, or parsimony (Euclio's qualities) but out of sheer selfishness in that Megadorus wants a wife who will toe the line, be subservient to him, and please him. *Although Euclio and Megadorus seem to agree, how are their motives different?*

526–531: *Why has the soldier come? How is the fact that he comes last given significance in this passage?* All of the household's money has been squandered on the wife's luxuries; then along comes the soldier, protector of the state, and he gets nothing. There is a perversion of values here in that luxuries come first and civic duties and necessities are ignored and come last. The household has been bankrupted by luxuries.

The extravagant life of the wealthy matron, scored by Megadorus to Euclio's delight, is brought into sharp and sad perspective by reference to the begging soldier who waits unfed in the midst of plenty. The fortunes made by businessmen in supplying war material, the booty from Carthage, and the contemporary profitable campaigns against Philip V of Macedon contrasted sharply with the plight of veterans of the Hannibalic War, who had lost their small farms as a result of continuous overseas service. Even officers of aristocratic families faced economic hardship because of neglect of their estates, including the great Scipio himself. The circumstances of some veterans were so serious that by the end of 201 B.C. a commission was appointed to allocate public land in Samnium and Apulia for them; they were to receive two iūgera (somewhat less than two acres) for every year served in Spain or Africa (Livy, XXXI.4.1–3 and XXXI.49.5).

532–535: Conclusions: wives with large dowries bring (1) disadvantages and (2) intolerable expenses. The wife without a dowry is in the power of her husband. The last line repeats the thought of lines 532–533 and adds nothing new.

The extravagant spending of the dowered wife leads to trouble for society in neglect of the soldier, but Megadorus' greater concern seems to be the trouble caused to the husband and in particular the financial ruin caused by the intolerable expenditures of the freely spending wife.

Lines 536–560

536–544: Euclio has listened attentively and with great pleasure to everything Megadorus has said, but while the two men agree in their dislike of extravagant women, they are still separated by the gap between rich and poor and by irreconcilable differences of personality and character. The latter are brought out in Megadorus' criticism of Euclio's appearance and in Euclio's reply. The irony of Euclio's reply should not go unnoticed. The ostensible reason he is not well dressed and well groomed is that he is poor and has nothing more than what one would expect a poor man to have (542–544), but while he gives this explanation he clutches his pot of gold.

545–548: Note that Megadorus' innocent and cordial reply revives Euclio's suspicions that he is after his gold and that Staphyla has revealed his secret. This suspicion that Megadorus is after his gold will increase in the course of the scene and lead Euclio to his decision to hide the gold somewhere outside the house (the next stage in the development of the plot).

550: Note the irony in Euclio's words. He was indeed contemplating an accusation, namely, that Megadorus was after his gold. He in fact voices another set of accusations concerning the cooks, the flute girl, and the provisions for dinner. The accusation about the cooks is that Megadorus filled his house with thieves (551–552) in the form of cooks, whom we know Euclio had thought were sent by Megadorus to steal his gold (463–464).

This is an excellent opportunity to discuss dramatic irony: Euclio's words will be understood one way by Megadorus and another way by the audience, which knows his real anxieties and paranoia.

554–559: Since mythological references here and in other plays could easily have been omitted by the playwright, we can take it for granted that the average Roman was familiar with a number of Greek myths. He probably gleaned his knowledge from tragedy, which was based on Greek models, and from temple murals. Geryon might have been mentioned in plays about Hercules, and he might have been familiar from the festival of Hercules at the Ara Maxima (see note to line 40). Argus, Io, and the peacock might have been known from adaptations of tragedies such as Aeschylus' *Prometheus Bound*. The fountain of Pirene in Corinth could have been familiar from plays dealing with Bellerophon, who caught Pegasus there and rode him in his mission to kill the Chimaera.

Lines 561–586

569–578: The next stage in the plot—Euclio's decision to hide the gold someplace outside his home—is motivated by Megadorus' invitation to drink (569) and his promise to get Euclio very drunk (573). Euclio is naturally afraid that Megadorus intends to make him drunk so he can steal his gold (575–576). Compare his earlier fear that Megadorus had sent the cooks to steal his gold and that the cooks had bribed the cock to find it. Euclio was happy to have thwarted that supposed attempt on his money, and he is happy now to envision thwarting Megadorus. Megadorus will lose both his effort and his wine (578), chuckles Euclio.

580–586: Euclio decides to hide the gold in the temple of Fides. The goddess Fides embodied a traditional Roman aristocratic ideal; the concept of fidēs was of paramount importance in family life, political life, the patron–client relationship, and international relations. The implausibility of a temple of this Roman deity being situated in Athens, the ostensible scene of the play, would not have been noticed by the original audience, used as it was to a constant blending of Greek and Roman elements in comic dramas.

583: Fideī: this Plautine spelling with a long e is retained here (see also lines 615, 617, 667, and 676); the spelling with a short e, to which students may be more accustomed, is given in the end vocabulary.

Lines 587–615

587–604: *How does Plautus establish the character of Lyconides' slave? What are the qualities of a good slave as described by L.S.?* There is special emphasis here on the relationship between the slave and his master. Virtue for a slave is equivalent to obedience to the will of his master. Note that the good slave's reward is stated only in negative terms: not being beaten or shackled.

Students should note L.S.'s actions as the play progresses and come back to this passage to judge how well his actions harmonize with his words. Do his actions always carry out the wishes and will of his master?

A similar and longer exposition of the duties and attitudes of the good slave appears in the *Menaechmi* (966–984), where Messenio details his philosophy. The better known alternative to such an attitude is the clever and manipulative slave who plots to help his young master and deceive his father, as seen in the *Mostellaria* and the *Pseudolus*.

Note that lines 592–598 have been omitted because they are thought to have been an interpolation added for a later production of the play.

603–605: Be sure that questions 6, 7, and 8 below the Latin text are answered carefully. Some students may wonder why Lyconides has not taken any initiative earlier if, as his slave says, he loves Euclio's daughter. Discussion may lead to the conclusion that Plautus has deliberately shifted the focus of the play away from the romance and onto Euclio's obsession.

608–615: Note the irony of the scene with the slave watching while Euclio absentmindedly addresses the temple of Fides about the gold he has hidden within. Further irony: in the very act of warning Fides not to reveal the gold to anyone (608), Euclio is himself revealing its hiding place to L.S. Euclio is so obsessed with the gold that he blabs on about what a great find (**praedam**) it would be (610–611), thus only whetting L.S.'s appetite.

Who is to blame for the attempted theft of the gold, Fides or Euclio?

612–613: Note Euclio's attention to the amenities: washing, sacrifice. Compare line 579.

614–615: *Why does Euclio again speak of the gold?* Because he is so obsessed with it? The result is, of course, that L.S. is told in even more explicit terms that gold is hidden in the temple.

Note that Euclio's prayer in line 614 is actually answered. He will take the gold safe and sound from the temple. Is it Fides who makes the raven crow (next scene) to warn Euclio?

Lines 616–638

616–623: *How does L.S.'s warning that Fides not be faithful to Euclio but instead to himself pervert the very concept embodied by this goddess? How seriously does L.S. regard the goddess?*

Is L.S. sincere in his promise to reward Fides for her infidelity to Euclio? How equivalent will his reward be to the gift he will have received from Fides? How does L.S. mock the true reciprocity expected in normal give and take between men and gods?

Is L.S. insincere and hypocritical? What do his remarks reveal about his character?

624–627: *What action of the raven points to L.S.'s planned digging up of the pot of gold?*

628–638: *How many times before in the play has Euclio driven someone out of doors?*

Why does Euclio not want to mention what he thinks L.S. has stolen?

Lines 639–660

642: *Who elsewhere in the play has thought that Euclio was insane?*

Lines 661–681

661–662: *What motivates L.S. now?*

667–676: Note that Euclio never realized that L.S. had overheard his earlier talk; this may explain his lack of hesitation in talking aloud further about the gold now.

667–669: *How does Euclio express his disillusionment with Fides? Did the goddess actually cheat him? What does Euclio mean by using the adverb* **paenissimē** *(668)? To what does he attribute his salvation?*

670–672: *How is Euclio's attitude toward rewarding the raven similar to L.S.'s attitude toward rewarding Fides (621–623)? How seriously does either of them take religion or superstition?*

673–676: *Why does Euclio determine on the grove of Silvanus as the next hiding place for his gold?* He thinks it will be more secure there for three reasons: (1) the grove is outside the city walls, (2) it is pathless (and therefore inaccessible and unfrequented), and (3) it is covered with a protective grove of willows.

The teacher may want to raise the question of whether there is any further significance to the choice of the grove of Silvanus. One could also ask why Plautus did not simply allow L.S.'s attempt to steal the gold from the temple of Fides to be successful. *Why the second hiding of the gold?* Part of the answer lies in the fact that there are now three important deities: the Lar (the household god), Fides (the goddess who protects agreements between men in the city), and Silvanus (the god of the woods and of wild, uncivilized life outside the city).

Central questions that are useful to address here are where the pot of gold belongs and how it should rightly be used. Clearly, it belongs in the context of the household and the city, as a dowry to cement a faithful marriage relationship between two families. Note that Megadorus is wrong in wanting to take a wife without dowry, i.e., without use of money as a symbol of the shared interests between families represented by the institution of marriage; that Euclio is equally wrong in wanting to give his daughter away without a dowry and that he is making a perverse use (or nonuse) of the gold; and that the well-dowered wives who use the fact that they come with dowry to bludgeon their husbands into submission and extravagant expenses are also wrong—they make a use of dowry money that is just as bad in its own way as Euclio's is in his way. Money neither should be hidden away for some unspecified future private use, nor should it be used as a weapon to reduce husbands to servitude. On the other hand, the withholding of dowry money is equally wrong if it leads (as Megadorus proposes) to subjugation and servitude for the wife. The proper use of Euclio's money is as a dowry to cement a marriage relationship that will lead to a happy family life and a trusting relationship between families in the context of the social life of the city as a whole.

Taking the pot of gold totally out of the familial context (protected by the Lar) and out of the civic context (protected by Fides) is both wrong and a counsel of despair or admission of defeat—of the fact that Euclio is unable to conceive of any good use for the money. His views of family and society are bankrupt, and he deserves to forfeit the money, which, by taking it to the grove of Silvanus outside the city walls, he has removed from the protection of society and from any possibility of its right use within society. See *Roman Comedy*, "Aulularia," pp. 33–46.

680–681: L.S. disobeys his master; compare his introduction of himself as totally responsive to his master's will (587–602). He will now welcome even "punishment" (**malam rem**), since he sees a possibility for profit (**cum lucrō**). He thus makes his initial portrayal of himself seem hypocritical. Compare his insincere promise to reward Fides if she allows him to find the pot of gold (621–623).

Lines 682–700

682–689: Lyconides had sent his slave on ahead to reconnoiter the situation; he now enters with Eunomia, having already been talking with her for some time. The important thing here is that Eunomia takes the side of her son, who has admitted his violation of Phaedria and expressed his honorable intentions. She is on his side (686), even though this means going against the marriage plans of Megadorus that her earlier actions had prompted.

688–690: The question of whether Lyconides has been telling Eunomia the truth is resolved by the labor pains of Phaedria (691–693).

691–692: Phaedria's voice is heard from inside Euclio's house. A free-born, unmarried daughter of a citizen never appears on the Roman stage. Matrons, slaves, flute girls, and prostitutes, however, appear in abundance.

694–695: With this proof of the truth of Lyconides' confessions, Eunomia is now ready to go in to Megadorus and ask that he give up his plans to marry Phaedria.

696–700: Lyconides will follow to help persuade Megadorus, but he first looks for his slave. He had commanded him to wait there (697–698), but he does not see him. Lyconides is willing to give his slave the benefit of the doubt: if the slave is attending to Lyconides' interests, it is unfair to be angry with him (698–699). Note the irony here: the slave went off to steal the pot of gold thinking only of his own potential profit and weighing that against any punishment he might receive from his master for disobeying his orders (681). So in one sense Lyconides is wrong here in supposing that his slave is attending to his (Lyconides') affairs. Yet, in the long run it is exactly the slave's theft of the gold that triggers Euclio's despair and ultimately his change of mind or character that results in Euclio's giving Lyconides both the hand of his daughter and the gold as dowry. So, the slave, unbeknownst to himself, is actually attending to the long-term best interests of Lyconides.

697: The manuscripts of the play give **Strobīlum** here and **Strolum** in line 804, as the name of Lyconides' slave. However, since **Strobīlus** is the name of Megadorus' slave (264), it is best to assume that mistakes in the transmission of the text have occurred in lines 697 and 804; we simply do not know what name Plautus gave to Lyconides' slave, hence the gaps left in the text in lines 697 and 804 and our designation of the slave as merely **Lyconidis servus**.

Lines 701–726

701–711: *What has happened to L.S., who introduced himself as a slave attentive only to the* *interests of his master? How has he been corrupted by his newly discovered wealth? How has his estimate of himself been reversed? What concern, if any, does he show for his master? What had his master ordered him to do, and how do his actions now violate those orders?*

713–726: This song climaxes one line of the plot, namely, the theft or loss of Euclio's gold. The dramatic illusion is shattered, and the action on stage is brought to real life by the audience being brought into the play. This is a favorite device in Plautus. Is the audience supposed to be a group of Athenians? Or are they understood to be Romans? This crossing of illusion and reality along with the mixture of Greek and Roman elements in the play as a whole creates a particular kind of ambiance peculiar to Plautus in our extant Latin literature.

The monologue may contain reminiscences of the diction of tragic lyrics as Euclio attempts to gain sympathy for his suffering, anguish, despair, and loss. Note, however, the purely personal focus with an emphasis on the first person: **Ego mē . . . animumque meum geniumque meum** (724a–725); **meō malō et damnō** (726); and **Patī nequeō** (726). The loss affects Euclio and Euclio alone, since he had no intention of sharing the gold with anyone and had no familial or societal use for it.

Lines 727–751

727–751: Lyconides assumes that Euclio is wailing over the ruin of his daughter when he is really wailing over loss of his money. Euclio has tried to keep the fate of his money separate from the fate of his daughter. He never even considered giving the money as a dowry; he took the money away from the house when wedding preparations were being made, and he finally lost it. He has shown no real concern for his daughter but has been concerned only with how to get her married off at the least expense to himself (incense and flowers for the Lar were as far as he was willing to go). Now the two themes of loss of his money and ruin of his daughter are dramatized simultaneously with Euclio speaking of his pot of gold and Lyconides speaking of Euclio's daughter. The two talk at cross purposes with no comprehension of what the other is talking about, thus emphasizing the gulf that separates the obsessive miser Euclio from the normal young man with wholesome feelings and honorable intentions.

Students should carefully note the concerns of Lyconides in this exchange:
  to express his feeling of being miserable
  to confess what he did

  to explain why he did what he did (a god was the cause)
  to accept blame personally in spite of the workings of the god
  to come to ask for pardon
  to explain what happened as the result of intervention by the gods (of wine and love)

What does this exchange contribute to our understanding of Lyconides' character? How does it expand on and develop the glimpse of Lyconides that we had earlier in his dialogue with Eunomia? Is he a sympathetic character? a credible character? an admirable character? Is he a strong enough character to steal the limelight from Euclio, or do you feel that the play will remain focused on Euclio?

Euclio and Lyconides are talking about two different crimes. Euclio uses **illa** *to mean the pot of gold, Lyconides uses* **illa** *to refer to Phaedria. How could you handle this in English translation?*

Lines 752–776

752: Note that Lyconides emphasizes his voluntary approach to Euclio (**ultrō supplicātum veniō**) and his admission that it was his fault (**stultitiam meam**).

757–758: Note the emphasis here on the fact that **illa** ought to be Lyconides', thus highlighting his wholly honorable intentions. But at the same time this leads to resolution of the misunderstanding between the two speakers, as Euclio insists that Lyconides "give back" what he "stole" (759).

763: The turn that the dialogue takes finally forces Euclio to mention the pot of gold (**aulam aurī**) publicly for the first time in the play. Euclio is now so desperate that he proposes a 50/50 split of the gold (767).

775: neque fūrem excipiēs: Lyconides' swearing to this will preclude him from sheltering his slave when he discovers that he has stolen Euclio's gold.

Lines 777–802

777–780: Before he explains his case, Lyconides introduces himself and his family. Why? Compare Megadorus' "introduction" of himself to Euclio in lines 212–214. Does Lyconides' introduction of himself appear to help?

783: The abruptness of this announcement by a third party is not in character for the genial, courteous, and responsible Megadorus. In adapting his Greek model, Plautus may have chosen to omit details that were not directly related to his own theme.

786: *When Lyconides announces that Megadorus is repudiating his marriage intentions,* to what do Euclio's thoughts immediately jump? The loss of his gold, which he blames on Megadorus. *What does this reinforce about Euclio's character?*

787–795: Through what stages does Lyconides reveal what has happened, his involvement, his intentions, and his wishes? What efforts does he make to reassure Euclio and soften the blow?

Do you think Lyconides wants to marry Phaedria because of her own qualities, or to "do the right thing", or a combination of the two? What does he recognize as his legal responsibilities? Why do you think he did not seek to marry Phaedria before this last minute, especially since he has known all along who his victim was (29), although she did not know who attacked her (30)?

Lyconides, like many of Plautus' young lovers, is a weak hero. His late entrance on the stage, his relative unimportance in the entire drama, and his previous inertia reveal how little concerned Plautus is with the romance.

796–802: How does Euclio react to Lyconides' confession?

Lines 803–823

808–817: Note the unusually lengthy process by which master and slave recognize and approach one another.

817: Note that L.S. has a specific purpose in mind here—to seek his freedom. Again, compare his first appearance as the dutiful, subservient slave. Was that all a mirage, and was he talking about "the ideal slave" and not really about himself? Was he bluffing?

823: Again, L.S. expresses his desire to be set free. *Until now has L.S. done anything to "deserve" to be set free? Has he really been looking out for his master's interests, or has he been pursuing his own advantage and profit?*

Would it be possible to rehabilitate L.S. at the very end of the play by having him perform some truly generous action that would warrant giving him his freedom?

Lines 824–831

824–825: So far, L.S. has performed no generous action; thus, Lyconides' enraged response to his request to be set free.

831: L.S.'s refusal to return the gold: *How do you think this could be resolved? Could it work out so that L.S. would bring back the gold and at the same time convince Euclio that his previous handling of the gold was against his own best interests and that he should present it as a dowry? Could this then be regarded as a generous and noble enough action to warrant manumission? These*

are just a few of the questions students should consider in thinking about how the play might have been brought to a satisfying conclusion.

*   *   *

TRANSLATION

Note: the full stage directions included in the Latin text are not reproduced here. This translation is intended to serve only as a fairly literal guide to the meaning of the Latin.

Lines 1–22
LAR   So that no one will wonder who I am, I will
    tell you in a few words.
I am the Lar Familiaris of this household
from which you saw me come. I
have inhabited this home now for many years and
    watched over
the father and grandfather of the man who now
    lives here.
His grandfather prayed to me and entrusted to me
a treasure of gold in complete secrecy; in the mid-
    dle of the hearth
he buried it begging me to guard it for him.
When he died—so greedy a nature was he—
he never was willing to reveal the treasure to his
    son,
and he preferred to leave him destitute
rather than to show the treasure to his son;
he left him only a moderate-sized piece of land
so that he could make a poor living by a great deal
    of work.
When the man who entrusted the gold to me died,
I began to observe whether the son in any way
would give me any more respect than his father
    had.
And in truth he cared for me less—
much less— and gave me less honor.
I did the same in return, so he likewise died.
He left a son who now lives here,
a man of the same character as his father and
    grandfather were.

Lines 23–39
This fellow has one daughter. To me daily
she always prays either with incense or wine or
    something else.
She gives me wreaths. Out of consideration for her
    honor
I have enabled this Euclio to find the treasure
in order that he might more easily give her in mar-
    riage, if he wished.

For a young man of highest rank has raped her.
This young man knows who it is whom he has
   wronged.
She doesn't know him nor moreover does her father
   know that she has been raped.
Today I shall make this old man from next door
ask for her as his wife. I shall do so with this in
   mind
that he who raped her may more easily wed her.
And this old man who will demand her as wife for
   himself
is the uncle of that young man
who violated her by night at the festival of Ceres.
But now this old man is shouting inside as usual.
He is forcing the old woman outside so that she
   won't know his secret.
I think he wants to check on his gold, to be sure it
   hasn't been stolen.

Lines 40–54

EUC. Get out, I say, go on, get out. By Hercules,
   you've got to get out of here,
you spy with prying eyes.
STA. Now why are you beating me, a poor
   wretch? EUC. So that you may be miserable,
and so that, wicked as you are, you may spend an
   old age worthy of yourself.
STA. Now why have you shoved me out of the
   house?
EUC. Should I give an accounting to you, you crop
   of whips?
Move back there away from the door. See, if you
   please,
how she creeps along. But do you know how
   things are with you?
By Hercules, today if I get hold of my club or whip,
I will increase that tortoise-like gait of yours.
STA. I wish the gods would drive me to hang
   myself
rather than to be a slave under these conditions at
   your house.
EUC. But how that cursed woman mutters to
   herself!
By Hercules, you insolent creature, I will dig out
   those eyes of yours,
so that you can't observe what I'm doing.

Lines 55–84

Go away now a little—a little more—a little—
   whoa!
Stand over there. By Hercules, if you move
a finger's breadth or a nail's breadth from that
   spot
or if you look around before I order you to,
by Hercules, immediately I will hand you over as a
   pupil to the cross.
I know that I have never seen anyone

more wicked than this old crone. I am terribly
   afraid
that she will trick me unawares from ambush,
or that she may become aware of where the gold is
   hidden.
She has eyes in the back of her head too, the bitch.
Now I have to go see whether the gold is where I
   hid it.
That gold troubles me, poor wretch that I am, in
   very many ways.
STA. By Castor what misfortune shall I say
has happened to my master or what madness
I cannot think; ten times a day just like this
he so often drives me out of the house, poor thing.
By Pollux, I don't know what disorder possesses
   that man.
He stays awake all night; then moreover in the
   daytime
he sits at home all day long, like a lame cobbler.
How shall I hide the disgrace of my master's
   daughter
whose time for giving birth is near
I cannot think; there is nothing better for me,
I think, than to make of myself one long letter
and bind my neck in a noose.
EUC. Now at last I am coming out of my house
   with an easy mind,
after I saw that all was safe within.
Go back inside right now and guard the house.
   STA. Of course?
I should keep guard inside? Lest someone steal
   the house?
For here at our house there is nothing else worth-
   while for thieves;
it is so full of nothingness and cobwebs.

Lines 85–119

EUC. It's a wonder that Jupiter doesn't make
   me King Philip
or Darius for your sake, you witch.
I want those cobwebs guarded for me.
I'm poor; I admit it, I endure it. What the gods
   give I bear.
Go on inside. Shut the door. I'll be back any
   minute.
Take care that you don't let any outsider into the
   house.
In case anyone asks for a light, I want the fire extinguished,
so that there will be no reason for anyone to try to
   obtain it from you.
For if the fire is alive, you will be extinguished at
   once.
Then say that the water has run out, if someone
   asks for any.
Knife, hatchet, pestle, mortar—

the kinds of utensils neighbors always ask to borrow,
say that thieves have come and stolen them.
Certainly I want no one to be let into my house
while I am absent. And I'm also telling you this:
even if Good Fortune comes along, don't let her inside.
STA. By Pollux, I think that even she would beware coming inside.
For she has never come near our house in any way.
EUC. Be quiet and go inside. STA. I'm quiet
and I'm going inside. EUC. If you please,
lock the doors with both bolts. I'll be back any
minute.
I'm tormented in my mind because I must go away
from home.
By Hercules I leave very unwillingly. But I know
what I'm doing.
For the official who is the master of our curia
said that he would distribute money to each man
individually.
If I pass it up and don't ask for it, everyone immediately
will suspect, I suppose, that I have money at
home.
For it is not likely that a poor man
would regard even a small amount of money of
such little value that he would not seek it.
For although I carefully keep all in ignorance so
they don't know,
everyone seems to know and to greet me
in a more friendly fashion than they used to before.
They come up to me, stand around, shake hands.
They keep asking me how I am, what I'm doing,
what affairs I carry on.
Now I'll go where I've started out for. Afterwards I
will
take myself home again as fast as I can.

Lines 120–150

EUN. Brother, I want you to think that I am
speaking these words
out of my loyalty and for the sake of your welfare,
as is right for a true sister to do,
although I am not unaware that we women are
considered tiresome.
For rightly we are all considered too talkative,
and certainly they say no quiet woman has been
found
either today or in any age.
But nevertheless, brother, think over this one
thing:
that I am the closest to you and you likewise are
closest to me.
So it is proper that we consider what is to the advantage of both of us,

that you look after and advise me and that I do
likewise for you.
Nor is it right that anything be kept hidden or
suppressed out of fear,
but rather we should share it equally with each
other.
For this reason I have led you outside here in private,
so that I could talk over your family business with
you here.
MEG. Give me your hand, best of women.
EUN. Where is she? Who is that best of women?
MEG. You. EUN. You say so? MEG. If you
deny it, so will I.
EUN. Indeed it befits you to speak the truth,
for no one can be chosen the best woman.
One is worse than the other, brother. MEG. I
agree with you,
and I have decided never to argue with you about
that.
EUN. Please
pay attention to me. MEG. My attention is yours.
Use it and
command if you want anything.
EUN. I am thinking of something which is to
your best interest.
I come to give you advice.
MEG. Sister, you are acting in your usual way.
EUN. I want to see this thing done.
MEG. What is it, sister? EUN. Something that
will be an everlasting
blessing to you—for the purpose of begetting children—
MEG. So may the gods grant— EUN. I want
you to get
married. MEG. Oh, I'm done for! EUN. Why is
that?

Lines 151–177

MEG. Because your words have knocked out my
brains,
sister. You are speaking stones.
EUN. Oh, do what your sister bids. MEG. If it
were pleasing, I would do it.
EUN. It is to your advantage. MEG. Indeed I
would die before I got married.
But under these conditions, if you are willing to
provide someone, I'll marry her—
who will come tomorrow and the day after, sister,
she'll be borne out for burial.
Are you willing to give me someone under these
conditions? Come on! Prepare the wedding
festivities!
EUN. I can give you [a bride] with a very large
dowry, brother,
but she is rather old, a woman of middle age.

If you bid me ask for her on your behalf, I will do so.

MEG. Are you willing for me to ask you a question? EUN. Yes, if you want to, ask.

MEG. The man who marries a middle-aged woman after his middle age,

if by chance this old woman becomes pregnant,

do you doubt that the name of Postumus is in store for the child?

Now, sister, I would cut short and diminish this labor of yours.

Thanks to the gods and our ancestors, I am rich enough.

Those great social connections, airs, abundant dowries,

shouting, commands, ivory-trimmed carriages, gowns, purple-dyed clothing—

I have no patience with these things which reduce husbands to servitude with such expenditures.

EUN. Tell me, if you please, who is it whom you wish to wed? MEG. I'll tell you.

Do you know this old man Euclio next door—a poor man?

EUN. By Castor, I do know him, not a bad fellow. MEG. I wish

to be engaged to his unwed daughter. Don't interrupt, sister.

I know what you are about to say: that she is poor. This poor girl pleases me.

EUN. May the gods make it turn out well. MEG. I hope the same. EUN. Well, do you want anything else with me? MEG. Good bye.

EUN. Goodbye to you too, brother. MEG. I will approach Euclio, if he's at home.

But there, I see him. The fellow is coming home from some place or other.

Lines 178–203

EUC. My mind had a foreboding that I was going for no purpose when I left home,

and so I went off unwillingly. For no one of the officials

came nor did the man in charge who had to distribute the money.

Now I am hastening to hurry home, for I am now here but my thoughts are at home.

MEG. Euclio, may you always be in good health and good fortune.

EUC. May the gods love you, Megadorus. MEG. How are you? Are you in as good health as you wish?

EUC. It is no accident when a rich man addresses a poor man cordially.

That fellow knows I have gold. For that reason he greets me rather cordially.

MEG. Do you say that you are well, Euclio? EUC. By Pollux, I'm not very well as to my financial circumstances.

MEG. By Pollux, if you have a contented spirit, you have enough to live life well.

EUC. By Hercules, the old woman has told him about the gold; it is plainly common knowledge.

I'll cut out her tongue and dig the eyes out of her head when I get home!

MEG. What are you saying to yourself? EUC. I'm complaining about my poverty.

I have a grown daughter, lacking a dowry and hence unmarriageable.

I can't marry her to anyone. MEG. Quiet, Euclio, cheer up!

A dowry will be given. You will be helped by me. Tell me if you need anything. Command me.

EUC. Now when he promises, he's after something. He gapes at my gold in order to swallow it.

In one hand he carries a stone, in the other he presents some bread.

I trust no rich man who is so markedly fawning upon a poor one.

When he stretches out his hand politely, he is heaping up some loss for me.

I know those octopuses who stick to anything that they have touched.

MEG. Listen to me for a moment, Euclio, if you can spare the effort. What I want

to address you about concerns our common interest, mine and yours. EUC. Oh, poor me,

the gold inside has been stolen from me. Now what he wants is this, I know,

to make an arrangement with me. But I'm going home.

MEG. Where are you going? EUC. I'll come back to you in a moment; for there is something I must go home and see.

Lines 204–235

MEG. I suppose, by Pollux, when I mention his daughter,

that he betroth her to me, he will think that he is being made fun of by me.

There is no one else in the ranks of the poor who is stingier than he.

EUC. The gods preserve me, my treasure is safe. It is safe if nothing is gone.

I was terribly afraid. Before I went inside, I was out of my mind.

I'm coming back to you, Megadorus, if you want me for anything. MEG. Thank you.

Please tell me what I ask you, unless it irks you.

EUC. Provided you don't ask me anything that it does not please me to answer.

MEG. Tell me, of what kind of family was I born? EUC. Of a good one.

MEG. What about my trustworthiness? EUC. Good. MEG. What about my actions? EUC. Neither bad nor wicked.

MEG. Do you know my age? EUC. I know it is great, just like your fortune.

MEG. Certainly, by Pollux, I have always thought you a citizen without any

evil vice and I still think so. EUC. He smells the gold.

What do you want of me now? MEG. Since you and I both know what the other is like—

may things turn out well for me and for you and for your daughter—

I ask your daughter's hand in marriage. Promise that this will be.

EUC. Ah, Megadorus, you are doing something not in keeping with your [previous] deeds:

mocking me, a poor man and one blameless in relation to you and yours.

For I have deserved from you neither in fact nor in words that you should do what you are doing.

MEG. By Pollux, I do not come to make fun of you, nor do I mock you,

nor do I think you worthy of such conduct. EUC. Why then do you ask for my daughter for yourself?

MEG. So that things might be better for you on my account and for me on account of you and yours.

EUC. This thought comes to my mind, Megadorus, that you are a rich man,

a powerful one, and likewise that I am a very impoverished poor man.

Now if I will have married my daughter to you, it occurs to me

that you are an ox and I am an ass: when I am yoked to you,

[and] when I am not able to carry my share of the burden, I, the ass, would lie in the mud.

You, the ox, would pay me no more attention than if I had never been born.

I would find you quite unfair and my own class would make fun of me.

I would have no firm footing with either group if there should be a divorce.

The asses would tear me with their bites, the oxen would gore me with their horns.

This is a great danger—to climb up from asses to oxen.

Lines 236–264

MEG. The closer you have joined yourself in kinship to the upper class

the better. Accept these terms, listen to me,

and promise her to me. EUC. But I have nothing to give as a dowry. MEG. Don't give one.

Provided she comes to me well brought up, she is sufficiently dowered.

EUC. I am speaking for this reason so you won't think I've found a treasure.

MEG. I know, don't tell me. Promise her. EUC. So be it! But by Jupiter,

am I destroyed? MEG. What's the matter? EUC. What clinked like metal just now?

MEG. I ordered them to dig up a garden at my house here. But where is the man?

He went off and didn't inform me. He scorns me,

because he sees that I want his friendship; he acts the way people do.

For if a wealthy man goes to seek a favor from a poor one,

the latter fears to go near him. Out of fear he takes it badly.

The same fellow, when the opportunity is gone, later desires it—too late.

EUC. By Hercules, if I do not hand you over to have your tongue torn out by the roots,

I command and am myself the authority for you to give me to whomever you wish to be castrated!

MEG. By Hercules, Euclio, I see that you think me a suitable person

to make fun of in my old age, and I don't deserve it.

EUC. No, by Pollux, Megadorus, I'm not doing so, nor, if I desired to, is there any chance of it.

MEG. What about it? Now will you betroth your daughter to me? EUC. On these terms,

with that dowry about which I told you. MEG. Then you do betroth her? EUC. I do.

MEG. May the gods favor this match. EUC. So may the gods act! See that you remember this,

that it is agreed that my daughter brings you no dowry.

MEG. I remember. EUC. But I know how you people are accustomed to twist things:

what has been agreed is not agreed and what is not agreed is agreed, just as it suits you.

MEG. There will be no controversy between us. But is there any reason

why the marriage can't take place today? EUC. On the contrary, by Pollux, it's a wonderful idea.

MEG. Then I'll go and make preparations. Do you want anything else of me? EUC. Just what we agreed. Go and farewell.

MEG. Hey, Strobilus, quickly follow me to the market—briskly now.

Lines 265–279

EUC. He's gone off there away from here. Immortal gods, I beg you, how powerful gold is!

I believe that he had already heard that I have a treasure at home.

He gapes after it. For this reason he had his mind set on a marriage connection.

Where are you, you who have now blabbed to all the neighbors

that I would give my daughter a dowry? Hey, Staphyla, I'm calling you.

Do you hear at all? Hurry and wash clean the utensils inside.

I have betrothed my daughter; today I will give her in marriage to Megadorus.

STA. May the gods favor it. But, by Castor, it's not possible. It's too sudden.

EUC. Shut up and go away. See to it that things have been taken care of by the time I return home from the forum.

And lock up the house. I'll be back here any minute. STA. What shall I do now?

Now disaster is close upon us—upon me and my master's daughter.

Now her disgrace, her giving birth, is at hand so that it will become public knowledge.

That which was concealed and hidden up to now, can no longer be so.

I'll go inside so that what my master has ordered will be done when he comes.

For, by Castor, I fear that I'm drinking ruin mixed with sorrow.

Lines 280–294

STR. After my master had shopped and hired these cooks

and flute girls in the forum, he told me

to divide up the provisions into two parts.

AN. By Hercules, I will tell you very openly you will not divide me.

If you want the whole of me to go anywhere, I will do it.

CON. Indeed, you pretty and chaste prostitute of the people,

if anyone wanted your behind, you would wish to be divided.

STR. And I had spoken in an entirely different sense there, Anthrax,

not what you allege. But my master is going to have

a wedding today. AN. Whose daughter is he marrying?

STR. The daughter of his neighbor, Euclio, from next door here.

Hence he ordered half of these provisions to be given to him,

and likewise one cook and one flute girl.

AN. Of course you are saying half there and half at home?

STR. Surely, just as you say.

Lines 294–326

AN. What? Couldn't the old man

shop for his daughter's wedding from his own pocket?

STR. Bah! AN. What's the matter? STR. You ask what's the matter?

Pumice isn't as dry as this old man.

AN. Do you say so? CON. It's just as you say! STR. . . . he thinks

that his fortune has perished and that he has been utterly destroyed.

Why he continually calls on the faith of gods and men

if any smoke escapes from a small log fire.

In fact, when he goes to sleep, he ties a bag over his mouth.

AN. Why? STR. So he won't perchance lose any breath while he sleeps.

AN. Does he even block up his lower opening

so that he won't perchance lose any wind while he sleeps?

STR. I believe it is right that you believe me just as I believe you.

AN. Nay I certainly do believe you. STR. But do you know what else he does?

By Hercules, he grieves over pouring out the water when he washes.

AN. Do you think that a big sum of money can be begged

out of this old man, that he will give it to us so that we can be freed?

STR. By Hercules, if you should ask to borrow his hunger, he'll never give it.

Why once the barber had cut off his nails.

He collected them and carried away all the clippings.

AN. By Pollux, you're talking about a mortal who is a really miserly miser.

STR. But do you think that's as stingy and wretched as he is?

Once a kite snatched an appetizer from him.

That man went complaining bitterly to the magistrate.

There he began to demand, complaining and wailing,

that he be permitted to arraign the kite.

There are six hundred more examples I could mention if I had time.

But which of you is quicker? Tell me.

AN. I am, and much better, too. STR. I am asking for a cook, not a thief.

AN. Well, I mean a cook. STR. What do you say? CON. I am just as you see.

AN. That one is only a market day cook. He's accustomed

to go to cook on market day. CON. Do you, a five letter man, insult me? You t h i e f ! AN. You are also a thief—a triple rogue.

Lines 327–330
STR. Shut up at once, you, and take whichever lamb is fatter.

Away from here and go on inside to our house. AN. Okay. STR. You, Congrio,

take this one and go inside there, and you follow him.

The rest of you go here to our house.

Lines 330–349
CON. By Hercules, unjustly

you have made the division: they have the fatter lamb.

STR. But the fatter flute girl will be given to you.

Go on with him, Phrygia. But you, Eleusium,

go in here at our house. CON. O clever Strobilus, have you shoved me off here on the stingiest of men?

Where if I ask for anything I will ask to the point of hoarseness before

anything is given to me. STR. You're a fool and there's no gratitude

in doing a favor for you, since what one does is of no avail.

CON. How so? STR. You're asking me? Now in the first place at that house

over there there will not be a crowd in your way. If you want to use anything,

bring it from your own house so you don't waste your effort in asking.

However, here at our house there is a great crowd and a whole household—

furniture, gold, clothes, silver vessels.

If anything is lost there, certainly (because I know

that you can easily restrain yourself, if nothing is available)

they would say: the cooks have stolen it, catch them,

tie them up, beat them, put them in a pit.

None of this will happen to you there since

there is nothing to steal. Follow me this way.
CON. I'm following.

Lines 350–370
STR. Hey, Staphyla, come out and open the door. STA. Who's calling?

STR. Strobilus. STA. What do you want? STR. That you receive these cooks

and flute girl and food for the wedding.

Megadorus ordered me to send them to Euclio.

STA. Are they going to arrange a marriage for Ceres?

STR. How so? STA. Because I know that no wine has been brought.

STR. But it will be brought if he himself returns from the forum.

STA. There's no wood here at our house. CON. Are there rafters?

STA. There are, by Pollux. CON. Then there is wood. So don't hunt for it outside.

STA. What's that, you filthy scum? Although you're devoted to Vulcan,

for the sake of dinner and because of your wages are you asking to burn down our house?

CON. I'm not asking that. STR. Take them inside. STA. You follow me.

STR. Take care. I'll go see what the cooks are doing.

By Pollux, it is my greatest concern today to look after them.

Unless I could arrange this one plan that they cook dinner in a pit;

hence we might bring the cooked dinner up from below in baskets.

If, however, they eat below what they cooked,

those above are unfed and those below, fed.

But I'm just talking here as if there were no work to be done,

when there are so many robbers in my house.

Lines 371–397
EUC. Now, I did want to strengthen my spirits today,

so that I would enjoy myself at my daughter's wedding.

I go to the meat market, I ask for fish; they turn out to be

expensive; so too is the lamb, the beef,

the veal, the dolphin, the pork: all expensive.

And all the more so because I have no money.

I go away from there angry because I have nothing with which to buy.

Thus I cheated all those dirty fellows.

Then I began to think to myself

on the way home: if you squander money on a holiday,

you must go without on an ordinary day, unless you live sparingly.

After I declared this reasoning to my stomach and to my heart,

my mind came to this conclusion,

that I should give my daughter in marriage with as little expense as possible.

Now I have bought a little frankincense and these floral garlands;

these will be placed on our hearth for the Lar

so that he may make my daughter's marriage a prosperous one.

But why do I see our house standing open?

And a racket within. Am I, poor thing, being
   robbed?
CON. Get a larger pot, if you can, from a
neighbor. This is too small, it can't hold it all.
   EUC. Oh gods,
I'm done for, by Hercules! My gold is being taken.
   A pot is being sought.
Surely I'm ruined, unless I hurry to run inside
   here.
Apollo, I pray, help and aid me!
Pursue with your arrows these thieves of my trea-
   sure,
you who already before now helped in such an af-
   fair.
But do I hesitate to rush in before I am thoroughly
   ruined?

Lines 398–405
AN. Dromo, scale the fish. You, Macherio,
debone the eel and the moray as fast as you can.
I will try to borrow a breadpan next door
from Congrio. You'll return that cock to me, if you
   have any sense,
smoother than a plucked dancer.
But what clamor is arising next door?
By Hercules, the cooks, I suppose, are doing their
   duty.
I shall flee inside so that the same tumult won't
   spread here.

Lines 406–424
CON. Oho, citizens, people, residents, neighbors,
   foreigners, all of you
make way where I can flee! Clear the streets!
I have never except today come to a bacchanal to
   cook for Bacchantes.
They have badly beaten wretched me and my
   pupils with clubs.
I am sore all over and am completely done in.
   That old man has used me as a punching bag.
Oho, by Hercules, I'm ruined, wretch that I am!
He's opening the bacchanal. He's here.
He's pursuing me. I know what I shall do.
The master himself has taught me,
for I have nowhere in the world seen wood fur-
   nished so prettily.
And so he has driven all of us, me and these
   pupils, outside loaded with clubs.
EUC. Come back! Where are you fleeing now?
   Stop him! Stop him! CON. Why are you
   shouting, stupid?
EUC. Because I will now report you to the au-
   thorities. CON. Why?
EUC. Because you have a knife. CON. It befits
   a cook. EUC. Why did you threaten
me? CON. I think it was badly done that I
   didn't stab your side.

EUC. There is no man alive today more wicked
   than you,
nor anyone whom I would more willingly ill treat
   more—and deliberately.
CON. By Pollux, even if you were silent, the situation is clear: the facts themselves are witness.
Your beatings have made me much softer than any
   dancer.
But why have you touched me, you beggarly fellow?
   EUC. What's that?
Do you even ask? Or because I have acted less
   than fairly?

Lines 425–448
CON. Stop that! But, by Hercules, it will be
   with great harm to you, if this head has any
   sense.
EUC. By Pollux, I don't know what may be afterwards. Now your head senses.
But what business did you have in my house
in my absence, unless I had so ordered? I want to
   know. CON. Quiet then.
Because we came to cook the wedding feast.
   EUC. What the devil do you care
whether I eat raw or cooked food, unless you are
   my guardian?
CON. I want to know whether you will allow or
   not allow us to cook the dinner here?
EUC. Likewise I want to know whether my
   property will be safe in my home?
CON. I'd like to take back my property safe and
   sound that I brought to your house.
I'm very well satisfied with my own things; still
   less do I seek yours. EUC. I know, don't lecture me, I know.
CON. What is it on account of which you prohibit
   us from cooking the dinner here?
What have we done, what have we said to you
   otherwise than as you would wish?
EUC. Do you even keep asking, you rascal, who
   turn all the corners
of my house and rooms into a thoroughfare?
If you had been at the hearth, there where your
   business was,
you would not be carrying off a broken head. It
   was done to you as you deserve.
So that you can now know my opinion,
if you approach hither nearer to the door, unless I
   order it,
I will see to it that you are the most miserable
   man alive.
Now you know my opinion. CON. Where are you
   going? Come back again.
So may Laverna love me well, unless you at once
   order my utensils returned

to me, I will slander you in a shrill voice in front of your house.

What shall I do now? By Pollux, I certainly came here under an evil omen.

I was hired for a wage: I need more than my pay [just] for the doctor's bills.

Lines 449–474

EUC. This pot, by Hercules, wherever I go will be with me. I will carry it with me,

and I will never allow it to be in such great danger there.

All right, now all of you, go on inside, cooks as well as flute girls.

Even take inside, if you wish, a crowd of young slaves as well.

Cook, act, hurry around now as much as you wish.

CON. Just on time, after you have filled my head with cracks with your club.

EUC. Go on inside. Your work was hired here, not a speech.

CON. Hey, old man, by Hercules, I'll seek reimbursement from you for that beating.

I was hired just now to cook, not to be beaten!

EUC. Take me to court, don't be a pain. Go cook the dinner,

or go away from the house to the devil. CON. You go to hell.

EUC. He has gone off from here. Oh, immortal gods, that fellow begins a bold deed

who, as a poor man, has any dealings or business with a rich man,

just as Megadorus tempts me, poor thing, in every way,

who pretends to send me cooks here out of regard for me;

he (really) sent them for this reason, that they might steal this pot from me, unfortunate fellow.

Just as badly did my domestic cock inside

very nearly ruin me, that cock that was the private property of the old woman.

Where this [pot] had been buried, he began to scratch about with his nails

on all sides. Why waste words? He excited my heart so!

I grab a club, I knock off the cock's head, a thief caught in the act!

I believe, by Pollux, that the cooks promised a reward to that cock

if he had revealed this [gold]. I took the opportunity out of their hands.

Why talk on? I had a fight with the cock.

But look, Megadorus my neighbor is coming from the forum.

I wouldn't dare to pass him by now, but I must stop and chat.

Lines 475–504

MEG. I have told many friends my plan
about this arrangement. The daughter of Euclio
they praise. It was wisely done and with good planning.

For in my opinion if the rest of the wealthier
men should do the same thing, namely marry
undowered daughters of poor men,
the state would become much more harmonious,
and we would experience less envy than we do,
and our wives would fear punishment more than they do,
and we would have less expense than we do.
That is best for the majority of the people.
Argument arises against the minority of greedy men
to whose greedy and insatiable minds
there is neither law nor cobbler who can set a limit.
For should anyone say, "Where would those wealthy dowered women
wed if this right is granted to poor women?"
Wherever they please, let them marry, provided a dowry is not made their companion.
If it were done this way, they would prepare for themselves better
habits, which they would bring instead of a dowry—better habits than they bring now.
I suppose that mules, which now exceed horses in price,
would be cheaper than Gallic nags.
EUC. So may the gods love me! How gladly I listen to him!
He speaks very charmingly in support of thrift.
MEG. Therefore no woman would say, "Certainly I brought a dowry to you
much larger than your own fortune.
Of course it is fair that purple cloth and gold be given to me,
slaves, mules, mule-drivers, man servants,
young salutation carriers, vehicles in which I may ride."
EUC. How well he knows the actions of matrons!
I wish he were made the overseer of women's morals.

Lines 505–535

MEG. Now wherever you go, you may see more wagons in front of a [city] house
than in the country when you go to your farm.
But this is fine compared to when tradesmen seek their money.
There stands the launderer, the embroiderer, the goldsmith, the wool dealer,
dealers in borders for tunics, [dealers in] outer tunics,
dyers of flame-colored, violet, and brown shades,

or makers of long-sleeved garments or . . . ,
retailers of linens, cobblers,
sedentary shoe and slipper makers.
Sandal makers stand around, as do sellers of
    mallow-colored garments.
Dyers are seeking their money, as are clothes
    menders.
Lingerie makers stand about along with makers of
    underwear.
Now you might think them paid off. There come
    and ask for money
three hundred more, when there stand in the
    atrium creditors,
weavers of fringes, box makers.
They are led in, money is paid. Now you may
    think them paid off,
when in come dyers of saffron-colored robes,
or there is always some other nuisance seeking
    some money.
EUC. I would speak to him, if I weren't afraid he
    would stop
mentioning the customs of women; now I will let
    him alone.
MEG. When the money is paid out to all these
    sellers of trash,
then finally comes a soldier. He is seeking money.
You go to your banker and make up an accounting.
The soldier stands there without breakfast; he
    thinks money is going to be paid.
When the account has been argued out with the
    banker,
the master in addition even owes money to the
    banker.
Hope is postponed for the soldier for another day.
These and many other inconveniences and un-
    bearable expenses
occur in cases of large dowries.
For she who is undowered is in her husband's
    power;
dowered wives punish their husbands with pain
    and loss.

Lines 536–560

But look! My neighbor in front of the house. How
    goes it, Euclio?
EUC. I have devoured your words with the
    greatest of pleasure.
MEG. Did you really hear them? EUC. Every-
    thing all the way from the beginning.
MEG. In my opinion, however, you would be act-
    ing considerably more properly
if you would spruce yourself up for your daughter's
    wedding.
EUC. People who have elegance in proportion to
    their assets and
pomp in accordance with their wealth remember
    whence they have come.

By Pollux, Megadorus, neither for me nor for any
    poor man
has a fortune been piled up at home any better
    than people think.
MEG. Nay, what you have is enough, and may
    the gods make it
more and more, and may they protect that which
    you now have.
EUC. That phrase, "which you now have," does
    not please me.
He knows that I have this [gold] as well as I do
    myself. The old woman has made it known.
MEG. Why do you remove yourself from our dis-
    cussion off by yourself?
EUC. By Pollux, I was intending to level a just
    complaint against you. MEG. What is it?
EUC. You ask me what it is? You who have
    filled
all the corners in my house with thieves, poor me,
you who have sent inside into my house five hun-
    dred cooks
with six hands apiece, of the race of Geryon.
If Argus were to watch over them, Argus who was
    all eyes,
whom once Juno assigned as a guard for Io,
he never would be able to watch over them. In
    addition, the flute girl,
who all by herself, if the Corinthian spring of
    Pirene
gushed with wine, could drink it dry.
Then, moreover, the food— MEG. By Pollux, it's
    enough for a legion!

Lines 561–586

MEG. I even sent a lamb. EUC. I know well
    enough that
nowhere is there any beast more curious than that
    lamb.
MEG. I want to know from you how that lamb is
    a cūriō.
EUC. Because it is all skin and bones, it is so
    thin from care.
Why you can see the guts of that living beast in
    the sunlight;
it's as transparent as a Punic lantern.
MEG. I bought it to be slaughtered. EUC.
    Then it is best
that you arrange for its funeral; for I believe it is
    already dead.
MEG. Euclio, I want to drink with you today.
EUC. By Hercules, I will certainly not drink with
    you today. MEG. But I will order
a large jar of old wine to be brought from my cellar.
EUC. By Hercules, I don't want it, for I have de-
    cided to drink water.
MEG. I'll make you nicely drunk today, as I live
    and breathe,

you who have decided to drink water. EUC. I
know what he's up to.

His purpose is to put me down with wine

so that afterwards he'll change the dwelling place
of this (gold) that I have.

I will prevent it, for I will hide it elsewhere outside.

I'll see to it that he wastes his effort and his wine
at the same time.

MEG. I'm going home to wash up in order to perform a sacrifice, unless you want me for anything.

EUC. By Pollux, pot, you certainly have many
enemies,

as also has that gold that has been entrusted to
you.

Now this is the best thing for me to do, to carry
you away,

pot, into the shrine of Faith. There I'll neatly hide
you.

Faith, you know me and I know you. Beware, if
you please,

that you don't change your name, if I entrust this
to you.

I shall go to you, Faith, relying on your trust.

Lines 587–615

L.S. This is the act of an honest slave, to do that
which I persist in doing,

so that he may not consider his master's command
as a delay or burden to himself.

For the slave who expects to serve his master to
his (master's) satisfaction

engages speedily (as is fitting) in his master's affairs and slowly in his own.

And if he becomes drowsy, let him do so in such a
way that he [still] thinks himself a slave.

Let him thoroughly learn his master's wish so that
his eyes may see what his expression indicates.

What his master orders let him hasten to pursue
more quickly than four-horse chariots.

The one who will take care for these things will
avoid the punishment of a whipping.

Nor will he ever by his effort shine up shackles
[i.e., by rubbing his chained limbs against the
fetters].

Now my master loves the daughter of this poor
man Euclio here.

It has been announced to my master that she is
being married to Megadorus there.

He has sent me hither to watch so that he may
share in [knowledge of] what is happening.

Now without suspicion I will sit here on the sacred
altar;

from here I will be able to observe what they do
both in this house and in that.

EUC. You must be careful not to point out to
anyone that my gold is there, Faith.

I don't fear that anyone may find it, so well has it
been secreted in its hiding place.

By Pollux, truly he would get a pretty reward there
if anyone finds

that pot loaded with gold; but I ask you this,
Faith, that you prohibit it.

Now I'll wash up so that I may perform the sacrifice and not delay my neighbor

from leading my daughter home immediately when
he summons her.

Faith, now earnestly [I beg]; see to it that I may
carry off the pot safe and

sound from you.

I have entrusted my gold to your trust. It has
been placed in your grove and shrine.

Lines 616–638

L.S. Immortal gods, what deed have I heard this
man mention?

That he has hidden a pot full of gold here inside
the shrine of Faith.

Take care, I beg you, not to be faithful to that fellow rather than to me.

And he is the father, as I think, of the girl whom
my master loves.

I'll leave here and go inside. I'll examine the
shrine thoroughly (and see) if I can find anywhere

the gold, while this fellow is busy. But if I find it,
O Faith,

I will dedicate to you a full quart jar of mixed wine
and honey.

So will I do for you, but I'll drink it myself when
I've done it.

EUC. It is not by accident that a raven cawed to
me just now on the left;

at the same time he scratched the ground with his
claws and croaked with his voice.

Immediately my heart began to dance

and to give a jump into my breast. But do I delay
to run?

EUC. Come outside, you worm, who have just
now crept from under the earth,

you who just now were able to be found nowhere.
Now when you are found, you perish.

By Pollux, you trickster, now I will welcome you in
miserable ways.

L.S. What in the world is agitating you? What
business have you with me, old man?

Why are you striking me? Why are you dragging
me away? Why do you beat me?

EUC. You most-worthy-of-a-beating, do you even
ask, you who are not [just] a thief but a triple
thief?

L.S. What have I taken from you? EUC. Give it back here, if you please. L.S. What do you want me to give back? EUC. You ask?

L.S. Indeed I have taken nothing from you. EUC. But that which you had taken for yourself, hand it over!

Are you going to do it? L.S. What should I do? EUC. You can't carry it away. L.S. What do you want for yourself?

EUC. Put it back. L.S. By Pollux, I believe that's where you are accustomed to give it, old man.

EUC. Put it back, if you please. Stop making jokes. This is no trifling matter.

Lines 639–660

L.S. What shall I put back? Say what it is by name.

By Hercules, I certainly have not taken or touched anything. EUC. Show me your hands.

L.S. Here you are. I've shown them. Here they are. EUC. I see. Come show the third hand also.

L.S. Devils, intemperance, and madness are stirring up this old man.

Are you doing injury to me? EUC. I admit it, the greatest, because you are not being hanged.

And this will also happen, unless you confess. L.S. What shall I confess to you?

EUC. What have you taken from here? L.S. May the gods destroy me, if I have taken anything of yours,

or if I hadn't wished to have taken something. EUC. Come then, you must shake out your pallium—

L.S. As you wish. EUC. I'm afraid you have it in your undergarments. L.S. Try wherever you please.

EUC. Bah, you rascal, how kindly [you allow me], so that I may not know you've stolen it!

I know these tricks. Come on, again, show me your right

hand. L.S. Here. EUC. Now show the left. L.S. Why I even offer you both together.

EUC. Now I'll stop searching. Return it to me. L.S. What should I return? EUC. Oh, you're acting like a fool.

Certainly you have it. L.S. I have it? What do I have? EUC. I'm not saying. You're too eager to hear.

What you have of mine, return it. L.S. You're crazy. You've searched

as you wished and you haven't found anything of yours in my possession.

EUC. Wait, wait! Who's in there? Who else was inside with you at the same time?

By Hercules, I'm done for. That fellow is now causing a disturbance within. If I let this fellow go, he'll get away.

After all I have already searched this one thoroughly. He has nothing. Go where you wish.

L.S. May Jupiter and the gods damn you. EUC. Not badly did he give thanks.

I'll go inside and throttle the throat of your partner.

Are you fleeing away from my sight? Are you going or not? L.S. I'm going.

EUC. Watch out, if you please, that I don't see you again.

Lines 661–681

L.S. I would prefer to perish of an evil death
rather than to fail to trick that old man today.
For he will not now dare to bury the gold here.
I suppose he will now carry it out with him and change its location.
Aha, the door creaked. See the old man is carrying the gold outside.
Meanwhile I'll move over here near the door.
EUC. I thought that there was by far the greatest trust
in Faith, who has very nearly cheated me.
Unless that raven had come to my assistance, I would have perished, poor thing.
By Hercules, I wish terribly that that raven would come to me,
the one who gave evidence, so that I might say something good
to it; for giving it something to eat is the same as throwing food away.
Now I'm considering a lonely spot where I can hide this.
The grove of Silvanus is remote, outside the wall [of the city],
crowded with a thick clump of willows. There I'll find a place.
I've decided I'll trust Silvanus rather than Faith.
L.S. Oh, good, good, the gods want me safe and sound.
Now I'll run ahead there, and I'll climb into some tree,
and from there I'll observe where the old man puts the gold.
Although my master ordered me to await him here,
I've decided I prefer to seek punishment—along with profit.

Lines 682–700

LYC. I've told you, mother; you understand equally with me
about Euclio's daughter. Now I beg you

and implore you again, mother, what I had already begged.

Tell it to my uncle, my mother.

EUN. You know that I want done what you want done,

and I'm sure that I can gain that request from my brother;

and the cause is just, if it is as you say

that you were drunk and raped the girl.

LYC. Would I lie to your face, my mother?

PH. I am dying, my nurse! I beg you, my womb aches.

Juno Lucina, [I ask] your trust! LYC. Oh, my mother,

I see something more convincing to you. She cries out, she is giving birth.

EUN. Come along inside with me, my son, to my brother,

so that I may get from him what you beg me to obtain.

LYC. Go along, I'll follow you in a moment, mother. But my slave

. . . I wonder where he is, the one whom I had ordered

to wait for me here. Now I am thinking to myself:

if he is carrying out his task, it is wrong for me to be angry at him.

I'll go inside where an assembly about my life is being held.

Lines 701–726

L.S. The griffins, who inhabit the golden mountains, in riches

I alone surpass. For the rest of those kings

I do not wish to mention, beggarly fellows.

I am the renowned King Philip. Oh delightful day!

For as soon as I left here, I arrived much before him

and hid myself in a tree way ahead of him,

and there I waited [to see] where the old man was hiding the gold.

When he went off, I climb down from the tree,

I dig up the pot full of gold. Then from that place

I see the old man return; he doesn't see me,

for I turned a little away beyond the road.

Aha, there he is. I'll go home to hide this.

EUC. I'm ruined! I've perished! I'm done for! Where shall I run? Where shall I not run? Hold him, hold him! Whom? Who?

I don't know! I see nothing! I'm going blind and indeed where I am going or where I am or who I am

I cannot search out for certain in my mind. I beg you, I implore,

I invoke you, aid me and show me the man who stole it away.

What do you say? I have decided to trust you, for I know from your expression that you are a good man.

What is it? Why do you laugh? I know you all, I know that there are many thieves here

who hide themselves in whitened garments and sit as if they were honest men.

Ah, no one of these has it? You have killed me. Tell me then, who has it? You don't know?

Alas, poor me, I have perished miserably.

Terribly ruined, I go in sorry plight;

so much of moaning, misfortune, and grief

this day has brought me—and hunger and poverty.

I am the most ruined man of all in the world.

What need have I for life, I have lost

so much gold that I guarded

carefully? I have cheated myself

and my soul and my Genius.

Now others rejoice

at my misfortune and loss. I can't stand it.

Lines 727–751

LYC. What man, tell me, is wailing, complaining

and sorrowing here in front of our house?

It is Euclio, I think. I am completely a goner. The whole thing is out in the open.

He knows that his daughter has already given birth, I think. Now I don't know

whether I should go away or stay or go up to him or flee. What should I do? By Pollux, I don't know.

EUC. What man is speaking here? LYC. It's I—[and I'm] miserable. EUC. No, I'm

[the one who's] miserable, and utterly destroyed,

a man to whom so many evils and sadness have befallen. LYC. Cheer up.

EUC. How, I ask you, can I? LYC. Because that outrage that

troubles your spirit, I did it and I confess it. EUC. What do I hear from you?

LYC. That which is true. EUC. What evil have I earned from you, young man,

that you would act thus and ruin me and my children?

LYC. A god was my instigator, he attracted me to her. EUC. How?

LYC. I confess that I have done wrong and I know that I fully deserve the blame.

So I come to beg you this that you pardon me with equanimity.

EUC. Why did you dare to do this, to touch that which was not yours?

LYC. What do you want to happen? It was done; it cannot be undone.

I believe the gods wished it; for if they did not wish it, it wouldn't have happened, I know.

EUC. But I believe that the gods wished that I chain you up at my house and kill you.

LYC. Don't say that. EUC. Why then did you touch what was mine against my will?

LYC. Because I acted through the fault of wine and love. EUC. Most brazen fellow,

that you have dared to come here to me with such an excuse, shameless one!

For if this is justice—that you can excuse this [crime]—,

we could openly snatch gold from women in broad daylight.

Afterwards, if we were caught, we would make the excuse that we were drunk

and had acted out of love. Too cheap are wine and love,

if we were allowed to do whatever we wish without punishment while drunk or in love.

Lines 752–776

LYC. But I come on my own to pray to you on account of my stupidity.

EUC. Men are not pleasing to me who apologize when they have done wrong.

You knew that she was not yours. You ought not to have touched her.

LYC. Therefore because I dared to touch her, I do not in the least object to

having her. EUC. You would have what is mine against my will?

LYC. I do not demand her against your will, but I think she must be mine.

In fact you will soon find, I tell you, that she must be mine, Euclio.

EUC. Unless you bring back— LYC. What should I bring back to you? EUC. That of mine that you stole.

By Hercules, I'll now take you to the praetor and bring a charge against you.

LYC. I take something of yours? From where? What is it? EUC. May Jupiter love you just as much as you don't know. LYC. [I don't know] unless you tell me

what you seek.

EUC. The pot of gold, I say, I am demanding back from you, that you confessed

you have stolen from me. LYC. By Pollux, I neither said nor did so. EUC. You deny it?

LYC. Of course I flatly deny it. For neither the gold nor what that pot is

do I know or have I known. EUC. That pot which you stole from the grove of Silvanus, give it to me!

Go, bring it back! Rather I will share half of it with you.

Although to me you are a thief, I will not be troublesome. But go, bring it back.

LYC. You're crazy to call me a thief. I thought, Euclio,

that you had found out about something else that does concern me.

There is something very important that I want to talk to you about at your leisure, if you're free.

EUC. Speak out in good faith. You didn't steal that gold? LYC. I swear it.

EUC. And you don't know who stole it? LYC. That also I swear. EUC. And if you learn

who stole it, you'll tell me? LYC. I will. EUC. And you won't get

a share for yourself from him who has it or protect the thief? LYC. So I swear.

EUC. If you are lying about it? LYC. Then may great Jupiter do with me what he wishes.

Lines 777–802

EUC. That's enough. Come now tell me what you want. LYC. If you don't know who I am,

to what family I belong— This Megadorus here is my uncle,

my father was Antimachus. I am called Lyconides.

My mother is Eunomia. EUC. I know your family. Now what do you want? I wish

to know. LYC. You have a daughter. EUC. Yes, she is at home there.

LYC. I believe you have betrothed her to my uncle. EUC. You understand the situation.

LYC. He ordered me to announce to you now the cancellation of this engagement.

EUC. A cancellation with wedding arrangements prepared and ready?

May all the immortal gods and all the goddesses damn that man,

on account of whom today I lost so much gold, poor thing that I am.

LYC. Cheer up, don't curse. Now may this situation turn out well and

happily for you and your daughter—so may the gods bring it about!. Say it.

EUC. So may the gods bring it about! LYC. May the gods bring it about on my

behalf also. Now listen.

A man who admits blame in himself—no such one is of such little worth,

but that he is ashamed and apologizes. Now I beg you, Euclio,

that if I have foolishly sinned against you or your daughter,

that you pardon me and give her as a wife to me, as the laws order.

I confess that I did an injury to your daughter

at the night festival of Ceres because of wine and the prompting of youth.

EUC. Alas, what crime do I hear from you? LYC. Why are you exclaiming,

you whom I have made a grandfather at your daughter's wedding?

For your daughter has given birth ten months later; count it up.

For this reason and for my sake my uncle has sent the cancellation.

Go inside, see whether it is as I say. EUC. I'm completely ruined!

So very many misfortunes attach themselves to my troubles.

I'll go inside that I may know what part of this story is true. LYC. I'll soon follow you.

Lines 803–823

LYC. This affair seems nearly to be in the shallow waters of safety.

Now I do not know where I should say my slave . . . is.

Unless I wait here, however, for a little; afterwards

I'll follow him inside. Now in the meantime I'll give him time to inquire into

my actions from the old nurse and attendant of his daughter. She knows the situation.

L.S. Immortal gods, with what joys and with what great ones you have endowed me!

I have found a four-pound pot loaded with gold. Who is richer than I?

What man in all Athens is there to whom the gods are more propitious?

LYC. Just now I seem to hear the voice of someone speaking. L.S. Aha,

do I see my master? LYC. Do I see this slave of mine?

L.S. It is himself. LYC. It is no other. L.S. I'll approach him. LYC. I'll step up to him.

I believe that he, as I ordered, has approached the old woman herself, the nurse of the girl.

L.S. Why don't I tell him that I have found the booty and speak out?

Then I'll beg him to free me. I'll go and speak to him.

I found— LYC. What did you find? L.S. Not what boys shout

that they have found in a bean. LYC. Still your usual self? You're joking with me.

L.S. Master, wait. Now I'll speak to you. Listen. LYC. Come, then speak. L.S. I have found today,

master, extraordinary riches. LYC. Where? L.S. A four-pound pot, I say, full of gold.

LYC. What deed do I hear from you? L.S. I stole it from this old fellow, Euclio.

LYC. Where is the gold? L.S. In a chest at my house. Now I wish to be freed.

Lines 824–831

LYC. I should free you,

you rascal, abounding in crime?

L.S. Go on, master, I know what you're doing.

By Hercules, I have cleverly tested your mind. You were already planning to snatch it away.

What would you have done, if I had found it? LYC. You can't get away with joking.

Come on, hand over the gold. L.S. I should hand over the gold? LYC. Hand it over, I say, so it may be returned to him. L.S. From where?

LYC. What you just now confessed was in a chest. L.S. By Hercules, I am accustomed to chatter nonsense.

Such is the way I talk. LYC. But do you know how [I will handle you]? L.S. By Hercules, even kill me. Never will you take it away from me.

I.   For those saffron dresses, girdles, a wife's expense

II.   How it gnaws at a man.

III.   EUC. I was digging ten holes at a time in one day.

IV.   EUC. Neither by night nor by day was I ever at rest; now I'll sleep.

V.   L.S. Those who serve raw vegetables to me, let them add a fish sauce.

*　*　*

TRANSLATIONS OF EXERCISES

The following are sample translations of the exercises on pages 80–82 of the student's book. Specific line references are given after the translations below to passages that may serve as models for vocabulary and syntax.

1–39

1. Ego sum Lar familiāris quī avum patremque virī nunc in hāc domō habitantis servāvit. (2–5)

2. Ubi avus thēsaurum aurī in focō dēfōdit, rogāvit (mē) ut eum (or id) servārem. (6–8)

3. Ille erat tam avidus ut aurum fīliō suō nōn indicāret neque fīlius Eucliōnī (id) indicāvit (or commōnstrāvit). (9–12)

4. Quamquam mē honōribus nōn impertīvērunt, cotīdiē fīlia familiae mihi supplicat et dōna dat. (18–25)

5. Eucliō auxiliō meō aurum repperit ut adulēscēns Phaedriam dūcat. (26–28)

6. Phaedria ab adulēscente dē summō locō quem nōn scit compressa est. (28–30)

7. Hodiē avunculus illīus adulēscentis Phaedriam uxōrem sibi poscet. (34–36)

40–119

1. Eucliō suam servam Staphylam ex aedibus extrūdit ācribus cum verbīs. (44)

2. Metuēns nē Staphyla thēsaurum reperīret, Eucliō eum esse salvum scīre magnopere voluit. (65–66 and 79–80)

3. Cum Staphyla dē probrō Phaedriae sciat, prō puellā et prō sē timet. (74–78)

4. Thēsaurō īnspectō, Eucliō ad forum abīre parat anumque nēminem in aedīs mittere iubet. (90–100)

5. Eucliō omnīs dē thēsaurō domī absconditō scīre et ergō sē benignius salūtāre sentit. (113–115)

120–279

1. Eunomia suum frātrem Megadōrum uxōrem domum dūcere dēbēre arbitrātur. (149–150)

2. Megadōrus fēminam cum maximā dōte ab Eunomiā oblātam negat sed sē domum dūcere fīliam pauperis Eucliōnis etiam sine dōte velle dīcit. (158–174)

3. Ut Eucliō dē thēsaurō sollicitus ab forō redit, Megadōrus fīliam eius uxōrem poscit. (178–181 and 219)

4. Eucliō Megadōrum dē aurō repperisse crēdit quod hominem dīvem grātiam pauperis petere temerārium nōn est. (184–185 and 247)

5. Tandem senex fīliam dēspondet hīs lēgibus, ut nē quid dōtis dētur. (255–258)

280–475

1. Coquī in forō ab Megadōrō conductī cum tībīnicīs et agnīs et obsōniīs ab Strobīlō īnferuntur. (280–282)

2. Variīs fābulīs dē Eucliōne parcō nārrātīs, Strobīlus comitēs et obsōnia inter familiās Megadōrī Eucliōnisque dīvidit. (280–330)

3. Congriō ūnā cum discipulīs forās (or domō) exēgitur (or extrūditur) ab Eucliōne quī ā forō rediit cum tūsculō modo et corōnīs flōreīs minimō sūmptū ēmptīs. (384–385 and 414)

4. Aulā aurī domō ēlātā, Eucliō Congriōnem coctum inīre sinit. (449–453)

5. Eucliō gallum Staphylae obtruncāvit, quod eum fūrēs adiuvāre cōnārī putāvit. (469–471)

475–587

1. Amīcī Megadōrī putant cōnsilium dē uxōre indōtātā esse bonum. (475–477)

2. Megadōrus hoc cōnsilium prōpōnit ut cīvitās multō concordior fīat cum dīvitēs pauperum fīliās indōtātās domum dūcant. (478–484)

3. Eucliō auscultāns Megadōrum, verba dē mōribus mulierum dōtātārum probat. (496–497 and 503–504)

4. Eucliō satis nitidus nūptiīs fīliae nōn vidētur. (539–540)

5. Megadōrum dē aurō intellegere suspicāns, Eucliō thēsaurum Fideī cuius fānum est proximum concrēdere cōnstituit. (548 and 580–586)

588–681

1. Lyconidis servus missus est speculātum quae fīunt. (603–605)

2. Hic servus thēsaurum in fānō Fideī ab Eucliōne abstrūsum surripere cōnātur. (616–623)

3. Croccientī corvō monitus, Eucliō servum rogat num quid ē fānō Fideī surripuerit. (624–625 and 628–638)

4. Postquam Eucliō aurum in lūcō Silvānī abstrūdere cōnstituit, servus praecucurrit ut ubi senex thēsaurum dēfossūrus esset vidēret. (673–676 and 678–679)

682–end

1. Eunomia, quod vērum nunc est nārrātum, frātrem rogābit (or ab frātre petet) ut dē nūptiīs repudium remittat (or renūntiet). (694–695, 783, and 799)

2. Aurō surreptō, servus Lyconidis maximō cum gaudiō domum it ut id abstrūdat (or condat). (712)

3. Eucliō et Lyconidēs frūstrā colloquuntur, alter dē aulā surreptā, alter dē Phaedriā compressā. (see 29–30)

4. Eucliō, ubi suam fīliam peperisse et Lyconidem eam uxōrem dūcere velle reperit, tandem ad nūptiās avus cōnsentit. (797–798)

5. Dum Lyconidēs servum dē fūrtō interrogat, in dubiō relinquimur fīne fābulae perditō.

* * *

BIBLIOGRAPHY

Editions of the Plays

Menander

The Dyskolos: Menander, translated with an introduction and notes by Carroll Moulton. New American Library, New York, NY, and Scarborough, Ontario, 1977. Excellent introduction; spirited translation.

Plautus

Aulularia: A Videotape in Latin, by the Department of Classical Studies, University of Richmond. Order from Stuart L. Wheeler, Department of Classical Studies, North Court, University of Richmond, Richmond, VA 23173. A videotape (VCR 1/2 inch) of the play as performed by faculty and students at the University of Richmond.

*Plautus' Aulularia: The Pot of Gold: An Adaptation for Production by High School Latin Students, ed. by Gilbert Lawall. *NECN* Publications, 71 Sand Hill Road, Amherst, MA 01002. An adaptation of the play with some sections in English and others in Latin for a thirty- to forty-minute production.

T. Macci Plauti: Aulularia, ed. by E. J. Thomas. Oxford University Press, Oxford and New York, NY, 1913. Edition of the play with introduction, Latin text, and notes.

*The Pot of Gold (adapted from Plautus' comedy for use in first year Latin), by Erika Rummel. *NECN* Publications, 71 Sand Hill Road, Amherst, MA 01002. A simplified version of the play suitable for a fifteen-minute enactment.

Molière

*The Miser and George Dandin: Two Plays, tr. by Albert Bermel. "Actor's Molière Series," Vol. 1. Applause Theatre Book Publications, New York, NY, 1987.

*The Miser and Other Plays, tr. by John Wood. "Classics Series." Penguin Books Inc., New York, NY, 1953.

General

*Life and Literature in the Roman Republic, by Tenney Frank. "Sather Classical Lectures," No. 7, 1930. University of California Press, Berkeley, CA, 1971. Comedy as one important cultural vehicle in the formative years of Rome.

"Menander (ca. 342–ca. 291 B.C.)," by Carroll Moulton. In *Ancient Writers: Greece and Rome*, ed. by T. James Luce. Vol. I, pp. 435–447. Charles Scribner's Sons, New York, NY, 1982. Includes discussion of the *Dyskolos*.

"Plautine Stage Settings," by V. J. Rosivach. *Transactions of the American Philological Association* 101 (1970) 445–461. Locations of houses, the temple of Faith, and Silvanus' grove.

"Plautus (254–184 B.C.)," by John Wright. In *Ancient Authors: Greece and Rome*, ed. by T. James Luce. Vol. I, pp. 501–523. Charles Scribner's Sons, New York, NY, 1982. A useful survey of Plautus' plays.

"Plautus and Popular Drama," by Alan Little. *Harvard Studies in Classical Philology* 49 (1938) 205–228. The influence of native Italian drama on Plautus' adaptation of New Comedy.

Post-Aristophanic Comedy: Studies in the Social Outlook of Middle and New Comedy in Both Greece and Rome, by P. S. Dunkin. University Press of Illinois, Urbana, IL, 1946. An analysis of the changing role of comedy in reflecting contemporary life and standards.

*Roman Comedy, by David Konstan. Cornell University Press, Ithaca, NY, 1983. Chapter titled "*Aulularia*: City-State and Individual," pp. 33–46, deals with the state or society and the individual in the *Aulularia*.

Roman Drama, ed. by T. A. Dorey and D. R. Dudley. "Studies in Latin Literature and Its Influence." Routledge and Kegan Paul, London, 1965. A collection of essays on various aspects of comedy and tragedy, including "Plautus and His Audience," by W. R. Chambers (pp. 21–50).

*Roman Laughter: The Comedy of Plautus, by Erich Segal. Harvard University Press, Cambridge, MA, 1968; Oxford University Press, Oxford and New York, NY, 1987. A lively study of comedy as a celebration of the relief of tension.

*Roman Life, by Mary Johnston. Scott, Foresman and Company, Glenview, IL, 1957. A basic resource book for information on the daily life of the Romans; fully illustrated.

Roman Perspective Painting and the Ancient Stage, by Alan M. G. Little. Star Press, Kennebunk, ME, 1971. The influence of Roman painting on the scenery and staging of plays.

"Scholarship on Plautus: 1965–1976," by Erich Segal. "Special Survey Issue." *The Classical World* 74.7 (1981). An annotated bibliography of work on Plautus.

*Social and Private Life at Rome in the Time of Plautus and Terence, by G. W. Leffingwell. Columbia University Press, New York, NY, 1918. A comprehensive look at the Romans and their customs in the society for which Plautus and Terence wrote.

"The Comedy of Plautus," by M. M. Henderson. *Akroterion* 20 (1975) 2–13. Discussion of the importance of the "Romanness" of the plays.

The Greek "Aulularia": A Study of the Original of Plautus' Masterpiece, by W. E. J. Kuiper. "*Mnemosyne* Supplement," 2. Leiden, 1940. An imaginative reconstruction that attempts to explain, for example, Megadorus' sudden wish to marry Phaedria and his abrupt change of mind.

*The History of the Greek and Roman Theater, by M. Bieber. Princeton University Press, Princeton, NJ, 2nd ed., revised and enlarged, 1980. A thorough investigation of all aspects of ancient drama.

"The Lost Ending of Plautus' *Aulularia*," by E. L. Minar. *The Classical Journal* 42 (1946–1947) 271–275. A discussion of the way in which the play could have ended to the satisfaction of the characters and the audience.

The Nature of Roman Comedy: A Study in Popular Entertainment, by George E. Duckworth. Princeton University Press, Princeton, NJ, 1952. The basic study of all aspects of Roman comedy: its origin, authors, plots, characters, meter, and later influence.

*The New Comedy of Greece and Rome, by R. L. Hunter. Cambridge University Press, Cambridge and New York, NY, 1985. A general, topical treatment of New Comedy.

"The Number of Slave Roles in Plautus' *Aulularia*, by D. Lange. *Classical Philology* 68 (1973) 62–63. The problem of Strobilus and the slave of Lyconides.

"The Original of the *Aulularia.*" *Studies in Menander,* by T. B. L. Webster, pp. 120–127. Manchester University Press, Manchester, 1950, 1960. Speculation on Plautus' changes of the original.

The Roman Stage: A Short History of Latin Drama in the Time of the Republic, by W. Beare. Methuen, London, 1950, 1964 (3rd ed.); Rowman & Littlefield, Totowa, NJ, 1977. Careful analysis of the development of Roman drama.

"The Social Theme in Plautus' *Aulularia*," by David Konstan. *Arethusa* 10 (1977) 307–320. An earlier version of the chapter on the *Aulularia* in *Roman Comedy* (see above).

SELECTIONS FROM OVID'S METAMORPHOSES

INTRODUCTION

Ovid's Life and Times

Publius Ovidus Naso was born in 43 B.C., the second son of an affluent middle-class family, in the humble rural town of Sulmo, which was located on the slopes of the Apennines less than 100 miles east of Rome. The name Ovidius had earned no political or public distinction before our man; the cognomen Naso came from an ancestor who had a nose that attracted attention. We have no idea how Ovid actually looked. To be born at this particular time in Italy, close to Rome, was to be involved in the troubled era that followed the murder of Julius Caesar in 44 B.C. But Ovid was lucky: Sulmo remained unscathed while other parts of Italy became the scene of battles, sieges, and confiscations of land. He was too young to experience the nervousness that his parents probably felt when they anxiously awaited the outcome of two great conflicts: first, that between the so-called "Liberators," on the one hand, who had successfully conspired against Caesar, and, on the other hand, the self-styled heirs and avengers of the dictator; second, the conflict between the two successful "Avengers," Mark Antony and the young Octavian, who fought to determine who would be sole heir and ruler. From about 39 B.C., Octavian was in control of Italy, while Antony held power in the East, making his headquarters in Athens and subsequently with the friendly Queen of Egypt, Cleopatra. The rumors of growing tension between Octavian and Antony no doubt penetrated to Sulmo, but Egypt was far away, and the Battle of Actium, which in effect ended the threat of Antony in 31, spared Italy entirely and cost few casualties. To judge from Ovid's silence about his home and boyhood, his youth was quiet and untroubled.

By the time Ovid was a teenager, Octavian had clearly begun to make his impression on the world of Italy, and Ovid's father developed ambitions for his two sons that required them to pursue their education and training in Rome. Octavian, as part of his emphasis on the peaceful revival of political and economic stability, drew much of the actual power of the state into his own hands but managed his program through the traditional machinery of the Republic. In 27 B.C., about the time that the young Ovid came to Rome to study, Octavian took for himself the honorary title of Augustus, and for the next forty years, until his death in A.D. 14, he presided over what we now call the Augustan Age. That age corresponded almost exactly with the vital and productive career of our poet: he survived the Emperor by only three years.

In one sense, then, Ovid deserves more than any other writer to be considered *the* Augustan poet, because his life and creative career coincided with the rule of Augustus. In another sense, however, he is often viewed as the least Augustan, for he seems to have had little admiration for Augustus and for the miracle of peace and prosperity that was achieved in his time. It is Augustus' contemporaries, Vergil, Horace, and Livy, who provide us with the most sensitive and complex appreciation of what Augustus meant and achieved, good and bad, for the Roman world. They had a perspective similar to his, qualified by thirty years of unrest while they were growing up. Horace, as a young student, had even served in the armies that resisted Octavian and Antony, and he experienced the bitter defeat and rout at Philippi in 42 B.C. Ovid, however, grew up a generation later in the protected environment of Sulmo and never knew or showed sympathetic understanding of what Octavian went through to become Augustus. Ovid knew and wrote about the Augustan world that opened before his eyes only from the time that he arrived in Rome at the age of sixteen.

The great poets Vergil and Horace were admirable, remote, and too old to seem imitable to the young man from Sulmo. Vergil was at work on his formidable epic, the *Aeneid,* and Horace had nearly completed his collection of Odes, soon to be published in 23. Neither was writing for teenagers, and so it was natural that Ovid turned from their kind of poetry to the more congenial verse produced by the elegiac poets, of whom today Tibullus and Propertius survive as prime examples. These two, perhaps ten years older than Ovid, had only just begun to publish, and their subject was calculated to excite the admiration and imitation of the younger generation. They featured a young lover who could easily be imagined as in his twenties or a bit younger, who rejected all demands that he participate in the responsible adult world of politics, war, and business, who turned his back on a "career" in order to throw himself heedlessly into passionate but unproductive love affairs with beautiful and exciting prostitutes. There was no future in such affairs, not the slightest chance of marriage: such involvements were only in the present. But that is exactly the way most young people would prefer and indeed, we must admit, need to live for a while. Elegiac poetry, then, swept much of Rome, Ovid included, off its feet. His father had sent him to the city to learn the practical art of rhetoric and then start on a responsible political career. But elegiac poetry, in its ostentatious cult of irresponsible love, provided Ovid an alternative lifestyle that he early embraced and a genre of verse that came almost instinctively to him. Although in deference to his father's wishes he did study with some of the greatest rhetorical teachers and practitioners, he spent much more effort and interest in studying the works of Tibullus and Propertius, chiefly the latter.

By the time Ovid was twenty, he was composing elegy, reading it in the receptive circles of sophisticated Rome, and actively publishing. First, he wrote as a lover in the first person, but he innovated by creating a lover of considerable polish who appears more in love with himself and his wit than with any of the numerous women who catch his eye. Ovid published these elegies in a collection of five books, not long after 19 B.C., when the death of Tibullus evoked a lamenting poem from him. Then, inspired by a novel Propertian elegy in the form of a letter from a Roman wife to her soldier-husband on campaign in the East, Ovid devised his *Heroides:* a collection of letter-elegies from heroines of myth to the heroes who had deserted them (e.g., Dido to Aeneas or Medea to Jason). An even more brilliant innovation in elegy was the *Art of Love*, which may have been published, as Syme has recently suggested, in a first version as early as 9 B.C. Ovid's innovation here was to abandon the pose of ardent lover, male or female, and assume the manner of an expert in

love, **praeceptor amōris**, who confidently instructs young men (Books I and II) and women (Book III) how to succeed in the tricky field of love. Since verse instruction or didactic poetry traditionally used the hexameter and was serious, Ovid's shift to elegiac meter warns his audience that something is not quite straight. Indeed, the more his "teacher" reduces love to a series of rules and manipulative strategies, the less convincing he becomes. In effect Ovid deliberately exposes this teacher's distorted view of love so as to imply a better alternative, namely, love as a relationship of mutual giving and receiving, of mutual commitment. The *Art of Love* implicitly prepares for the fuller presentation of love's richness in the *Metamorphoses*.

After experimenting with a tragedy on Medea (successful but now lost), Ovid set to work on two major projects, at the start of our era. One of these was still another elegiac novelty, again inspired by Propertius and the influential Alexandrian poet Callimachus: it was to be called the *Fasti*, and it consisted of a series of clever comments, in varying manner, on the days of the months. Ovid never finished the full year of twelve months, stopping at the end of June and Book VI. It used to be thought that it was his exile that cut the project short, but Syme now proposes that Ovid stopped earlier, in A.D. 4, when the adoption of Tiberius as Augustus' heir seemed to negate the hopes of Ovid and his friends that Germanicus, a younger and more congenial prince, might be named. The second project was our poem, the *Metamorphoses*, on which Ovid worked steadily up to the time of his exile in A.D. 8, at which point it was virtually finished. This is Ovid's only hexameter poem, and it represents a blending of the familiar manner and matter of elegy with the style and some topics of epic: it is, as some critics describe it, an "epic of love."

For reasons that will probably never be fully known, though they certainly involved crucial political concerns of the Emperor Augustus, Ovid was sent, without public trial, into what proved to be permanent exile in A.D. 8, to the shores of the Black Sea at Tomi, now ironically a Rumanian seaside resort called Costanza. There, he reverted to still another kind of elegy, lament for separation from wife, friends, and beloved Rome. And there he died at about age sixty in A.D. 17.

The *Metamorphoses*

Ovid's *Metamorphoses* is a huge poem of fifteen books. In size, meter, and importance, it fits some of the conditions of epic, but we must be careful, when we call it an "epic of love" or simply an epic, that we do not measure it by the same generic standards that we successfully apply to Vergil's *Aeneid.* Vergil adhered to the traditional format and produced a magnificent epic on a single grand narrative plot, namely, the wanderings and struggle of Aeneas to found a new homeland in Italy after the destruction of his native Troy. Ovid rejected any such grand scheme, spurned heroic figures, and addressed not the Roman feeling for the past and patriotic traditions, but rather the immediate sense of the present and the most vital emotions. He collected a series of more than two hundred stories about metamorphoses or physical transformations, of which we have selected four for this reader. At first reading, these stories seem to have little in common except the usually terminal metamorphosis, and even the metamorphoses vary in detail and significance. Thus, Baucis and Philemon, central characters, receive their transformation, lovingly described by the narrator, as a reward for their simple piety, whereas in the story that focuses on the monstrous lover Polyphemus, told by the nymph Galatea, who spurns his affection, it is a third, clearly minor character, Acis, who experiences metamorphosis, when he escapes death (though crushed under a boulder hurled by the jealous Cyclops) and instead is turned into a river, his blood becoming water, through the divine care of Galatea. We hardly respond to Acis, turned as he is into bodiless, inanimate water, since the story gives him no personality and only the weak act of flight. We do, however, see considerable significance in the final form of the elderly couple, Baucis and Philemon—trees with affectionately interlaced branches.

Sometimes, then, Ovid makes the metamorphosis an integral part of his narrative theme, and sometimes the physical transformation of a minor character merely punctuates the narrative so that another story can take over our attention. Of course, we do not usually expect the ending of a tale to be its most important feature. The theme, the narrative manner, and the response of the audience are what really count; when we look at these, we start to discern a common Ovidian denominator for the poem. In both the Baucis and Polyphemus episodes Ovid involves us with a sentimental narrative about simple feelings. These feelings have no social, patriotic, or heroic context, and it is a mark of Ovid's irreverence when he calls the fleeing Acis a "hero" (XIII.879). The characters we hear about are somewhat simplified versions of people we have known from our own personal experience or from familiar literature. Galatea is the woman who repulses unwanted admirers, and Polyphemus is a gross exaggeration of the unwanted suitor. Putting this everyday situation

into the imaginary world of myth encourages us to distance ourselves and be critically amused by the naive narrative. Galatea, the narrator, tries to interpret her tale, but unwittingly she is made by Ovid to give us the means to a fuller insight into her situation. For her, the story supposedly illustrates her own pathetic experience when she was punished for spurning the ardently proffered passion of Polyphemus. In fact, though, because she is made to quote extensively from the wooing words of the Cyclops, we begin, in spite of her, to minimize her pathos and rather to concentrate on this gargantuan lover whom she ignores. He is very interesting and amusing indeed, and his clumsy sense of himself and of the nature of love leads him to appeal to Galatea by arguments that are comically inept and frustrating. Yet Ovid does not let us rest with our patronizing indulgence of this ridiculous, misunderstood lover. Unlike Theocritus, who earlier popularized an amatory Polyphemus and allowed him to be finally consoled by his own song, if not by happy love, the Roman poet goes on to describe the murderous jealousy of the Cyclops, the would-be killer of Acis. We do not respond to the story with the simplistic bias of Galatea, but Ovid enables us to discover a more satisfying, if not exactly cheerful, meaning in the series of misunderstandings that love generates. He even compels us to revise our first responses when Polyphemus, whom we have generously tolerated because he amused us, turns into a brutal murderer out of jealousy, that perversion of love.

It is Ovid's genius in the Polyphemus episode and in the other three stories that makes a seemingly naive story into a compellingly complex narrative, a tantalizing blend of humor and seriousness. He engages us as intelligent, sympathetic, but critical readers, who must not be content with the easiest, most obvious interpretation. We must go beyond Galatea's self-serving self-pity, and we must not treat the Baucis episode simply as a goody-goody tale of piety rewarded. Aghast at the impious incredulity of his table companion, the elderly and reverent Lelex offers his tale as proof that the gods are omnipotent and capable of carrying out metamorphoses among human beings at will (VIII.618–625); he concludes by praying that the pious may be rewarded with reverence themselves (724). However, as told, the story shows much greater concern with the uncritical goodness of the human couple than with the power of the gods. Indeed, the gods' exertion of power causes us problems. Disguised as men, Jupiter and Mercury knock at various doors and request hospitality, which all but Baucis and Philemon refuse. Thus, when the gods reveal themselves to their elderly hosts and in the same breath declare themselves and their intention to destroy the impious neighbors (689), we have to wonder about such small-minded deities and about Lelex's ingenuous reverence that can blandly recount and accept such attitudes. Baucis and Philemon show far more humane and creditable feelings when they weep for their exterminated neighbors (698). As a result, we tend to alter Lelex's emphasis, dissatisfied with his gods and their arbitrary use of power, and we find in the story an admirable account of simple humanity. It is not piety that in the first place triggers the self-sacrificing hospitality of the old couple, and it certainly is not Lelex's conception of piety that makes the same pair, in spite of the gods and morally superior to these gods, regret their neighbors' deaths. (In fact, the Roman audience of Ovid's entire poem would recall earlier stories when these very gods went about reprehensibly in disguise in order to pursue their lust for desirable females, to get their way by deception.)

The discussion above has emphasized the individual significance of each story rather than the wider context in which Ovid sets it. In the contiguous stories of Narcissus and Pentheus, students can get some sense of how Ovid arranges the narratives to set each other off. Although there is no suspiciously simple-minded person who functions as biased and inept narrator, as Galatea and Lelex do, there is a narrator who does not see the deeper meanings of what he recounts. He seems to think that the amazing reliability of the prophet Tiresias constitutes the common theme of both stories. To be sure, Tiresias occupies a prominent position at the start of both, with his menacingly ambiguous prophecy, and he implicitly earns our credit at the end when Narcissus and Pentheus meet destruction. Ovid, however, makes us far more concerned with the confused and conflicting feelings of the human characters, and he gives their passions, acts, and dooms a significance that the narrator does not define, but that we discover. Here, some of the common features suggested by the juxtaposed tales should be noted. Both Narcissus and Pentheus are headstrong, self-centered young men, and in their respective stories Ovid carefully contrasts them with a mild, selfless, and honorable character whom the young man instinctively tries to eliminate. Narcissus spurns Echo and causes her reduction from a fully physical nymph to a mere voice, and Pentheus tries to destroy Acoetes, devotee of the Bacchus whom the king loathes. Both meet their doom when they venture into the wild countryside, Narcissus to hunt and Pentheus to track down and spy on the ecstatic Bacchantes. Both are destroyed because they see something that is forbidden, mysterious, and fatal to behold. Narcissus sees his own reflection, falls in love with himself, and in that fatal error declines into nothing. Pentheus spies on religious rites that no outsider can be permitted to observe, and his body is literally torn limb from limb by the worshiping Bacchantes. In the destruction of these egoists' bodies, Ovid suggests a terrible but fit punishment. (A third tale of this book, to which reference is made in the notes, involves Pentheus' cousin Actaeon, who is torn to pieces by his own hunting dogs after he sees another forbidden sight, the nude goddess Diana bathing in a forest pool.) Thus, Ovid's organization and placing of the stories of Narcissus and Pentheus enhance the individual significance of each by artful reuse of narrative details.

Style and Meter

Although superficially the stories of the *Metamorphoses* are naive fairy tales about simple characters, in fact they prove to be complex and often unsettling accounts of human beings with whom the Romans in their sophisticated culture and we in ours can easily identify. Ovid contrived a unique style that enhanced his purposes: it is smooth, perspicuous, grammatically easy, structurally transparent, and metrically swift, regular, and unimpeded. Thereby, he lulls us into the expectation of a naive narrative, all the more to disturb us by the final depths of his interpretation.

Probably the best way to demonstrate succinctly the principal characteristics of Ovidian style is to use a short passage for illustration. The following verses start from the point in Narcissus' tale where the young hunter comes upon the clear spring that is to be the instrument of his doom. The lines (III.413–417) are here numbered 1–5.

1 Hīc puer et studiō vēnandī lassus et aestū
2 prōcubuit faciemque locī fontemque secūtus,
3 dumque sitim sēdāre cupit, sitis altera crēvit,
4 dumque bibit, vīsae conreptus imāgine fōrmae
5 spem sine corpore amat, corpus putat esse quod unda est.

Although this is a single sentence spread over five lines, it has none of the interlocking word order and complicated structure that we find in Vergilian and Horatian hexameters. In effect, every line provides us with an adequate unit of sense, and the sentence builds by clear additions and coordination more than subordination. In line 1, Ovid announces the boy as subject and uses the adverb hīc ("here") to connect this sentence with the previous description of the spring. An adjectival phrase that rapidly summarizes the boy's situation fills out the line: lassus is artfully placed between the two ablative nouns that depend on it, and Ovid uses the double et to make sure that we are ready for their relationship in spite of their separation. Line 2 begins with the main verb, which **puer** has led us to expect, and the remainder of line 2 consists of a participial clause, **secū- tus** with its double objects, which achieves emphasis not only by alliteration but also by the double **-que**.

Here, the sentence could have been complete, but Ovid added to it some new coordinated units. His is a story of clauses connected by "and." Still, though this is the simplest of organizations, do not be fooled by it: what Ovid now adds is really of a different order from the picture he has built up in lines 1 and 2. We can infer from the heat (**aestū** 1) and from Narcissus' pose over the pool in line 2 that he is eager to satisfy his thirst. In line 3, loosely connected to line 2 by the **-que** attached to **dum** (whereas logic requires connection between the two main verbs), Ovid transfers our attention from the literal thirst to a "second thirst" and starts exploiting the paradox of the boy's self-infatuation. Each of the clauses in line 3 has a form of **sitis** and a verb beginning with the letter *c,* to enhance the parallelism and contrast. However, line 3 seems too witty and potentially obscure for our narrator, and so he adds lines 4–5 to explicate his thirst metaphor. Line 4 repeats the initial **dumque** of line 3 (a device known as anaphora and popular with Ovid: repeating an initial word). In **bibit,** he contrives a précis of the first clause of line 3, and in the remainder of the two lines the second clause becomes clear. A participial clause fills out line 4 with the necessary background information so that in line 5 Ovid can once again, in a new fashion, formulate wittily Narcissus' predicament. Instead of describing in detail the exact procedure by which the boy, as he drank, looked into the pool and saw a reflection of a handsome boy, which was only himself, Ovid lets us grasp the essence of the scene: Narcissus was utterly enraptured by the image or reflection of the form that he saw in the pool. The wit of line 5 uses two successive clauses, which are separated by only comma and caesura, but no conjunction. Enraptured as he is, Narcissus loves a mere hope that has no body (since it is only a reflection); or, to put it another way, he thinks that what is only water (the physical substance that reflects) is a body (the solid that is reflected). This is the fatal moment when, according to Tiresias' prophecy, the boy "knows himself" and seals his doom. But the wit of the narrator, based on his simple structure and choice of words, distances us from the scene and invites us, too, to limit our sympathy for Narcissus.

In the precise and clear organization of this sentence, Ovid has moved from physical to psychological interest, with two lines for the objective description and three for the more intriguing subjective. The wit concentrates on the last three lines, where the paradox of self-infatuation, of puerile "self-knowledge," receives its first sketch. It should also be noted that, in the course of the sentence, Ovid moves in on his scene, having started in the past tenses but ending in the narrative present. From this point, the narrator and we are going through the experience simultaneously with Narcissus.

The metrical organization supports the general narrative clarity and fluidity. (The easy, unproblematical syntax is adequately covered in the Grammar Review on pages 139–142` of this handbook.) Since around 180 B.C., when Ennius introduced the Greek hexameter to Latin verse, poets had steadily developed the art with which that meter could be employed, until finally in the *Aeneid* Vergil achieved the ultimate in expressivity and epic seriousness. Ovid does not want Vergil's density or utter seriousness, and he does seek speed to fit the flowing smoothness of his storytelling manner and to support his wit. He aims to avoid such epic hexameter strategies as would complicate or obscure the clarity of his tale. Latin naturally had many long syllables and so produced spondees more easily than dactyls. Vergil found dactyls all right, but he preferred the slower, heavier rhythm of spondees, and in his epic he uses roughly ten spondees for every six dactyls. When we compare Ovid's text, we discover that in the *Metamorphoses* he has totally reversed the preference: he restricts the proportion of spondees to six for ten dactyls. (In this passage, counting only the first four feet of each line, we find seven spondees and thirteen dactyls.) Ovid regularly begins each line with a dactyl to establish the dominant rhythm, and he tends to assign a dactyl to the fourth foot, just before moving to the expected rhythm of the final two feet (dactyl and spondee or trochee). Dactyls, because they add syllables to the line, which is read with a regular pace, force a reader to speed up and thereby convey a sense of movement to a passage.

Ovid likes conjunctions and has an almost flippant method of adding **-que** to *any* nearby word rather than to the logically coordinate word. This obviousness of connections with its emphasis on additive organization could have been reduced or clouded had the meter not used the structural devices available to it in full support of the stylistic goals of speed, perspicacity, and wit. Metrical structure depends on elision, caesurae, and movement from line to line. Although we cannot simplify the effect of elision into one or two easy descriptions, it is evident that it produces a clash of syllables and sounds which often serve to enhance a scene of effort and conflict. That effect was congenial to Vergil's subject, but not to Ovid's or to his desire to give it speed and clarity. Therefore, whereas Vergil welcomed elisions, Ovid drastically reduced their number, and students will find the Ovidian hexameter very easy in this respect. Where Vergil elides in at least half his lines, Ovid can go long stretches without elision. Thus, this passage shows no elision in lines 1–4, then elides twice in line 5 at the end of each of the parallel clauses. The elision, after four lines of uninterrupted rhythmical flow, slows down our reading and brings the sentence to a calculated emphasis as it closes with wit.

The caesura cuts through a metrical foot, separating words within the line. The normal caesurae in the hexameter occur in the second, third, or fourth feet. We expect at least one such cut in every line, but the tradition behind Ovid, especially that of Vergil, did not require that a caesura be an emphatic break in the structure of meaning. Ovid, on the other hand, treats the caesura as a means of clarifying the articulation of his narrative in each line. This may be seen most obviously in lines 3–5, where the internal commas all mark caesuras. In line 3, the line moves, with perhaps a subordinate caesura after sitim, to the break in the fourth foot that nicely separates the two kinds of thirst, the slaking of the physical and the firing of the erotic. In line 5, the central caesura in the third foot effectively divides the two coordinate flashes of Ovidian wit. In line 4, Ovid starts out with the same word as in line 3 and with the same rhythm into the second foot, but now the subordinate caesura becomes the principal one. However, it is supported by a secondary one in the third foot (after vīsae) that enhances the structure of the participial clause. In line 2, another editor might have placed a comma in the second foot, after prōcubuit, for the line's structure closely resembles that of line 4 (key verb, then long participial clause after early caesura). A secondary caesura marks off the two alliterative objects of secūtus, splitting faciemque locī slightly from fontemque. Line 1, at the start of this swiftly flowing sentence, has the least pronounced caesura: it would come after studiō and presumably emphasize the two separated causes of fatigue, the loss of energy and the heat of the day. Ovid thus employs caesurae to reinforce the clarity of sense units.

Anyone who has ever tried to write poetry according to a traditional metrical (and rhyming, for English verse) scheme will know how one's first efforts result in a series of end-stopped lines. It is about all one can do to limp along with the meter and sense to the end of the line. That was how Ennius wrote the first Latin hexameters. Poets gradually tested the advantages of moving from line to line by overlapping syntactical structures, and so the periodic structure of the hexameter developed, to reach a high point, of course, in Vergil's epic. The movement from one line to another is referred to by the French word *enjambement* or, more easily, by the English "run-on." Vergil often forces run-on, because he breaks a phrase or leaves necessary syntax incomplete at the line end. By contrast, these five lines illustrate typical Ovidian practice: lines 2 and 3 have commas that mark the end of an independent clause before the poet continues with "and"; line 5, of course, has a period; and lines 1 and 4 also end with intelligible sense-units, participial clauses that in English would often be separated by commas from what follows. Thus, Ovid consciously restricts elision, caesurae, and run-ons, which Vergil had used with maximum epic effect, and Ovid's narrative style gains thereby. As students read and enjoy Ovid's narrative, they should pause here and there to give him credit for the art that went into the creation of this unique and disarming style.

* * *

DISCUSSIONS OF THE EPISODES

Baucis and Philemon

Interaction between the Frame and the Tale. It is fitting that Lelex, an older man (mātūrus, 617), should be the one to defend pious belief in the gods by means of a story about the pious actions of two old people. To reinforce the sense of Lelex's maturity, Ovid has introduced him earlier as having thinning white hair at the temples (rārīs iam sparsus tempora cānīs, VIII.568). At the end of his tale he tries to add further support to his assertions by saying that the story was told to him by reliable old men (nōn vānī . . . / nārrāvēre senēs, 721–722).

A different connection between story and frame is the topic of dining. In the third section, when the dinner begins, students should remember that the story of Baucis and Philemon is being told *at* a dinner, a situation that invites comparisons between the frame and its contained tale.

Ring Structure. Related to the poet's use of frames is his strategy of ring structure. The end of this fable will recall the beginning. In the first lines Ovid seemingly casually introduces the elements (**tiliae, quercus, collibus, stagnum,** 620–624) that will be found in the concluding metamorphoses: the hill that Baucis and Philemon ascend to safety (692), the swamp they look back over their shoulders to see (696), and the "neighboring" trees they eventually become (715–720). Similarly, the "thousand homes" (628–629) will reappear submerged in the laconic pronoun **suōrum** (698), while their own thatched roof (**cannā tēcta palustrī**, 630) will be seen to be gilded (**aurāta . . . tēcta**, 702).

As the story reaches its climax in section VI, it begins with these verbal echoes to circle back to themes introduced from the beginning. Students should be alerted to these repetitions and their functions. As the theme of hospitality and its contrast was earlier punctuated by the phrase **sed pia**, placed at the beginning of its line (631), so at the conclusion the complementary theme of reward and punishment is signaled by the contrasting word **inpia**, again at the beginning of the line (690). The phrase **dominīs etiam casa parva duōbus** (699) likewise recalls the first description of the household (635–636) and reiterates the theme of smallness and poverty, developed particularly at 638–678.

Dining in Antiquity and Comparative Sources. The details about food preparation and serving in sections II and III have to be read against the contemporary audience's expectations of a company dinner. Instead of a boiled bacon and cabbage stew (646–650), accompanied by fruit and nuts (674–678), a fashionable dinner party could include half a dozen courses of poultry, meat, and fish, most of it elaborately prepared, some of it merely ornamental. Although the number of courses varied, it was conventional to define the conclusion of the first part of any dinner by eggs (**ōva**, 667) and the end of it by apples (**redolentia māla**, 675). From this convention came the proverbial saying, **ab ōvō usque ad māla**, "from eggs to apples," that is, from beginning to end. Wines, frequently of ancient vintage, were changed from course to course. In contrast, Baucis and Philemon's wine defies fashion on two counts: not only is it of recent vintage (**nec longae vīna senectae**, 672), but it is of only one kind (**referuntur vīna**, 672). To eat all this food, Romans reclined (**adcubuēre**, 660), supporting themselves on one elbow and lying three to a couch on three couches arranged in a horseshoe. From a table in the center, slaves offered food and drink. Against this pattern of hospitality, that of Baucis

and Philemon becomes more vivid: only the gods recline to eat; the old people, having no slaves, serve their guests themselves. (For a fuller description of Roman dining, see *Life in Ancient Rome*, pp. 76–80.)

For primary sources and a comparison with the satirists, see Trimalchio's dinner in Petronius' *Satyricon*, Juvenal's *Satire* XI, Horace's *Epistle* I.5, *Satires* II.3, II.4, II.6, and II.8. These show explicitly the contrast that Ovid here makes implicitly: between an ethically superior simplicity of menu and entertainment on the one hand, and a jaded, luxurious wastefulness on the other. According to the code of simplicity outlined by the satirists, conversation (**sermōnibus**, 651) and the reading aloud of poetry provided the best entertainment at a dinner. By contrast, according to Juvenal, aristocratic dinners offered not merely singers and dancers, but even sex shows. Furthermore, in the claustrophobic court society of the first century, conversation at dinner parties tended to be stifled by the fear that one's words might be found inappropriate and betrayed to the Emperor. Horace's *Satire* II.6 is a particularly good comparative text. Both in this satire and in the story of Baucis and Philemon, food and hospitality are topics that represent larger philosophical issues; material poverty, in particular, is a sign of philosophical richness. In Horace, a fable about dining (the story of the country mouse and the city mouse) is told at a dinner party to point up a moral ("Be happy where you are and with what you have"). In the same way, the story of Baucis and Philemon is also, at its center, a tale about dining told by Lelex at another dinner party, that of the river god Achelous, to point up a different moral ("The gods must not be mocked"). Ovid may be "quoting" Horace in the participle **succincta** (660). To move about and serve the gods more easily, Baucis has tucked her skirts up. The same adjective describes the city mouse in Horace's *Satire*, dashing about offering his rural friend gourmet leftovers (**velutī succinctus cursitat hospes**, *Satire* II.6.107).

Architecture and Furnishings. The little house of Baucis and Philemon (**parva . . . casā**, 630–633) is not only the place where they live in philosophic contentment, it also represents that way of living. It contrasts with the larger houses (**domōs**, 628) of their neighbors and also, implicitly, with the houses that most of Ovid's audience would be likely to live in—in quality and materials more like the temple the little hut eventually becomes (700–702). Well-to-do Romans of the Empire built their houses and villas (frequently they had more than one) with a liberal use of marble, gold, and columns imported from the Hellenic world. (For a fuller discussion and illustrations, see *Houses, Villas and Palaces in the Roman World.)*

The house may also be seen as a representation of Baucis and Philemon in that it contains within it, so to speak, the temple seen in the metamorphosis in section IV (**casa parva . . . vertitur in templum,** 699–700), just as they bear within themselves the potential for priesthood. The house was a post-and-lintel construction (**furcās,** 700), and we must assume it had the same floor plan as the temple. Roman temples typically had a longitudinal floor plan with a peaked roof. Columns (**columnae,** 700) supported the roof out over a porch, which was reached up a flight of steps (**gradūs sacrōs,** 713). Doors were wooden but could be sheathed (as here, evidently: **caelātae,** 702) with metal plates. (For a general discussion and photographs, see *Etruscan and Early Roman Architecture.)*

Within their houses Romans had, by our standards, relatively few furnishings. Not every room, for example, might have chairs and table, for slaves could move the furniture from room to room for the master in order to take advantage of daylight or seasonal changes. (Note the actions of Baucis and Philemon: **positō . . . sedīlī,** 639; **mēnsam . . . pōnit,** 660–661.) But what furniture the rich had was made of valuable materials such as imported woods, gold, silver, or ivory. Footed pieces, like a bed, would have the feet made of a different material from the frame—hence the pointed reference to Baucis and Philemon's wooden bedstead with wooden feet. Similarly, the Roman elite drank from cups made from metal and jewels; the old couple's cups are not only wooden, but so old and porous as to need wax patching (**pōcula, quā cava sunt,** 670).

Poetic Strategies and Ovidian Style. *Line Beginnings.* The beginnings and ends of lines are emphatic positions in Latin poetry. "Myself, I saw the place" (**ipse locum vīdī,** 622), says Lelex in the opening lines, trying to add first-person authority to his narrative. Similarly, in order to emphasize the first of several themes of contrast (see below), Ovid places the key words in the turn from 624 to 625: **ōlim, / nunc.** When Lelex describes the house, he points out that it is small—but pious (**parva . . . / sed pia,** 630–631).

Word Placement. Related to word position in the line is the way an arrangement of words in Latin poetry can contribute to meaning. When the old people chase their goose, the opposition of quick and slow is supported by the contrast between adjacent pairs of adjective-plus-noun (**celer pennā tardōs aetāte,** 686).

Repetitions. Since Latin poetry depends for its shape on meter rather than rhyme, repetition of sounds (either words or letters) is relatively less expected and can therefore be used emphatically for rhetorical purposes. In section I the repetition of **mīlle** (628, 629) emphasizes the contrast between the many and the one (**ūna,** 629) and between the great (**domōs,** 628, 629) and the humble (**casa,** 633). Similarly, in section II the triple alliteration of **vīlisque vetusque / vetus** (658–659) draws attention to the adjectives, emphasizing the humbleness of the old people's furnishings.

Personification. Throughout the *Metamorphoses,* personification attributes human action to objects: for example, from section II, **mentae tersēre** (663). There are two possible explanations for the frequency of this poetic device. One is that in a long narrative about the endless metamorphoses of men and women, the boundary between human and nonhuman thins. Moreover, in this particular story it is almost as if Ovid is saying wittily that in the absence of the usual household of slaves, animated objects take their place.

Themes of Contrast. Besides the contrast between the many and the one and between the great and the humble, mentioned above, we find the following contrasts: the difference between appearance and reality (**Iuppiter . . . speciē mortālī,** 626; the hut evolving into a temple, the old people into priests); the difference between the gods' response to the destruction of the neighborhood and that of Baucis and Philemon (section VI); and the fact that material poverty is coupled with philosophical richness.

Tone. Finally, students may consider Ovid's tone. What prevents this tale of elderly piety from becoming merely saccharine is his tendency to undercut from time to time with comical observations, such as the listing table (**pēs tertius inpār,** 661) and the spectacle of the old people scampering about after the goose (686). Students may have difficulty negotiating Ovid's tone, but the question they need to ask is, What would happen if these comic elements were omitted? What therefore is their rhetorical function?

[For the interpretation of the story from Genesis 18–19 on page 78 of the student's book, see *The Anchor Bible, Genesis,* pp. 128–144.]

Acis, Galatea, and Polyphemus

Ring Structure. Three words introduced in section I (**ūritur,** 763; **amor, cruor,** 768) encapsulate the conflicts and intensity in Polyphemus' story. Love of slaughter and thirst for gore are in the past, Galatea says; love of herself is all that remains. But these three words foreshadow the story's conclusion, when the Cyclops burns even hotter (ūror, 867), both with an unrequited desire for Galatea (cūr . . . amās, 860–861) and an equally strong desire to tear Acis in pieces (865–866). During Acis' metamorphosis he is seemingly reduced to **cruor** (887), which first drips red from the rock, then clears. Thus, with verbal echoes, the story returns to its beginning. Compare also the repetition of the phrase Ācis erat in lines 750 and 896. If students look back to the story of Baucis and Philemon, they will see there, too, how the story concludes by recalling particular elements introduced at its beginning. One way the poet gives shape to his long narrative is by this technique of marking a "ring" around the individual tales.

Use of Sources. Contemporary audiences would recognize in Ovid's Polyphemus both Theocritus' literary lover (*Idyll* XI) and Homer's ferocious giant. From Theocritus Ovid has made a number of precise borrowings (though not all are carried over straight: it is Polyphemus who has the "new down on his lips" in *Idyll* XI). Other borrowings include Polyphemus' sitting on a high rock to sing his love song seawards to Galatea, the series of comparisons between Galatea and objects precious to the giant, the self-portrait, the list of possessions, the list of gifts, and the fact that Polyphemus is an artist—*Idyll* XI contains his song. From Homer's *Odyssey* come the theme of gigantism, Polyphemus' hostility to strangers, his scorn of the gods (especially Jupiter), and his murderous violence. The weird mix in the *Metamorphoses* is Ovid's own, and by combining in this character both physical ferocity and aesthetic sensibility (however excessive), he manages, as he often does, to define a psychological reality that is plausible, if unattractive, to a modern audience.

Poetic Strategies. *The Catalog.* Polyphemus' song contains three catalogs: the first an extended series of comparisons (section III), the second a list of gifts (sections IV and V), and the third a catalog of reasons (section V). A catalog in poetry is a list of persons, places, things, ideas, or other items, which all have a common denominator. In ancient poetry the catalog was a familiar device and could have several functions: for example, educative, if the catalog was a genealogy (to answer the question, who were the ancestors?). In Homer's *Iliad* II, the catalog of ships may serve a different purpose: to demonstrate how great the power of Agamemnon was to be able to command this fleet. Polyphemus' catalogs do at least two things. They are, first, like the visible pine-tree staff (782), verbal representations of his gigantism. A comparison with Theocritus' *Idyll*, where

Polyphemus is not represented as a giant and where his comparisons, list of gifts, and reasons for deserving love are tastefully restrained, makes this point clearer. The catalogs also reveal aspects of his character, particularly his surprising sensitivity to the world around him, as well as his gigantic vanity and mercenary streak.

Presentation of Character: Description versus Revelation. Since the story of Acis' metamorphosis is really a story about Polyphemus—a long monologue by him, preceded by a short introduction to him and followed by a brief description of the consequences of his violent actions—students need to be attuned to the continuous unfolding of the Cyclops' character. He is not at any point (as Acis is) described *in toto* by an omniscient narrator. In particular, although events reveal that he is Homer's giant, Ovid nowhere explicitly says so: the pine-tree staff, the one-hundred-reed pan-pipe, the gigantic songs, and the piece of mountain he hurls at Acis are our clues to his gradually revealed size. Galatea, who introduces him, focuses on his habits, former and present (760–767), and reveals his uncouth appearance. Subsequently his words and actions—his encounter with Telemus, his songs, and his murder of Acis—are the means by which we gradually perceive the many attributes of this complex character: gigantic, but minutely observant of the world around him; generous in passion, but mercenary in his possessions; submissive as Samson before the allurements of his lady, but—like that other giant—appallingly violent and cruel when thwarted.

Themes. *Hospitality.* As in the story of Baucis and Philemon, the issue of hospitality and its opposite is related to contempt for the gods. In both stories we see that such contempt is followed by death or disaster. In the story of Baucis and Philemon, the neighbors who refuse hospitality to Jupiter and Mercury are drowned in a flood and their homes destroyed. In Homer's *Odyssey* Polyphemus shows his contempt for the gods in a scornful speech and then by refusing to show hospitality to Odysseus. He kills and eats six of Odysseus' shipmates who have entered his cave; Odysseus and the surviving crew members blind the Cyclops' one eye, in revenge and to expedite their escape. In the *Metamorphoses* these future events are only alluded to by means of Telemus' prophecy, but their presence in even this form suggests their importance to Ovid's version. We are also told twice (once by Galatea, 761, and once by Polyphemus, 843–844) that Polyphemus despises the gods, Jupiter in particular. As a result, we must believe that disaster will come sooner or later to this proud giant. The presence of this interrelated issue of hospitality and the gods in two widely spaced stories in the *Metamorphoses* (from Books VIII and XIII) may persuade students that themes provide one kind of unity in the poem.

Self-knowledge. In the stories of both Narcissus (the third selection in this book) and Polyphemus, self-examination in a mirror, literally in a pool of water, is a parody of self-knowledge. Although Narcissus' passion for his own reflection in the pool leads to his death, he at least becomes aware of his paradoxical predicament before he fades away (**Iste ego sum! Sēnsī; nec mē mea fallit imāgō!** III.463). Polyphemus, too, gazes at himself in standing water, but further self-delusion rather than clarification is the result. His report of what he sees contrasts pointedly with what Galatea describes. Where she sees ferocity and crudeness (765–768), he sees admirable bulk and luxuriant hair (842–850). If, in examining his worst features—his gigantism, hairiness, and Cyclopean eye—he had acknowledged them as such and passed on to his other attractions (his wealth, for example, as does Theocritus' Polyphemus), we could grant him a modicum of self-awareness. The rationalizations of Ovid's Polyphemus, however, are yet another indication of monstrous vanity. His blindness to Galatea's point of view (**cūr . . . Ācin amās,** 860–861), that is, his inability to see himself as another sees him, seems to adumbrate the physical blindness he will eventually endure.

Narcissus and Echo

This is one of the great stories of the *Metamorphoses,* and it was so superbly composed by Ovid that it effaced all previous versions of the myth and exercised a dominant influence on literature and art in the Middle Ages and Renaissance. In the twentieth century it has given rise to a standard term of psychoanalysis, the adjective "narcissistic." Self-love, however, forms but part of Ovid's interests in this complex tale. He chose to link Narcissus with Echo—he *may* have been the first to do so, but we cannot be sure—and thereby to represent two kinds of constrained and ultimately frustrated love; and he placed his story in a larger structure of narratives about doomed young men who share, with variations, some of the themes here developed.

Structure. We can see how the poet might have ignored Echo entirely and concentrated exclusively on Narcissus. After recounting the birth and fatal oracle, he moves to the sixteenth year, when Narcissus spurns all love, both male and female (355). It is at this point that Ovid inserts Echo (356–401). Since Echo is such a vivid victim of

Narcissus' indifference, later writers, like the medieval poet Guillaume de Lorris, from whom a passage is quoted in the Passages for Comparison, naturally made her the cause of the boy's destruction: they had her invoke vengeance from the gods. Ovid, on the other hand, drops Echo now from his main account of Narcissus, motivating the boy's doom with a prayer from an unidentified male whom he has rejected (404–405). Only when the boy alone has experienced the full frustrations of his passion for his reflection and has started to waste away does Echo return (493–507), both to comment on the death of Narcissus and to remind us of the thematic links between their vain loves. Thus, a simpler, less artistic and significant narrative could have been written without the inserted tale of Echo by being focused solely on Narcissus throughout.

But the combination greatly enriches this story. Apart from the interrelated motifs of self- and other-love, of reflection and echo, of frustration and wasting away, Ovid has also contrived to direct our sympathies by his use of Echo. Already disabled by what Juno has done to her, Echo serves as a pathetic victim to define the harsh selfishness of Narcissus. She wastes away in lonely misery, uttering no complaint, indeed unable to express herself because Narcissus gives her no thought and no words to which she can respond in some personal way. Thus, as de Lorris failed to see, not only does she not bring a curse down on the boy whom in fact she still loves (395), but she *cannot* do so because of the constraints on her speech. Later, however, Ovid deliberately brings her back to demonstrate that her kind of love persists and, in spite of her personal grief (494), continues to respond to the unworthy Narcissus. Her intervention at the time of his death and metamorphosis guarantees that we feel the superiority of a love that is "other-directed" over the "self-love" of the boy.

The Theme of Love. It is often said that Ovid's *Metamorphoses* is an "epic of love." Not that every tale deals with romantic love: the next story, about Pentheus, and that about Philemon and Baucis demonstrate that fact. However, a large majority of the most memorable tales do focus on love. Ovid is interested in the many ways that human beings grope for love and fail to achieve it. He uses a predictably simple scheme to initiate the passion, as the beauty (**fōrma**) of young Narcissus arouses the desire of those who see him, both young men and girls (353). In stories earlier in the poem, he has described love relations that were crude and one-sided, where a god saw a lovely nymph (Io, Callisto), approached her with obvious lust, and simply raped her when she resisted. The god was ruthlessly excited by the beauty and utterly indifferent to the person of his victim. Obviously, Ovid expects us to see the viciousness of such love between responsible human beings, and normally, in later stories about human love, the lover does show a greater sensitivity to the beloved and a desire for more than merely brief exploitation of the physical beauty. We might be in doubt here about Echo's motives if she were not shown to pine away after rejection and then return to prove her persistent love as Narcissus dies (even though he has no thought of her).

From his very birth, then, Narcissus' beauty was capable of generating love in others (345), and, when he was sixteen, his slender, handsome form aroused erotic feelings in many. What concerns Ovid now is the curious disability of the most significant lover, Echo, the way she is frustrated first by her own physical constraints and then by the harsh rejection of Narcissus. After that, he continues with the predicted and invoked doom of Narcissus, whose own capacity for love, twisted by his selfishness, becomes distorted into suicidal self-love. Echo's disability originates in her misuse of her voice: she has interfered with Juno's vengeance against her sister nymphs, a kindly but dangerous act where Juno is concerned, and Juno has taken away her independent power of speech. When, therefore, she falls in love with Narcissus' beauty, she has no way of conversing with him and of interpreting her own feelings to him except by responding to his words, repeating them exactly. This rapidly leads to tragic misunderstanding.

Words that the boy speaks out of mere curiosity Echo tries to impress with erotic meaning, and she then reacts to the erotic opportunity she has imagined, most obviously in **hūc coeāmus** (386). Ovid does not say what Narcissus thinks about the echoed response—since here he presents the story exclusively from Echo's viewpoint—, only that he is deceived by the "image" of the repeating voice (385). However, we may well imagine that he was expecting in this "person" who spoke exactly like himself someone who had no strong feelings, certainly none of love. For him, then, when Echo emerges from the woods and rushes eagerly toward him with arms extended (389), she seems in the role of the rapist attacker, and accordingly he flees to escape the danger. He cannot see her as what she wants to be, a devoted lover. Her effort to change dispassionate and loveless words into erotic material fails dismally. The echo-image of Narcissus' words can have no independent existence, any more than, later, the reflected image (416) of his handsome form has independent substance.

If the rejection of Echo were a single instance in the course of Narcissus' adolescence, it could be sympathetically understood. As it is, Ovid has made clear that the boy has systematically spurned all offers of love because of his hard pride (354), which coexists with his soft beauty. Far from being exceptional, the rejection of Echo exemplifies the unfeeling character of the boy. The last words he ever addresses directly to Echo assert his death-wish rather than a willingness to be open to her feelings in any way (391). He will get that wish. Her sad effort to use some of the same words to express her entirely different feelings, her readiness for openness and affection, compound the pathos of the situation. So Ovid sees to it that we do not interpret Narcissus here as a youth heroically fighting for his chastity, but rather as a heartless young man whose hard pride inflicts such damage on Echo that she utterly wastes away, to become mere voice. The marvelous **fōrma**, because of his twisted character, avoids its natural destiny of love: it is, as Ovid later suggests (419), like a cold, lifeless, and useless statue. It will become the means of Narcissus' punishment.

Incapable of loving anyone else or responding generously to others' warm feelings, Narcissus implicitly can love only himself. Ovid's story now spells out explicitly that "diminished capacity" and makes that self-love, focused on his handsome body's bodiless reflection, the answer to the puzzling oracle and to the curse of a rejected admirer. The oracle (spoken by the venerable and reliable Tiresias) produced a parody of the famous response Delphi had once given (urging self-knowledge) and warned that knowing himself would cut Narcissus' life short (348). You and the students should discuss the ambiguity of this oracle. Normally, the ancient Greeks and Romans believed that people should try to know their own characters and the way personal feelings and motives operate, so that self-knowledge could limit corruption and bias and, hopefully, lead to self-improvement and a richer life. Modern psychology has refined this procedure of self-understanding. There are, of course, dangers in the process today, and these were recognized long ago, as the tragedy of self-discovery by Oedipus suggests.

None of this turns out to apply aptly to Narcissus. Because of his profound lack of thought and feeling for others, he can achieve no true self-knowledge of the ordinary sort. The "self-knowledge" that destroys him has no ethical basis and involves only the most superficial kind of knowledge: he sees himself, that is, his image or reflection, in a clear pool and first ignorantly falls in love with it as though it were another real human being; then, even when he realizes that it is only his own reflection, he persists in his now-foolish passion and so wastes away, like Echo, to nothing. It is, of course, appropriate that Narcissus should be punished by himself, that the unfeeling **fōrma** that was denied to all others should finally, when denied to him, cause his doom and simultaneously "self-destruct." There is a common verb of "knowing" in Greek, Latin, the Bible, and Shakespeare, which refers to knowing another by the mutual discoveries of sexual intercourse. The Latin verb is **cognōscere**, and the prepositional prefix **cog-** (= con-, cum) is essential. It shows that love's knowledge involves others. Narcissus never knows another person, least of all sexually, but only himself in this trivial fashion: his verb, then, is simply **nōscere**.

Narrative Patterns. Ovid likes to repeat dramatic situations for similar stories or sequences. When Echo fell in love with Narcissus, he was hunting (356); when Narcissus first sees his reflection in the pool and falls in love with it (and himself), he has just been hunting and, tired and thirsty, looks for a place to rest in the woods (413). In earlier stories (Daphne, Callisto, and Actaeon), Ovid has established the hunter as a virginal figure, devoted to Diana, goddess of both hunting and virginity; and resting from the hunt meant being exposed to assault by love. But Ovid has built variations into his story pattern. Daphne was unsuccessfully pursued, but Callisto was raped; Actaeon was falsely accused by Diana, hunter by huntress, and destroyed by his own hunting dogs when he saw *her* in a pool. In our story, Narcissus has avoided what he imagines as "rape" and sees himself in a pool. This of course is no crime: he has not seen what is forbidden, the nude body of the deity. But this is the weird process that Nemesis, goddess of vengeance, has determined for his destruction, because seeing himself turns out paradoxically to be like the disastrous results of self-discovery.

Narcissus falls in love with what is forbidden to him by nature, and he cannot employ the usual routine of self-understanding to recognize and reject his impossible passion. Ovid spends considerable detail on the description of the pool (407–412), putting most of his items in negative terms. You might ask the students to talk about what the description suggests to them, and then you could have them compare, in the Passages for Comparison, the account of the pool where Diana was bathing when Actaeon saw her (III.155–164). In effect, this pool symbolizes virginity in both its beauty and sterility, and so it is the perfect mirror for Narcissus: he already sets too much value on his sterile beauty, and, when that is reflected to him, sterile beauty doubled, he cannot help but fall helplessly for it.

A pool in the woods that has never been visited by another human being, never touched by animal, never even disturbed by bird, beast, or branch has not performed any function: it is full of lovely, fresh, cool water that nobody, human or animal, has ever tasted. It is plenty (**cōpia**) which has never been accessible to others, which might as well be nonexistent. Does that not sound like what Narcissus declared as he spurned not only Echo's love but also her very touch (**ante ēmoriar quam sit tibi cōpia nostrī**, 391)? He will die because of his stubborn insistence on fruitless virginity, which here equals self-love. Though he can eventually define his predicament in paradoxical terms— his very plenty has left him impoverished (**inopem mē cōpia fēcit**, 466)—he can do nothing to escape it. He is the first to violate the pool (416), and, as if this were a ritual sin, he simultaneously feels for the first time a passion that can never be gratified. Fourth in the series of tired hunters in the poem, he suffers neither rape nor physical outrage from outside himself: self-loving, he self-destructs—both he and his useless **fōrma**.

Elegiac Themes. In giving his own unique coloring to the extensive development of Narcissus' doomed self-love, Ovid instinctively refers to standard amatory situations and motifs that are familiar to himself and his audience, for they serve as foil to clarify the situation and to direct our attitude. It is, of course, generally true that love stories have dramatic interest only so long as the lovers are not united, while one pursues, woos, expresses jealousy, threats, despair, and so on, and the other spurns or responds in ways that keep the two apart. Nevertheless, the presupposition of all love stories is that love for another is both natural and satisfiable.

Roman comedy usually ends with boy getting girl. Vergilian pastoral regularly refers to instances of shepherds who have won their shepherdesses' affection, even though most of the speakers in the *Eclogues* do not themselves have much amatory success. Roman elegy, the genre in which Ovid served his apprenticeship and of which he was the last great master, has the occasional poem in which the lover exults over a night's rare happiness, but the overwhelming mass of elegies emote over love failure, love desired. Narcissus, by his location in the countryside, reminds us of the lovelorn swain of pastoral, and by his articulate manipulation of familiar erotic themes he reminds us of the lover in Propertian or Ovidian elegy. However, because of his essential selfishness, his refusal to make himself accessible to others, Narcissus can only parody the words of the pastoral and elegiac lover, can only abuse the basic assumptions of their passion, and thus only condemn himself to total failure. Self-love is ungratifiable love, love that is not love. It ends in suicide.

Ovid spends more than twice as many lines on Narcissus' failed passion as he has on Echo's. He sets the scene of the virginal fountain to mirror the virginal boy (407–412). Then, as narrator, he describes the onset of the passion for a reflection (413–431). With little or no sympathy for the boy, he devotes his efforts to capturing the fascinating aspects of this crazy predicament where, in terms of amatory vocabulary, Narcissus is both lover and beloved, the one who both arouses the heat of passion and burns with it (426). Using the familiar words to render the stunning effect of love at first sight (**adstupet, vultūque inmōtus eōdem haeret**, 418–419), Ovid also seems to play upon the etymology of Narcissus' name, which refers to the narcotic effect (a use to which the narcissus was sometimes put). Like Echo earlier, Narcissus reaches out his arms to embrace his beloved (428–429) and suffers total frustration, not because the beloved spurns him, of course, but because he can never touch a physical substance or a person behind his reflection and, in fact, can only dissipate the reflection by touching it.

As if finally impatient with the ignorant folly of this boy (**inprūdēns**, 425; **nescit**, 430; **dēcipit**, 431), the poet then intrudes on his dramatic situation and tries to address the fictional Narcissus (432–436). He does not find this love either touching or pathetic, in contrast to such Renaissance painters as Caravaggio: for him, Narcissus is a credulous fool who needs to grow up, wake up, smarten up. His unsympathetic intervention naturally accomplishes nothing: Narcissus ignores him and prefers to establish a kind of communication with nature, which will neither criticize nor answer him and thus will leave him his self-centered illusions. His long soliloquy (442–473) is one of the fine examples of Ovid's skill in rendering the lover's complaint in novel manner; Polyphemus' speech is another variation on the convention. After twenty lines, Narcissus at last realizes that the person he thinks he loves there in the pool is merely a thing, his reflection, a hopeless object of passion (463–468). For a while, then, he uses neuters to refer to it (**quod cupiō**, 466; **quod amāmus**, 468), but his self-love proves too strong, and once again he relapses into his passionate personification of this image without substance. All the articulateness of the boy's speech, as he describes almost elegiacally his symptoms and the paradoxes of the situation, only goes to emphasize his fanatic fixation. The separation of lover from beloved constitutes a favorite elegiac theme: Narcissus contrasts the usual types of separation with the minuscule film that seems to part him from his desire (448–453). Then, as he refuses to fight the love that he knows is irrational, he extracts a grain of irrational comfort from another elegiac commonplace: at least the lovers will be united in death (473).

The death of young Actaeon earlier in Book III, unfairly punished by Diana and torn apart by his own dogs, stirred our sympathy. The death of his cousin Pentheus, which will follow our story, will not be sympathetic because, though torn apart by his own mother and aunts, the young man will have deserved punishment for his savage irreverence to Bacchus. Somewhere between these two in his claim on our feelings stands Narcissus: he has naively sinned against the essential power of Love, but he certainly has not knowingly blasphemed like Pentheus. In death, he does not suffer the wild violence of assault by external forces, as Actaeon and Pentheus do. He wastes away, occasionally beating himself with despair, weeping inconsolably into the pool. For the most part, we remain cold to all this silly emotionality and self-destruction in the boy who himself was once so cold to others. Ovid, however, reminds us that Echo still retains enough love for the other to lament the boy's death, even to beat herself in response to his self-flagellation (497–498).

Metamorphosis. In keeping with the title and announced subject of his poem, Ovid ends with the transformation of Narcissus' corpse into a pretty but insignificant flower. In many of his stories, a person who has lived fully and often suffered much in failure of some kind is metamorphosed and continues to live in another form, say, that of an animal, bird, or plant. Philemon and Baucis turn into two lovingly intertwined trees; Acis will become a river deity. Despite the change of outer form, something of the human personality persists in the new shape, and as a result the transformation strikes us as a way of escape from death. Even Echo, though she lost her body, continued to exist, with her loving, abused spirit. She was ready and waiting at the end to respond with affection to anything that Narcissus spoke in her direction. But Narcissus did not have a personality that could survive apart from his physical form: the two were inextricably connected. As his body declines, his life sinks away, and finally his body and spirit separate. What remains of the body turns into the yellow flower; the futile spirit descends to the Shades and there continues its futility, staring at its shade, somehow still admirable to Narcissus' warped judgment, in the supremely sterile waters of the Styx. That is the final emblem of self-love's uselessness. You might encourage students to compare the different ways that Ovid presents metamorphosis in the stories they have read and to compare the different meanings the poet sees in change.

Pentheus

The story of Pentheus concerns the punishment of a young man who persists in his wrong-headed opposition to the god Bacchus, using his position as king to force his tyrannical viewpoint on his subjects and the religious supporters of the genuine god. We have chosen it not only because Ovid tells it well but also because it gives us an opportunity to observe how the poet arranged his stories in this long poem. Young Pentheus exhibits some significant similarities to and differences from Narcissus.

Structure. Ovid uses the same device of ring structure as in the Narcissus story: he begins with a prophecy from Tiresias about Pentheus' death, that he will be torn apart (**lacer,** 522) and scattered in a thousand places in the woods, and he ends with the obvious fulfillment of that prediction: in the woods of Mt. Cithaeron, Pentheus is torn limb from limb (**lacerāta,** 722). The cause, too, follows the prophecy. As Tiresias warned, the king would some day wish he were not spying on the Bacchic rites (518), and, sure enough, he does not reverently welcome and carry out the **sacra** but goes out to spy on them with profane eyes (710) and so pays the penalty for irreverence. There is even some similarity in what causes the doom of the two young men. Both see something which then produces their destruction. However, Narcissus sees his own reflection and, fixated on himself, wastes away with useless love, self-destroyed, whereas Pentheus spies on rites forbidden to outsiders, becomes involved in a perverse way (not with himself but with his own female relatives), and is killed by others. The story of Actaeon, partially cited in the Passages for Comparison, offers still another item of comparison.

Within this frame of prophecy declared and then fulfilled, Ovid sets his main narrative. It consists of an alternation of warnings to Pentheus and violent rejections, until at last, when the most cogent warning is spurned, Pentheus' next blasphemous act can only receive its just punishment. The first warning is Tiresias' prophecy, which the king rejects, literally knocking the old man over as he predicts the truth (526). We are all familiar with folk tales in which the rejection of prophecy is an important motif and aligns the audience against the one who scorns warnings. When next the king harangues the Thebans and denounces Bacchus for un-Theban ways, his male relatives try to reason him out of his folly (564–565). Their admonitions serve only to increase his fury, and he orders his guards to arrest the leader of the Bacchic group. They return not with the **dux,** but with someone they present as a mere **comes** or follower. In answer to the hostile demands of the king, this man identifies himself as Acoetes and then proceeds to explain why he follows the **sacra** of Bacchus (582–691). We can see, though Pentheus cannot, that Acoetes' long account of how the god revealed himself and made him a devout follower is another veiled warning to Pentheus, a reminder that he is fighting against a real deity who has immense powers to punish those who oppose him or violate his rites. Unimpressed by Acoetes' experience, indeed infuriated by the length of his pious tale, Pentheus now commands that the stranger be tortured and put to death (694–695). When the guards try to carry out these orders, a miracle occurs: the chains fall away from Acoetes, the prison doors open by themselves, and he escapes unscathed (699–700). It is Pentheus' final warning, but he predictably persists (**perstat,** 701) in his irrational antagonism. Going out, then, to spy on the Bacchic rites, he meets his end.

Ovid does not make all these episodes of the same length. In fact, straight narrative forms a very small portion of the more than 220 lines in this story. The encounter with Tiresias at the beginning illustrates his methods: 6 lines of narrative, 9 lines of Tiresias' speech, and one final line of narrative. In the next episode, Ovid shifts the proportions of narrative to speech sharply: 4 lines of narrative (527–530) lead into Pentheus' ranting denunciation of the **sacra,** which the Thebans have accepted with simple piety, a tirade of 33 lines (531–563). The capture and speech of Acoetes again show the bias in favor of direct speech over indirect narrative: 100 versus 18 lines. Only the last section, where Pentheus meets his fate, uses more narrative than speech. By their very length, the two major speeches, those of Pentheus to his people (531–563) and of Acoetes to Pentheus (582–691), form the heart of the story. They serve to define the two principal antagonists and their opposing values. Because the speech of Acoetes is so much longer than Pentheus' and his tone more gentle and reverent, it is apparent that Pentheus loses the implicit contest for our sympathy, as Ovid plans it. We shall come back to the contrast of these two.

Sources. We had practically no earlier materials on Narcissus, and so it was not safe or useful to conjecture how the poet used his sources to create his inimitable tale. In the case of Pentheus, we do have some of the material once available to Ovid, and it helps us to see more sharply some of his methods and thematic emphasis. Pentheus the blasphemer was a primary figure of Greek art and literature, and he early entered the repertoire of tragedy. Although several such tragedies have disappeared utterly or come down to us as a few

131

disconnected lines, we do possess the final play of Euripides, the *Bacchae,* completed about 406 B.C. It is almost certain that Euripides' text was available in Rome and known to the Augustan poets, whose Greek was impeccable and whose passion to assimilate Greek literature unquenchable. In any case, we know that Roman tragedians in the second century B.C. adapted the story to the Roman stage at least twice: Pacuvius in mid-century produced a tragedy entitled *Pentheus,* and some years later Accius wrote a *Bacchae.* The latter seems to have followed closely the Greek text of Euripides. Among other things, these facts indicate that Ovid was working with material that defined itself as tragic and encouraged him to utilize any applicable dramatic techniques, and particularly the contrast of character and themes that is exploitable in paired speeches.

The teacher should be familiar with Euripides' play: it can be read in an hour. A quick reading easily demonstrates that Ovid did *not* use Euripides as a major source. More important, it shows how the Greek, by different emphasis and organization as well as by different details, made the story an extremely powerful tragedy, whereas Ovid's story, in the end, escapes tragic emphasis. Here are a few key features of Euripides' play. The principal opposition rages between on the one hand the god Dionysos himself, at work in the action from the opening lines, where he speaks the Prologue and establishes his purposes, and on the other hand young Pentheus, who first appears after two hundred lines to denounce the god and his adherents. Euripides has no character parallel to Ovid's Acoetes to make any convincing effort to dissuade the king from his folly. Indeed, Dionysos, when he allows himself to be temporarily captured, does not identify himself and toys maliciously with the doomed Pentheus, first defying him to do his worst and then luring him with sinister pleasure to spy on the women's rites and die.

In Euripides, Pentheus makes a speech, cited in the Passages for Comparison, accusing the god and his followers of practicing sexual debauchery; in Ovid, that charge may be implicit, but it fades behind the main attack, namely, that the god undermines the martial essence of Theban society. (That special stress probably derives not from any tragic sources but rather from Ovid's interest in adapting some contemporary Roman topics from the *Aeneid* and the propaganda of Augustus.) Pentheus' tyrannous power, such as it is, never seems to be a serious threat to Dionysos, whom Euripides makes convincingly confident and menacing in his divinity. A messenger describes with vivid horror the death of the king, but that is not the end for Euripides. Ovid lets the story trail off with two final lines, which announce that the Thebans sensibly take these events as a warning and revere the god. In the Greek play, however, Pentheus' mother Agave comes to center stage brandishing the severed head of her son, which she in her delusion believes and boasts triumphantly is the head of a lion. Slowly she recovers her senses and realizes the terrible thing she has done. As she discovers this wretched truth, Dionysos reappears to exult over all the human characters and pitilessly declares his victory and future miseries for every member of the royal house of Thebes. We are appalled, fully struck with the tragic effect, which is manifest in the contrast between the blood-stained, horror-stricken mother with her son's head and, on the other hand, the untouched, untouchable, and vengeful god.

It is of the very essence of tragedy when a human being tries and fails to make himself more than a human, to become like a god. Different tragedies emphasize this attempt and failure differently. Sometimes we accept without protest the necessity for an arrogant man to be crushed; sometimes, again, we tend to feel the colossal waste that destroys a mainly good person (as in *Hamlet).* Euripides forces on his audience both the feeling of horror that Pentheus' mother had over the cruel death that she has unwittingly perpetrated and a powerful sense of dismay that a god could act in such an inexplicably inhuman manner. We know that Pentheus was wrong, but we cannot comprehend the person of Dionysos. It is a disturbing experience to watch and hear the god in the Greek play.

Ovid had other goals. Although in a few other stories he approached the tragic mode, he really did not want it here. The play of Pacuvius *may* have encouraged his different interpretation: that depends on whether we trust a late plot-summary which ignores Bacchus entirely and says that Pacuvius opposed Pentheus and Acoetes. No lines of the Latin drama survive. At any rate, Ovid, if not Pacuvius, did construct his plot on the antagonism between king and a mere follower of the god; Ovid hardly mentions the god except in Acoetes' narrative and never gives him a role, so that we cannot claim that the god himself engineers Pentheus' destruction or that he chooses the mother as his instrument because he is also punishing her for blasphemy. Acoetes, because he is not a god but an ostentatiously weak, humble, non-threatening human being who faces an obvious tyrant with saintly mildness, emerges as the weaker opponent. Consequently, Pentheus quickly loses our sympathy, as the rhythm of warning and contemptuous rejection is played out before us. We do not like his words, ideas, or actions. He is a tyrant, which no Roman would admire. He distorts the grandiose words and ideas of Roman patriotism in a way that makes him almost obscenely objectionable. His stubbornness, threats, and infantile anger against innocent people ensure that we approve his death and waste no pity on him. Though Ovid lets the prophecy be fulfilled along the lines prescribed by myth, he avoids bringing the mother on stage in the finale and does not risk a mood that would be tragic.

Pentheus. The king is the dominant character of Ovid's story; at least he behaves as though he is dominant, with angry, tyrannous words and actions, until he discovers his powerlessness (long since predicted) as a victim of women, especially of his mother and aunts. To make this tyrant particularly obnoxious, Ovid borrows motifs from the recent *Aeneid* (which had appeared in 17 B.C., a mere twenty years before Ovid composed this episode). In the second half of his epic, Vergil presents a blasphemous tyrant, Mezentius, formerly an Etruscan ruler, whose tyranny was overthrown, whose defiance of the gods takes a tragic course at the end of *Aeneid* X. In calling Pentheus **contemptor superum** (514), Ovid invites his audience to recall Mezentius **contemptor dīvum** (same metrical position, *Aeneid* VII.648). Moreover, by having Pentheus remind the Thebans of how they came as exiles from a foreign land, of their ancestor Mars, and of their military heritage, Ovid turns Pentheus into a travesty of Aeneas and the epic values he embodies.

What effectively sabotages the ranting rhetoric of the king is his comically inept effort to turn the dragon (which reluctantly in death provided the "seed" from which sprang the first people of Thebes) into a "hero" who died fighting for the country, thus affording a militaristic paradigm for the future. Furthermore, nothing in Ovid's story supports the claim that the followers of Bacchus are corrupt effeminates. On the contrary, though the king is brutal and a bully, the followers are peaceful, mild, and yet endowed with a residue of strength that eventually overpowers a man who is more a bully than a hero. In Acoetes' story, the villainous crew of kidnappers provides a clear parallel to Pentheus and further defines his nature. During the final episode, Ovid describes the king as a warhorse at the outset (704–707). That comparison quickly proves ironic. When the women notice him, they perceive him as a wild boar (715). A boar might seem similar to a warhorse, immensely powerful and virile, but Pentheus as a boar only brings out his own weakness and the fanatic strength of the women who attack him. Torn limb from limb, he ends up compared to a tree stripped of its leaves by the autumn wind (729–731).

Acoetes. Euripides opposed Dionysos to Pentheus and thus declared the defeat of the king by the god from the beginning. Ovid chooses a humble human follower of Bacchus to represent the opposition. He has taken his cue from an unnamed helmsman in the Homeric *Hymn to Dionysos*. In his fearless but simple response to Pentheus' ugly demands (582–691), Acoetes describes his poor origins as a fisherman on the Aegean coast of Asia Minor and his efforts to improve himself as a ship's captain. He plainly stands as a sharp contrast to the spoiled young ruler who has never done hard work in his life. The main portion of his account, which answers the question of why he is a follower of Bacchus, presents a warning parallel to Pentheus. Like the king, the crew of his ship had scornfully rejected the divinity of Bacchus, confidently mocking his trust and eventually provoking his punishment. Acoetes, on the other hand, had instinctively recognized the god in the boy, had alone protested at the crew's impiety, and thus had witnessed the epiphany of Bacchus unhurt. He is plainly not the degenerate type that the king's diseased imagination has proposed in his speech: he is simple, rugged, and virile. His narrative not only proves the existence of the god but also attributes to him a nature that is calculated to appeal to us.

Bacchus. Bacchus never actually appears in the main narrative; he has a role only in Acoetes' story. Earlier in *Metamorphoses* III, Ovid has briefly described how Bacchus was born, the son of Jupiter and Semele (an aunt of Pentheus, now dead); thus, the poet guarantees the divine nature of Bacchus before he (or his followers) appear in Thebes. But Pentheus hates his divine cousin. Sneering at him as an unarmed boy (553–586), he goes on to accuse him of soft and decadent interest in perfume, fine robes, and jewelry. However, none of the details that Ovid himself provides about the worship of Bacchus supports this prejudice. Then, when Acoetes reports his own experience of the god, we accept it as true, though the king clings to his perverse bias. At first sight (607), Bacchus appears indeed as an unarmed boy, but there is nothing corrupt about his dress. He has the somewhat girlish face of a teenager, and he staggers uncertainly as if drowsy or a little tipsy from drink (608–610). There is no un-Roman degeneracy in this appearance and definitely no barely concealed menace (as in Euripides). To the simple piety of Acoetes, the divinity of the boy seems likely. But the god acts guilelessly, like a boy, asking for help trustingly, crying with disappointment when the crew's deception is exposed. When finally he does punish the crew, he says nothing (unlike Euripides' all-too-articulate, menacing Dionysos):

his actions speak for him. The ship miraculously stops dead in the water and then is covered with ivy and filled with the forms of fierce beasts. Gradually each of the crew turns into a dolphin.

Since Ovid makes sure that the god takes no direct part in the metamorphosis and that the process of change is marvelous rather than fearsome or pathetic, to readers as well as victims, we end up concluding that in fact the god has been rather gentle toward the brutal crew. In their final scene, they are "playing" in the water, exactly as people today imagine dolphins (683–686). Now, the death of Pentheus is, by contrast, very cruel. Euripides not only makes sure that *his* audience knows that Dionysos is responsible but even has him boast of his role. Not so Ovid. Nobody apparently accompanies Pentheus to Cithaeron, not Acoetes, certainly not Bacchus. Nowhere does Ovid imply that the god acted through the women in pursuit of private vengeance. Rather, it seems that the death of Pentheus results from his own violation of the rites of Bacchus and from his own misunderstanding of the physical power and religious commitment of even the female disciples. Therefore, Bacchus is at most only indirectly involved in the destruction of the king. Ovid does not invite us, as Euripides does, to speculate about the darker, inhuman, or subhuman aspects of the deity.

Principal Themes. Ovid has appropriated the age-old tragic theme of the conflict between man and god, but he has attenuated it from its tragic mode. By representing Pentheus as a tyrant and by replacing Bacchus with Acoetes, he has produced an all-human conflict between absolute ruler and simple worshipers or, to put it in abstract terms, between tyranny and religion. In a somewhat similar situation in a story in *Metamorphoses* VI, the imperious queen Niobe interferes with the worship of gods, but she tries to claim that it is she who deserves the worship. Pentheus is not so rash as to arrogate divinity to himself. He is not trying to replace one god with another or one conception of religion with another that he considers "higher" or "more holy." His view of Bacchus is totally negative and irreligious: the god threatens his state and power. Thus, beside his negative view of Bacchus (which Ovid makes out to be perverse and wrong), Pentheus places his "positive" view of the Theban state and the national character. Only it does not convince. To further alienate us from the viewpoint that Pentheus espouses, Ovid emphasizes the parallelism between him and Acoetes' villainous crew.

On the side of religion stands the entire population of Thebes, it would appear, with the exception of the king's soldiers—the military regu-

larly collaborates with political power—plus Acoetes. Of the Thebans, Ovid says little, primarily as a frame for the violence of Pentheus. When the god first arrives, they swarm out to his rites, and the fields roar with festive shrieks (528). The Latin words **fremunt ululātibus** do have negative overtones connected with animal sounds, but no details support the king's wild charges. As for Acoetes, who serves as Ovid's main representative of Bacchus, he is, as we have seen above, simple, manly, honest, and a reliable witness for the god. Thus, by means of Acoetes, we correct the king's prejudice and view the Bacchic rites as a valid expression of religious feeling. If Pentheus does become a victim of the Bacchantes, it is not because they are automatically corrupt, but because he violates their worship as a declared enemy. He has initiated the hostility, which results in his death.

Metamorphosis. In the other three stories selected, metamorphosis comes at the end to punctuate the narrative effectively. It saves a pious couple (Philemon and Baucis) and a lover (Acis) from the annihilation of death; it marks the disappearance of Narcissus with a commemorative flower. For Pentheus, death—and a most horrible one, as predicted—is final. Nothing attenuates it; nothing should. However, we do not know that the god himself acted to cause this death, for the human explanation is quite adequate, and so we need not expect any softening of the king's fate. Before violating the rites, he had more than one warning, all of which he furiously rejected. Where we know that the god did act, from the pious report of Acoetes, a metamorphosis is recorded. When Bacchus was personally affronted by the blasphemous sailors, he retaliated by changing them into dolphins. Ovid lovingly describes the multiple metamorphoses, focusing on partial aspects of the total transformation in individual cases (671–682). The god did not kill those savage men, and by metamorphosis treated them most mildly, converting them, so to speak, from murderous pirates into playful beasts, an emblem of his kindly majesty. In these two different ways of treating blasphemers, the known action of Bacchus toward the sailors may be designed by Ovid not as a preface to the god's merciless destruction of Pentheus, but rather as an indication that the god did *not* destroy the king. The bloody mutilation of the young man by his mother and aunts reflects the irrational savagery with which human beings treat each other.

*   *   *

TRANSLATIONS

Baucis and Philemon

[I.] All were stunned, nor did they approve of such words, and before all of them Lelex, ripe in mind and age, speaks thus: "The power of heaven is immense and has no end, and whatever the gods above have wished, it is done. And in order that you may doubt less, on Phrygian hills there is an oak adjacent to a linden, encircled by a wall of medium height. I myself have seen the place; for Pittheus sent me into Pelopeian territory ruled formerly by his ancestor. Not far from this place is a lake, once habitable land, now waves crowded with sea-birds and marshland waterfowl. To this place Jupiter [came] in mortal disguise and with his father came the descendant of Atlas, the caduceus-bearer, though he had put aside his wings. A thousand homes they approached, seeking a place to rest; a thousand homes shot their bolts; nevertheless, one received them, small indeed and thatched with swamp-reed, but pious. Baucis, an old woman, and Philemon, of equal age, were united in their youthful years in that hut; in it they grew old together, and by confessing their poverty and bearing it with not uneven mind, they made it light.

[II.] "Nor does it make a difference, whether you ask for the masters or the servants: they two are the whole household; the same two both command and obey. Therefore, when the gods reached the little house and with bowed head entered the humble doorway, the old man ordered them to rest their limbs after he had put out a chair, on which the attentive Baucis threw a rough woven cloth; and on the hearth she pushed aside the warm ashes and arouses yesterday's fire and nourishes it with leaves and dry bark and draws it forth to flames with her old woman's breath and brought down from the ceiling torch-material broken into little pieces and dry branches and made them smaller and applied them to a small copper pot; and the vegetable which her husband gathered from the well-watered garden she trims of its leaves. With a two-pronged fork she lifts down a sooty side of bacon hanging from the blackened beam and cuts off a small piece from the back, saved for a long time, and cooks it in the boiling water. Meanwhile they beguile the passing hours with conversation and prevent the delay being felt.

[III.] "A beechwood trough was there, suspended from a nail by its hard handle; this is filled with warm water and receives the feet [of the guests] in order to soothe them. In the middle a mattress made of soft grasses is placed on a bed with willow-wood frame and feet. They cover this with cloths which they were not accustomed to lay out except at festive times, but even so this cloth covering was old and cheap, not likely to be disdained by a willow-wood bed. The gods reclined to eat. The old woman, her skirts tucked up, tremulously puts the table in place, but the third foot of the table was unequal: a broken potsherd made it even, which, after it had been put under the leg, eliminated the tilt; green mint rubbed the leveled table clean. Here is placed the mottled olive of pure Minerva and wild autumn cherries preserved in liquid wine-lees, and endives and radish and a lump of cheese and eggs turned lightly in temperate ashes, all things in pottery vessels. After these things a crater, embossed in the same silver, is set in place and cups fashioned from beech-wood, which are smeared with yellow wax in the places where they are porous.

[IV.] "There is a small delay, and the hearth sent forth the warming feast, and the wines—not of an old vintage—are brought back and give way a little, once they've been set aside, to dessert. Here nuts, here dried figs are mixed with wrinkled dates and plums and fragrant apples in broad baskets and grapes collected from purple vines; in the middle a honeycomb shines; in addition to all these their good faces approached and their good-will, neither sluggish nor meager. Meanwhile they see that the crater, as many times as it is drunk up, is refilled of its own accord and the wine rises up from below. Astonished by the strangeness, Baucis and fearful Philemon are terrified and with upraised hands begin their prayers and pray for pardon for their meal and the insignificant preparations. They had only one goose, the guardian of their tiny farmhouse, which its masters were preparing to sacrifice to their guests, the gods. He, quick of feather, exhausts them slowed by age and eludes them for a long time and at last seemed to flee to the gods themselves.

[V.] "The gods forbade its being killed, and said, 'We are gods, and this impious neighborhood will suffer a deserved punishment; to you will it be given to be immune from this evil. Only, abandon your house and accompany our steps and go together onto the high place of the mountain!' They both obey and, supported on walking sticks, strive to place their footsteps on the long incline. They were as distant from the top as an arrow, sent once, can go: they looked behind and catch sight of all the other houses submerged by a swamp; only their own house remained. And while they marvel at these things, while they bewail the fates of their neighbors, that old hut, small for even two masters, is changed into a temple: columns have replaced the forks, the thatching turns gold, the earth is seen to be covered over with marble, the doors embossed, and the roof gilded. Then the son of Saturn proclaimed the following words from his kindly mouth: 'Say, just old man and woman worthy of a just spouse, what you desire!' Having spoken a few words with Baucis, Philemon reveals their joint decision to the gods:

[VI.] " 'We ask to be your priests and to guard your temple, and since we have lived out harmonious years, let the same hour take us two away, nor let me ever see the funeral pyre of my spouse nor let me be buried by her.' Fulfillment follows the prayer: they were the guardians of the temple, as long as life was granted; weakened by years and old age, while they were standing before the sacred steps and by chance relating the history of the place, Baucis caught sight of Philemon putting forth leaves, Philemon the elder saw Baucis leafing out. And now over both their faces, as a tree top was growing, while it was permitted, they exchanged mutual words and said at the same time, 'Farewell, O spouse,' while at the same time bark covered their hidden mouths. Up to the present time the Bithynian native points out there the neighboring trunks [growing] from a twin body. These things old men—not foolish (nor was there any reason why they would wish to deceive)—recited to me; I for my part saw entwined garlands hanging over the branches and, placing fresh ones, said, 'Let those who care for the gods be gods, and, those who have worshiped, let them be worshiped!' "

Acis, Galatea, and Polyphemus

[I.] "There was Acis, sprung from Faunus and a nymph, the daughter of Symaethus, a great pleasure indeed to his father and mother; nevertheless, to me a greater one; for he had united me to himself alone. Handsome, and, twice eight birthdays having been passed, he had marked his soft cheeks with uncertain down. Him I [was pursuing], [and] me the Cyclops was pursuing with no limit; nor, if you were to ask whether hatred of the Cyclops or love of Acis was more present to me, would I [be able to] say: both were equal. Oh! how great is the power of your kingdom, kindly Venus. For he, merciless, who must be feared by the very forests and is seen safely by no visitor and is a despiser of great Olympus, together with its gods, what might be love, he felt, and, seized by a desire for me, he burns, unmindful of his herds and caves. And now you have care for your beauty, you have care of pleasing, now you comb, Polyphemus, your rigid locks with rakes, now it is pleasing to you to prune

your shaggy beard with a sickle and to gaze upon your fierce countenance in the water and to compose it. Love of slaughter and ferocity and immense thirst for gore cease, and ships come and go safely.

[II.] "Telemus meanwhile, carried towards Sicilian Etna, Telemus, the son of Eurymus, whom no bird had deceived, approached the terrible Polyphemus and said, 'That one eye which you bear in the middle of your forehead, Ulysses will steal from you.' He laughed and says, 'O most stupid of prophets, you are deceived. Another has already stolen it.' Thus in vain he spurns the one warning him of the truth, and either walking with huge step he presses heavily on the shore or exhausted returns beneath his shady cave. A wedge-shaped hill with a long promontory projects out into the sea, the wave of the sea flows around on either side. To this place the wild Cyclops ascended and sat down in the middle, his wool-bearing herds having followed, with no one leading them. By whom [i.e., the Cyclops] after the pine tree, which furnished him the use of a walking stick, was placed at his feet, though suitable for bearing yardarms, and the pan-pipe, of a hundred reeds bound together, was taken up, all the mountains heard his pastoral whistling, as did all the waves. I, hiding under a cliff and sitting idly in the lap of my Acis, drank up from a distance the following words with my ears, and what was heard, noted.

[III.] " 'Whiter than the snowy privet leaf, Galatea, more flowery than meadows, loftier than the tall alder tree, brighter than glass, more playful than a tender young goat, smoother than shells worn down by the continuous ocean, more pleasing than winter suns, than summer shade, finer than apples, more visible than a tall plane tree, shinier than ice, sweeter than a ripe bunch of grapes, softer than both the feathers of the swan and cheese, and (if you should not flee), fairer than a well-watered garden; the same Galatea [is] more savage than untamed bullocks, harder than aged oak, more deceptive than waves, tougher than both rods of willow or white bryony, more immovable than these rocks, more violent than the river, prouder than the praised peacock, fiercer than fire, more prickly than brambles, more aggressive than a bear that has just given birth, deafer than the ocean, more pitiless than a trampled snake, and— what especially I would wish I might take away from you—swifter not only than a stag driven by loud barkings, but even than winds and the winged air! (But if you knew [me] well, it would displease you that you fled, and you yourself would curse your delays and strive to hold me back!)

[IV.] " 'I have, part of a mountain, caves vaulted by living rock, in which is felt neither sun in the middle of a heat-wave nor winter; I have fruit weighing down the branches; I have bunches of grapes like gold, on long vines; and I have purple ones: both these and those I save for you. Yourself with your own hands you will pick the soft wild strawberries, sprung up under woodland shade, [you] yourself [will pick] the autumn cornel cherries and plums, not only purplish with dark juice, but even the superior ones, imitating new beeswax. Nor will there be lacking to you—when I am your husband—chestnuts or the fruit of the strawberry tree: every tree will serve you. All this herd is mine; many kine also graze in the valleys; many the forest covers, many are stabled in caves. Nor if by chance you were to ask, could I tell you how many there are: it is the mark of a poor man to number his herd! About the praises of these cattle you should not believe me at all: in person you can see them yourself, how scarcely they can get around the swollen udder with their legs. There are young offspring, lambs in warm sheepfolds; there are also, of equal age, young goats in other pens. I always have snowy white milk: part of it is saved to be drunk, a part dissolved rennet solidifies [into curds].

[V.] " 'Nor will I give you only easy toys or common gifts, deer and hares and a billy goat, a pair of doves or a nest taken from a tree top: I have found twin bear cubs, who can play with you, indistinguishable between themselves, so that you can scarcely tell them apart, belonging to a shaggy she-bear on the highest mountain. I found them and said, "I will save these for my mistress." Now, just poke your shining head out of the blue sea, now, Galatea, come, and do not despise my gifts! Certainly I know myself and have recently seen myself in the reflection of clear water, and my form pleased me as I gazed. Look, how big I am! Jupiter in the sky has no bigger body—for you are accustomed to tell tales about how this Jupiter fellow reigns. Many a hair sticks out over my fierce face and shades my shoulders, like a grove. And do not think my body shameful, because it bristles very thickly with rigid hair; a tree is shameful without leaves; a horse is shameful if the mane does not cover his yellow neck; feathers cover birds; to sheep their own wool is a distinction; a beard and shaggy hair on the body suit men! I have one eye in the middle of my brow, but it is the equal of a huge shield. What [of that]? Does not the great sun see all these things from the heavens? Nevertheless, the sun has only one eye!

[VI.] " 'Consider additionally, that my sire reigns in your ocean; him I give you for a father-in-law! Only, take pity on [me] and pay heed to the prayers of a suppliant. To you alone I yield. And I, who spurn Jupiter and the heavens and the pene-trating thunderbolt, worship you, daughter of Nereus: your wrath is fiercer than a thunderbolt. But I might be more able to undergo this contempt if you fled from all [suitors]; but why, if the Cyclops is rebuffed, do you love Acis, and prefer Acis to my embraces? Nevertheless, although he pleases himself and—what I would not prefer—although he pleases you: provided the opportunity be granted [to me], he will feel the strengths I have, in proportion to so big a body! I will drag his living entrails, and sprinkle his scattered limbs through the fields and through your waves—thus may he mingle himself with you. For I am burning, and my wounded passion burns more fiercely, and I seem to carry Etna in my breast, transferred with all her forces: and you, Galatea, are not moved!' Having lamented such words in vain—for I saw all this—he rises up, and, like a raging bull deprived of its cow, he is unable to stand still and wanders in the forest and well-known woodlands. When the wild one sees me and Acis unaware nor fearing any such thing, 'I see [you],' he cries out, 'and I will see to it that that union of your love is the last.'

[VII.] "That was the voice, just so great as an enraged Cyclops ought to have. Etna trembled greatly at the outcry. But I, terrified, submerge myself under the neighboring ocean; the Symaethian hero had turned his back in flight and had said, 'Help me, Galatea, I pray, help me, parents, and admit me, about to die, to your kingdoms.' The Cyclops follows and throws a part of a mountain which he had torn loose, and although [only] the extreme corner of the mass reached him, nevertheless it buried Acis totally. But I, what only was permitted through the fates to be done, I did, so that Acis could assume his grandfather's powers. Purple gore was dripping from the boulder, and within a short space of time the redness began to fade away and becomes the color of a river muddied by the first rain and with a delay is cleaned; then the boulder gapes where it had been touched, and through the cracks a tall living reed rises up and the hollowed out opening of the stone resounds with dancing waters, and the amazing thing [was], suddenly a youth stood forth up to the middle of his stomach, his new horns girt with woven reeds, who, except that he was larger, except that he was blue in his whole face, was Acis. And thus also was Acis nevertheless converted into a river, and the river kept his former name." Galatea ceased to speak.

Narcissus

[I.] The very lovely nymph gave birth from her full womb to a baby who even then could be loved, and

she names him Narcissus. When consulted about him whether he would live to see a long period of ripe old age, the prophetic seer said: "If he does not know himself." For a long time the word of the prophet seemed empty, but the outcome, events, the type of death, and the novelty of madness all prove it true. When the son of Cephisos had added a year to his fifteen and could appear both a boy and a young man, many youths and girls desired him. But such was the hard arrogance in that tender shape, no young men or girls touched him.

As he is driving frightened deer into his nets, the talkative nymph sights him, she who did not know how to be quiet in response to another's talk nor how to initiate talk: responsive Echo. Echo was still a body, not yet mere voice, yet this talkative person had no other use of her mouth than she has today: to be able to repeat the last of many words. Juno had caused this because, when she might have caught nymphs often lying on the mountain under her husband Jupiter, Echo deliberately detained the goddess with her long conversation, until the nymphs escaped.

[II.] When Juno realized this, she said, "Little power and the briefest use will be granted you of this tongue by which I have been tricked," and she confirms her threat with action. Nevertheless, Echo repeats words at the end of speeches and returns the words she has heard.

So when she saw Narcissus wandering through the lonely countryside and grew hot with passion, she follows his tracks unnoticed and, the closer she follows, the hotter she becomes from the proximity of the flame, just as when inflammable sulphur that has been smeared about the tops of torches catches fire as a flame is moved close. O how often she wanted to approach with winning words and use soft prayers. Nature refuses and does not let her begin. But she is prepared to wait for sounds, as Nature allows, to which she can respond with her own words. By chance, the boy, separated from his loyal band of comrades, had said, "Is anyone present?" and Echo had answered: "Present." He is surprised and, as he looks in every direction, he shouts in a loud voice, "Come!" She calls the one who is calling [her]. He looks back and, when in turn nobody comes, said: "Why do you flee me?" and received as many words as he had spoken.

[III.] He persists and, deceived by the image of the answering voice, says, "Let's get together here." Never more happy to respond to a sound, Echo repeated, "Let's get together" and, acting on her words, she emerged from the woods and moved forward to throw her arms around the neck she desired. He fled and, as he fled, said: "Take your hands off me. I will die before I would give myself to you." She answered only: "I would give myself to

you." Rejected, she lurks in the woods and conceals her shamed face with leaves and lives after that in lonely caverns. But her love clings to her and grows with the grief of rejection. Wakeful passions waste away her unhappy body, thinness draws her skin tight, and all the juices of her flesh evaporate into the air. Only voice and bones remain: the voice survives; the bones, they say, took the shape of a rock. Thereafter, she lurks in the woods and is never seen on the mountain, but is heard by all: it is voice alone that lives in her.

Thus Narcissus had disappointed her, thus other nymphs born from the waves or in the mountains, and throngs of men earlier. One of those he had spurned lifted his arms toward the sky and said, "May he himself love this way and similarly fail to possess his beloved." Nemesis sided with these just prayers.

[IV.] There was a clear spring, silvery with glistening water, which neither shepherds, nor goats grazing on the mountain, nor other kind of cattle had touched, and no bird nor wild animal nor branch fallen from a tree had disturbed. Around it grew grass, which the nearby water nourished, and woods which never allowed the spot to grow warm from the sun. Here, the boy, tired from energetic hunting and from the heat, leaned forward, attracted by the beauty of the spot and the spring, and, while he desired to slake one thirst, another thirst grew. And while he drinks, caught by the image of beauty he sees, he loves a bodiless hope, he thinks what is water is body.

He is stunned at himself and is fixed motionless in one expression like a statue of Parian marble. Prone on the ground, he looks at those twin stars, his own eyes, at the hair worthy of Bacchus or Apollo, at the beardless cheeks, the ivory neck, the attractive mouth, the red mixed with snowy whiteness, and he admires all the features for which he himself is admired. Unwittingly he desires himself, and he who approves is the person approved; while he seeks, he is sought, and simultaneously he sets afire and burns.

[V.] How often he vainly kissed the deceptive spring. How often he plunged his arms into the middle of the water to clasp the neck he saw, but did not catch himself in it. He doesn't know what he sees, but he burns for what he sees, and the very mistake that deceives his eyes arouses them. Trusting fool, why do you vainly grasp at fleeting reflections? What you seek exists nowhere; what you love, you will destroy if you turn away. That is the shadow of a reflected image that you are looking at. It has nothing of itself: it comes with you and stays [with you] and with you will depart, if you could depart.

Concern for food or rest cannot tear him away from there, but, sprawled in the dark grass he stares at the deceptive shape with insatiate vision and perishes by his own eyes. Lifting himself slightly and stretching his arms toward the surrounding woods, he says, "Is there anyone, o woods, who has ever loved more cruelly? You know and have been a convenient hiding place for many. Is there anyone that you remember wasting away similarly in the long age during which so many centuries of your existence have passed? He both pleases and I see him, but what I see and like, I can't find: such confusion possesses me in my love.

[VI.] "To make me even sadder, it isn't the vast sea that parts us nor a journey nor mountains nor walls with barred gates: we are separated by a tiny bit of water. He himself desires to be held. For as often as I strain toward the water to kiss him, he stretches toward me with his face upward. You'd think he could be touched: the slightest obstacle stands in the way of us lovers. Whoever you are, come out here. Why do you trick me, one and only boy? Where do you go when I seek you? Surely it is not my looks nor my age that you flee; nymphs have also loved me.

"You promise me some hope with your friendly expression and, when I have stretched my arms toward you, you willingly stretch yours. When I have laughed, you laugh back. I have also noticed your tears as I was crying. You also signal with a nod and, as far as I can guess from the movement of your handsome mouth, you are replying with words that do not reach my ears. I am that person. I have figured it out, and my image no longer deceives me. I burn with love for myself, I rouse and suffer the fires. What should I do? Should I be asked or ask? What then shall I ask? What I desire exists as part of myself: my wealth has made me destitute.

[VII.] "If only I could escape from my body! Here's a new wish for a lover: I would wish that what I love were absent! Now pain destroys my strength, and my lifetime does not last long. I am snuffed out in early youth. But death does not bother me, since death will end my pain: I only wish that he whom I love could live longer. As it is, the two of us will die together, united in one soul." He stopped and irrationally turned back to the same face and disturbed the water with his tears. At the motion of the pool, the beauty faded. When he saw it vanish, he cried out, "Where are you fleeing? Wait! Don't abandon me in my love, cruel one. Let me at least look at what I can't touch and feed my wretched madness."

As he grieved, he tore his robe open from the top and beat his bared breast with his marble hands. The beaten breast took on a rosy blush, as apples do that are partly white and partly red, or as grapes in varicolored clusters take on a purple color before maturity. As soon as he saw this in the water once again made clear, he endured it no further, but, as golden wax melts in a light fire or morning frosts in the warming sunshine, so he dissolves weakened by love, and little by little is eaten away by hidden fire.

[VIII.] No longer is his complexion one of white mixed with red, nor does he retain the vitality, strength, or features that pleased on sight, and the body does not remain, which Echo had once loved. However, when she saw this, though she was angry and pained by her memories, as often as the pathetic boy had said, "Alas," she repeated in response, "Alas." When he pounded his arms with his hands, she echoed back the very sound of the beating. His last words, as he gazed at the water to which he had grown accustomed, were: "Alas, boy loved in vain!" And the place repeated the words; and when he said, "Goodbye," Echo also said, "Goodbye."

He lowered his tired head to the green grass, and death closed the eyes that were admiring their master's beauty. Even then, after he was received in the world below, he kept looking at himself in the water of the Styx. The naiads, his sisters, beat their breasts and cut their hair for their brother. The dryads beat their breasts; Echo responded to their beating. Now they prepared a pyre, torches that are shaken, and a bier: the body had disappeared, and instead of the body they find a yellow flower, whose center is ringed by white petals.

Pentheus

[I.] The story, when it became known, had brought deserved fame to the prophet throughout the cities of Greece, and the name of the seer was great. However, the son of Echion alone of all despises him, Pentheus the scorner of gods, and laughs at the prophetic words of the old man and mocks his blindness, the disaster of deprived light. Tiresias, shaking his white-haired head, says, "How lucky you would be if you too were orphaned of this light, so that you would not see the rites of Bacchus. For the day will come, which I predict is not far off, when Liber, son of Semele, will arrive here as a stranger. Unless you treat him as worthy of the honor of a temple, you will be torn to pieces and scattered in a thousand places, polluting with your blood the woods and your mother and mother's sisters. It will come to pass. You will not treat the god as worthy of honor, and you will complain that in this blindness of mine I saw all too clearly."

The son of Echion drives him away as he says this. But confirmation attends the words, and the prophecies of the seer are carried out. Bacchus arrives, and the fields roar with festive howling. A crowd rushed out, mothers and fathers together, daughters-in-law, the masses, and the nobility proceeding to the unfamiliar rites.

[II.] "What madness, snake-born descendants of Mars, has confounded your minds?" Pentheus asks. "Does bronze cymbal struck by cymbal have so much power, and the flute of curved horn and the tricks of magic, that men whom no warlike sword or trumpet or troops with poised spears have frightened are conquered by womanish cries, by madness provoked through wine, by obscene throngs, and hollow drums? Should I be surprised at you, elders, who, after sailing the broad sea, established on this site Tyre and on this [site] your exiled Penates, but now allow it all to be captured without a fight? Or [should I be amazed at] you young men, a more vigorous age and closer to my own, who should wield weapons, not wands, and wear helmets, not leaves?

"Please remember from what stock you were born, and adopt the spirit of that dragon who alone slew many. He perished in defense of a spring and pool: you conquer on behalf of your glory. He sent brave men to their death: you drive out weaklings and maintain our father's honor. If the fates forbade Thebes to stand for long, would that siege weapons and men were destroying our walls, that iron and fire roared.

[III.] "Then we would be wretched but guiltless, our destiny would be [one] to be lamented but not to be concealed, and our tears would be free of shame. Now, however, Thebes will be taken by an unarmed boy who delights not in wars, weapons, and horsemanship, but in hair dripping with incense, cowardly crowns, purple, and gold woven into embroidered robes. Yet I personally right now will compel him—you just stand aside—to confess his father falsified and his rites counterfeit. Does Acrisius have enough courage to scorn this fake god and close the gates of Argos to his approach, and will Pentheus and all Thebes be terrified by this stranger? Go, on the double"—so he orders his servants—"and bring the leader here in chains. Let there be no sluggish delay for my commands."

His grandfather, Athamas, and the rest of the throng of his relatives reprove him with their words and vainly struggle to stop him; he becomes fiercer at their rebukes, his madness is provoked and increased by restraint, and controls were only aggravating. Thus I have seen a torrent, where nothing blocked its passage, running rather smoothly, with mild uproar; but wherever logs and piled up boulders checked it, it became foamy and seething and proceeded the more violently because of the obstruction.

[IV.] But look, the servants return all bloodied, and when their master asked where Bacchus was, they said they had not seen Bacchus. "Still," they said, "we have captured this companion and attendant of the rites," and they deliver, hands bound behind his back, a man once of the Tyrrhenian race who practiced the god's rites. Pentheus stares at him with eyes that anger had made fearsome, and, although he scarcely postpones the moment of punishment, he says, "You who are doomed and will set an example for others by your death, tell me your name, that of your parents, your native land, and why you participate in rites of a new kind."

Fearlessly he replied, "My name is Acoetes, my native land Maeonia, my parents from the humble masses. My father did not leave me fields for tough bullocks to cultivate nor wool-bearing flocks nor any herds. He himself was a poor man and used to deceive fish with hooks and pull them in with a rod when they jumped. His skill was his source of income. When he handed on the skill, he said, 'What wealth I have, receive as heir and successor of my profession,' and dying he left me nothing but the water. That is the only thing I can call my father's.

[V.] "In order that I might not be stuck forever on the same rocks, I soon learned how to steer a boat with controlling right hand, and I marked with my eyes the rainy constellation of the Olenian Goat, Taygete, the Hyades, the Great Bear, the homes of the winds, and ports fit for ships. One time, as I was steering for Delos, I put in toward the shores of Chios, am pulled to land by skillful use of oars, give a light leap and jump on to the damp sand. When night was over (Dawn had begun its first blush), I rise, direct the sailors to bring aboard fresh water, and point out the way that leads to the springs. I myself from a tall mound check to see what the breeze promises, call my comrades, and head back to the ship.

" 'Here we are,' said the first of the crew, Opheltes, and, having seized what he thinks is plunder in the abandoned fields, leads along the shore a boy of girlish appearance. The child, weighed down by wine or sleep, seems to stagger and follow with difficulty. I look at his clothes, face, and gait. I saw nothing there that could be believed mortal. I both understood and said to my comrades: 'What god is in that body, I'm not sure, but there is a god in that body. Whoever you are, grant us your favor and assist our toils. Grant these men also your mercy.'

[VI.] " 'Stop praying for us,' says Dictys, than whom none was swifter in climbing to the top yardarms and sliding down a grasped rope. Libys approves his words and so does blonde Melanthus, guard of the prow, so also Alcimedon and Epopeus, who set with his voice the time and the period of rest for rowing, encourager of spirits, and so do all the others. Such is the blind greed for plunder. 'But I shall not allow this ship to be profaned by the holy weight,' I said; 'I am in command here,' and I block the approach. The boldest of the whole crew goes wild, Lycabas, who, driven from his Etruscan city, was paying the penalty of exile for savage murder.

"While I stood in the way, he smashed my throat with his youthful fist and would have knocked me off into the sea if I had not held on tight, though dazed, to a rope. The impious crew cheer the deed. Then at last Bacchus (for it *was* Bacchus), as if his sleepiness had been dispelled by the noise and his senses were returning to his breast [= head] after the wine, said, 'What are you doing? What is this noise? Tell me, sailors, how did I get here? Where are you planning to take me?' 'Don't be afraid,' said Proreus, 'and tell us what port you wish to reach. You will be set down at the land you seek.' 'Steer your course for Naxos,' said Liber. 'That is my home and will be hospitable land for you.'

[VII.] "The liars swear by the sea and all the gods that it will happen and they order me to set the sails of the painted ship. Naxos was on the right; when I steer to the right, everyone fears for himself and says: 'What are you doing, you fool? What madness [possesses] you, Acoetes? Head left.' Most of them indicate by head movement what they mean, but some whisper in my ear. I was shocked and said, 'Let someone else take over the steering,' and I resigned from practice of crime and my skill. I am rebuked by everyone, and the entire crew mutters against me. Of them, Aethalion said, 'I suppose you think our whole safety depends on you alone,' and he moves forward and takes over my duties and heads in the opposite direction, leaving Naxos behind.

"Then the god, play-acting as though he has only just figured out the deception, looks out over the sea from the curved stern and, pretending to cry, says, 'These are not the shores you promised me, sailors, this is not the land I asked for. What did I do to deserve punishment? What honor do you earn if you young men, so many, trick a boy all alone?' I was already crying. The impious crew laughs at our tears and beats the sea with driving oars.

[VIII.] "I swear to you by him (for no god is more present than he) that I am relating things as true as they are beyond belief. The boat stopped dead in the sea as though held in drydock. Amazed, the sailors persist in their oar-strokes,

unfurl the sails, and try to race by doubled means. Ivy interferes with the oars and snakes about with curving knots and dots the sails with heavy clusters. Bacchus himself, his head crowned with a wreath of grape-clusters, waves a spear tipped with vine leaves; around him lie tigers and empty shapes of lynxes and wild bodies of spotted panthers.

"The men jumped up, whether madness or terror caused it, and Medon was the first to start to turn black over his body and to be bent as the spine was forced into a curve. Lycabas starts to say to him: 'Into what monster are you turning?' As he spoke, his mouth grew wide and his nose snubbed, and his skin hardened and took on scales. But Libys, while he tried to turn the resisting oars, saw his hands shrink into a small space, no longer hands but what could be called fins.

[IX.] "Another sailor, desiring to give his arms to the twisted ropes, had no arms, and snub-nosed, with truncated body, leapt into the waves. The end of his tail was sickle-shaped as the horns of the half moon are curved. From all sides they jump and are soaked with much spray. They emerge and plunge back under the water and play about like a chorus, tossing their playful bodies and blowing out the sea through open nostrils. Of the crew of twenty (that was what the ship carried) I alone remained: fearful and shivering with trembling body and hardly myself, I was steadied by the god who said, 'Dismiss fear from your heart and make for Dia.' When I landed there, I joined the worship, and thus I participate in the rites of Bacchus."

"We have listened to your long-winded speech," said Pentheus, "enough that anger might lose its force by the delay. Servants, rush him off headlong and, after you have afflicted him with cruel tortures, send him down to Stygian night." Immediately Tyrrhenian Acoetes is dragged away and imprisoned behind solid walls. While iron and fire were being prepared as the cruel instrument of ordered execution, the story is that of their own accord the doors opened and the chains slipped from his arms, although nobody released them.

[X.] The son of Echion persists, and now he does not order others to go, but himself marches to Cithaeron, which was chosen for the ritual practices and resounded with the clear cries of the Bacchantes. As a high-spirited horse neighs, when the trumpeter in war gives the signal with his tuneful brass instrument, and takes on passion for battle, so Pentheus is stirred when the air is struck by prolonged shrieking and, when he heard the noise, his anger blazed up. Almost in the middle of the mountain is a field visible from all sides, free of trees, its edges ringed by woods.

Here, as he watches the rites with profane eyes, the first to see him, the first to rush at him in a wild race, the first to injure her Pentheus by throwing the thyrsus was his mother. She cried out, "Come here, my two sisters. This huge boar, which wanders over our field, I shall have to strike down." The whole wild company rushes on the one: they all come together and pursue fearful [Pentheus], now at last fearful and uttering less violent speeches, now damning himself and admitting his sin. When wounded he said, "Help me, Aunt Autonoe. Let the shade of Actaeon stir your feelings."

[XI.] She does not know who Actaeon is and yanked off the right arm of the suppliant; the other arm was torn off in the grasp of Ino. The poor wretch has no arms to hold out to his mother, but, since his limbs are lost, showing his mutilations, he says, "Look, mother!" At the sight, Agave howled, tossed her neck, shook her hair in the air, and, after tearing away his head, embracing it with gory fingers, shouts, "Hurray, friends. This achievement is a victory for me." No sooner are leaves, touched by the autumn cold and barely clinging, snatched from a tall tree by the wind than the limbs of the man were torn away by unspeakable hands. Warned by such examples, the Theban women participate in the new rites, giving incense and decorating the holy altars.

* * *

GRAMMAR REVIEW

For the experienced Latinist, Ovid's grammar seems relatively simple: just as his meter is designed to give the impression of ease and flowing movement, so his grammar avoids complicated or unusual structures and rarely puzzles the reader. Nevertheless, at this stage in students' acquaintance with Latin, it would be well to use Ovid to review some of the basic grammar that they are learning. In the sections below, brief examples will be given of each construction. Students would be well advised to keep a notebook with additional examples that will be encountered in the course of reading Ovid.

SYNTAX OF CASES

Nominative

This is the case of the subject of a main verb, of all adjectives that modify it, of participles that refer to it, and of nouns, pronouns, and adjectives that are linked to it by a verb of being, seeming, or the like, or in apposition with it.

Adspicit hunc trepidōs agitantem in rētia
    cervōs
vōcālis nymphē, quae nec reticēre loquentī
nec prius ipsa loquī didicit, resonābilis
    Ēchō.
Corpus adhūc Ēchō, nōn vōx erat.
(III.356–359)

The subject of adspicit is nymphē, in the Greek nominative form (which Ovid often uses with direct Greek derivatives). Its adjective, vōcālis, agrees with it. There follows a relative clause, which begins with the nominative quae (referring to the nymph) and contains the pronoun ipsa. Then, in apposition to this subject Ovid adds resonābilis Ēchō, adjective and name. In the next line, Ēchō now becomes subject, and Ovid describes it with two predicate nouns: "Echo was still body, not merely voice."

Genitive

1. Possession. This is the commonest use of the case.

   foedābis mātremque tuam *mātris*que
       sorōrēs. (III.523)
   "You will pollute your mother and the sisters *of your mother.*"

2. Partitive or genitive of the whole. In a sentence like, "I have enough money," the Romans thought of "enough" as part of the noun "money" (the whole). They therefore put "money" in the genitive case.

   nīl habet ista *suī.* (III.435)
   "It has nothing *of its own.*"

   an satis Ācrisiō est *animī?* (III.559)
   "Does Acrisius have enough *spirit?*"

3. Objective genitive. The Romans put in the genitive a noun dependent on another noun or adjective when that noun or adjective contained a verbal sense (the first noun then functioned as its object).

   crēscit . . . dolōre *repulsae.* (III.395)
   "It grows with grief *over rejection.*"

   contemptor *superum* Pentheus. (III.514)
   "Pentheus, despiser *of the gods above.*"

contemptūs essem patientior. (XIII.859)
"I would be more tolerant *of contempt.*"

4. Genitive with special adjectives. The adjectives on which the noun in the genitive depends are less specifically verbal in origin than those in group 3 above.

lūminis huius / orbus . . . fierēs. (III.517–518)
"You would be devoid *of this light.*"

Dative

In addition to its basic usage for the indirect object (e.g., *mēnsīs*, VIII.673), Ovid employs:

1. Dative of reference. Often a proper noun or pronoun in the dative is inserted to remind us of the person referred to in a sentence where the verb is generally intransitive.

sit *tibi* cōpia nostrī. (III.392)
"There might be access to me *for you.*"

2. Dative of possession. The person referred to in the dative is the possessor of the thing that is the subject: used with forms of **esse**:

an satis *Ācrisiō* est animī? (III.559)
"Does *Acrisius* possess enough spirit?"

3. Dative with adjectives of likeness, fitness, nearness, etc.

et *flentī* similis . . . / ait. (III.652–653)
"And acting like *one who cries* he says."

4. Dative with verbs of favoring, helping, pleasing, trusting, etc.

et *verbīs* favet ipsa *suīs.* (III.388)
"And she favors *her own words.*"

5. Dative with special compounds. Many verbs compounded with **ad-, con-, in-, re-**, etc., govern the dative.

quae nec reticēre *loquentī* / . . . didicit. (III.357–358)
"Who had not learned how to be quiet in response *to someone speaking.*"

parvōque admōvit *aēnō.* (VIII.645)
"And she moved it up to *a small cauldron.*"

6. Dative of agent. You have learned that the future passive participle (or passive periphrastic) often takes a dative of agent without a preposition, e.g.:

vestis erat *lectō* nōn indignanda *salignō* (VIII.659)
"There was a cloth that would not be resented by *a bed made of willow.*"

Ovid and other poets extended the use of the dative of agent and freely employed it with any passive verb:

omnibus audītur. (III.401)
"She is heard *by all.*"

mīsit in arva *suō* quondam rēgnāta *parentī.* (VIII.623)
"He sent me into fields once ruled over *by his father.*"

Accusative

Ovid uses this case in a very normal fashion, for the object of a finite verb and with prepositions. You should have no trouble with it.

Ablative

This is the most versatile case in Latin, and hence also in Ovid.

1. Means or instrument is expressed by the ablative without a preposition.

ad flammās *animā* prōdūcit *anīlī.* (VIII.643)
"She urges it to ignite *by her elderly breath.*"

2. Cause is also expressed without a preposition.

quōque magis sequitur, *flammā propiōre* calēscit. (III.372)
"The closer she follows, the more she grows warm *because of the nearer flame.*"

3. Agent. The agent of a passive verb is expressed by the ablative with the preposition **ā** or **ab**. (See the Dative of Agent.)

at nunc *ā puerō* Thēbae capientur *inermī.* (III.558)
"But now Thebes will be captured *by an unarmed boy.*"

4. Manner. The ablative conveys manner with the preposition cum, which may be omitted when an adjective modifies the ablative noun.

spem mihi nescio quam *vultū* prōmittis *amīcō*. (III.457)
"You promise me some hope *with friendly expression.*"

effēcēre levem *nec inīquā mente* ferendō. (VIII.634)
"They made it light by enduring it *with no hostile attitude.*"

5. Specification. A noun in the ablative indicates in what respect a verb, noun, or adjective applies: used without a preposition.

Lelex *animō* mātūrus et *aevō*. (VIII.617)
"Lelex, mature *in attitude* and *age.*"

nunc celebrēs *mergīs fulicīsque palustribus* undae. (VIII.625)
"Waters now frequented *with divers and marsh coots.*"

6. Separation. Verbs of separation, removal, deprivation, etc., take the ablative, often with the preposition ab or ex in prose, but usually with none in Ovid.

mēque *ministeriō* scelerisque artisque remōvī. (III.645)
"I removed myself *from the service* of crime and skill."

7. Place where. Ovid regularly omits the preposition in, which is expected in prose.

hāc Tyron, *hāc* profugōs posuistis *sēde* Penātēs. (III.539)
"*In this place* you have settled Tyre and your fugitive Penates."

8. Comparison. The ablative of comparison provides poets with an economical substitute for the structure that requires quam + noun or pronoun in the same case as the comparative adjective.

quō nōn alius cōnscendere summās / *ōcior* antemnās. (III.615–616)
"*Than whom* no one else was swifter in climbing the highest yardarms."

Ovid uses this device playfully for fifteen successive lines in XIII.789–804.

9. Description. When a noun itself is modified by an adjective, it may be used in an ablative phrase, without a preposition, to describe a person or thing.

Baucis anus *parilī*que *aetāte* Philēmōn. (VIII.631)
"Old Baucis and Philemon *of like age.*"

10. Verbs such as ūtor, fruor, potior, and dignor and the adjectives dignus and indignus take the ablative.

sīc non potiātur *amātō*. (III.405)
"Thus may he not possess *his beloved.*"

quem nisi templōrum fueris dignātus *honōre*. (III.521)
"Unless you have regarded him as worthy *of the honor* of temples. . . ."

et dignōs *Bacchō*, dignōs et *Apolline* crīnēs. (III.421)
"And hair worthy *of Bacchus*, worthy also *of Apollo.*"

11. Absolute. A noun or pronoun in the ablative and a participle agreeing with it may be used "absolutely" to replace an entire dependent clause.

rūrsus *nūllō veniente* . . . inquit. (III.383)
"Again, *when nobody was coming*, he said."

vēnit Atlantiadēs *positīs* . . . *alīs*. (VIII.627)
"The grandson of Atlas came *after putting aside his wings.*"

The Subjunctive

1. Deliberative question. Such questions indicate hesitation or doubt.

quid *faciam*? (III.465)
"What *am I to do?*"

2. Clauses of wishing take utinam or vellem + subjunctive.

hic quī dīligitur, vellem diuturnior *esset*. (III.472)

"I could wish that he whom I love *might live* longer."

3. Hortatory subjunctive. Prayers and commands may be expressed with the present subjunctive in independent clauses.

quisquis es, ō *faveās* nostrīsque labōribus *adsīs*. (III.613)
"Whoever you are, *be favorable* and *at hand* for our efforts."

4. Purpose. Purpose is expressed in a dependent clause introduced by ut or nē.

ībat, *ut iniceret* spērātō bracchia collō. (III.389)
"She advanced *in order to throw* her arms around his desired neck."

5. Relative purpose. Here, the clause is introduced by a relative pronoun, adjective, or adverb. The relative is quō with a comparative adjective or adverb.

exspectāre sonōs, *ad quōs* sua verba *remittat*. (III.378)
"To await sounds *to which she might send back* her own words."

quō*que *magis doleam*, nec nōs mare sēparat ingēns. (III.448)
"And *in order that I may grieve* all the more, no huge sea separates us."

6. Result is expressed in a dependent clause introduced by ut or ut nōn.

inter sē similēs, vix *ut* dīnōscere *possīs*. (XIII.835)
"So like each other *that you could* scarcely distinguish them."

7. Indirect questions are introduced by interrogative words.

quid *videat*, nescit. (III.430)
"He does not know *what he sees*."

ēde . . . / cūr sacra *frequentēs*. (III.580–581)
"Tell me *why you attend* the rites."

8. Characteristic clause. A relative clause in the subjunctive marks some characteristic of the antecedent of the relative pronoun.

diēs aderit . . . / quā novus hūc veniat . . . Līber. (III.519–520)
"The day will arrive *on which* Bacchus *will come* here as a stranger."

9. Temporal clauses with dum, antequam, or the like indicate that an action is anticipated or intended.

illa deam . . . tenēbat, / *dum fugerent* nymphae. (III.364–365)
"She detained the goddess *until* the nymphs *could escape*."

"ante," aﾖait, **"ēmoriar, *quam sit* tibi cōpia nostrī."** (III.391)
" 'I would die,' he said, '*before there would be* access to me for you.' "

10. Contrary to fact conditions. The imperfect subjunctive expresses present contrary to fact, and the pluperfect expresses past.

quam fēlix *essēs*, sī . . . lūminis huius / orbus . . . *fierēs*. (III.517–518)
"How happy *you would be if* you became deprived of this light."

* * *

BIBLIOGRAPHY

Studies on Ovid, Especially the *Metamorphoses*

Changing Forms: Studies in the Metamorphoses of Ovid, by Otto Due. Gyldendal, Copenhagen, 1974. Excellent general literary analysis.

*History in Ovid, by Ronald Syme. Oxford University Press, Oxford and New York, NY, 1978. Reviews the people and events that were connected with Ovid's career and offers some important new dates for some of the poetry.

Landscape in Ovid's Metamorphoses: A Study in the Transformations of a Literary Symbol, by C. P. Segal. "Hermes Einzelschriften," 23: Wiesbaden, 1969. Studies the use of landscape, e.g., the pool of Narcissus or Galatea's refuge, as a thematic symbol.

*Metaformations: Soundplay and Wordplay in Ovid and Other Classical Poets, by Frederick K. Ahl. Cornell University Press, Ithaca, NY, 1985. A daring proposal of an elaborate level of mean-

ing in the *Metamorphoses*, achieved in the interplay of syllables and puns. Not entirely reliable.

Narcissus and the Invention of Personal History, by K. J. Knoespel. Garland Press, New York, NY, 1985. Gives a careful reading of Ovid's story, then devotes its major interest to medieval adaptations.

"Narcissus in the Text," by J. Brenkman. *Georgia Review* 3 (1976) 293–327. A useful reading of this story.

Ovid, ed. by J. W. Binns. Routledge and Kegan Paul, London and Boston, MA, 1973. This contains a series of essays on all the works of Ovid, including an excellent one by Kenney on the *Metamorphoses*.

Ovid: a Poet between Two Worlds, by H. Fraenkel. "Sather Classical Lectures," 18. University of California Press, Berkeley, CA, 1945. Contains an appreciation of all the works of Ovid as mediating between the Classical world of the first century B.C. and the new interests of the next century; also, a seminal analysis of the story of Narcissus and Echo.

Ovid as an Epic Poet, by Brooks Otis. 2nd edition. Cambridge University Press, Cambridge and New York, NY, 1970. Emphasizes the special "epic" features of the *Metamorphoses* and argues forcefully that the poem exhibits a carefully symmetrical (hence epic) structure.

Ovid Recalled, by L. P. Wilkinson. Cambridge University Press, Cambridge and New York, NY, 1955. Urbane, highly readable general study of Ovid, his poetry, and his subsequent influence on literature.

"Ovid's *Metamorphoses*: A Bibliography, 1968–1978," by A. G. Elliot. *The Classical World* 73 (1980) 385–412. The latest critical bibliography of the poem.

"Ovid's *Metamorphoses*," by A. H. Griffin. *Greece and Rome* 24 (1977) 57–70. Short general appreciation.

Ovid's Metamorphoses and the Traditions of Augustan Poetry, by Peter Knox. "Cambridge Philological Society," Supplemental Volume 11, 1986. Emphasizes that Ovid was more in debt to Callimachus and the elegiac tradition than to epic.

*Ovid's Metamorphoses: An Introduction to the Basic Aspects, by G. K. Galinsky. University of California Press, Berkeley, CA, 1975. Useful study for the general reader. Emphasizes the playful qualities of the poem a bit more than necessary.

*Ovid's Metamorphoses, Books 6–10, with Introduction and Commentary, by William S. Anderson. University of Oklahoma Press, Norman, OK, 1972. A full commentary on the Latin text (including the story of Baucis and Philemon).

"Ovid's Polyphemus Idyll," by R. E. Colton. *The Classical Outlook* 56 (1979) 59–62.

The Death of Procris: "Amor" and the Hunt in Ovid's Metamorphoses, by Gregson Davis. Edizioni dell' Ateneo, Rome, 1983. An important examination of the way Ovid uses love and hunting as mutually exclusive themes.

*The Metamorphoses: Ovid's Roman Games, by Edgar Glenn. University Press of America, Lanham, MD, 1986. Intelligent reading of the poem with special interest in allegory.

*The Motives of Eloquence: Literary Rhetoric in the Renaissance, by R. A. Lanham. Yale University Press, New Haven, CT, 1976. Uses Ovid's *Metamorphoses* as the classic example of the presentation of the "rhetorical self" that reappears in several forms in Chaucer, Shakespeare, Rabelais, and others.

Additional Resources

*Etruscan and Early Roman Architecture, by Axel Boethius and J. W. Ward-Perkins. Penguin Books, New York, NY, 1970.

*Euripides, Bacchae, edited with Introduction and Commentary, by E. R. Dodds. Oxford University Press, Oxford and New York, NY, 1944. The best modern study of the play.

*Golden Latin Artistry, by L. P. Wilkinson. University of Oklahoma Press, Norman, OK, 1986.

*Greek Pastoral Poetry: Theocritus, Bion, Moschus, The Pattern Poems, tr. by Anthony Holden. Penguin Books, New York, NY, 1973.

*Houses, Villas and Palaces in the Roman World, by A. G. McKay. Cornell University Press, Ithaca, NY, 1975.

Life in Ancient Rome, by F. R. Cowell. G. P. Putnam's Sons, New York, NY, 1961.

*Reading Latin Poetry, by Roger A. Hornsby. University of Oklahoma Press, Norman, OK, 1967.

*The Anchor Bible: Genesis, ed. by W. F. Albright and D. N. Freedman. Doubleday and Co., Garden City, NY, 1964.

*The Bacchae, in *The Tragedies of Euripides*, Vol. V, tr. by William Arrowsmith. University of Chicago Press, Chicago, IL, 1959.

*The Odyssey of Homer: A Modern Translation, by Richmond Lattimore. Harper and Row, New York, NY, 1965.

*The Pronunciation and Reading of Classical Latin, by Stephen G. Daitz. Jeffrey Norton Publishers, Inc., Guilford, CT, 1984.

SELECTIONS FROM VERGIL'S AENEID BOOKS I, IV, VI DIDO AND AENEAS

INTRODUCTION

This volume of selections from Vergil's *Aeneid* is designed with two purposes in mind. First, it will serve as an introduction to Vergil for any third- or fourth-year Latin class or for a second-year class that has mastered basic Latin grammar. The facing vocabulary and notes will be most helpful in guiding the student to a correct translation and an understanding of the material. The passages have been divided into sections of fifteen to twenty lines with comprehension questions at the end of each selection to help the student in understanding the passage. Grammar exercises in the back of the student's book have been tied to specific passages and serve as a grammar review and as an aid to comprehension and translation. The fact that the 600 lines taken from Books I, IV, and VI tell the love story of Dido and Aeneas will enable the student to grasp and appreciate the material more easily. Second, this volume also contributes to the materials available to teachers of the Advanced Placement Vergil Course. Teachers of the AP Vergil Course will have to use additional instructional materials and resources, but this volume will be a valuable supplement to the study and understanding of Vergil's *Aeneid*.

Historical Background

Vergil's lifetime (70–19 B.C.) spanned the final years of the republic and the beginnings of the Augustan era. His homeland, in Cisalpine Gaul, was a land of lakes, lagoons, and plains. Family prosperity, derived from productive farming, enabled him to enjoy a proper education in northern Italy, Rome, and Naples. He soon developed a sense of the diversity of Italy and a respect for the mosaic of traditions and cultures. The activities of Julius Caesar, at home and abroad, were pulse-stirring events of his youth and adolescence.

Civil war was the staple of his adult years. Born during the consulship of Crassus and Pompey, he was to witness the gradual breakdown of senatorial government and antique institutions during his lifetime. The First Triumvirate, an unconstitutional but effective union of Pompey's prestige, Crassus' wealth and influence, and Caesar's military genius and family name, accelerated the dissolution of constitutional authority and the inevitability of violence. Formed originally in 60 B.C., the league of generals was renewed in 55 B.C., when Vergil was a student in Rome. A constitutional crisis in 50–49 B.C. signaled the end of any hopes for "peace in our time." Caesar's response to Pompey's resistance and to senatorial objections to his re-entry into Italy with his legions was to cross the Rubicon River on 11 January 49 B.C. with a gambler's abandon (ālea iacta est, "the die is cast"). Pompey's flight from the capital was prelude to war overseas on Greek territory. Pompey met defeat at the hands of Caesar, his father-in-law and one-time partner, at Pharsalus in Thessaly in 48 B.C. The defeated general fled to Egypt, where he was assassinated by his former centurion. Caesar followed shortly after and entered Alexandria and Cleopatra's life.

Hostilities between the defeated senatorial clique, which had declared for Pompey, and the Caesarians continued. Resistance to Caesar was spirited and desperate, particularly in North Africa and Spain. The defeat of the Pompeians at Alexandria, at Thapsus in Tunisia, and ultimately at Munda in Spain cost Caesar dearly but ended the conflict. Caesar returned to Rome to celebrate a triple triumph and to assume the office of Dictator, finally for life. A skillful reformer, an ambitious administrator of a vast public works program, and a bold refounder of Carthage, Caesar won enormous popular support but alienated the Republican die-hards. Fears that he had designs on Hellenistic monarchy after the pattern of Alexander the Great and his successors and that he would lead his victorious legions to the Middle East and Parthia (Mesopotamia) were deep-seated among the opposition. Indignation over the presence of Cleopatra in the capital and the lodging of her gilded statue in the Temple of Venus Genetrix was inevitable. Conspiracy and murder were the sequel, and on 15 March 44 B.C. Caesar's death in Pompey's theater reverberated throughout the world. Vergil's passionate epilogue (37 B.C.) to the first book of the *Georgics* (lines 498–515) accented the omens and prodigies that attached to the death of the Dictator and signaled, no doubt, Vergil's admiration for the great general and popular statesman.

The aftermath of the assassination was yet another coalition, a constitutional arrangement this time, the Second Triumvirate, which comprised Mark Antony, Octavian (Caesar's grandnephew and heir), and Marcus Lepidus. Self-styled avengers of Caesar and restorers of constitutional law and order, they launched a campaign against the "Liberators," Brutus and Cassius. The defeat and deaths of Brutus and Cassius at Philippi in 42 B.C. left the triumvirate unopposed except within their own ranks.

Octavian and Antony turned to their commitments at home and abroad. After rewarding their veterans with land assignments in Italy, a procedure that deprived both Vergil and Horace of lands, the triumvirs had to meet the assaults and claims of Gnaeus and Sextus Pompey, militant and ambitious sons of Pompey the Great. Sextus Pompey proved to be a vigorous, often successful opponent of the triumvirate. By repeated raids on the supply lines of Rome, particularly on the shipping lanes between Alexandria and Puteoli (in Campania) and Ostia (the port of Rome), Pompey weakened and embarrassed the status of the triumvirs. There were repeated attempts to patch up an alliance and resolve difficulties inside and outside the triumviral ranks. On one occasion, during the spring of 37 B.C., Vergil joined a diplomatic mission, headed by Maecenas, his patron, with Horace, Varius, Plotius Tucca, and others bound for Brindisi or Taranto. Horace's account of the journey (*Satires* I.5) offers valuable sidelights on the passage through Latium, Campania, and the southern reaches of the peninsula.

Sextus Pompey, who always had misgivings about the reliability of the triumvirate, finally resorted to military action. The resistance offered by Octavian, in concert with his naval genius, Marcus Agrippa, brought about the defeat of Sextus Pompey at Mylae (in Sicily) in 36 B.C. Antony seized the opportunity to launch his own campaigns in the Middle East between 36 and 32 B.C., during which time he married Cleopatra VII. Their **coniugium** and the lavish territorial settlements made by Antony to their offspring (Cleopatra Selene, Ptolemy Philadelphus, and Alexander Helios) roused considerable discontent in Rome and fanned the fire of civil war again. The ultimate encounter at Actium on the Adriatic on 2 September 31 B.C. brought Octavian and Agrippa into conflict with Antony's eastern contingents and with Cleopatra's armament. The battle was terminated abruptly with the flight of Cleopatra and with Antony's inept withdrawal from the action. Octavian pursued the nation's public enemy (**hostis**) to Alexandria, where Antony, followed by Cleopatra, committed suicide to avoid the indignity of Octavian's triumphal procession in Rome. Egypt was annexed, and Octavian occupied the limelight henceforth.

Vergil, resident meanwhile in Rome and Naples, published his collection of *Bucolics* in 37 B.C. and his verse treatise on agriculture, the *Georgics*, in 29 B.C. Octavian's triple triumph as a result of his victories in Dalmatia (35–34 B.C.), at Actium (31 B.C.), and in Egypt (30 B.C.) was celebrated in the same year. Within two years Octavian was assigned the exceptional title of Augustus, a cognomen with religious implications, and engaged himself in reorganizing the Roman state and rebuilding the capital.

Vergil's recourse to Campania and the Bay of Naples provided a welcome and secure haven from the tumult and shouting of Rome during the fifties and forties. He found solace and inspiration in the "Garden" Academy of Siro, the Epicurean teacher whose influence on aspiring writers and the intelligentsia was evidently profound. Campania was a veritable hotbed of Epicureanism at that time and subsequently. The materialistic ethic, founded on the scientific argument of atomism, found ready acceptance among the Romans who favored the "ivory tower" and the companionable ethic of Epicureanism that Lucretius made available in verse form to an ardent following. Vergil was evidently sufficiently impressed to borrow inspiration and phraseology from the Roman poet and interpreter, and scholars have detected Epicurean traits in the character of Dido conflicting with the Stoic nature of Aeneas. The carbonized rolls of Philodemus' philosophical works, discovered in the villa of the Pisones near Herculaneum in 1787, offer marvelous testimony (still largely unread) to the presence and vitality of Epicurean teaching and alignment in the Campanian area. The original owner of the villa, L. Calpurnius Piso, was father-in-law to Julius Caesar, also an avowed Epicurean.

The poet's involvement with the diplomatic mission of 37 B.C. signaled his attachment to the Second Triumvirate during its happier days. His fourth *Bucolic (Eclogue* IV) extolled the harmony between Antony and Octavian as a consequence of the Peace of Brundisium (40 B.C.) and the marriage of Antony to Octavia, sister of Octavian. The *Georgics,* particularly the second book, reflect the time of troubles after Caesar's assassination and during the struggles with Sextus Pompey (*Georgics* II.161–164). Vergil hailed the advent of Octavian as restorer of peace and order and as guarantor of the recovery of Italian agriculture. The "war to end all wars," at Actium, provided Vergil with the incentive and inspiration for his **magnum opus,** the *Aeneid,* which occupied him between 29 and 19 B.C.

Literary Background

Vergil's choice of epic was carefully deliberated and courageous. Adaptation and creativity were always closely allied in Roman literary craft. Vergil's obviously thorough grounding in classical Greek, in Hellenistic verse, and in early Latin poetry gave him a distinct advantage and had a profound effect on his epic verse. The *Aeneid* was repeatedly indebted to Homer's *Iliad* and *Odyssey,* supreme paradigms of the genre unparalleled from the standpoint of scale, characterization, and humanity. Vergil's response to the *Odyssey* in *Aeneid* I–IV and to the *Iliad* in *Aeneid* VII–XII is an established fact. Correspondences in form, narrative patterns, and details are manifold and manifest. To some degree, Aeneas simply re-enacts Homer's *Odyssey* in *Aeneid* I, III, V, and VI. *Aeneid* II (The Fall of Troy) and IV (The Tragedy of Dido) show no significant coincidences with either epic, and *Aeneid* VI (The Underworld and the Revelations), although it offers strong reminiscences of *Odyssey* XI in setting, motivation, and occasional incidents, remains unique in its content and message, which are more often indebted to Stoic and Orphic-Pythagorean doctrine than to the poetry of Archaic Greece.

The *Aeneid* was hailed by Propertius, Vergil's younger contemporary, as "something greater than the *Iliad"* (*Elegies* II.34.66), and Horace's tribute to his **animae dīmidium meae** (*Odes* I.3.8) and his frequent echoes of Vergil's epic verses in his *Odes* are token of the admiration and affection Vergil awakened in his fellow poet and close contemporary (65–8 B.C.). "Greater than the *Iliad"* inclines toward hyperbole, but it does underline the unique character of Vergil's epic as Homeric in form but Hellenistic or contemporary in style. Vergil, with two other Transpadanes, Cinna of Brescia, and Catullus of Verona, was intensely devoted to the fresh experiments and the disciplined style and mannered structure of Callimachus (ca. 305–ca. 240 B.C.) and the Alexandrians.

Vergil found the four books of Apollonius' *Argonautica* of the third century B.C. particularly fertile and inspirational. The Dido and Aeneas books are notably indebted to Apollonius' Jason and Medea episode (Books III and IV) and serve frequent notice of the Roman's respect for the mastery of psychology and imagery of the Hellenistic poet. Among the nine Passages For Comparison included in the student's book, Extract I, Homer's *Odyssey* VI.102–109, and Extract II, Apollonius' *Argonautica* III.876–886, include a simile that Vergil used to enhance Aeneas' first encounter with Dido (I.498–504). In Extract IV, Apollonius' *Argonautica* IV.1139–1145 and 1149–1155, the cave of Macris, where the marriage of Jason and Medea was consummated, is reflected in the cave where Juno officiates at the **coniugium** of Dido and Aeneas (IV.165–172).

Dido's character alone is an astonishing amalgam of earlier heroines. Fashioned after the youthful Calypso (Homer, *Odyssey* V.1–128), the radiant Nausicaa (*Odyssey* VI, VII, and VIII), and Circe the sorceress (*Odyssey* X.135–574), she also exhibits traits of the tragic heroines of Euripides (e.g., Phaedra in the *Hippolytus* and the Colchian princess in the *Medea).* Apollonius Rhodius was a major influence, as has been shown already. Closer in time, Vergil found inspiration in Catullus' epyllion on Peleus and Thetis, particularly in the love story of Theseus and Ariadne, which is caught up in its textual fabric (Catullus LXIV.50–266, part of which is given in Extract V).

Clearly, it would be superficial to read Vergil's tragic story of Dido and Aeneas as entirely derivative, as a plagiarizing composite of gatherings from exemplary forebears in Greek and Roman literature. The hallmarks of the poet's genius are legion and pervasive: the haunting beauty of his poetic lines, which must often be read aloud to yield their beauty and majesty; his profound sympathy with human suffering; his understanding of the human condition; his remarkable psychological insights; his strength as architect and formal designer of episodes like the Dido and Aeneas story; and the supreme craft of enlivening literary echoes with emotional immediacy. The *Aeneid,* at first encounter, appears to be overly austere and solemn, even depressingly melancholic at times; the burden of politics and the agony of war, particularly of civil war, seem depressing and overly grave. This initial reaction and uncertainty about Vergil's success are soon dispelled by the power and suggestion of his lines and by the unforgettable characters he has created. The *Aeneid* is much more than an anachronistic recreation of past authors. Vergil has also, in the tradition of Ennius' verse *Annales* of the second century B.C., embraced the aims and ideals and the triumphs and failures of the new society of Augustan Rome. Clio, the Muse of History, and Melpomene, the Muse of Tragedy, are inextricably bound into the epic. Echoes of the times of national strain, of the unification of Italy in days of yore, of more recent civil war, and of the sacrifice of youth and great personalities in the march of time are never far removed from the progress of the poem. Dido and Aeneas have their temporal associations in Cleopatra and Julius Caesar, and Ascanius-Iulus is surely the ancestor of Octavian, Caesar's heir after 44 B.C.

On one occasion, duly recorded in the poet's life (Donatus, *Vita* 32), Vergil read completed portions of *Aeneid* II, IV, and VI to Augustus and his sister Octavia, once married to Marc Antony. Vergil's eulogy of the recently deceased Marcellus, nephew and son-in-law of Augustus, won the tearful gratitude of the youth's mother. Vergil encountered the emperor again in Greece in 19 B.C. The poet had apparently traveled to Greece to complete and refine his epic and to resume his philosophical studies in its academic capitals. Augustus invited Vergil to join the imperial party in Greece. During their visit to Megara, the poet contracted an illness that brought about his death after landing in Brindisi, Italy, on 21 September 19 B.C. (Donatus, *Vita* 35). Vergil was buried in his beloved Naples, and although he expressed the wish that his epic be burned upon his death, his literary executors and friends, Varius and Plotius Tucca, oversaw the publication of the *Aeneid* with some minor revisions (Donatus, *Vita* 37). The epitaph that identified his sepulchral urn was, according to tradition, his own composition:

Mantua mē genuit, Calabrī rapuēre, tenet nunc
 Parthenopē: cecinī pascua, rūra, ducēs.

Mantua gave me birth, Calabria (Brindisi) stole me away, Parthenope (Naples) now has me. I sang of pastures, the countryside, and leaders.

(Donatus, *Vita* 36)

* * *

TEACHING NOTES

Book I.338–368

1. **Pūnica** (338), the adjective, **Poenus**, the noun, and **Phoenissa** all equate with Phoenician, although **Pūnica** would suggest "Carthaginian" to a Roman.

2. **Tyriōs** (338) refers to the colonial party that set out from Tyre, an important Phoenician, therefore Semitic, city south of Beirut, Lebanon, and a major port. Tyrian influence reached the western Mediterranean by 800 B.C., the approximate foundation date for Carthage, which tradition assigned to 814 B.C. By Vergil's time, Tyre was part of the Roman province of Syria.

3. Dido's original name was Elissa (= Semitic, "princess"). The name Dido (340) (= "heroine," according to Servius) was assigned to her after her suicide, which (again according to Servius) she undertook as a desperate alternative to marrying an African suitor and breaking her marriage vows to her dead husband, Sychaeus. Vergil adopts the "heroic" name Dido but replaces the African suitor with Trojan Aeneas.

4. Some editors replace **agrī** (343) with **aurī**, which seems to suit Sychaeus' tragedy and the treasure better than agricultural land.

5. Pygmalion (347), the Tyrian ruler, bears the same name as the sculptor who fell in love with the beautiful statue that he made and named Galatea (Ovid, *Metamorphoses* X.243–297). George Bernard Shaw, in his *Pygmalion*, adapted the Ovidian story; his cockney heroine is, however, named Liza (compare Elissa).

6. The ghost of Sychaeus prompts flight (355–359) and plays a highly melodramatic role comparable to that of Hamlet's father in Shakespeare's tragedy. Notice too how revelations (**nudāvit**, 356; **retēxit**, 356; and **reclūdit**, 358) play a major role in the "drama." Scholars have suggested that Vergil borrowed from Plautus' *Mostellaria* (*The Haunted House*) in designing the spectral scene.

7. The Byrsa story (367–368) underscores ancient interest in etymology; Punic **Bosra**, which means "citadel," was confused with Greek *byrsa*, which means "bull's hide," and so produced the story of the bull's hide and the land purchase. The Libyans told the Phoenicians they could have as much land as a bull's-hide would cover. Dido and her

companions then cut the hide into long thin strips and thereby enclosed a fairly large area. That Vergil was familiar with the Semitic place name *Qart Hadasht*, which means "New City," is evidenced by the use of the phrase **novae Karthaginis** (I.336, not included in these selections). Julius Caesar's colonial foundation on the site, which was devastated by Rome after the Third Punic War (149–146 B.C.), was favored by Augustus in Vergil's lifetime. Recent excavations at the Tunisian site show spirited building activity in Augustan times comparable to the construction in Vergil's "sight-seeing" account. The map (page 8) will enable students to picture Dido's voyage and to locate the areas pertinent to the story of Dido and Aeneas.

Book I.375–401

1. Aeneas' frank revelations about himself (378–380) imitate the self-praise of Homeric heroes; Achilles, for example, calls himself "the bravest of the Greeks" (*Iliad* I.244).
2. Aeneas' explanation for the shipwreck (**forte suā**, 377) is actually correct. Although Juno raised the storm with the connivance of Aeolus, ruler of the winds, to delay Aeneas' passage to Italy, the shipwreck on Carthaginian shores was unintentional and undesirable for Juno.
3. Hector had entrusted the Penates (378) of Troy to Aeneas. They were eventually exhibited in sanctuaries on Rome's Velian Hill and in the Temple of Vesta in the Forum Romanum. These old Italian deities figure in the relief of Aeneas engaged in sacrifice on the Altar of Augustan Peace. They were the protective gods of sailors and of the storage-cupboards of households.
4. Aeneas' search for the land of his fathers (380) recalls the tradition that Dardanus, Troy's founder, came from Italian Corythus (= Tarquinii) in Tuscany. He was the son of Jupiter and Electra, hence Aeneas' quest for the race sprung from Jupiter. Aeneas' voyage, like that of Odysseus, is a homecoming: as Odysseus returned to Ithaca, so Aeneas will return to his ancestral land.
5. Although Aeneas acknowledges Venus' role in his travels, her help in the quest for the Golden Bough at Lake Avernus (*Aeneid* VI.190–197) is her major intervention; Apollo, god of prophecy and patron of colonial enterprises, is most often Aeneas' guide. Venus, however, has to be highlighted at the outset of the epic because of her Julian ties.

6. **data fāta secūtus** (382): recall the prelude to the epic, **fātō profugus** (2; see the Introduction to this teacher's handbook, page 15). Vergil emphasizes that Aeneas is directed by fate and by Jupiter's prophecy (*Aeneid* I.257–296). Protected by his goddess mother and with Jupiter's guarantees, Aeneas moves steadfastly toward his fulfillment.
7. **ignōtus** (384): Aeneas' heroic past has not assured him of recognition at the extremities of the Mediterranean, but the temple murals in Juno's sanctuary prove him wrong.
8. Venus' interruption of her son's complaints (385–386) has a motherly touch about it, although she pretends not to know the name of Aeneas or Troy, as evinced by **Quisquis es** (387). Her sure knowledge is illustrated by the augury of the swans (393–398). The comparison between the missing ships and the dispersed swans is quite precise; twelve ships (swans) have been dispersed by a storm (eagle) through the open sea (sky); some ships (swans) have already reached harbor (landed); some enter the harbor with full sails (some swans hover in the sky preparing to land).
9. **strīdentibus** (397): a vivid epithet more appropriate to creaking, straining cordage on ships, as bellying sails strain ropes and timbers, than to the wings of birds.
10. When the Trojans arrive in Carthage they are prefigured by swans, the birds of Venus and Apollo; but when they prepare to leave, they are compared to ants who dismantle (i.e., pillage) a heap of grain (*Aeneid* IV.393–400).
11. Encourage students to respond to metrical effects in the passage. Contrast the rhythms of 375 and 383 with 390; observe the dactylic rhythm of the eagle's swoop in line 394.
12. The climax in the comparison lies with the joyful return to safety of both the swans and the Trojans. The alliteration in lines 395 and 399 and the assonance in line 399 heighten the happiness of the deliverance of both the swans and the Trojans.
13. The repetition of **perge modo** (389 and 401) has the effect of a refrain, at the beginning and end of the paragraph.

Book I.419–437

1. **Plūrimus** (419) suggests the scale and length (a match for the walls) of the hill; the words **adversās . . . arcēs** (420) imply that the city's defenses tower almost as high.

2. The passage has many alliterative words such as **mīrātur mōlem . . . māgālia** (421), **strepitum . . . strāta** (422), **subvolvere saxa** (424), and **sanctumque senātum** (426). The work "flows" like honey (432).

3. By using **sānctum** (426), "sacred," "holy," "inviolate," Vergil is attempting to show the importance and authority of the senate. This corresponds to Augustus' attempt to restore the Republic in which the preservation of the senate's prestige was vital.

4. Vergil's simile of the bees is carefully constructed; the Carthaginians begin with defensive measures (423–424), and the description of the bees ends with a corresponding motif (434–435); the labor of the Carthaginians (426–429) corresponds with the labor of the bees (431–434).

5. Aeneas' arrival leads to disruption of everything, symbolized by the simile of the bees. The purpose of Aeneas' mission or quest does not include cooperation in the construction of Carthage, and in fact his arrival leads ultimately to a cessation of activity and a disintegration of order in the "hive."

6. Vergil seems to detect four virtues in the community of the bees: (a) responsibility, (b) practicality, (c) adherence to the laws, and (d) discipline. All are cardinal Roman virtues.

7. Aeneas' expression at the close (437) is a combination of pathos and complaint. His quest, to found a new Troy, is an obsession, and the rise of Carthage captures his imagination and envy. The simile suggests all the sweetness of security and joyous employment in contrast to Aeneas' unhappy condition after seven years of wandering and frustration.

Book I.494–508

1. Aeneas is portrayed here as a sympathetic, modest hero who is overcome by memories of the Trojan War. These memories are reinforced by the temple murals, which include pictures of many Greeks and Trojans who perished in the war. In lines 494–495 many words express this emotion: **mīranda . . . stupet, obtūtū,** and **haeret dēfīxus in ūnō.** Both verses contain spondees, which contribute to the effect of sadness. The fact that the scenes from the Trojan War appear on the walls of the temple would indicate that the Carthaginians not only are aware of the war and of the heroes involved but also wish to honor those heroes.

2. Dido is portrayed sympathetically, and, like Diana, she is very beautiful, walks in a stately manner, is surrounded by many followers, and, no doubt, carries a symbol (the quiver) of her rule. **iūra dabat lēgēsque virīs** (507): Dido dispenses justice and law, and she assigns tasks calmly and fairly or assigns them by lot. Vergil places her high on a throne in the center of the temple of Juno, thus emphasizing her power as a queen.

3. The description of the goddess managing her dancers, with her mountain nymphs, a thousand strong, and her distinction (**superēminet,** 501) match and enhance the status of the Punic queen. The allusion to Diana the huntress will find its realization in the fateful hunting episode later (*Aeneid* IV.129–159).

4. Dido's administrative role is extraordinary in a sacred building and would be more appropriate in a law-court. Vergil seems to blend temple and basilica (law-court) in the setting. There are folding doors to the sanctuary where Juno's cult image should be located, elevated, with a stepped approach; the throne of Dido, as lawgiver and city administrator, is set in the center of the sanctuary (505), at a lower level than Juno's cult image.

5. Dido's dramatic entrance and her concern for her people and their welfare must have impressed Aeneas. She is regal but modest and sympathetic, qualities also apparent in Aeneas in this passage (494–495).

6. Scholars disagree on Dido's age. Some imagine her as middle-aged and seriously engaged with a civic career, others as characteristically Roman, married at the customary age of fourteen or fifteen and recently widowed. Aeneas is probably in his early thirties. Considerable pathos attaches to the younger queen.

7. The passages for comparison with *Aeneid* I.498–504, namely, Extract I: Homer, *Odyssey* VI.102–109 (student's book, page 76), and Extract II: Apollonius Rhodius, *Argonautica* III.876–886 (student's book, page 77), should be introduced, read, and discussed with students at this point.

Book I.561–578

1. Dido certainly presents a picture of modesty as with downcast face she points out to the Trojans that ruling a kingdom is difficult and that as queen she must protect her bound-

aries and her people. She is simple and forthright, the picture of an ideal leader.

2. Dido's "trying position" (rēs dūra, 563) no doubt includes her loss of Sychaeus, the hostility of Pygmalion, and threats of retaliation for the theft of the treasure as well as the menace of African tribes. The precarious position of Carthage is made emphatic by repeated references to protective measures as Vergil presents Dido's awareness of the need to put her state first.

3. Dido not only shows familiarity with the Trojan War but also speaks of the war with strong words: virtūtēs . . . tantī . . . bellī. The story of the Trojans has greatly impressed her.

4. Pūnica fidēs always lies just beneath the surface of the story of Dido and Aeneas and frequently provides an ironical twist to the account. Both of the principal actors cite fidelity (and infidelity) as implicit in their relationships. Venus fears treachery both inside Dido's palace and from without.

5. This first encounter between the Trojans and the Carthaginians allows Aeneas to observe the queen and the rescued Trojans from the protective mist. Ilioneus' remarks that precede this passage (I.544–549, not included in these selections) give a picture of loyalty and affection for his leader and allow the qualities of Aeneas to be set forth clearly and explicitly. In her response, Dido echoes and reinforces the qualities and virtues of Aeneas and the Trojans.

6. This passage offers a good introduction to the character of Dido, who is so often seen as merely a romantic heroine overcome by passion. Students might discuss the role of the queen, her youth (fifteen to eighteen years old?), and the importance of this particular portrait of Dido.

Book I.588–610

1. Aeneas' physical appearance is given in more detail than Dido's: godlike features and shoulders, size, and exceptional beauty. Vergil repeatedly emphasizes his physical beauty, perhaps because Julius Caesar had encouraged people to regard his youthful bloom as the gift of Venus, and Augustus, though short, was very conscious of his good looks. Aeneas must be about thirty-three, a general, a high priest, a prince, and a widower with child.

2. caesariem (590) suggests beautiful, luxuriant hair; purpureum (591) suggests a

countenance glowing with youth and physical well-being.

3. Aeneas' remark, urbe domō sociās (600), seems to enlarge Dido's earlier statement—urbem quam statuō vestra est (573). urbe domō: an example of asyndeton, the omission of a conjunction, which emphasizes the closeness of the city and the palace of Dido.

4. Rhetorical devices are plentiful: exclamatory questions appear at 605 and 606; anaphora, 599, 603, 605–606, 607–608, 612; asyndeton, 600, 603; alliteration, 605, 607.

5. Aeneas' prayer includes Dido among the piōs (603) for her humanity to the castaway Trojans. Pietās is commonly identified with Aeneas, implying devotion to family, gods, and state. Aeneas' prayer also signals his trust in divine justice and in consciousness among the divine powers of Dido's moral qualities. mēns sibi cōnscia rēctī (604): the equivalent of the metrically unacceptable cōnscientia. Aeneas believes in a meaningful universe: if there is divine Justice, Dido's reward will be certain. His blessing is nullified by the bitterness of her final tragedy.

6. Aeneas' oath invokes the pattern of sea, earth, and sky, all with intimations of eternity, although Destiny has guaranteed Italy and Latium as his final home and Lavinia as his Italian bride. The prevailing tone of the passage is one of joy and infinite gratitude.

Book I.657–694

1. Venus combines powers of supplication, persuasion, and, of course, seduction. She flatters Cupid's irresistible power and excites his affection for his harassed half-brother, Aeneas. Ascanius, Venus' maxima cūra (678), balances her magna potentia, Cupid (664).

2. Cupid's merger with Ascanius is signaled by the design of the verse, a chiasmus of composition:

676–682 Ascanius ╲ ╱ 689–690 Cupid
683–688 Cupid ╱ ╲ 691–694 Ascanius

Venus' directions to Cupid are followed with evident success (IV.83–85). When Dido hugs and kisses Ascanius later, she is thinking of Aeneas.

3. Venus' sanctuary at Idalium on Cyprus (681, 692–694), where Dido's father Belus had a career of conquest (621–622), evinces the

warmth, color, and perfume appropriate to the Love Goddess. Amaranth (celōsia cristāta) in line 693 is identified as cockscomb and was commonly used in garlands.

4. Venus' design touches Dido's most sensitive area, her frustration at having no heir (cf. īnfēlīx, "unfruitful," "barren," at line 712). The queen will have fire insinuate her bones, and then, ablaze, she will be driven to madness. To defeat Juno's devious and destructive designs for Aeneas, Venus proposes to forestall Juno's "attack" (671–672) by her own treachery (673) and to ring her with flame (673). Cupid will breathe fire into her (688) and trick her with poison (venēnō also means "love charm," "aphrodisiac"). The cruelty of Venus and her son, armed with the "fire" of insanity, military strategy, and eroticism, hardly excites admiration for her divinity.

Book I.707–722
1. The Carthaginians marvel at the gifts and at the glowing features not, as they suppose, of Ascanius-Iulus, but of Cupid. Dido, love's victim, looks ardently at the boy and the presents. Austin comments on line 714: "Significantly, the child is named first; he is more important than any of the gifts." The acquisitive Carthaginians are concerned mainly with the offerings.

2. The fondling of Cupid by the unsuspecting Dido causes some concern about the age and scale of Ascanius-Iulus. Dido's attention to the false Iulus is patterned after the display and uses of dēliciae ("love objects") at Roman banquets and symposia. Catullus assigns a similar function to Lesbia's sparrow (Poem II). Ascanius seems to hover between the age of eleven and twelve; he rides a horse, hunts deer, and longs for a boar and a lion later on (IV.156–159).

3. Vergil's words praecipuē īnfēlīx, pestī dēvōta futūrae (712), and miserae (719) show his sensitivity to Dido's pathetic lifestory. īnfēlīx: "ill-starred," "unfruitful," "unhappy" is an adjective that appears repeatedly (I.719, 749; IV.68, 450, 529, 596; and VI.456). It is Dido's permanent epithet, just as pius characterizes Aeneas.

Book IV.1–30
1. Encourage students to respond to the repeated imagery of wounding (2 and 3) and of fire (2, 18, 23) in descriptions of Dido and her condition.

2. lūstrābat (6) implies purification and movement; Dawn "purifies" the world from darkness by her rising and by the sun's rays.

3. armīs (11) is ambiguous. Austin (1970) translates it as "shoulders" (armus, -ī m), but editors generally favor "martial exploits" or "martial prowess." Courage and heroic behavior are certainly the hallmarks of Aeneas' narrative of the fall of Troy (Aeneid II) and of his adventurous odyssey (Aeneid III).

4. The dactyls of line 13 suggest excitement; the spondees of line 14 are indicative of amazement in response to Aeneas' account of heroic adventures.

5. culpae (19) means a fault or infidelity to Sychaeus' memory. The word need not imply moral condemnation. Dido's culpa is weakness in yielding to the temptation of another love.

6. The passage for comparison with Aeneid IV.8–30, namely, Extract III: Geoffrey Chaucer, The Legend of Good Women (student's book, page 77), should be read and discussed with students at this point.

Book IV.56–89
1. Ceres (Demeter), Phoebus (Apollo), and Lyaeus (Dionysus-Bacchus) are all concerned with civilization, with the foundation of cities, and with life in general. They are also associated with marriage rites. A Roman proverb of indeterminate date includes two of the trinity of deities in an erotic context: sine Cerere (bread) et Līberō (wine) friget Venus (love is cold). Juno, called prōnuba (nuptial goddess) at line 166, presided over marriage rites and was also patron goddess of Dido and of Carthage.

2. Roman (and Etruscan) priests customarily studied the livers of sacrificial animals for any unusual markings or conditions in order to determine whether impending actions would have a favorable outcome or a catastrophic sequel. The details of this autopsy (called hepatoscopy, "liver-examination") are gruesome but fascinating.

3. vātum ignārae mentēs (65): this does not suggest disbelief in either religious practices or prophetic wisdom on Vergil's part. Dido's offerings and sacrifices follow conventional practices at Rome and elsewhere in the Mediterranean world. The point is that soothsayers (vātēs) cannot alleviate or alter Dido's frenzied condition (furentem, 65).

4. The correspondences between Dido's condition and that of the wounded deer are worthy of study. Dido's distracted wandering

(68–69) corresponds to the desperate movements of the doe (72); both Dido and the doe share a common vulnerability (**incautam**, 70), and both share a common doom (**īnfēlīx**, 68; **lētālis**, 73). Finally, Dido and the doe share a common gentleness and weakness. The shepherd's arrow, which cannot be withdrawn, almost certainly refers to the arrow of Cupid.

5. **nescius** (72) is placed at the end of its clause and at the beginning of a verse for emphasis. It is followed by a marked pause which enhances the emphasis. The implication is that Aeneas is unaware of the impression he has made on the passionate young queen.

6. Vergil's similes are always much more than superficial analogies. The simile of the wounded doe is a fine example of comparison not only in externals but in internal and psychological aspects as well. The simile anticipates the divinely contrived deer hunt later (IV.151–159).

Book IV.129–172

1. Encourage students to read the passage aloud to become aware of Vergil's deployment of metrical effects. There are prevailing dactyls at the outset (132–135), suggestive of vehement action and high spirits, combined with alliteration and assonance; dactylic rhythms suit the quickened pace of the hunt and the vehemence of the rain storm. Thereafter (160–172), spondaic rhythms are in accord with the gravity of the event. Vergil's metrical effects are as suggestive and manipulative as are the rhythms of Hector Berlioz' operatic epic, *The Trojans at Carthage.*

2. The cave scene mimics a Roman marriage ceremony, with the natural elements as witnesses and the nymphs as a high-spirited wedding party.

3. Some readers detect an ambiguity in the syntax of verse 165 ("Dido and the Trojan leader" or "Dido, as leader, and Trojan Aeneas"). Scholars generally prefer the former as the correct meaning. Direct students' attention to the ambiguity and clarify the meaning for them. Juno and Venus are the designers and the executors of the encounter. The humans appear to be divinely manipulated, but human desires are involved as well, and the tragic love story is consequently more pathetic.

4. Note the way the words **Spēluncam . . . eandem** enclose Dido and Aeneas within the cave and how the verb **dēveniunt** is given emphasis by being placed at the end of the clause and at the beginning of the next verse.

5. "Marriage by consent" was a Roman institution that could lead to complications. Marriage was a remarkably informal arrangement, and the ceremonies that were celebrated at the time were not regarded as legally binding. Consent and intention were basic to the marital relationship. If the intention to form a lasting union came to an end for any one of a number of reasons, the marriage could be regarded as terminated. Wives normally retained ownership of their property or dowry, and if the husband and wife separated, the wife recovered her contribution to the marriage. Divorce became increasingly common among upper-class Romans during the late Republic.

6. Arrange to have students hear a recording of Berlioz' "The Royal Hunt and Storm" from *The Trojans at Carthage.* The excitement of both events is admirably illustrated by the dactylic frenzy of the music and by skillful sound effects in the orchestral score.

7. The passage for comparison with *Aeneid* IV.160–172, namely, Extract IV: Apollonius Rhodius, *Argonautica* IV.1139–1145 and 1149–1155 (student's book, page 78), should be read and discussed with students at this point.

Book IV.238–278

1. Mercury plays a major role in the action. A Roman agnostic who did not believe in Mercury or Jupiter would probably not be disturbed by Vergil's divine interventions. Gods are not only visible actors in the drama, they are also sometimes personifications of psychological forces working within human agents. Ask students to consider whether the events of lines 265–278 might be interpreted in terms of Aeneas' wakening conscience without reference to the supernatural.

2. Atlas had conspired with his brother Titans to bring down the Olympic deities. When the attempt at violence failed, he was condemned to stand forever supporting the heavens on his head and shoulders. Another legend explains that Perseus turned Atlas into stone with the head of Medusa (Ovid, *Metamorphoses* IV.655–662).

3. Mercury's stopover on his grandfather's slopes may suggest the piety and respect Romans showed toward their ancestors.

Vergil's personification of Mount Atlas as a white-haired, bearded old man wearing a white cloak may seem grotesque to modern readers, but Greek and Roman writers often endowed their mountains and rivers with animate, divine beings. In ancient art, rivers and mountains are frequently represented as divinities. Later in the epic (XII.701-703), Vergil pictures Aeneas as being as huge as Mount Athos or Eryx or Father Apenninus.

4. Aeneas is guilty of a double fault in Mercury's accusation: a sin of commission (with respect to Dido's Carthage) and a sin of omission (with respect to his own true glory and Ascanius' future).

5. Try to make students aware of the irony of Aeneas' situation: he is busy assisting the foundation of a city (his own ultimate mission) but in the wrong territory. The general welfare of Carthage appears to be thriving with Aeneas hard at work helping to build the city, but it is not the right (i.e., his "fated") city—Rome.

Book IV.279-295

1. Help students to analyze lines 279 and 280 for evidence of spondaic rhythm, the repeated use of *a* and *o* sounds, doubled *r*'s, assonance (**Aenēās aspectū**), and harsh elisions—all accenting Aeneas' sense of horror.

2. Raise with students the question whether or not Aeneas has for the first time realized that, with or without the **deus ex māchinā**, there is a conflict between his mission and his amorous liaison with the Queen of Carthage.

3. Encourage students to forecast how Aeneas will discuss his departure with Dido. Dido will ultimately discover, of course, what is going on behind her back, will assume that Aeneas plans to desert her, and will finally force him to plead his case under very disadvantageous circumstances.

4. **optima Dīdō** (291): difficult to translate: "kindest," "generous," "gracious," "dear," "excellent woman," and "Her Highness" have all been suggested. One needs to be aware that the word may be more respectful and formal than emotional.

5. The contrast between the disarray of Aeneas and the enthusiasm of his shipmates merits discussion. How does this reflect on Aeneas' qualities of leadership?

Book IV.304-330

1. Dido's rhetoric needs to be examined carefully. Draw students' attention to emphasis by position (**dissimulāre**, 305; **perfide**, 305; **mēne . . . tē**, 314; **ōrō**, 319; **tē**, 320; **hospes**, 323; anaphora, 307, 312-313, 314-316, 320-321, 327-328; alliteration, 298, 307, 322; and a prevalence of dactyls.

2. Explore the ramifications of the idea expressed in the words **moritūra . . . crūdēlī fūnere** (308). Do these words imply that Dido will die of grief, or that she will commit suicide, or is she making a rhetorical threat of suicide to force Aeneas to remain?

3. The passage for comparison with *Aeneid* IV.305-319, namely, Extract V: Catullus, poem LXIV.132-144 (student's book, pages 78-79), should be read and discussed with students at this point.

4. Dido's reference to her earlier reputation (320-322) calls for some re-examination of her past to heighten the present crisis.

5. Lines 327-330 should prompt discussion among students; are they truly poignant, or are they simply special pleading by Dido in an emergency, her final attempt to stall Aeneas' departure? Study the speech for additional insights into Dido's love of children (her earlier conduct with Ascanius and Cupid provides insights); note also her reference to her home (**aulā**, 328), family activity (**parvulus . . . lūderet**, 328-329), and the cherished likeness of father and son (329-330). Vergil seems intent on winning the reader's sympathy for Dido at this juncture. Apollonius, *Argonautica* I.888-909, would provide a useful comparison.

Book IV.331-361

1. Use a diagram to detail Aeneas' formal defensive arguments. His reply will appear to be carefully structured and to follow reasonable lines. How persuasive are his statements? He responds to lines 305-306 in lines 337-338; but he shows little reaction to Dido's lines 317-319. The speech may be regarded as a masterpiece of courtroom oratory, specious and sophistical, or as a polite rejoinder to Dido's direct accusations. Certainly, Dido's reaction to his defense is irate and explosive.

2. T. E. Page in his school edition remarked that "not all Virgil's art can make the figure of Aeneas appear here other than despicable. His conduct has been vile, and Dido's heartbroken appeal brings its vileness into strong relief." One might argue that Aeneas was enthralled with Dido and that, in spite of everything he stated in his defense, he nearly renounced his design to desert her. There

are obviously divergent opinions about the sincerity of Aeneas' defense and the true nature of his regard for Dido. Editors generally regard the protestations of Aeneas in lines 335–336 as cold and excessively formal. The earlier promise of everlasting gratitude seems more genuine and sincere. A class debate might be organized with the following alternative themes: (1) Did Aeneas really love Dido? (2) Did Aeneas merely use Dido during a critical time and then abandon her when he no longer needed her?

3. How similar and how dissimilar are Dido and Aeneas? Both are honest and forthright. Both Aeneas and Dido express their true feelings—Aeneas with cold reason and logic, Dido with a range of feelings encompassing fury, regret, longing, and entreaty.

4. Ask students to debate the truth or falsity of Aeneas' half-line (361) at the close of his defense. Aeneas argues that he leaves unwillingly, but he does make a conscious decision to leave. Is the statement empty rhetoric to exonerate him from the charge of discarding Dido in order to pursue his own ambitions? Or is he sincerely and selflessly pursuing a higher calling?

Book IV.362–396

1. Readers respond differently to Dido's passionate outburst: some regard it as a magnificent speech condemning Aeneas, others as a piece of hysterical ranting. Read the speech aloud to heighten student interest and response.

2. The passage for comparison with *Aeneid* IV.373–381, namely, Extract VI: Homer, *Odyssey* V.129–140 (student's book, page 79), should be read and discussed with students at this point.

3. Argue for or against the notion that we are less sympathetic to Dido's cause at line 392 than earlier at line 330. The moral ascendancy that she had established by the close of her previous speech has been reduced considerably by this speech.

4. In what ways does Dido misunderstand Aeneas? Ask students to analyze the hero's words and actions to this point to arrive at a verdict. Does Dido, on the other hand, understand Aeneas too well?

5. Why is Aeneas "hesitant with fear" (390)? Do his fears attach to possible reprisals by Dido against him, by the Carthaginians against his Trojans, or to possible suicide by Dido? Or is he uncertain and apprehensive about himself, fearing that he might break

down and surrender to his love and sympathy for Dido? As Dido is carried away following her collapse, Aeneas considers going after her and solacing her (393–394). He chooses to leave and return to the ships (395–396), and Dido dies believing that Aeneas does not love her truly. Encourage students to read the Latin very carefully and reconstruct exactly what is happening.

Book IV.397–449

1. cernās (401) "you could see (if you were inclined to look)" sets the reader alongside Dido by direct invitation and so heightens the immediacy of the action.

2. The ant simile heightens the sense of hustle and bustle along the shore and the Trojans' distance from Dido's palace. The military associations, particularly of hauling away booty, recall Dido's own flight from Carthage with Pygmalion's treasure and also accentuate the militant character of the Trojans, ancestors of the Roman conquerors and later destroyers of Carthage in 146 B.C.

3. Vergil's asides (408–411 and 412), the address to Dido, and the interrogative apostrophe to Amor provide insights into the poet's feelings about Dido and underline the universality of love's sufferings.

4. Students should be alerted to the elements of detachment and of humor in the ant simile (402–407). Proverbs VI:6–8 offers a fruitful parallel: "Go to the ant, thou sluggard; consider her ways, and be wise: which having no guide, overseer, or ruler, provideth her meat in the summer, and gathereth her food in the harvest." Aesop also contributes a fable of the ant and the grasshopper.

5. frūstrā moritūra (415): these words need careful examination. Dido is resorting to every expedient to reach Aeneas. If she fails and so cannot save herself, her death will not be in vain. Vergil's use of the future participle is also an ironic (but not unsympathetic) comment on her hopeless tactic; Dido will die finally without accomplishing anything.

6. Dido's reference to the Greeks at Aulis (426), departure point for the Trojan War, recalls the sacrifice of Iphigenia by her father Agamemnon, to enable the fleet to sail. The sacrilegious act of disturbing cremated remains and so the departed spirits of the dead (Mānēs) was universally condemned. Dido's argument is simply that she had never done anything hateful or heinous to induce Aeneas to abandon her.

7. **hoc mūnus** (429) is explained in the following line (430).

8. The alliteration in line 430 reflects Dido's impatience and scorn. The *m* sounds in the preceding line are equally impressive.

9. Line 432 is ironic, a customary ingredient of rhetorical exercises.

10. Lines 435–436 are effective and ambiguous. The presence of twelve *m*'s, initial, medial, and final, may suggest the sound of speech half-stifled by sobs (*The Speeches in Vergil's Aeneid*, p. 137). The meaning is difficult. Dido asks for the favor of time and promises to repay the favor with interest by means of her death. She will permit Aeneas to leave Carthage without accusations after they have finally parted, and her death will allow him to escape the feelings of guilt for his desertion. The imagery is financial, a detail that should not go unnoticed in the Punic queen.

11. Line 440 underscores Vergil's reading of the episode; Aeneas wanted to listen as a sympathetic human being, but as an agent of destiny he is not his own master. Aeneas offers no response, but later (VI.450–476), he apologizes to Dido only to meet the same silence.

12. The tears of line 449 have been disputed by scholars. The falling of the leaves of the shaken oak tree seems to provide identification. Since the **lacrimae** are a parallel manifestation to the leaves, the poet may be indicating that they are Aeneas' tears, the visible sign of the turmoil raging within him. Some prefer to see the irreconcilable, obdurate nature of Aeneas opposed to the useless tears of Dido (and Anna). The ambiguity, if it really exists, simply universalizes the tragic nature of the relationship and of the separation of Dido and Aeneas.

13. There are interesting contrasts between Dido's earlier appeal (305–330) and this later and final message (416–436). In the earlier speech, Dido asked Aeneas to remain with her forever and so ignore his quest for Hesperia; her heart was set on marriage and progeny. Now she pleads for a delay in his departure to make the divorce less abrupt, and, equally important, she addresses him indirectly, through Anna. Although Aeneas makes no reply on this occasion, Vergil takes pains in line 448 to detail Aeneas' emotional stress (**magnō . . . pectore cūrās**, the last word having a wide range of connotations, "impact of grief in his great heart") to underscore his compassion and his heroic

stature at the same time. The force of **persentit** (448) accents the depth of the emotional stress he undergoes.

14. The simile deserves some close inspection for repetitions, which are numerous and are part of the orchestration of the passage: **flētūs** (437), **flētibus** (439), **flātibus** (442); **nūllīs** (438), **ullās** (439); and obstant (440), **obstruit** (440).

15. The passages for comparison with *Aeneid* IV.441–449, namely, Extracts VII and VIII: Homer, *Iliad* XII.131–134 and *Iliad* XVI.765–771 (student's book, pages 79–80), should be read and discussed with students at this point.

Book IV.584–629

1. Notice the contrast between the lovely new dawn and the tormented emotions of the deserted queen.

2. Explore with students the reasons for Dido's curses on Aeneas and his descendants: thwarted power, injured pride, discarded love, ineffectual favors, and passion for revenge. The example of Euripides' *Medea* and of Catullus' Ariadne (poem LXIV) could be introduced effectively at this point.

3. Dido's speech merits close scrutiny. At the outset, she suggests that her dignity as a royal person has been outraged and humiliated by Aeneas' withdrawal. Then she senses an incipient madness (595–599). She regains control of herself, and Vergil signals the effort involved in the slow spondees of line 596. The next seven verses mingle anger and remorse (600–606) when she wishes she had acted like the demonic heroines of tragedy (Medea and Procne) or had annihilated Aeneas, Ascanius, and his company and included herself in their funeral pyre. There are indications of her deadly hatred in the repetition of the letters *f* and *s* in these lines. The curses on Aeneas ensue with four slow lines (607–621) as prelude to her outburst. Dido's prayer to the gods to punish Aeneas is followed by her address to her Carthaginians (622–629) when, with the style of a dying queen (**cinerī . . . nostrō**, 623; **nostrīs ex ossibus**, 625), she invokes hatred between the nations and a future avenger. The final lines (628–629) pray for total hostility, and the speech concludes with a crescendo of hissing *s* sounds. The order of this speech is not so much rhetorical as emotional. Help the students to detect the four individuals and groups: Dido herself and her lover, the gods, and her people: Ae-

neas (590–594), Dido (595–606), the gods (607–621), and the Carthaginians (622–629). The fury and despair of the abandoned queen are transformed into generalized hostility and violence between two nations.

4. The long series of pluperfect subjunctives (604–606) conveys Dido's concern with what might have been, with what she might have done and did not.

5. The appeal to the Sun, Juno, Hecate, and the Furies (the avenging demons) is entirely appropriate to Dido's desperate condition. She asks for supernatural help, for the protection of her city and of marriage bonds, for chthonic assistance (Hecate was the patron of Medea), and for the power of vengeance.

6. Comment on the efficacy of Dido's curses: Aeneas will be harassed in war by Turnus and his Rutulians in Latium (*Aeneid* VIII); he will leave the Trojan camp and the embrace of Ascanius-Iulus to gain help from Evander, at the future site of Rome (*Aeneid* VIII); he will see the deaths of many of his men, particularly of Pallas, Evander's son, and his special charge (*Aeneid* VIII, X–XII); he will accept peace terms that favor the Italians over the Trojans (*Aeneid* XII.834–837); and he will not rule long, a span of only three years.

7. Elissa appears to be Dido's original Phoenician name, probably suggesting her "royal" nature. Aeneas used it at lines 335–336. Dido's role as queen requires divine intervention to avenge the insult to her dignity.

8. Aeneas' death (620) as forecast by Dido is troublesome. Will he lie unburied in the middle of the sand (as Priam, *Aeneid* II.557–558, and Palinurus, Aeneas' helmsman, at the end of *Aeneid* V)? According to one version of the Aeneas legend, the hero fell in battle and, when his body was not found, Ascanius-Iulus claimed that he had been received among the gods. Dido prays not that Aeneas lie unburied, but that he fall (so as to be) unburied. Her curse is therefore consistent with the legend that Aeneas was transported to heaven. Jupiter's address to Juno (*Aeneid* XII.791–795) confirms Aeneas' apotheosis.

Book IV.630–662

1. The tragic character of Dido's last moments and her parting words are reminiscent of the Greek tragic theater. To provide background, refer to Euripides' *Alcestis* (175–182), which highlights a wife's sacrifice of her life in order to ensure the survival of her husband and to guarantee the security of her children. There is another example of nobility comparable to that of Dido in the final words of Ajax before his suicide in Sophocles' *Ajax* (815–865).

2. Dido's concern for ritual exactitude as expressed in her instructions to Barce suggests that she retains control of herself at this final juncture. The magic and ritual are really nonexistent, and Dido no doubt hopes to die instantly (like Ajax in Sophocles' *Ajax*, 831–834). Anna is summoned in order that Dido's next of kin may be the first to discover her dead body and so prepare it for burial. She plans to use the sword of Aeneas, her one-time lover, now her enemy, as Ajax used the sword of Hector, his enemy.

3. The trappings of Dido's funeral pyre are the garments and sword of Aeneas, which he had seemingly entrusted to her for safekeeping during happier times. The details seem to be quite specific: she lies on the "marriage bed" they once shared, alongside the effigy of Aeneas evidently wearing his own clothes (648); she kisses the bed when she takes her life, and she uses his weapon, as an indication that he was responsible for her death (646–647, 663–665).

4. Vīxī (653) is normally used in contexts of a satisfactory completion of a life-span with some assurance of glory thereafter. In fact, of course, Dido's life has been disastrous and her reputation ruined. Instead of children, she raised a city; her distaste for injustice was embodied in her retaliation for Sychaeus' murder (656). She expects that her name will be memorialized as the founder of a great city (654).

5. Although Dido hoped and prayed for vengeance, her confidence slips with the expression **moriēmur inultae** (659). Desperate, unable to take a life for a life, she takes her own life. Her avenger will appear in the historical Hannibal.

6. The final words, beginning with **Dulcēs exuviae** (651–660), are exceptional for their musicality (Baroque composers often set them to musical accompaniment), their solemnity (accented by the use of spondees), and rhythmic repetition.

7. The repetition of **sīc** (660) can be interpreted in different ways. Some would argue that it signals that Dido stabs herself twice, at this moment; others, that it signifies "by my own

hand" and so underscores her voluntary choice.

Book IV.663–692
1. Ask students to analyze lines 665–671, describing the momentum attaching to the news of Dido's death: from the **ātria**, with traditional sky-light, and then through the city with ensuing uproar that suggested that Carthage was being sacked by an enemy and was collapsing in flames. The onomatopoeia of line 667 is noteworthy in **gemitū** and **ululātū**. The hiatus between **fēmineō** and **ululātū** heightens the effect by introducing a break in the verse.
2. Remind students that the description of a city in flames has already appeared in the Fall of Troy (*Aeneid* II.624–632). Tyre is introduced because it was the mother-city of Carthage. The repetition of **perque . . . perque** suggests the repeated surge of the engulfing flames (671).
3. Anna's quick realization of Dido's deceit is followed by a string of complaints, the recourse of someone who has been caught up in actions that have had a catastrophic outcome. Her reaction to Dido's suicide is to forecast her own doom and that of Carthage. Homer, *Iliad* XXII.410–411, provided Vergil with a model for the wailing and Anna's outburst: comparable wailing followed after the death of Hector, as if all Ilium (Troy) were burning. Homer indicated that the sequel to Hector's death at the hands of Achilles ensured the downfall of Troy; Vergil's imitation implies that Carthage will soon fall, to Pygmalion perhaps, or Iarbas.
4. The structure of this passage is carefully designed: the death of the queen is described at the beginning and the end; Anna's grief occupies the center and so highlights particular and general grief over Dido's suicide.
5. The fall of the city (669–671) was realized later in Rome's siege and destruction of Carthage in 146 B.C.
6. Vergil's use of **bacchātur** (666) recalls Dido's own frenzied activity earlier (IV.301, not included in these selections).
7. Help students to reflect now on Dido's tragedy, her regal character, her administrative strengths, her passionate nature, her "guilty" surrender to Aeneas, her denunciation and vituperation when deserted, and, at the supreme moment, her dignity and self-control.
8. To complement the review of Dido's nature and behavior, ask students to collect their thoughts on the characterization of Aeneas in connection with Dido. They should be ready now to provide a reasonable estimate of his strengths and weaknesses.

Book IV.693–705
1. Iris combines several functions: as minister to the queen of the underworld because Proserpina (Greek, Persephone) cannot intervene with the "untimely dead"; as a glorious "curtain" to the tragic story, a polychrome final display; and as emphatic contrast between the light that Dido sought and the darkness of death.
2. Dido's story, like Greek tragedy, ends with a tranquil, serene episode. The drama of human suffering and physical pain has come to an end. Iris, arching through the sky with colorful beauty and compassion, leaves the reader with a sense that Juno's patronage includes compassion for her favorite.
3. The ultimate intrusion of Juno into Dido's tragic career in Carthage is justifiable on many grounds. Discuss with the students whether this intrusion of Juno represents Vergil's own sympathy with his heroine. Certainly Juno's final mercy accomplishes more than Anna's mortal attempts to ease her sister's passing.
4. Vergil's epithet for Juno, **omnipotēns** (693), should give rise to a discussion regarding the powers and relative success of the two competing goddesses, Venus and Juno, in the careers of their favorites. Just how effective has Juno been with respect to Dido's experience with Aeneas?
5. **nec fātō meritā nec morte** (696) "neither in the course of fate nor by a death earned (by herself)" implies a natural death (in accordance with destiny) and a violent death (earned in battle) rather than suicide. **misera ante diem subitōque accēnsa furōre** (697): these words indicate, by contrast with line 696, that Dido died prematurely and suddenly, the consequence of her unhappy condition (**misera**) and sudden frenzy (**subitō . . . furōre**). Her impetuous nature finally brought her to suicide. Vergil's lines read like an epitaph for the tragic queen. Her death was her own choice.
6. The concept of the soul imprisoned by the body (cf. *Aeneid* VI.734—not included in these selections but given on page 41 of this handbook—and Cicero, "Somnium Scipionis," XIV) derives from Orphic belief that the body

was a prison (or a tomb) for the soul. Death enables the imprisoned, struggling soul to escape and enter upon a new cycle of existence (transmigration of the soul). Anchises instructs Aeneas in this mystery in the course of his sermon in the underworld to his son on the soul's relationship with the body and on what happens to the soul after death (VI.703–751, not included in these selections but see page 41 of this handbook).

7. The final line has a single word (**ventōs**) providing the fourth foot. This has the effect of bringing the final cadence (literally, "falling") with its alliteration (**ventōs vīta**) to a gentle but decisive close. Dido's life-spirit or soul lightly vanishes into thin air.

Book VI.450–476

1. The Dido episode of *Aeneid* VI provides a marvelous epilogue to *Aeneid* IV, and there are many echoes of the earlier book in this passage. Encourage students to compile a list of them: VI.455 and IV.395; VI.456 (**īnfēlīx**) and IV.596 (cf. 68); VI.461 and IV.345–346, 376–378; VI.463 (**imperiīs . . . suīs**) and IV.356; and VI.466 (**quem fugis?**) and IV.366–367. Many of the echoes are also reversals of the original situations with ironical implications. For example, VI.460, **invītus, rēgīna, tuō dē lītore cessī**, is a restatement of Aeneas' earlier apology, **Italiam nōn sponte sequor** (IV.361).

2. The simile of the moon is marvelously evocative of the haunting character of the place and the episode. Dido's first appearance was heightened by the simile of Diana, goddess, inter alia, of the moon (I.496–507). When Aeneas first saw Dido he was cloaked in a cloud of invisibility (I.411–414, 586–587, not included in these selections).

3. **Rēgīna** seems excessively formal to most critics. Aeneas used the royal title earlier (IV.283) when he sought ways and means of getting around the impassioned queen; in direct discourse, when he was on the verge of leaving her (IV.334); and now he uses it in the underworld (VI.460). The respectful adjective seems unexpectedly remote.

4. Dido's response to Aeneas' defense is inevitable. Aeneas is trying to defend and redeem himself by his passionate, earnest, and remorseful, if somewhat formal, declaration. His grief is visible in his tears. At this juncture, Dido can only remain adamant. Their roles have been reversed; where Dido once put the questions, now Ae-

neas puts the question (VI.466, **quem fugis?**) and gets no response.

5. The final simile of the rock recalls Dido's earlier description of Aeneas (IV.366–367). The simile underlines the finality of the situation, its dead end; there is no way that Dido can respond positively to Aeneas. The ironical recollection of the earlier accusation simply underscores the termination of the affair.

6. Dido's reunion with Sychaeus is poetic recompense for her terrible sufferings and her disenchantment with Aeneas' love. Dido has no further need of Aeneas; her indignation is deep-seated and her passionate nature still incensed (VI.467, **ardentem et torva tuentem**); she has reawakened her devotion to her first husband, and their mutual devotion is complete.

7. Aeneas' tears accompany his speech of persuasion and apology. His desperation at this last encounter, with his arguments that he had not made his departure willingly and that he had not believed that it would result in her death, would undermine the most stoical character. His tears are token of the sincerity of his declarations; they are aroused particularly by Dido's somber figure deserting him. They are a clear indication of his heartbroken condition.

8. Dido's surrender to a passionate relationship with Aeneas was transitory and ill-starred. Her brief, evidently happy, marriage with Sychaeus is unique in the epic, but it ended violently.

9. Spondees, with melancholy suggestions, occur at lines 450, 451, 452, 456, 460, 464, and 474. Alliteration also adds to the emphatic and passionate character of Aeneas' speech and to the poignancy of the episode.

10. Students may be curious about Vergil's underworld and Aeneas' other adventures. Have them read other sections of *Aeneid* VI in translation: the first stages of the journey (268–336); Charon, Cerberus, and the untimely dead (384–449); Tartarus (548–636); Elysium (637–702); and Marcellus and the Gates of Sleep (854–901).

11. The passage for comparison with *Aeneid* VI.456–474, namely, Extract IX: Homer, *Odyssey* XI.541–547 and 563–567 (student's book, page 80), should be read and discussed with students at this point.

* * *

TRANSLATIONS

Book I.338–368

"You see a Phoenician realm, Tyrians, and Agenor's city. But the hinterland is Libyan, a race unmanageable in war. Dido wields the sovereignty, having set forth from her city of Tyre in flight from her brother. It is a long story of crime, long and complicated, but I shall trace the main points. Her husband was Sychaeus, wealthiest landowner among the Phoenicians, loved with deep passion by the pitiable [girl]. Her father had given her to him as a virgin and had joined her to him in this her first marriage ceremony. But her brother held the rule of Tyre, Pygmalion, more brutal in crime than all others. Between them there came a hatred. Sacrilegiously before the altars, and blinded by his lust for gold, Pygmalion secretly struck down Sychaeus unawares with a sword, caring nothing for his sister's love. He concealed the deed for a long time, and wickedly, by making up many false stories, deceived the lovesick bride with empty hope. (353) But the very specter of her unburied husband appeared in her dreams, raising his death-pale face in marvelous fashion. He laid bare the cruel altars and his chest pierced by the sword, and he revealed all the secret crime of the household. Then he induces her to hasten her flight and to leave her fatherland; and as a help for her journey he brings to light, from the earth, ancient treasures, a forgotten weight of silver and gold. (360) Shocked by these revelations, Dido was preparing for flight and collecting companions. And there come together persons who either had a hatred or an acute terror of the inhuman ruler. They commandeer ships which happened to be ready and load them with gold. So the resources of greedy Pygmalion are carried overseas, and a woman is commander of the enterprise. They reached areas where you see now enormous walls and the rising citadel of new Carthage; they bought as much land as they could enclose with a bull's hide and called it Byrsa from the event."

Book I.375–401

"By pure chance a storm drove us, already carried over far-off seas from ancient Troy—if perhaps the name of Troy has reached your ears—to Libyan shores. I am faithful Aeneas, well-known in heaven above by reason of my fame, and I carry with me, in my fleet, our household gods snatched from the enemy. I am searching for Italy, my father's land, and the race descended from highest Jupiter. In twice ten ships I embarked upon the Phrygian sea, following my allotted destiny while my goddess mother showed me the way. Scarcely seven survive, shattered by the waves and wind. I myself wander, a stranger, destitute, over Libya's wasteland, rejected by Europe and Asia." (385) Venus would not listen to further complaints and interrupted him in the middle of his lament. "Whoever you are, in no way hateful, I think, to the heavenly powers, you draw the lifegiving breezes, you who have reached the Tyrian city. Carry straight on and go from here to the queen's threshold. For I bring you word that your comrades have returned and that your fleet has been restored, driven to safety by a shift of the winds—unless deceitful parents taught me augury in vain. (393) Look at those twelve swans, jubilant in their formation, which the bird of Jupiter, swooping down from the tract of high heaven, was just now scattering in the open sky. Now they can be seen in a long line either settling on the ground or gazing down on the [ground] settled on [by others]. Just as these swans, playful now with their whirring wings, have returned, and have circled the sky in a flock and have given song, so your ships and the young men of your crew have either reached the harbor or are drawing near its mouth under full sail. Press on now, and direct your steps wherever this path leads you."

Book I.419–437

Now they were climbing a hill, which looms large over the city and from above confronts the towers facing it. Aeneas marvels at the vast size of the buildings, once mere shepherds' huts; he marvels at the gates, the turmoil, and the paved streets. The enthusiastic Tyrians are pressing on their work; some are building walls; they labor at constructing a citadel and roll up rocks with their hands; some choose a spot for a building and enclose it with a furrow. They enact laws and choose magistrates and a reverend senate. Here some are excavating harbors; in this place some are laying the deep foundations for theaters and are cutting mighty columns from quarries, lofty adornment for stages to come. (430) Like the busy activity that engages bees under the sun in early summer through the flowering countryside, when they bring forth the young of the breed, full-grown; or when they pack the flowing honey and fill to bursting the honey-comb cells with sweet nectar; or else take over loads from the new arrivals; or sometimes, having formed an assaulting column, they drive away the drones, an unproductive herd, from their hives. Their work is alive with activity; and the thyme-scented honey spreads its perfume. "O fortunate people," says Aeneas, "whose city walls are rising!"

Book I.494–508

While these wondrous things are being viewed by Dardanian Aeneas, and while he stands astounded and concentrates [on her] motionless with one long gaze, Dido, the queen, most beautiful of all in her figure, walked in state to the temple with a large retinue of youths in attendance. She was like Diana, when she leads her dancers on the banks of the Eurotas or along the ridges of Cynthus, and a thousand mountain nymphs follow her and crowd round on this side and that. She wears a quiver on her shoulder, and as she walks she towers over all other goddesses (feelings of joy thrill Latona's silent heart). Like her was Dido, and in such a way she carried herself joyfully through the crowd pressing on with her work and her future realm. Then, at the folding-doors of the goddess's shrine, beneath the center of the vaulted roof of the temple, escorted by warriors, positioned on a high throne, she took her seat. She announced laws and statutes for her people, and she apportioned with balanced justice the division of toil or assigned it by lot.

Book I.561–578

Then, with eyes lowered, Dido speaks briefly: "Remove fear from your hearts, Trojans, and lay aside your anxieties. My difficult position and the newness of my kingdom drive me to devise such precautions and to protect my boundaries, far and wide, with guards. Who could be unaware of the race of the Aeneadae, Troy's city, her brave deeds, her heroes, or the holocaust of that terrible war? We Phoenicians do not have such dull minds, nor is the Sun, when he harnesses his horses, so remote from our Tyrian city. (569) Whether you choose mighty Hesperia, the Saturnian ploughlands, or the regions of Eryx with King Acestes, I will send you off safe with my assistance, and I will help you with my resources. Or rather, do you wish to settle in my kingdom, on equal terms with me? The city that I am establishing is yours. Beach your ships; Trojan and Tyrian will be treated by me with no distinction. And would that your king, Aeneas himself, might appear, driven here by the same wind. Indeed, I will dispatch reliable men along the coast and will order them to range over the remotest parts of Libya in case he has been cast ashore and is lost in some forests or cities."

Book I.588–610

Aeneas stood there and shone in the bright light; his face and shoulders were like a god's; for his mother had breathed upon her son and given him beautiful hair and the radiant glow of youth and a joyous luster in his eyes, like the beauty that artists' hands give to ivory, or when silver or Parian marble is surrounded with yellow gold. Then, suddenly, to everyone's surprise, he addresses the queen as follows: "Here I am, in your presence, the one for whom you are looking. I am Trojan Aeneas, rescued from the Libyan waves. (597) O you alone have pity for the unspeakable ordeals of Troy: now, remnants from the Danaan destruction, with our strength drained away by all our misfortunes on land and sea, in need of everything, you offer to associate us with your city, your home. To repay [you] to the full, Dido, is not within our power; nor in the power of any Dardanian race anywhere dispersed throughout this vast world. But may the gods, if indeed there are any divine powers at all who have regard for dutiful persons, if indeed there is any justice at all anywhere, and if [your] mind is conscious of what is right, bring you proper rewards. What so happy an age gave you birth? What illustrious parents gave birth to so wonderful [a child]? As long as rivers flow into the sea, as long as on the mountains the shadows shall move over the slopes, as long as the heavens shall nourish the stars, for ever shall abide the honor [which is due], your name, and [your] praises, whatever lands summon me."

Book I.657–694

Meanwhile the Cytherean goddess turns over in her mind fresh devices and fresh plans, how to make Cupid alter his appearance and aspect and come instead of sweet Ascanius and inflame the queen to passion with his gifts and entwine the flames of love around her bones. Because, you see, Venus fears for the deceitful house and the two-tongued Tyrians. Cruel Juno worries her and her anxiety returns toward nightfall. Therefore she addresses winged Amor with these words: "Son, you alone are my strength, and all my mighty power; you [even] scorn the Typhoean thunderbolts of the highest father. Now I flee to you for help and as suppliant beg [aid from] your divine power. You know how your brother Aeneas is storm-tossed on the sea around every coast through the hatred of merciless Juno, and you have sympathized often with my sorrow. (670) [Now] Phoenician Dido detains him and delays him with coaxing words. I fear the outcome of this hospitality inspired by Juno. She will not be inactive at such an important turning point. Therefore, I plan to forestall the queen by tricks and to encompass her with fire so that she may not change her mind by any divine influence but may be kept on my side by her deep passion for Aeneas. To enable you to effect this, listen now to my plan. At the summons of his dear father, the royal youth, my greatest love, is preparing now to go to the Sidonian city bearing gifts which have survived from the sea and the flames of Troy. When he has been lulled into a profound sleep, I will lay him away in my hallowed seat high on Cythera, or on Idalium, lest he may be able to know my tricks and appear right in the middle of things. (683) Assume by trickery his shape no longer than one night, and put on the familiar features of the child, child as you are, so that, when Dido, at her happiest, takes you into her lap, during the royal banquet when the wine is flowing, and embraces you and plants sweet kisses, you may breathe into her invisible fire and poison her without her realizing it." Amor obeys the commands of his dear mother; he takes off his wings and in delight walks like Iulus. Venus now pours soothing sleep over Ascanius' limbs and, snug in her bosom, carries him to the upland groves of Idalia where soft marjoram breathes its fragrance over him and wraps him round with its blossoms and sweet shade.

Book I.707–722

And the Tyrians came together in crowds through the festal doorways, invited to recline on embroidered banqueting-couches. They marvel at Aeneas' gifts; they marvel at Iulus, at the radiant face of the god and his dissembling words, the mantle and the veil embroidered with a yellow acanthus pattern. But the Phoenician, in particular, ill-starred, doomed to a disaster to come, cannot satisfy her heart. She catches fire as she gazes at him and is thrilled equally by the boy and the gifts. After Cupid in the embrace of Aeneas has hung around his neck and satisfied the great love of the deluded father, he makes for the queen. Her gaze and all her thoughts are riveted upon him, now and then she caresses him in her lap, for she does not know what a powerful god settles there to her sorrow. Then Cupid, remembering [the instructions] of his Acidalian mother, begins gradually to blot out [the memory of] Sychaeus and plots to occupy with a living love her long slumbering affection and unused heart.

Book IV.1–30

Meanwhile the queen, already wounded with the deep suffering of love, nourishes the wound with her lifeblood and is consumed by a fire she keeps hidden. Again the manliness of the hero, again the glory of his race keep recurring to her mind. His looks and his words cling buried deep in her heart, nor does grief allow her body quiet rest. The next day's dawn was moving across the earth with Phoebus' torch and had already scattered the dewy shades from the heavens when she spoke, distraught, to her loving sister as follows: (9) "Anna, my sister, what dreams frighten my trou-

bled heart! Who is this foreign guest that has come to our settlement? What a noble appearance, how brave in heart and arms! Indeed, I believe, nor is my confidence groundless, that he belongs to the race of the gods. Fear reveals a lowly born spirit. Alas, by what bad fortune he was tossed about! What wars undergone has he related! If it were not fixed and immovable in my mind never to wish to join myself with another man in wedlock, after my first love deceived me by dying, if I were not sick of the bridal chamber and torch, perhaps I might have been able to yield to this one temptation. (20) Anna, I will confess it, since the death of my unfortunate husband Sychaeus and the spattering of my household gods with murder committed by my brother, only this man has moved my feelings and caused my mind to waver. I recognize the traces of the old flame. But I would wish either that the earth would yawn open for me or that the all-powerful father would drive me with his thunderbolt to the shades, the pale shades and the bottomless night in Erebus, before I would violate you, Pudor, or break your laws. He who first joined me to him carried away my love with him. Let him hold it for himself and preserve it in the tomb." After she spoke these words, she filled her bosom with streaming tears.

Book IV.56–89

First they approach the shrines and pray for divine assent at the altars; following custom, they sacrifice choice two-year-old sheep to the lawgiver Ceres, to Phoebus [Apollo], to father Lyaeus [Bacchus], and above all to Juno, who has special concern for marriage bonds. Most beautiful Dido, holding a bowl in her right hand, pours [wine] between the horns of a white cow, or in front of the statues of the gods, approaches the altars rich with sacrifices, and daily renews her gifts and intently examines the palpitating entrails when the breasts of the victims are split open. Alas, the ignorant minds of soothsayers! How can offerings, how can temples help [Dido] maddened with love? All the time a flame devours the soft marrow of her being, and the silent wound lives deep in her breast. (68) Ill-starred Dido is afire [with love] and wanders madly through the city like an arrow-pierced doe, caught off-guard, which a shepherd, hunting with weapons, has shot from a distance in Cretan woods; though unaware, he has left his flying shaft [in the wound], and the animal wanders in her flight through the forests and woodlands of Dicte with the deadly arrow clinging to her side. Now Dido takes Aeneas with her through the midst of the city and shows him the rich Sidonian resources, the city all readied [for him]. She begins to speak, but stops when the word is begun.

Then, as the day slips away, she asks for the banquet all over again, and in her madness asks to hear once more the sufferings of Troy and again hangs on his words as he tells the story. (80) Later, when he and she have parted and the dimmed moon in turn sinks her light and the setting stars suggest sleep, she is alone; she grieves in the empty hall and flings herself on the couch he has left. Though they are apart, she hears him, she sees him, or, captivated by his likeness to his father, she holds Ascanius in her lap to see if she can solace a passion beyond words. The towers, already begun, cease to rise, and the young men do not practice their military exercises, nor do they make ready the port and the defenses as a protection against war. All works and the huge threatening walls and the crane that towers sky-high are broken off and hang idle.

Book IV.129–172

Meanwhile rising Dawn leaves Ocean behind. When the sun's rays had risen, a picked group of young men streams out from the gates; Massylian horsemen with wide-meshed nets, snares, wide-bladed hunting spears, and powerful, keen-scented hounds rush out. At the threshold the noblest of the Carthaginians await their queen delaying in her bedchamber. There stands her charger, resplendent in purple and gold, and he fiercely champs his foaming bit. At length, in the company of a great troop, she comes forth, clothed in a Sidonian cloak with an embroidered edge. Her quiver is golden, her hair is tied up in a golden clasp, and a golden brooch fastens her purple dress. (140) Happy Iulus and his Phrygian companions also join the train. Aeneas himself, more handsome than all the others, steps forth to join her and unites his troop [with hers]. As when Apollo leaves wintry Lycia in winter and the streams of Xanthus and comes to Delos and starts up the dances again, while thronging Cretans, Dryopians, and tattooed Agathyrsi raise a din around the altars, the god himself, his arrows clanging on his shoulders, walks along the ridge of Cynthus and with a soft [laurel] wreath shapes and confines his flowing hair and entwines it with gold, no less vigorous than his was Aeneas' movement, and equal grace shines forth on his noble face. (150) After they came into the high mountains and trackless forest lairs, see! wild goats, dislodged from the rocky peaks, race down from the ridges; from another direction, deer scurry across the open fields, mass their dusty columns in flight, and leave the mountains behind. Now the boy Ascanius rides gleefully through the mist of the valleys on a spirited horse, passes one after another as he races along, and wishes that in answer to his prayers a foaming boar would appear among all the timid herds and that a tawny lion would come down from the mountain. (160) Meanwhile the heavens begin to be disturbed with loud thunder, and a cloud-burst with hail follows. The Tyrian companions, everywhere, the Trojan youths, and the Dardanian grandson of Venus, terrified, made for shelter at scattered points in the fields as torrents race down from the mountains. Dido and the Trojan leader came to the same cave. Primal Earth and Juno as matron of honor give the sign [to begin the rite]; lightning flashed, and Heaven is witness to the marriage, while the nymphs screamed from the highest peak. That day was the original cause of doom and of sufferings; for Dido is not disturbed by appearances or reputation, and no longer does she plan a clandestine love affair; she calls it marriage, and with this name she cloaked her wrongdoing.

Book IV.238–278

[Mercury] prepared to obey the order of his great father. First he ties on his feet golden sandals, which carry him air-borne on wings over the sea or the earth with speed equal to that of the whirling wind. Then he seizes his wand [caduceus]. With this he calls forth the pale spirits from Orcus and with it sends others down to dismal Tartarus; with it he gives sleep or takes it away and unseals men's eyes in death; relying on this, he drives the winds and floats through the turbulent clouds. Now in flight, he sights the peak and steep sides of long-suffering Atlas, who supports the heavens on his head, Atlas, whose pine-forested head, forever veiled in dark clouds, is beaten by winds and rain alike; a mantle of snow conceals his shoulders; in addition, streams rush down from the old man's chin, and his bristling beard is stiff with ice. (252) Poised on balanced wings, the Cyllenian first stopped here; from here he dived down seaward, plunging with all his body's force, like a bird that flies low up and down the shoreline and the fish-teeming reefs, close to the sea. In the same way he flew between earth and heaven near the sandy shore of Libya and cut through the winds, the Cyllenian offspring coming from his maternal grandfather [Atlas]. As soon as he touched the huts with his winged feet, he catches sight of Aeneas building battlements and making new dwellings; he [i.e., Aeneas] wore a sword, studded with tawny jasper; hanging from his shoulders glowed a cloak of Tyrian purple—gifts which wealthy Dido had made and whose texture she had interwoven with a fine golden thread. (265) Straightway the god attacks Aeneas: "Are you now laying the foundations of lofty Carthage and, under a wife's power, are you building a beautiful city,

forgetful, alas, of your kingdom and your own affairs? The ruler of the gods himself, who turns the heavens and the earth with his power, sends me down from bright Olympus to you; he orders me to bring these commands on the high winds. What are you constructing? What prospect is there in idly wasting your time on Libyan soil? If glory in great enterprises stirs you not at all and you undertake no exploit on behalf of your own fame, consider growing Ascanius, the expectations placed in your heir, Iulus, to whom a kingdom in Italy and Roman territory are owing." With such words the Cyllenian spoke, and while he was still speaking he left mortal view and vanished from sight far away into thin air.

Book IV.279–295

But Aeneas, distraught at the vision, was speechless. His hair stood on end from dread and his voice stuck fast in his throat. Shocked at this awful warning and command of the gods, he is on fire to leave in flight and abandon these sweet lands. Alas, what can he do now? With what words now should he dare to get around the queen [who will surely be] angry? How can he broach the matter? And he divides his thoughts swiftly this way and that, and turns them through every possibility. As he wavered, it seemed that this was the preferable tactic: he summons Mnestheus, Sergestus, and brave Serestus, and orders them to outfit the fleet without a word, to gather their mates together at the shore, to make ready the tackle, and to disguise what is the explanation for the change of plans. Meanwhile, he himself, since Dido, best [of women], knows nothing and would never expect such great love to be torn apart, will look for ways of approaching her, the kindest occasions for telling her, and the right method for the purpose. All quite speedily and joyfully obey his command and carry out what had been ordered.

Book IV.304–330

Finally, without waiting for him, she addresses Aeneas with these words: "Did you even expect, deceitful man, that you could conceal such a wicked action and steal away in silence from my land? Does not our love hold you, does not the pledge once given? Does not Dido about to die by a cruel death detain you? Why are you laboring over your fleet in the season of winter, cruel man, why are you hastening to go over the deep in the midst of northerly winds? Tell me this, if you were not making for foreign lands, for unknown homes, and suppose ancient Troy were still standing, would the fleet still sail to Troy over the tempestuous sea? (314) Is it I from whom you are fleeing? By these tears and the pledge you gave me (since I

have nothing else left to me in my misery), by our marriage ceremony, and by our wedlock entered upon, if I have well deserved anything at all from you, or if ever I held any sweetness for you, I implore you, have mercy on a falling house and put off your purpose, if there is any place at all for my prayers. Because of you the Libyan races and the rulers of the Nomads hate me; my Tyrians are hostile; again, because of you, the flame of my conscience has been extinguished along with my one-time reputation by which alone I was taking my path to the stars. For whom are you deserting me, who must [surely] die [because of your desertion], guest, since this is the only name that remains in place of husband? (325) Why do I delay? Until either my brother Pygmalion destroys my walls or Iarbas the Gaetulian leads me away captive? If somehow, at least, I had conceived a child by you before you left [and if it had been born and formally recognized by you], if only in my palace hall a baby Aeneas were playing whose features would, in spite of everything, bring you back to me, then I should not appear to be utterly taken and abandoned."

Book IV.331–361

She had finished speaking. Because of Jupiter's warning, he kept his eyes fixed and resolutely kept his pain hidden in his heart. Finally he speaks a few words: "I will never deny, queen, that you have deserved praise for the countless services that you can list in words, and I shall never regret the memory of Elissa as long as I have a memory of myself and breath rules these limbs. For my cause, I will speak a few words: I did not intend (never imagine that) to conceal this retreat by stealth. I never held the bridegroom's torch before me, and I never entered a contract of this kind. (340) If the Fates would allow me to live my life according to my own will, to arrange all that grieves me to my own liking, I would be cherishing the city of Troy first and foremost and the beloved relics of my people, the high roofs of Priam would still be standing, and I would with my hand have founded a reborn Troy for the vanquished. But now Grynean Apollo has ordered me to make for great Italy, and so have the oracles of Apollo in Lycia. This is my love, this is my homeland. If the citadels of Carthage and the sight of your Libyan city hold you, a Phoenician, tell me, why should you begrudge that Trojans settle in the land of Ausonia? It is right for us also to seek a foreign realm. (351) As often as night drapes the earth with its dewy shadows, as often as the fiery stars rise, the agitated ghost of my father Anchises warns me and terrifies me in dreams; my boy Ascanius, too, and the wrong to this beloved person in defrauding him of a kingdom in Hesperia and fated ploughlands. Even now, the messenger of the gods, sent by Jupiter himself (I swear by your head and by mine), delivered these orders through the swift breezes; yes, with my own eyes, in clear daylight, I saw the god entering the walls of the city and I drank in his voice with these ears of mine. Stop inflaming both me and yourself with your emotional appeals; I make for Italy not of my own free will."

Book IV.362–396

All the time he was saying such things, the queen had been watching him with sidelong glances; this way and that she turns her gaze, looking him up and down with silent eyes. Then she flares up and speaks her mind with these words: "Traitor! You had no goddess for a mother, no Dardanus began your line. You were surely born on the flinty crags of dreadful Caucasus, and Hyrcanian tigresses suckled you. For why should I pretend? Or keep myself for worse injustices? When I wept, did he give any sigh? Didn't he avert his eyes in shame? Was he won over, did he shed tears, was he sorry for me when I loved him [so]? What shall I say first, what last? For it is clear enough now that neither mighty Juno nor the Saturnian father looks with impartial eyes on all this. (373) Nowhere can I safely put my trust. He was shipwrecked on my shore, destitute, and I took him in. I gave him, fool that I was, a share in my kingdom. I rescued the fleet he had lost and saved his companions from death. (O, I am driven on by the Furies, and I am on fire!) So now Apollo, the prophet, now oracles of Lycia, and now the very messenger of the gods sent by Jupiter himself brings through the breezes the orders at which he shudders. Indeed! This, I suppose, is what heavenly beings busy themselves with, this is the concern that disturbs their tranquillity. I do not detain you, nor do I refute what you have said. Go, seek Italy on the winds, look for kingdoms over the waves. (382) As for me, I hope, indeed, that if the gods of righteousness have any power, you will drain to the dregs the cup of punishment on reefs that lie between, and that you will often call Dido by name. Though far away, I shall pursue you with dark firebrands, and when chilly death has severed body from soul I shall be at your side even though I am a shade everywhere you go. Cruel as you are, you will pay the penalty. I shall hear [of your suffering], and the report of it will reach me deep in the underworld." (388) With these words she breaks off her speech and sick at heart flees the light, bears herself off and removes herself from his sight, leaving him frightened and hesitant as he rehearses many responses. Her servants pick her up, carry her collapsed form to the marble bed-chamber, and lay her on the bed. But dutiful Aeneas longs to assuage her pain by comforting her and to dispel her agony with his words; although he gives many a sigh and is shaken to the heart by his great love, nevertheless he follows the commands of the gods and returns to his fleet.

Book IV.397–449

Then in truth the Teucrians apply themselves vigorously and draw down the high ships along the entire shore. The vessel, caulked with pitch, floats, and they bring oars with leaves still attached and unshaped logs from the forests in their eagerness to leave. You could see them moving out and hurrying from the entire city. Just as when ants plunder an enormous heap of grain, mindful of winter, and store it in their home, a black line goes across the plains and they carry their booty along a narrow path through the grass; some heave and push huge grains with their shoulders, some marshal the lines and punish the loiterers; the whole pathway is seething with activity. (408) What were your feelings then, Dido, on seeing all this? Or what groans did you give when you looked out from the top of the citadel at the shores seething far and wide and saw before your eyes the entire sea a confusion of such shouting? Cruel Love, to what lengths do you not drive mortal hearts? Again she is forced to resort to tears, to try again by entreaty, and humbly to make anger submit to love in case she should leave anything untried, fated to die in vain. "Anna, you see that there is bustling activity all along the shore: they have assembled from everywhere; now the sail calls for the breezes and the joyful sailors have set garlands on the sterns. If I was able to anticipate this blow, great as it is, I shall also be able to bear it. Perform, however, this one favor for me in my pitiable state, for that faithless man has been attentive to you alone and has also entrusted his secret feelings to you. You alone know gentle approaches and [proper] times [to speak to him]. (426) Go, sister, and as suppliant address that arrogant enemy. I did not swear an oath with the Danaans at Aulis to uproot the Trojan race, nor did I send a fleet to Pergama; I did not violate the funeral ash of Anchises or his Departed Spirits; why does he refuse to let my word fall into his resistant ears? Where is he rushing? Let him grant this last gift to a pitiful lover; let him wait for an easy departure and favorable winds. I do not appeal to our one-time marriage, which he has betrayed. I do not beg him to abandon his beautiful Latium or to deprive himself of his realm. I seek only a useless bit of time, a respite and breathing space for my madness, until my fortune can teach my vanquished heart how to grieve. I ask for this last favor (take pity on your sister) and when he has granted it to me I will pay it back with interest by my death." (437) With such pleadings as these she made her requests, and the unhappy sister takes such tearful messages again and again. But he is not moved by weeping, nor does he listen sympathetically to any speeches. The fates stand in the way, and the god blocked his kindly mortal ears. And just as when northern gales from the Alps struggle between themselves with blasts, now on this side, and now on that, to uproot an oak tough with the strength of years; a creaking is heard, and leaves from high up strew the ground as the trunk is shaken; but the tree holds firmly to its cliffs, and as high as it reaches up into the breezes of heaven with its top so far does it reach also with its roots downward towards Tartarus; not otherwise is the hero buffeted with continuous pleadings on this side and on that and deeply feels grief in his great heart; his resolution remains unmoved, the tears stream down in vain.

Book IV.584–629
And now, as Aurora left the saffron bed of Tithonus, earliest daybreak was beginning to dapple the earth with renewed daylight. As soon as the queen saw from her watchtowers that the first light was growing bright, and that the fleet was moving forward in even line of sail, and as soon as she realized that the shores were deserted and the harbor empty and that no rowers were left, three, four times she struck her lovely breast with her hand and tore her golden hair and said: "By Jupiter, shall he leave, this man, shall he make a mockery of our realms, this foreigner? Will others not bring weapons and from the whole city follow after him? Will they not tear the ships from their docks? Off with you, bring fire, quickly! Get weapons! Drive on the oars! (595) What am I saying? Where am I? What is this madness that distorts my purpose? Unhappy Dido, is it now that wicked actions come home to you? The proper time was when you were offering your scepter. Look at his right hand, his pledge! The man who (so the story goes) carries with him his ancestral Penates! The man who (they say) bore on his shoulders his father weary with age! Could I not have torn him away, rent his body asunder, and strewn his limbs over the waves? Or murdered his men with the sword, even Ascanius himself, and served him at his father's table as feast? But the outcome of the battle would have been uncertain. Suppose it had been. Whom should I have feared since I was about to die [anyway]? I should have brought torches against his encampment, filled the gangways with flames, and slain son and father along with their line, and then myself I should have flung my very self on top of it all. (607) Sun, for you with your progress light up with your flames all the works of the earth, and you, Juno, mediator of these sorrows of mine and witness, and Hecate, whose name is shrieked at crossways at night through the cities, and avenging Furies, and gods of dying Elissa, hear this and turn your divine power, merited by my sufferings, and hear my prayers. If it must be that this unspeakable person must touch port and sail into lands, if this is what the pronouncements of Jupiter demand, and if this boundary stone is fixed firm, then, let him be harassed in war by the arms of a valiant people, let him be an exile from his land, let him be torn from the embrace of Iulus, let him supplicate for help and see the shameful deaths of his people. And when he has surrendered himself to the terms of an unjust peace, may he never enjoy his realm or the light he craved, but may he die prematurely and lie unburied on the open sand. (621) This is my prayer; this is my last utterance, and I pour it out with my life blood. Then, Tyrians, harass his offspring with hatred and all the future generation, and send this as offerings to my ashes. Let there be no love nor any treaties between our peoples. Arise, some avenger, from my bones, to harass the Dardanian settlers with fire and sword, now, in the future, at whatever time strength will offer. I call on shores to clash with shores, waves with waves, this is my prayer, weapons with weapons; and let them fight, themselves, and their descendants.

Book IV.630–662
Thus she spoke, and she whirled her mind in every direction looking for the first moment to cut off the light of life that she loathed. Then she briefly addressed Barce, the nurse of Sychaeus, for the black ash [of the funeral pyre] encompassed her own nurse in her ancient homeland. "Dear nurse of mine, bring my sister Anna here; tell her to hasten to sprinkle her body with river water and to bring the animals and the offerings of atonement that have been prescribed with her. Let her come in this way, and you yourself, bind your temples with a woolen band of holiness. I have a mind to finish the sacrifice to Stygian Jupiter, the beginnings I have already properly prepared, to put an end to my troubles, and to commit to the flame the Dardanian person's pyre." (641) So she spoke. And Barce quickened her step with an old woman's eagerness. But Dido, shivering and wild with her monstrous designs, rolling blood-shot eyes, her trembling cheeks flecked with blotches of red, pale with imminent death, bursts into the inner

thresholds and in her frenzy climbs the high pyre and unsheathes the sword, the Dardanian sword, a gift that she had never sought from Aeneas for this purpose. Then, after she had looked at the Trojan garments and the familiar bed, she paused for a little in tears and reflection. Then she lay down on the marriage-bed and spoke her last words: (657) "Sweet relics, sweet as long as the fates and god permitted, take this my spirit, and free me from these sufferings. I have lived my life and have finished the course which Fortune allotted me; now, a majestic ghost of what I am shall go beneath the earth. I have established a glorious city; I have seen my own walls; I have avenged my husband and exacted punishment from my brother who was my enemy. Happy, O, too happy, if only the Dardanian ships had never touched our shores." With these words, she pressed her lips against the bed and cried: "I shall die, unavenged; but may I die; thus, thus I am glad to go down to the shades. May the cruel Dardanian drink in this fire with his eyes from the sea and carry with him the omens of my death."

Book IV.663–692
She finished speaking, and her attendants saw her fallen on the sword while speaking such words, the blade frothing with blood and her hands spattered. A cry rises in the high halls; Rumor runs madly through the stricken city. Houses resound with lamentation and moaning with the shrieking of women. The heavens reverberate with loud cries of grief, just as if all Carthage or ancient Tyre were falling with the enemy rushing in, and raging flames were rolling over the rooftops of men and gods. (672) The distraught sister heard and, terrified, in frantic haste, ravaging her cheeks with her nails and bruising her breast with her fists, rushes through the crowd and calls on her dying sister by name: "Was this what it was, my sister? Were you seeking to deceive me? Was this what that pyre was for, to my sorrow, was it for this the fires and the altars were prepared? What shall I lament first now that you have forsaken me? Have you scorned your sister's company in your dying? Had you called me to the same fate, the same agony by the sword and the same hour would have taken us both together. Did I even build this pyre with my own hands and call aloud on the ancestral gods, only to be far away from you, heartless one, when you lay thus? (682) You have blotted out yourself and me, my sister, your people, the Sidonian elders, and your city. May I wash [your] wounds with water and, if any last breath still flutters above, may I catch it with my lips." As she spoke, she finished climbing the high steps [of the pyre], caressed her dying sister in her lap, and

embracing her with a groan tried to staunch the dark blood with her dress. Dido tried to raise her heavy eyes again but fainted. Deep in her chest the wound hissed. Three times lifting, she raised herself by leaning on her elbow; three times she sank back onto the couch and sought with roving eyes the light in high heaven, and groaned when she found it.

Book IV.693–705
Then all-powerful Juno, taking pity on her long suffering and her difficult death, sent Iris [the rainbow] down from Olympus to set free her struggling spirit from her imprisoning limbs. For because she was not dying by fate nor by a death she had deserved, but wretchedly before her time, set on fire by a sudden frenzy, Proserpina had not yet taken to herself the golden tress from her head and had not yet assigned her person to Stygian Orcus. So dewy Iris flies down through the sky on her saffron wings trailing a thousand changing colors as she meets the sun, and she stood above her head: "As instructed, I take this tress, consecrated to Dis, and release you from that body of yours." She spoke thus, and with her right hand she cut the tress; and with it all warmth slipped away and her life departed into the winds.

Book VI.450–476
Among them [the victims of love] Phoenician Dido, her wound still fresh, was wandering about in the great woods; as soon as the Trojan hero stood nearby and recognized her, dimly outlined through the shadows, like the moon which one sees or thinks he has seen at the month's beginning, rising up through the clouds, he wept and spoke to her with words of sweet love: "Unhappy Dido, so the report that reached me was accurate, that you had taken extreme measures and met your end by the sword? Alas, was I the cause of your death? I swear by the stars, queen, by the gods above, and by whatever valid pledge there is in the depths of the earth, I left your shores unwillingly. (461) But divine commands, which now compel me to pass through these shadows and this wasteland rough with neglect and through utter darkness, drove me by their commands. I could not believe that by my leaving I was bringing such great distress as this upon you. Check your step, and do not withdraw yourself from my sight. From whom are you fleeing? This is the last word by Fate's decree that I speak to you." With such words, Aeneas tried to calm her fervent wild-eyed mind and was mustering tears. Her gaze averted, she kept her eyes fixed on the ground and was no more moved in countenance by what he had begun to say than if she were made of unyielding flint or the rigid cliff of

Mount Marpesus. Finally, she tore herself away and in hatred fled back to the grove that provided shade where Sychaeus, her former husband, answers her sorrows and gives her love for love. Aeneas, no less stunned by the unjust fate, gazes after her with tears from afar and pities her as she departs.

* * *

ANSWERS FOR EXERCISES

Book I.338–368
Pūnica: acc. pl., rēgna. intractābile: acc. sing., genus. profecta: nom. sing., Dīdō. longae: nom. pl., ambāgēs. magnō: abl. sing., amōre. prīmīs: abl. pl., ōminibus. immānior: nom. sing., Pygmaliōn. caecus: nom. sing., ille. vānā: abl. sing., spē. inhumātī: gen. sing., coniugis. pallida: acc. pl., ōra. veterēs: acc. pl., thēsaurōs. ignōtum: acc. sing., pondus. novae: gen. sing., Karthāginis.

Book I.419–437
Preposition Review
1. colle collibus, down from the hill(s). 2. rūs rūra, through the country. 3. agmine agminibus, out of the crowd(s). 4. opere operibus, away from the work(s). 5. aliō aliīs, with another (others). 6. pecore pecoribus, without herd(s). 7. portum portūs, around the harbor(s). 8. arcem arcēs, to the citadel(s). 9. mōlem mōlēs, behind the mass(es). 10. mūrum mūrōs, in front of the wall(s).

Book I.494–508
Meter
1. There are 2 dactyls. There are 4 spondees.
2. Elision takes place in the second foot. The principal caesura is in the third foot. There is 1 dactyl. There are 5 spondees. This gives it a slow, stately, marching rhythm.
3. Fert is long because the vowel is followed by two consonants.
4. The last syllable of tacitum is long because it is followed by two consonants.

Book I.494–508
Declension Review
1. templa, temples. 2. stīpantibus, crowding. 3. mīlia, thousands. 4. umerīs, shoulders. 5. tālēs, such. 6. operibus, works. 7. testūdinibus, arches. 8. sortibus, lots. 9. pectora, ribs. 10. pharetrās, quivers.

Book I.561–578
Verb Forms
1. profārī, to address. 2. dēmittis, you send down. 3. solūtus esse, to have been released. 4. coēgerat, he had compelled. 5. nesciēbāmus, we were unaware. 6. gestāvistī, you carried. 7. iunxisse, to have joined. 8. optābō, I shall wish. 9. velint, they may wish. 10. agī, to be driven. 11. adsumus, we are present. 12. iusserit, he might have ordered.

Book IV.238–295
Grammatical Forms
1. H. 2. D. 3. J. 4. F. 5. C. 6. E. 7. I. 8. A. 9. G. 10. B.

Book IV.522–528
Sight Passage
1. B. 2. A. 3. C. 4. D. 5. C. 6. A. 7. B.

Book IV.560–570
Sight Passage
1. D. 2. B. 3. C. 4. B. 5. A. 6. B. 7. C. 8. B. 9. C. 10. D.

Book IV.584–662
General Review
1. linquentium. 2. cūbila. 3. Iove. 4. loquerētur. 5. īnfēlīcī. 6. fideī. 7. corpora. 8. fax. 9. haec. 10. capita. 11. sanguis. 12. tegite.

Book IV.693–705
Adjective Agreement
1. acc. sing., dolōrem. 2. abl. sing., morte. 3. acc. pl., artūs. 4. nom. sing., subject "she" understood. 5. acc. sing., crīnem. 6. abl. pl., pennīs. 7. acc. sing., colōrēs. 8. abl. sing., corpore. 9. nom. sing., calor. 10. nom. sing., calor.

* * *

BIBLIOGRAPHY

Editions and Commentaries

*P. Vergili Maronis: Aeneidos Liber I, ed. by R. G. Austin. Oxford University Press, Oxford and New York, NY, 1971. *P. Vergili Maronis: Aeneidos liber IV, ed. by R. G. Austin. Oxford University Press, Oxford and New York, NY, 1955. These volumes provide scholarly commentary on Books I and IV with excellent introductions and expert guidance throughout.

P. Vergili Maronis Opera, ed. by R. A. B. Mynors. Oxford University Press, Oxford and New York, NY, 1969; 2nd edition, 1972.

P. Vergilius Maro: Opera, ed. by M. P. Geymonat. Paravia, Torino, 1973. This and Mynors's edition listed above have provided the basis for the Latin text, spellings, and punctuation used in the present textbook.

The Aeneid of Virgil: Books I–VI, ed. by R. D. Williams. St. Martin's Press, New York, NY, 1972. Edited with introduction and notes, this book by Williams provides the best available commentary on the *Aeneid* for schools, colleges, and universities. Williams is concerned with diction, meter, and construction as well as with poetic methods and intentions. He explains what Vergil says, how he says it, and why he says it in his own fashion. Required reference material, reliable and instructive.

Translations

The Aeneid, tr. by Robert Fitzgerald. Random House, New York, NY, 1983.

The Aeneid of Vergil, tr. by Allen Mandelbaum. Bantam Books, Inc., New York, NY, 1981. Both Fitzgerald and Mandelbaum have produced excellent verse translations of the epic. They should be consulted for additional episodes and larger contexts.

Literary Criticism

Aeneas and the Roman Hero, by R. D. Williams. Macmillan Education, Basingstoke, 1973. Highly recommended reading, especially Chapter 3, "Aeneas—the New Hero," and Chapter 4, "Virgil's Private Voice: Dido, Turnus, and Juno."

An Introduction to Virgil's Aeneid, by W. A. Camps. Oxford University Press, Oxford and New York, NY, 1969. This book offers helpful factual information. Camps's personal views of both Aeneas and Dido (Chapters 3 and 4) and Chapter 5, titled "Higher Powers: Fate and the Gods," make it particularly attractive for teachers and students. Essential reading.

Patterns of Action in the Aeneid: An Interpretation of Vergil's Epic Similes, by R. A. Hornsby. University of Iowa Press, Iowa City, IA, 1970. A valuable study of an important aspect of Vergil's poetic technique expressed in succinct, clear language. Scholarly and revealing, a valuable reference work for teachers and for students' essays.

Technique and Ideas in the Aeneid, by Gordon Williams. Yale University Press, New Haven, CT, 1983. Inter alia, treats Vergil's concept of Fate, the gods in the *Aeneid*, and Aeneas in Carthage. This is a complicated book that offers some valuable insights into the epic and provokes reflection and debate on a host of topics.

The Aeneid of Virgil: A Companion to the Translation of C. Day Lewis, by R. D. Williams. Bristol Classical Press, Bristol, 1985. Supplies explanations of fact and aids toward appreciation of Vergil. The commentary explores certain values or words that feature in the themes of the poem, such as **pietās** and **furor**. Convinced that Vergil has portrayed Dido with the utmost sympathy, Williams also provides helpful remarks on Aeneas as a new-style hero. Highly recommended reading.

The Art of the Aeneid, by W. S. Anderson. Prentice-Hall, Englewood Cliffs, NJ, 1969. This book has been called the classic book on the *Aeneid*. It is basic to an understanding of the hallmarks of the Vergilian epic. Essential reading.

The Art of Vergil: Image and Symbol in the Aeneid, by Viktor Pöschl (tr. by G. Seligson). University of Michigan Press, Ann Arbor, MI, 1962. This is an indispensable guide for an understanding of the *Aeneid*. This German scholar and critic analyzes basic themes and explores Vergil's unique artistry and creative imagination. Chapter 2, "The Principal Figures," treats Aeneas and Dido with exceptional insight.

The Speeches in Vergil's Aeneid, by Gilbert Highet. Princeton University Press, Princeton, NJ, 1972. Analysis of the structure and content of all the speeches; treats their importance in the portrayal of character. Vergil emerges as a master dramatist as well as a great epic poet. Highly recommended.

The Dido Episode and the Aeneid: Roman Social and Political Values in the Epic, by R. C. Monti. E. J. Brill, Leiden, 1981. Examines the Dido and Aeneas story with attention to Roman values as they are reflected in the episode. Useful for background and as incentive to discussion and further inquiry.

Virgil, by Jasper Griffin. Oxford University Press, Oxford and New York, NY, 1986. Offers a compact study of Vergil with a good chapter titled "Aeneid and the Myth of Rome." A useful compendium of information and criticism.

Virgil: A Study in Civilized Poetry, by Brooks Otis. Oxford University Press, Oxford and New

York, NY, 1963. A clever, innovative study with ingenious analyses of Vergil's techniques in building a new epic on antique (= Homeric) foundations. Strenuous reading, but revealing and helpful with respect to *Aeneid* I and IV.

Virgil's Aeneid: A Critical Description, by Kenneth Quinn. Routledge and Kegan Paul, London, 1968. Examines Aeneas and Dido with a critical eye and offers provocative views on their characterization.

*Virgil's Aeneid and the Tradition of Hellenistic Poetry, by Wendell Clausen. "Sather Classical Lectures," Vol. 51. University of California Press, Berkeley, CA, 1987. This volume studies Vergil's relationship to his Alexandrian sources. Clausen argues that Vergil's aims and procedures, his choices, emphases, and emotional content are those of a Hellenistic poet. Indispensable for comparative study of Apollonius' *Argonautica*.

Meter

"Teaching the Appreciation of Latin Metre," by H. F. Guite. *The Classical Journal* 81 (1986) 348–351. Useful suggestions for teaching the dactylic hexameter.

*The Pronunciation and Reading of Classical Latin: A Practical Guide, by Stephen G. Daitz. Jeffrey Norton Publishers, Inc., Guilford, CT, 1984.

Bibliographies

*The Classical World Bibliography of Vergil, by G. E. Duckworth and A. G. McKay (ed., Walter Donlan). Garland Press, New York, NY, 1977. Donlan assembles three major bibliographies by two North American scholars published originally in *The Classical World*.

"Vergilian Bibliography," by A. G. McKay. An annual feature in *Vergilius*, the journal of the Vergilian Society of America, Department of Classics, University of Maryland, College Park, MD 20742. Annotated bibliographies of Vergilian studies on a yearly basis with detailed listings, reviews, and assessments (since 1974).

Virgil, by R. D. Williams. "Greece and Rome: New Surveys in the Classics," No. 1. Oxford University Press, Oxford and New York, NY, 1967; reprinted with addenda, 1978.

CATULLUS AND HORACE SELECTIONS FROM THEIR LYRIC POETRY

INTRODUCTION

The poems in this reader are the work of the two greatest writers of Latin lyric poetry: Catullus and Horace. The poems have been selected for their intrinsic interest and inherent beauty but, perhaps not so coincidentally, they also teach Latin language and Roman culture. They are excellent reading for students in both high school and college, either as part of a course or as the texts for a class devoted entirely to Latin lyric. These readings are also the core of the Advanced Placement Lyric Syllabus and are appropriate as partial preparation for the Advanced Placement examination. These verses, however, present problems for the teacher and demand approaches different from those used to introduce the prose of Cicero or, for that matter, the epic poems of Vergil or Ovid.

The teacher who comes to this course must be able to answer four questions before presenting the material:

Who were Catullus and Horace?
What did Catullus and Horace write?
How should we read Catullus' and Horace's poems?
What are the goals of a course in Latin lyric?

These questions are preliminary, but they should also be addressed by teachers and students during and after the course .

Who Were Catullus and Horace?

The first question is biographical. For any poet, ancient or modern, biography is a problem since, in fact, two lives must be defined. The first life is that of the historical flesh and blood human being, the Catullus or the Horace who actually walked the **Forum Rōmānum**. The other life is more elusive; it is the character, the I—critics use the Latin word **persōna** (mask)—created in the poems, who is other than the poet even if they share the same name. Sometimes these lives may overlap or contradict, sometimes they may exist in parallel or in opposition. They are, however, never wholly the same. For example, the first poems in this reader concern the love that Catullus has for a certain Lesbia. This relationship becomes vivid as we read about it, and we are tempted to equate the Catullus in the poems with the Catullus who wrote the poetry. Then we discover that historians—Apuleius is their source—believe that Lesbia is a nickname for Clodia, wife of Metellus, the woman whom Cicero lambastes in the *Pro Caelio.* With this "fact" and what can be culled from other sources, we are ready to reinterpret the poems in terms of the historical Clodia. Yet here is the problem: we do not know enough—nor can we ever—about the historical Clodia to determine where Catullus has changed her by making her better or worse or where he has inadvertently fictionalized or even just plain lied. After all, Catullus creates his own world in his poetry, based on the one in which he lived but nonetheless different. And, of course, Horace does the same in the lyrics he wrote.

The practical problem remains. Should you, the teacher, give any biographical introduction? The answer is yes. You must place the poet in time and space: that is, you must explain the context in which the poet wrote. You should also be sure that you do not equate historical background with literary interpretation. Who then was Catullus?

The historical Catullus is little known to scholars. He was named Gaius Valerius Catullus, though debate exists even about this "fact." He was born about 84 B.C. and died about 54 B.C., but both dates are uncertain. He came from the northern Italian city of Verona, where his family was wealthy and politically influential enough to have entertained Julius Caesar. At some point, Catullus came to Rome, where he fell in with a group of poets, called "new poets," **poētae nōvī** in Latin, *neoteroi* in Greek. These young men admired greatly the work of Callimachus and the other Alexandrian poets and wanted to imitate that highly polished verse in Latin. They were eager to fill their poems with learned allusions and esoterica, to experiment in various meters, and to write for an "in-crowd." Catullus wrote in this tradition, but he was able to avoid its extremes and is only rarely obscure.

Catullus moved in the best social circles and knew Cicero and other people of significance, such as Memmius, who was to become governor of Bithynia. In fact, Catullus followed Memmius to that province, where he claims in his verse to have been unhappy, perhaps because he there mourned the death of his brother (see Catullus 101), perhaps because he disliked the pay, the commander, or military life (see Catullus 10). In Rome, however, Catullus lived more happily, went to parties, and learned the **fora** and **viae** of the capital, and he fell in love. With whom, when, how often, and how sincerely are questions that the historian cannot answer and that the literary critic should not try to.

Horace led a life better known to scholars. Quintus Horatius Flaccus was born on 8 December 65 B.C. in Venusia, a town in Apulia. He was the son of a moderately well-to-do freedman who provided him with a first-class education, first in Rome and then in Athens. As a young man, Horace served with Brutus and Cassius and fought against Octavian. After the battle of Philippi Horace was pardoned for being on the losing side, and he returned to Italy. There he attracted the attention of Maecenas, the most powerful man in Rome after Augustus and Agrippa. Horace impressed Maecenas with his talent to such an extent that Maecenas became Horace's supporter and patron. Horace also found favor with Augustus, who encouraged the poet's efforts and who figures in several of the odes. As a result of these relationships, Horace was given the famous Sabine Farm, not too far from Rome, where he lived quietly and wrote epodes, satires, lyrics, and verse epistles. He died in 8 B.C., shortly after Maecenas.

What Did Catullus and Horace Write?

Both Catullus and Horace wrote lyric poetry, a genre that began in the eighth century B.C. and has continued to the present. These poems are called lyric because they were originally written to be sung to the accompaniment of the lyre, but they share a more important characteristic. Although after the early Greeks most lyric was not sung, all lyric verse deals with a poet's personal sentiments, his own emotions. The "I," the ego, however fictionalized (and it always is), is the central actor.

Each poem places the ego in some dramatic moment which is begun and ended within just a few lines. Lyric verse, then, is short, personal, and musical, even if not sung.

These formal characteristics determine in large part the substance and content of the poems. Love and hate, joy and despair, the possibilities of life and the inevitability of death, that is, those circumstances that all people have to face in their lives, are articulated in lyric verse. The lyric poet is like us in what he experiences, but he can say what we feel more precisely, more poignantly, and more perceptively.

When he writes, the lyric poet ironically must move away from his own experience, which is, like our own, too limited and too specific to be truly understood by anybody else. To make his feelings accessible to all, indeed to be able even to communicate, the poet must transcend his experience and approach it with some objectivity. Catullus falls in love and discovers (poem 85) that he simultaneously hates. He is certainly no poet because he felt two conflicting emotions. We have all felt these. He is a poet because he can express what he felt with such precision that we can feel the emotion ourselves. Horace writes in *Odes* I.5 about the fickleness of love. The insight is not profound, but its expression is. Both Catullus and Horace may have felt what they wrote about. Both, however, took their feelings, cast them into bleak words (ōdī et amō) or powerful images (love as a stormy sea) and thereby made the emotion universal. Necessarily they ceased to write about themselves to the extent that they went beyond their own limited lives.

The lyric poet has available an important tool in his effort to get beyond the merely personal, namely the tradition in which he writes. Because Sappho wrote in particular meters about certain subjects, so does Catullus. Horace can follow an Archilochus. Both poets show acquaintance with a wide range of predecessors. Later lyric poets in turn base their work on Catullus and Horace. Poets use the tradition to shape their work, to give their experience a more readily understood form, and to deepen communication. In poem 51 Catullus translates a poem by Sappho into Latin. He retains the meter and much of the imagery, yet he changes words, adds a verse, and makes his poem say something that Sappho's did not. Elsewhere the poets may not use tradition so obviously, but never do they ignore it.

After you have told your students a little about the life of Catullus and Horace, you have to explain what they wrote. If you give them abstract definitions or critical theory, you will only bewilder them. Instead, present the students with a popular love song, perhaps one they could have heard that morning on the radio, take away the music, and have them study the form and the content. (Some of the Beatle's songs are useful.) Then give them a more traditional, more literary lyric, say, something by Robert Frost or Carl Sandburg. Then move back in time to Rome and to the not-so-different poems of the late Republic and early Empire. Have the students point out similarities in the various poems, and from these observations have them derive a working definition that they can test while reading Catullus and Horace.

How Should We Read Catullus' and Horace's Poems?

Although the poems in this reader are varied in content, style, and difficulty, you may want to approach each poem in the same way so that students acquire good habits of reading, translating, and interpreting poetry. First, read the poem aloud in Latin and perhaps read a particularly good literary translation. Second, have students translate the poem. Third, ask questions about grammar and vocabulary. Focus on any words or structures that are ambiguous or unusual. (Some teachers may prefer to give at least some of these comments before the students translate.) Fourth, explain the meter fully. Have students read the poem aloud, giving each student the chance to "perform." This practice consumes time, but if you skip this step, you will deprive your students of significant pleasure and, more important, of a full appreciation of the poem. Latin lyric was designed to be heard and much of its meaning is carried in the music of the lines. Ask students to note unusual sound patterns or ways in which meter reinforces or reflects meaning. Have students memorize sections of the poem. In this way, they will become sensitive to the role of sound in poetry and find prosody easier to understand. Fifth, after the poem has been translated and read aloud several times, you are ready to begin a discussion of the poem. Do not lecture. If you present your interpretation of the verses, students will accept it as the only right one. They will look for no other, nor will they come to realize that poetry never has one right meaning and that it is not some code waiting to be deciphered.

For every poem have students suggest what the occasion of the poem was: that is, ask why the poem claims it was written. Ask what the dramatic situation is. Ask how the ego relates to any second or third persons in the poem. These questions are almost universally applicable and are a good beginning to any discussion. Then use the questions that accompany each poem. These are designed to take the reader through the poem thoroughly. They are not meant to impose an interpretation on the poem. Encourage the students to see different meanings and approaches. Remember that poems are not problems in mathematics with one and only one solution. Instead, they do not have solutions at all. They are infinitely varied condensations of human experience, which, like rare gems or fine sculpture, appear different from different perspectives. Next, ask students to relate their now fairly sophisticated understanding of the poem to their own lives. This step will not always produce great criticism but will make the poem a part of the student's own experiences. Finally, read the poem aloud in Latin one more time.

What Are the Goals of a Course in Latin Lyric?

The goals of a course in Latin lyric can be as varied as the people teaching it. No two courses will be exactly alike. Nonetheless, at least two objectives should be met in any course in Latin lyric: (1) students should develop a deeper understanding of Latin and (2) students should acquire a more lively appreciation of poetry.

Many good suggestions for teaching Latin lyric and in particular the Catullus–Horace Advanced Placement course may be found in the *Teacher's Guide to Advanced Placement Courses in Latin*, Advanced Placement Program, The College Board, Princeton, NJ, 1986, especially on pages 60–86. This teacher's guide also has a complete bibliography that will be helpful in preparing for a Latin lyric or epic course. In addition, the College Board offers several publications, including an annual course description for both Catullus–Horace and Vergil, that may be purchased from them at the following address: Advanced Placement Program, CN 6670, Princeton, NJ 08541. Each year since 1983, *The Classical Outlook* has published in the December-January or March-April issue a complete discussion of the grading of the free-response section of the exam of the previous year. The multiple-choice section of the Advanced Placement examination, which tests students' ability to sightread, is not released annually; the 1980 multiple-choice section, however, containing five separate poetry passages and questions on them, is available from the College Board or may be found in *The Classical Outlook* 60 (1983) 112–116.

In a course on Catullus and Horace students may read less Latin than they usually do in an equivalent amount of time, but they will read more carefully and closely. They will have to pay particular attention to words: the range of their meanings, their expected contexts, and their history in the language. **Amīcitia**, for example, is a common enough word; students may be tempted to translate it with the English word *friendship* and move on. **Amīcitia**, of course, does mean friendship, but it also means political alliance, a force of the word with which Catullus plays. A poet almost by definition stretches language and does unusual and unexpected tricks with it. Students will have to become alert to all of this. Horace, for example, is particularly adept at ordering his words to reinforce the meaning of the verse. In *Odes* I.5.1, he writes, **Quis multā gracilis tē puer in rosā**. The **tē** is surrounded by **gracilis** and **puer**, while the **tē** and the **puer** are encircled by **multā** and **rosā**. The words are doing what the line is saying. Students who learn to read lyric well will read other genres more closely and, hence, with better comprehension.

Poetry is one of life's great joys, but one that most American students shy away from. Although they may listen endlessly to popular music and its lyrics, students rarely feel the power of more serious verse, in part because they do not know how to read it. All people, it is true, can understand best the poetry of their native language as it rings in their ears. Yet the person who can understand a poem almost immediately often fails to see through image and structure to deeper meanings and significance. Students of a foreign language must pay attention to multitudes of detail they would ignore in their familiar native language, and, thereby, they learn poetic method and meaning more readily. Students who learn to read Catullus or Horace will one day come to love a Berryman or a Plath.

* * *

TEACHING NOTES

The works of K. Quinn, S. Commager, E. Fraenkel, and M. O. Lee have been particularly helpful in preparing the following teaching notes. The interpretations and suggestions offered in these notes are limited by space and are meant to indicate only one or several out of many approaches to these poems. For bibliography on the individual poems of Catullus, see *Gaius Valerius Catullus: A Systematic Bibliography* and Quinn's edition of Catullus.

Catullus 5
Love is light (**lūx**) and life itself, to be defended against the gossip of jealous old men, too old themselves for love, against dark death (**nox**),

where suns do not shine, and against those wicked men who cast the evil eye. Although the themes expressed here are not difficult to convey in another language, no translation can capture the sound effects such as the *r*'s and *s*'s of the old men talking. Note how the repetition of words in lines 7–9 suggests the breathlessness of the two lovers' kissing and the emotion of their passion.

Several poems in this text are followed by translations or adaptations. A discussion may begin here with the poem by Ben Jonson of what the criteria are for a successful translation and at what point a translation becomes an adaptation and a poem in its own right. Jonson treats the question of Celia's love in a manner more consistent with the sonnets of Shakespeare than with the poems of Catullus: at issue for Jonson are "the sports of love," Celia's "gifts" (i.e., beauty), "household spies," and the "sin" of physical love—sixteenth-century notions and concerns.

Catullus 8
Poem 8 is an introspective meditation. As Catullus talks to himself, he moves from firmness (1–2) to hopeless memories (3–8) and back to the present in a crescendo of strength (10–14). He concludes with bitterness: love has become spiteful (15–18), or at least it seems to have. In fact, the very vividness of the description suggests that passion still burns and that Catullus must still remind himself to be firm and strong. His mind tries to command his heart (note the many imperatives), but its success is at best doubtful.

This poem uses the choliambic meter, employed traditionally in satiric verses, such as those of Archilochus and Hipponax, and appropriate for these lines, in which the poet abuses himself and his beloved. Catullus here makes himself the jilted lover who must come to realize that what is lost is lost and who must learn to be strong now that the brilliant light of love has set.

Catullus 12
The theft of a napkin is no great crime, perhaps not even wrong when committed by a friend. Catullus, however, rises to a mock fury here because what Asinius did is **invenustus** and **sordidus**. To somebody who has **lepos** and **facētiae**, like Pollio, the brother of Asinius, a million dollars (**talentum**) is a reasonable price to pay to hush up the whole affair. Why? **Venustās** and **lepos** are qualities highly valued in the world that Catullus and his fellow new poets were creating in Rome. They made a new society in which they were the sophisticates, trained in living and writing by the Hellenistic poets of Alexandria. Not to be charming or lovely was not to be part of this

world. Worse yet, if lack of charm somehow adversely affected love, as it does here, then the crime was all the greater. Line 1 demonstrates Catullus' playful humor as the name of the thief is echoed by the words **manū sinistrā**, which make the charge of gaucheness an element of the culprit's name.

On another level, this is a poem about friendship. The napkin has sentimental value because it is a token of the affection between Catullus and his friends, Veranius and Fabullus. The announcement, delayed until line 11, that it is this napkin that was stolen by Asinius is the poet's oblique admission that he, too, was one of the "rather careless" guests at the party. Perhaps Catullus is also admitting that he has not paid careful attention to the friendship this napkin embodied; in fact, the final two lines forcefully link his love of the napkin with his love for his friends.

Catullus 13
On a literal level this is a poem of invitation. Does the content, however, belie the form? Students should be asked to compare this poem with an invitation they might write. They would not ask their guests to bring all the food, nor would they explain their financial situation, nor would they talk about cologne or after-shave lotion, no matter how unusual. The question then should be asked: to what is the poem inviting Fabullus? The answer is not just to a party but to see what the deities of love have given to Catullus' girlfriend. The gift is an **unguentum**, a very sweet and very elegant perfume. Although its literal significance is clear, **unguentum** is best read as an example of metonymy. In classical Greek and Latin poetry a woman was said to be identified by her aura, her scent, and therefore her perfume could be said to identify her. Catullus, then, offers Fabullus this unusual gift that his beloved possesses or, at least, to witness the pure, undiluted love that she gives. This love is so intoxicating that Fabullus will want to experience it with his whole being, represented by synecdoche in the word **nāsus**.

Thomas McAfee's poem demonstrates how modern Catullus is for us. McAfee first admires the frank poetic disclosure that we associate with Catullus ("If I had your gall, Catullus") and the seamless artistry of the Latin poems ("you could live on ink and my sweat"; i.e., the master, Catullus, writes effortlessly and lives on inspiration, whereas the student, McAfee, writes with great effort). The abrupt transition to a paraphrase of poem 13 gives us an example of Catullus' "gall" and explains why Catullus need not worry about mundane finances: the poetry substitutes for real life. The trouble, as McAfee sees it at the end of

his poem, is that whether somebody shows or not, real life will somehow leave the poet unsatisfied and depressed.

Catullus 22
In poem 22 Catullus defines the world of the neoteric poet. Suffenus has all the attributes valued in the society of new poets. He is **venustus et dicāx et urbānus**, yet he lacks the more important quality: he cannot write poetry. When he tries, he sounds like some country hick, not someone suitable for a world of grace and charm.

Uncharacteristically, Catullus concludes kindly with a proverb that effectively cuts the harshness of the ridicule. The source of the proverb in lines 18–21 is a work of Aesop, which has come down to us in the following Latin version by Phaedrus (ca. 15 B.C.–ca. A.D. 50):

Pērās imposuit Iuppiter nōbīs duās:
proprīīs replētam vitiīs post tergum dedit,
aliēnīs ante pectus suspendit gravem.
Hāc rē vidēre nostra mala nōn possumus;
aliī simul dēlinquunt, cēnsōrēs sumus.

Jupiter has placed two sacks on us:
he put one full of our own faults behind us,
he hung the other filled with another's faults in
   front of us.
In this way we cannot see our own wrongs,
but as soon as others misact, we are critics.

Catullus 43
Catullus nowhere tells us what Lesbia looks like; here he comes closest. The catalogue of physical features in lines 1–4 implies that, if the unnamed **dēcoctōris amīca Fōrmiānī** does not have these qualities, then Lesbia does. She is, in fact, the subject of the poem, and therefore she alone is named. Note how the use of litotes and the repetition of the conjunction **nec** (1–4) build up the impression we initially receive of the unnamed woman that she really is not very attractive at all. We are well prepared then for the surprise we are meant to feel in lines 6–7 that she is even mentioned in the same breath with Lesbia.

This poem, though, is more than a comment on Lesbia; it is an attack on an entire era that cannot see the true beauty of Lesbia but is infatuated with the provincial charms of someone's insignificant girlfriend.

Ezra Pound's rendition of this poem is more faithful to the original than are his other translations. He retains the understatement and repetition of the opening lines. The man from Formiae becomes a person called Formianus, which both turns the person into a representative type and hints that he is a possessor or admirer of good looks (fōrma). That he is a "vendor of cosmetics" in Pound may be a pun on the Latin dēcoctor (from the verb dēcoquere, "to boil away") because it pertains to boiling liquids and it provides us with the English word *concoction*. Perfume, as we know from poem 13, was also highly prized and sought after, much like the women who wore such perfumes, so Formianus probably had a high opinion of himself and his wares, according to Pound. The poem may be further discussed as a personal statement from Pound, a controversial and opinionated poet and critic, that implicitly condemns the values of his time.

Catullus 46
In this poem Catullus bids farewell to Bithynia. Spring has come, people can again travel, and Catullus is excited at the prospect. Lines 1–2, which describe the external world of spring's arrival, are nicely mirrored by lines 7–8, where Catullus feels the internal restlessness that spring has evoked. The repetition of iam makes the connection more tangible. Catullus also engages us by naming specific places in lines 4–6. Here, we are treated to exotic sounds of the East (note the play in the words Zephyrī . . . Phrygiī . . . Nicaeae . . . aestuōsae . . . Asiae) and we learn the specific names of places from which Catullus and his friends will disperse in different and unnamed directions in lines 10–11. By the end of the poem, Catullus sadly realizes that he will be leaving the comrades with whom he has served. He uses words that begin with or contain the letter v (volēmus, avet, valēte, variē, and viae) and that indicate his concern with the impending departure and separation from friends.

Catullus 49
This poem should interest students, first because it is about Cicero, a Roman about whom most students know something, and second because it is an amusing piece of wit, heavy with irony. It begins as a seemingly sincere compliment. Few people, then or now, would disagree that Marcus Tullius Cicero was the most eloquent Roman. The poem, however, changes from compliment to flattery, and the fulsome words cast doubt on the sincerity of the lines. Finally, Catullus claims that his poetry is poor in inverse proportion to the greatness of Cicero's oratory—a claim that cannot be sincere. Indeed, if Catullus thought himself a good poet (and the evidence of poem 16, which is not included in this selection, and poem 76 suggests that he did), then here Catullus is calling Cicero the worst of all possible orators. Embedded in the final lines is a possible ambiguity. Optimus omnium pa-

trōnus can be translated "the best patron of all" or "everybody's patron." The first is the expected translation, but the other is possible and suggests that Cicero will defend anybody. (In fact, Cicero defended people whom he had once prosecuted.)

Christopher Smart's imitation reproduces the implicit humor and irony of the Catullian original. Such words and phrases as "the chief," "all eminence and goodness," and "thou transcend'st" for the British orator are examples of exaggeration, and they are purposely contrasted with the poet's description of himself as the "meanest of the tuneful train." Parallel exaggerations can be found in the Catullian original, for example, disertissime, pessimus, poēta, and optimus patrōnus. Although Catullus' poem is simpler and less bombastic, both poets delight in using alliteration and both seem to carry out the charge of inferiority they level against themselves by using obvious devices, such as anaphora and parallel phrasing, and, in Smart's case, a very monotonous iambic pentameter.

Catullus 51
Here, Catullus translates a poem by Sappho (fragment 31 in Denys Page's *Sappho and Alcaeus*, Oxford University Press, 1955) but makes some changes and appears to add an additional stanza. Sappho's poem is a fragment—it is not clear how much may be lost—and many critics argue that Catullus' poem 51 is also. In many editions the fourth stanza is printed separately as a stanza of an otherwise lost poem. In this reader it is printed as the conclusion to the poem with the assumption that it is not part of the translation from Sappho but rather a moral that Catullus has added. No certainty is possible.

Catullus 53
Like many Romans—Cicero, for example—Catullus had a gift for invective, particularly in his epigrams. Since invective is often topical, the object of the attack is often obscure. Here, however, the poet seems to abuse not only Calvus but also the oratorical techniques he used.

Catullus 70
This poem is a beautiful lament for love that is lost. Most take the woman to be Lesbia, but this need not be the case. Whoever the woman may be, she is not to be trusted. She may understand what she has promised and, therefore, may not be telling the truth. Or she may not realize the faithfulness that love demands. In either event, her words fly away like wind or water. The poem concludes with an *adynaton*, that is, an impossible act

(here, writing on the wind), a particularly effective hyperbole for this epigram.

This is a good opportunity to compare Catullus to the Hellenistic poet Callimachus, whose poem is given in translation. Although the themes of both poems are similar, Callimachus does not enter into the scene in the Greek version, whereas Catullus is very much the victim in the Roman love poem. The Greek version jokes about the Megarians and mentions love in a purely physical and masculine way; the girl disappears from sight at the end of the poem. Catullus, however, here and elsewhere reverses male and female roles (compare poem 11, lines 22–24, a poem not included in these selections, where he is the flower, she the plow) and turns the woman into the aggressor. The element foreign to Callimachus is the suggestion of marriage in line 1 of Catullus; here and in several other poems Catullus explores the meaning of a union that is more than physical.

Catullus 72

The poem's subject and its first word **dīcēbās** recall Catullus 70. Here, however, the exact nature of Catullus' love is defined more precisely. He does not merely lust after his girl but has a more profound love that can be compared only to a pure love that a father has for sons and sons-in-law. In the past, he both desired (**amāre**, 8) and loved (**dīlēxī**, 3) Lesbia; now he continues to burn (**ūror**, 5) but does not like (**bene velle**, 8).

Catullus 73

This poem comments on betrayed friendship and suggests that human relationships should be mutual and that kindness should be returned for kindness, love for love. This belief is at the heart of the Catullian view of love. By using the language of traditional Roman values (**mererī, pium, ingrāta, benignē**, and **prōdest**), Catullus proposes that relationships between people are of equal importance.

Two other instances of generalizing from particular experiences may be found in poems 22 and 43. In 22, Suffenus suffered from a blind spot; he had admirable qualities of character but he could not see that these were not transferred to his poetry. Catullus used this particular event to illustrate the truthfulness of the Aesop's fable of the two sacks that we all carry. In 43, the attention and favorable comparison to Lesbia that the unnamed woman received in the province compelled Catullus to condemn his entire generation for poor taste.

Catullus 75

Note how the chiasmus (**tuā . . . culpā . . . officiō . . . suō**) makes the word **culpa** become the antonym of **officium**. Duty is that which is done by a **pius vir**; fault is that which is done by the faithless, in this instance, Lesbia. The close connection between Lesbia and **culpa** is reinforced by the word order. Although Lesbia is at fault, Catullus cannot stop loving her, no matter what she does.

The word **omnia** in line 4 includes all present and future acts of faithlessness of which Lesbia, acording to Catullus, is capable. This couplet is more strongly worded and desperate than the final couplet of poem 72. Here, Catullus insists that Lesbia's faithlessness has so ruined him that he can never respect her again, no matter what she does to change herself for the better, but he is equally in the throes of a physical desire that will persist no matter what further injuries she decides to do to him. The despair is greater because, unlike in poem 72, there is the stated belief that no resolution can be found for his love–hate.

Catullus 76

This poem gives the fullest and most complete treatment of the Catullian notion of human relationships. A relationship should be based on **sancta fidēs** or a **foedus** that a **pius vir** maintains as his **officium**. The **pius vir** gives kind words and good deeds. In return, he has a right to expect the equal of what he gives. When such reciprocity does not occur, love becomes one-sided and turns into a sickness to be treated. Although it is stated here more clearly, this view of human love underlies the entire Catullian corpus.

The densely worded opening of this poem conveys the feeling of a Roman contract that is bound by law. Words such as **recordantī, benefacta, pium, sānctam, violāsse, fidem, foedere, fallendōs, dicta, facta,** and **crēdita** are ones that a Roman might have found in religious, political, and military documents. Such language strengthens the poet's claim that because he has lived by the terms universally recognized by Romans as binding and legal, he is entitled to the simple request from the gods at the end of the poem.

The various devices listed in question 6 intensify the sensation of being in a diseased state. Lines 21–22 clearly recall lines 9–12 of poem 51, where the intensity of a new passion penetrated deep into the poet's body and overcame him. Now, however, the protracted passion (**longum . . . amōrem**) has become a cancer that threatens to destroy him completely.

Many words and phrases from poems 8, 72, 73, 75, 85, 87, and 109 may be found in poem 76. Lines 11–12, in particular, reintroduce the **miser Catulle** theme of poem 8, and the word **redūcis** (11) is an echo of **quō puella dūcēbat** in line 4 of poem 8; Catullus must now journey back alone from the physical and spiritual place to which the woman had led him. A comparison of poems 8 and 76 will demonstrate the marked difference between a poet still bathing in the memories of physical love (poem 8) and one tortured by the physical and emotional symptoms that his love–hate for Lesbia has induced (poem 76).

Catullus 83
The actors here are Catullus, Lesbia, and her husband; one may compare the cast in poem 51. There, however, Catullus' emotions were the subject; here the subject is Lesbia's emotions, at least as Catullus sees them. In poem 51, Catullus' feelings seemed real. Here, Catullus may be deluding himself about Lesbia and her regard for him.

Each couplet of this poem is part of an equation that in the world of love makes perfect sense to Catullus: (1) Lesbia verbally abuses the poet, and her husband takes the greatest pleasure in the scene, (2) the husband must be blind to the true meaning of the scene, because if Lesbia were quiet and not mindful of his presence, she would be in her right mind (note the unreal condition), but, (3) in fact, she is mindful, she is not in her right mind, and the proof of that is her anger. The final words, **ūritur et loquitur**, with the weight of Catullus' proof behind us, bring the poem full circle: her verbal abuse (**loquitur**) of Catullus is a consequence of the burning passion she feels (**ūritur**) for him.

Catullus 84
Read this poem aloud to your students in Latin. More than any other, this poem shows the importance of sound in conveying meaning. Note how the poem begins with an improperly aspirated word, **chommoda**, and ends with another, **Hīoniōs**. About Arrius nothing is known, but he is clearly the sort of person who does not belong in the sophisticated society of the new poets.

Lines 5–6 and, in particular, the adjective **līber** (5) are the tip-offs that Arrius shares this oratorical pretense with other members of his family and that it is a failed attempt to cover up a humble origin. Humorously, Arrius inherits this verbal impediment socially and genetically, since the habit of aspiration apparently comes strictly from the maternal side of the family.

Catullus 85
This epigram is one of the most famous in Latin literature. It is simple in expression and profound in thought. It has been translated dozens of times, and each translation makes a different commentary on the poem. Ask your students to tell how each of the translations given brings out some particular aspect of the verses. Most translations miss the action in the epigram, which contains eight separate verb forms and no nouns or adjectives. Most translations also miss the starkness of the phrases **id faciam** and **fierī sentiō**, which express the pain of conflicting emotions brilliantly, and they usually create direct objects for **ōdī** or **amō** and thereby give the poem greater specificity than it actually has.

Catullus 86
Lesbia's physical appearance is never described in Catullus' extant verse. Here the reason for that omission is given. Lesbia's beauty is something more than the merely physical. The parallel between lines 1 and 5 strenghthens the contrast between Quintia, who has only some beautiful parts, and Lesbia, who is completely beautiful.

The antithesis between the words **multīs** and **mihi** in line 1 renews the poet's critique of the sensibility of his generation. The gossip of old men in poem 5 and the comparisons made between the woman of the province and Lesbia in poem 43 are two earlier examples of the distance between Catullus' tastes and values and those of society at large.

Catullus 87
Here the words **fidēs** and **foedus** occur again and recall Catullus 76. In fact, these two plain sentences treat the same theme as that poem but more elliptically.

To his translation of poem 87 Walter Landor has added the sentiments of poems 72 and 75. The effect is similar to that of poem 76, which incorporated a variety of different points of view presented elsewhere in shorter, more concise poems. Landor has joined Catullus' extreme physical and emotional devotion (poem 87) to expressions of Lesbia's faithlessness (poems 72 and 75), to show that, in the end, Catullus must endure the extreme suffering that his love for her has caused.

Catullus 92
Here, as in poem 83, Catullus interprets Lesbia's anger as a sign of her love. In this poem, however, he derives "proof" from analyzing feelings. His mistake, then, is in ascribing the same diagnosis of his behavior to hers. Such a projection of oneself onto another blocks true understanding and leads

one further down the path of self-delusion and misrepresentation. The irony of the situation is that the more Lesbia verbally abuses Catullus, the deeper is the conviction that she actually loves him. Verbal and physical abuse between lovers may be understood as symptoms of more deeply rooted, underlying causes, such as jealousy, fear of commitment, alienation, and feelings of enslavement and entrapment.

Catullus 96
All relationships, even marriage, must end. Quintilia and Calvus had an **amīcitia**, which has now been broken by death. Catullus holds out to Calvus the hope that if the mute graves are responsive to human grief (1–4), then Quintilia must derive joy from knowing that Calvus loves her still (5–6). The words **amōrēs** and **amīcitiās**, which end successive lines in the middle of the poem, appear elsewhere in Catullus as mutually supporting conditions of a complete love affair, the passion (**amor**) and a commitment (**amīcitia**) that lasts. See poem 109, where these two words appear at the beginning and end of the poem, indicative of how far apart Catullus and Lesbia are in this matter.

Catullus 101
This beautiful poem is a dirge. The *m*'s, the *n*'s, and the open vowels signified mourning to the Roman ear, and these sounds dominate the elegy. The sadness of this poem, different from the hopeful tone of poem 96, rests on the one-way conversation that Catullus must conduct with his brother. In lines 2–3, Catullus addresses his brother personally (**frāter . . . tē**); in line 4, the truth of the situation washes over the poet, namely, that it is in vain (**nēquīquam**) for him to address his brother and expect a reply since he is really speaking to mute ash (**mūtam . . . cinerem**), not his brother. The pain of his realization is most evident in lines 5–6, where the severing of the bond between the poet and his brother is emphasized by the repetition of the word **mihi**, the strong pronoun **tētē** used in conjunction with the intensifying **ipsum**, and the two words **abstulit** and **adēmpte**, which are weighted with prefixes that stress the action.

The words **heu miser indignē** (6) grow in feeling from a sense of resignation to pity to anger, but the ceremony must continue; the words **nunc tamen intereā** (7) bring us slowly and pensively back to the ritual at hand. The word **tamen** corresponds to **nēquīquam** in line 4. Although communication has been broken off between brothers, tradition demands that Catullus carry out this duty for the dead. The tears will transform the

ancient rite into a living and expressive act of love. The chief difference between this poem and poem 96 is the retreat from any anticipation of what may be felt on the other side; Catullus' brother is left nameless and unresponsive; we only learn what the poet feels. The **dolor** in poem 96 transcends the grave; in poem 101 it stops at the grave.

Catullus 109
This poem expresses Catullus' fondest hope that the promises of love that he hears from Lesbia will be transformed somehow, perhaps with the help of the gods, into a lifelong pact. The problem is that Lesbia is talking about physical love (**amor**), which is neither sustaining nor everlasting.

Horace I.3
Horace appears to be writing a traditional "sendoff" poem for his close friend and fellow poet Vergil. As the genre demands, Horace prays for a safe and secure journey (1–8), but he exploits the tradition to write about the ambitions of mankind.

In examining lines 9–12, we see that they offer not so much a curse on the inventor of sailing as a colorful commentary on human audacity. The clause **Illī rōbur . . . erat** (9–10) may refer to the material outfit of the sailor, but it also suggests the boat that protects him from the elements and the rugged disposition of the dauntless sailor himself. In the clause **quī . . . prīmus** (10–12), the nominatives **quī** and **prīmus** provide a frame, the verb is placed in the center, and chiasmus (**fragilem trucī . . . pelagō ratem**) and antithesis (**fragilem trucī**) are employed to emphasize the inordinate audacity of man's first attempt on the high seas in a flimsy craft. The catalogue of sins and sinners in lines 25–36 follows from a claim by the poet that man has transgressed natural bounds (21–24). The contrast between **deus . . . prūdēns** and **impiae . . . ratēs** in this stanza recalls a traditional Greco-Roman attitude dating back to Hesiod and Homer that human disobedience and disregard for divine ordinances have caused a breach in human and divine relations and are the cause of divine anger and punishment. Horace provides examples of such transgressions by alluding to Prometheus' theft of fire, Pandora's box, Daedalus' flight, and the theft of Cerberus from the underworld by Hercules (27–36). The consequence for humankind is neatly summarized in the final two lines: Jupiter's wrath and thunderbolt.

The relationship between the opening of the poem, a farewell to Vergil, and the remainder of the poem, on human audacity, is open for discussion. One interpretation expressed succinctly by Charles W. Lockyer, Jr. ("Horace's Propempticon and Vergil's Voyage," *The Classical World* 61, 1967, pp. 42–45) suggests that this is a literary propempticon wishing Vergil well on a most daring poetic undertaking, the *Aeneid*. In support of this interpretation, Lockyer and others point in the poem to Vergil's trip to Greece (a pilgrimage to the origins of epic), the presence of Venus, Helen, Aeolus, Hercules, and Daedalus, all of whom appear in the *Aeneid*), and the word **impiae** (23), which touches on one of the major themes of Vergil's epic. The first person plural verb **patimur** (39) may hint at Horace's poetic culpability, too, in bringing down the wrath of ancient Jupiters, namely literary critics and readers.

For discussion of all the odes from Book I and relevant bibliography, see *A Commentary on Horace: Odes Book I*.

Horace I.5

Horace often uses words like tesserae in a mosaic to create visually a picture of what the words are saying. In line 1 the words **multā . . . rosā** literally surround the words **gracilis . . . puer**, which themselves embrace **tē**. Similarly, in line 3, the words **grātō . . . antrō** completely enclose **Pyrrha**. Horace also uses the order of words to emphasize their meaning, as when he juxtaposes **simplex** and **munditiīs** in line 5. In line 1 Horace has made the boy surround and dominate the girl; in line 9, however, the girl, **tē . . . aureā**, surrounds the **crēdulus [puer]**: the placement of words gives a pointed commentary on the changes in the relationship between Pyrrha and the **puer**.

Liquids and fire dominate the imagery of the poem. The pleasant liquid odors of the boy and the golden hair of Pyrrha, whose name derives from the Greek word for fire, in the first stanza are transformed in the second and third stanzas into tears, black storms, and fatal attractions. All the confidence of a successful wooing in the first stanza is shattered in the second. Tears are the boy's reaction to Pyrrha's abrupt change of interest (**[mūtātam] fidem**, 5) and to a world of love that is topsy-turvy (**mūtātōs . . . deōs**, 6). The boy's inexperience in matters of love is vividly evoked by the words **aspera / nigrīs aequora ventīs** (6–7), which are interlocked and represent for us the rude discovery that the boy has made, namely, that love is not all smooth sailing. Finally, a pun on the words **aurae / fallācis** (11–12) that suggests false gold (**aurum fallāx**) ties the storm and Pyrrha's deceit together.

Horace I.9

Horace looks off into the distance and sees Mt. Soracte cold and white in winter's snow, like an old man with white hair. He realizes that he must be the good Epicurean and enjoy life now. He calls for wine, a symbol in these odes of life well lived.

Lines 9–18 provide a recapitulation of Horace's Epicureanism. Thaliarchus is first exhorted not to dwell on the bigger picture, questions such as suffering and death, which, according to Horace, are better left to forces beyond our control and knowledge, i.e., the gods (9). In imagery reminiscent of the opening stanza, the suppression of living elements such as winds and water (10) brings about the hardening of old age and death, symbolized in lines 11–12 by old oaks and cypress trees, which are motionless, like the rivers in the first stanza. Each day lived should be treated as profit (14–15); conversely, time lost on worrying about the future can never be enjoyed or reclaimed. This is especially true in one's youth, when the pleasures of love and physical exertion are still possible (15–16). Horace, in fact, groups fire, wine, winds, hot waters, love, dancing, and the color green over against trees laden with snow, frozen rivers, still cypress and oak trees, and the color white (or gray: **canitiēs**, 17). Thaliarchus is strongly encouraged to embrace the former and to leave discussion of the latter to those, like Horace, nearer the graying age of life.

As in I.5, Horace arranges the order of his words effectively. The first words in nearly all the lines are emphasized, but particularly those in lines 2, 3, 4, 5, 7, and 9. The complicated, interlocked order of words in the last stanza suggests two lovers embracing.

Horace I.11

In the previous poem, Horace turned Thaliarchus away from an external winter scene to the comfort of a warm fire and wine indoors. Had Thaliarchus been meditating on the future and neglecting enjoyment of the present? Clearly, Leuconoe in I.11 is guilty of such investigations into the future ("Babylonian numbers" in lines 2–3). Once again Horace uses nature and mythology (4–6) to express an Epicurean commonplace that human destiny is inscrutable. Our lives (the "sea") are worn down by the years ("winters"), and we can never know when destiny ("Jupiter") serves up our final hour ("the last winter"), which may even be upon us "now."

Lines 6–8 are the exhortation, expressed in wine imagery, to indulge in the present. Compare Catullus 5, lines 7–9, for such a request couched in kisses. The urgency of the present request is reflected in the reverse order in which Horace arranges the wine imagery: tasting is unexpectedly first, then the straining of the wine for sediment, and finally the pruning of the grape vines. Concrete and metaphorical intermingle. The verb **sapere** (6) generally means "to be sensible," but in this context it also connotes its original meaning, "to taste"; the clause vīna liquēs (6) literally refers to the process of removing impurities from the wine, but in keeping with the tenor of the word sapiās it suggests removing the impurities from wrong beliefs and behavior that get in the way of sensible living according to the Epicureans; and the third piece of advice, longer than the previous two and more obviously metaphorical, urges pruning of a hope that stretches too far into the future (6–7).

The urgency of the situation is greater than mere exhortations: time is wasted in even talking about these matters (7–8). Two words make this point. The verb fūgerit (7), in the future perfect, turns the completion of one's life (the word aetās in line 8, unlike tempus, expresses the idea of time in human terms) into a not-so-distant actuality, and the adjective invida (7) catches our attention by reversing the common notion that we are envious of time; instead, time, envious of us, begrudges us what little time we have.

Horace I.14
On the surface this poem is about a ship and expresses a point of view similar to that in Horace I.3. Quintilian believed, however, that the poem was an allegory in which the ship was Rome. Certainly the image of the ship of state was common in ancient poetry and was found, for example, in the works of Alcaeus and Theognis. Reading the poem in this way explains well the real concern the poet expresses for the ship's well-being.

A more controversial interpretation of the poem proposes that the ship be understood as an older woman and acquaintance of Horace who is contemplating new love affairs. In support of this reading, evidence is found in the correspondence between certain words with human references that are used to describe the ship and that could be used for an older woman. Such a woman might have a noble lineage (silvae fīlia nōbilis, 12) but her body has suffered the ravages of time and experience (nūdum . . . latus, 4), her bones creak (antemnae . . . gemant, 6), her clothes are in ill repair (nōn tibi sunt integra lintea, 9), and no cosmetic can hide her age from male companions (nīl . . . fīdit, 14–15). The impulse for such an interpretation comes from the appearance in the last stanza of two words from the love vocabulary of poets: dēsīderium and cūra. In support of such a view, see "The Craft of Horace in Odes I.14," by A. J. Woodman, *Classical Philology* 75 (1980) 60–67; in rebuttal, see "Boats, Women, and Horace Odes I.14," by H. D. Jocelyn, *Classical Philology* 77 (1982) 330–335.

Horace I.22
Although the opening lines of this poem once marked it for inclusion in a canon of serious and moral Latin works, there is evidence throughout that Horace is being playful here. Our first clue is in the third stanza, where the wolf runs from Horace; the reason: the poet is singing. Is it the content of the poem (i.e., love) or the poor quality of the poet's voice that scares off the wolf? The next stanza turns the incident in the Sabine forest into a fairy tale. The wolf becomes a beast of the imagination, more savage than those found long ago either in Horace's birthplace, Apulia, or in exotic Africa, where lions of legendary ferocity dwelt. We are prepared at this point for a further flight of fancy as Horace, fresh from his encounter with the wolf and feeling charmed, confidently orders that he be sent to any region of the world—to the north where all is lifeless without sun or to the south where too much sun has scorched the earth.

Will Horace, like the pure man in the first stanza, be free from anxiety and fear, thanks to a moral perfection? No. The twist at the end of the poem is that the charm of love allows him to make such outrageous claims. The allusion to Sappho and Catullus in lines 23–24, however, must make us wonder whether there is a hidden rebuke of carefree and careless lovers in this poem. Love does not, in fact, protect us from harmful reality, and, as Catullus had revealed, there is a painful difference between the ideal of love and its reality.

Horace I.23
Horace's gentle seduction of Chloe here may be compared with Pyrrha's seduction of the boy in I.5. Both Chloe and the boy are inexperienced at love. The boy stares in wonder at the storm of love (I.5, lines 5–8), and Chloe suffers from physical trembling (8). Chloē is Greek for "twig" or "green shoot" and is here a suitable name for a girl confronting her first sexual experience. The difference between the two situations is nicely expressed in the word order of lines 1 and 9 in each poem. In I.5 Pyrrha has turned the situation of the opening line, where the boy physically and in word order surrounds Pyrrha, to her favor by now mastering the boy (nunc tē fruitur crēdulus aureā). In I.23 Chloe surrounds the poet in line 1, although humorously she avoids him in reality. In line 9 of this poem Horace insists through a negation of such a word order that he is *not* going to control Chloe (nōn ego tē tigris) in the same way that Pyrrha did the young boy.

Horace I.37
This poem celebrates the suicide of Cleopatra in 30 B.C. The history which led up to this event is too

complicated to be recounted in this short space. You are well advised to check the relevant articles in the *The Oxford Classical Dictionary*. Cleopatra's death marked the triumph of Augustus and the end of civil war. Rome celebrated, ecstatic that the wicked queen was dead. In this ode Horace captures the first wild moments of drunken revel when at last Rome was free to dance (**lībero . . . pede**), but he also conveys in sober tones the dignity of the fallen queen. He contrasts the joyful drinking of line 1 with the final deadly drink that Cleopatra took. Rome defeated a great person, who fought, lost, and then faced death with Stoic fortitude. So great was this woman that a joyful celebration seems almost out of place.

For an excellent analysis of this poem, see *The Odes of Horace: A Critical Study*, pp. 88–98.

Horace I.38

This short poem on the pleasures of the simple myrtle tests our willingness to accept Horace at face value or to probe for deeper and perhaps disguised meanings. For instance, in some poems Horace openly discusses his evaluation of himself as a poet (e.g., I.1, not included in this selection, and III.30), and in others he may do so obliquely. If we see in the words **Persicōs . . . apparātūs** (1) a reference on the level of ancient literary criticism to prose or poetry that is overblown and excessive, then Horace is declaring that he is a worthy practitioner of a spare style, the value of which lies in its tightly woven artistry. The simple myrtle (5) and the dense vine (**artā / vīte**, 7–8), with its pun on **ars, artis**, are our clues for this interpretation.

The poem may also be an invitation to a youthful companion to forsake the allurements of the city and of a crowd whose excessive refinements miss the simple pleasures of life. The word **morētur** (4) may be a pun on **morietur**; postponement of simple pleasures in pursuit of a precious rose, that may or may not be found blooming late in the season, is a death warrant to the enjoyment of youth. In the second stanza, a pun on **vīte** (8), hinting at the word **vīta**, accents Horace's advice to the young man that he should join Horace in a leisure that puts the highest premium on life, adumbrated in the concluding word **bibentem**.

Horace II.3

The second stanza of this poem refers to the human condition and the third to the natural world, yet the two stanzas are intimately connected by the attributes they share. The unhappy life in line 5 is reflected in the laboring waters in lines 11–12; the life of contentment in lines 6–8 is reflected in the pleasant shade in lines 9–11. Furthermore,

the pleasures that Horace calls for in lines 13–14 have lines 6–8 and 9–11 as their antecedent; the grim reminder of the dark threads of the Fates in line 16 is anticipated by the word **maestus** (5), the future perfect **vīxeris** (5), and the adjective **fugāx** (12), the root of which means "to flee" and which is a frequent reminder in Horace of life's short duration.

The second half of the poem contains a darker message than the first. Lines 21–24 balance the rich man with the poor man as lines 5–8 did for the sad man and the happy man, but in the final stanza all differences are extinguished and all people are subject to death. The placement of **omnēs** and **omnium** at the beginning and end of line 25 effectively reduces everyone to the same mortal condition. The unusual elision of the words **aeternum** and **exsilium** (27–28) makes them seem a single term, somehow more frightening.

As Dellius is strongly urged in the first stanza to attain a balance in his life, so the deftly worded lines and balanced thoughts and images of this poem can be seen in the parallel phrasing, repetition, and rhetorical devices that are used. Here are some examples: **rēbus in arduīs / . . . nōn secus in bonīs** (1–2); **seu . . . vīxeris, / seu . . . beāris** (5–7); **pīnus ingēns albaque pōpulus** (9; chiasmus); **oblīquō labōrat / lympha fugāx trepidāre rīvō** (11–12; ablative, verb, nominative, verb, ablative); **Hūc vīna et unguenta et nimium brevīs / . . . dum rēs et aetās et sorōrum** (13–15); **Cēdēs . . . cēdēs** (17–19); **Dīvesne . . . ab Inachō, / . . . an pauper . . . / dē gente** (21–23).

For further discussion of this and the remaining odes (and for bibliography on them), see E. Fraenkel's *Horace*.

Horace II.14

This poem may be fruitfully compared with II.3. Although the latter poem to Dellius concluded with a vision of human mortality, earlier parts of the poem conceded to humankind the prospect of happiness and the enjoyment of life's pleasures. Familiar Horatian reminders of the **carpe diem** theme were present in that poem, too, through words for grass, wine, perfume, and roses. Poem II.14, in comparison, is relentless in its message to Postumus that death is inevitable and unavoidable; the final stanza of II.3 has been fleshed out and made into a single poem here.

The full power of this poem lies in the number of ways in which Horace surveys his one theme, the inevitability of death. The opening line effectively anticipates the theme. The sad and emphatic interjection **ēheu** is followed by the adjective **fugācēs**, which announces the quick flight of time.

The name Postumus is not only placed in the first line (Horace usually postpones the name of the addressee until later in the poem) but is also repeated to convey the urgency of the message and the sympathy for the victim, which, in this case, is all of us. Lines 2–7 expose a human weakness in thinking that any action can be taken against death. Pietās, the observance of one's duty toward human and divine, highly prized by the Romans, does not stop the onslaught of old age and death; daily sacrifices of three hundred bulls to Pluto—an absurd act of homage to the god of the underworld and an expensive one, too—cannot stop death, either. The power of death becomes greater when we learn who inhabits the underworld: mythological strongarming criminals such as Tityus and Geryon (8). Poor Postumus also learns who his companions in Hades will be.

An examination of the subversion of life-giving images in this poem also indicates the seriousness of Horace's theme. The years "flow" away, Pluto is "tearless," the "bull" is sacrificed to Pluto, the "waters" are Stygian or life threatening, the "winds" are harmful, the "cypress tree" accompanies one to the grave, and the "wine"—the foremost symbol of carpe diem—that Postumus never enjoyed will stain the pavement like blood and be wasted by the heir.

Finally, the three passive periphrastic constructions in this poem (11, 17, and 21) are integral to the message that death is obligatory. This is a fine example of grammar reinforcing meaning.

Horace III.13
Lines 1–12 contain strong and vivid contrasts. The fountain is translucent, placid, cold, and refreshing; the goat has swelling horns, hot red blood, and physical movement. The fountain is an object of worship, toasted with wine and flowers; the goat is sacrificed, cut off from a full life of celebration in love and battle. The emphatic placement of the word frūstrā (6) begins to sway our sympathy toward the goat. The third stanza, however, justifies for us the status of the fountain as we learn that it has received the goat so that it may refresh the herd of bulls.

One's understanding of lines 1–12 rests on whether one treats the fountain and goat literally, as metaphors for something else, or as symbols that are open-ended. If we take this poem as a poet's reflection on his work and the process of poetic creation, the fountain becomes a metaphor for art that transforms life (the goat) into a timeless artifact that is immune to the elements (9) and uplifting (10–12). The fountain and the goat may also reach out beyond art to speak to us about seemingly unjust sacrifices in nature and in life,

sacrifices that make sense only in a larger picture. Here, for instance, the cold waters that are stained with the innocent blood of a goat become amābile in line 10 once it is understood that the fountain—in whatever symbolic role it may have—is a source of life and renewal for the living.

The final stanza more clearly focuses on the power of the artist to elevate his or her subject. In a surprising reversal, Horace boldly proclaims that he the artist will make this obscure fountain famous and not, as the poetic tradition had normally expressed it, become a famous poet by drinking the waters of an inspiring fountain (the nōbilēs fontēs referred to in line 13). The simple beauty of lines 14–16 with their modulating c, m, and l sounds attests to the power of the poet and also deepens our appreciation for the fountain, which now, in the manner of great poetry, is deeply rooted with an oak tree and is dynamic (dēsiliunt) and expressive (loquācēs) as well.

Horace III.30
This poem is an open exploration of the poet's artistic worth. Horace's work will not be subject to the natural elements that obliterate metals of the earth and human constructions, such as pyramids. The order of the elements moves from the most concrete to the abstract and evanescent, time's flight (1–5).

Horace links his fame in lines 6–9 with two symbols of Rome's greatness, the Capitolium and the priestly tradition. What seems to be a contradiction here between Horace's opening claim that his work will outlast all physical expressions of a nation's power, such as a pyramid, and his reliance on the survival of such expressions for his fame, may be resolved by taking Horace's vision as similar in nature to Jupiter's promise to Venus in Vergil's Aeneid I.278 (hīs ego nec mētās rērum nec tempora pōnō, "I set neither limits nor constraints of time on them") or to Rome's bequeathment to the future, for as long as Rome's greatness and institutions are kept alive by succeeding generations, there will be an appreciative audience for Horace's work.

Lines 10–14 surprise us by their humility in contrast with the previous lines. Horace's fame begins in Apulia, where a raging river (10) vies with the parched earth (11). This oxymoron prepares us for the striking words ex humilī potēns / prīnceps (12–13) that describe Apulia's favorite son. In addition to expecting fame in the Italian hinterlands, Horace insists that his fame will rest not on the beauty or themes of his work but on the successful transposition of Sappho and Alcaeus to Roman poetry and meter (13–14). By forging the link between Greek and Roman lyric poetry, Horace feels entitled at the end to the Delphic laurel wreath (15–16).

Horace IV.7

The arrival of spring is treated in various ways by Catullus and Horace. Good comparisons may be made among Catullus 46, Horace I.9, I.23, and IV.7. Poem IV.7 opens with a fresh and dynamic description of the passage of winter and the return of spring. The Graces and Nymphs give the occasion a timeless quality as well. We are, in fact, seduced by the beauty of the divinities and their timeless play into forgetting our own mortality. Horace abruptly reminds us of the sad truth in line 7 by inverting the indirect command (nē spērēs, monet instead of monet nē spērēs) and by placing the deluding word immortālia outside the clause and first in the line. The poem takes a dark turn from here to the end.

The arrival of spring had falsely excited us in lines 1–6; in truth, the same spring that excited Catullus in poem 46, that evoked an image of adolescent playfulness in Horace I.9, and that presaged Chloe's coming-of-age in I.23 will now be treated as part of the inexorable revolution of seasons leading to lifeless winter (brūma . . . iners, 12), in other words, our death.

In the middle of the poem (13–16) and in the words cum semel occideris (21) Horace alludes to Catullus 5, lines 4–6. In Catullus, the fact that we are not immortal like the sun prompted an urgent request for countless kisses to deceive ourselves into a feeling of absoluteness; Horace taunts us instead. The moons (a darker, more nocturnal metaphor than the suns in Catullus), which regenerate, are called swift, to remind us of the swift *unregenerative* nature of our own lives, and we are reminded here and at the end of the poem through legendary and mythological examples that much greater and more worthy people than we could not escape death, so why deceive ourselves into thinking otherwise.

Lines 17–24 review themes that have appeared elsewhere in Horace. The uncertainty of tomorrow (17–18) appeared in Horace I.9, lines 13–15, and in I.11, lines 1–6; the figure of the heir (19–20), in II.3, lines 19–20, and in II.14, lines 25–28; and the futility of pietās to reverse death (23–24), in II.14, lines 2–4. Poem IV.7 stands beside II.14 as a classic poem that exemplifies the phrase mementō morī, "be mindful of dying."

* * *

TRANSLATIONS

Catullus 5

Let us live, my Lesbia, and let us love, and let us value all the stories of sterner old men at a single penny. Suns can set and return. By us, when once our short light has set, a single continuous night must be slept. Give me a thousand kisses, then a hundred, then another thousand, then a second hundred, then constantly another thousand, then a hundred. Then, when we will have made many thousands, we will stir them up so we may not know and so no evil person may be able to cast spells when he knows there exists such a great number of kisses.

Catullus 8

Wretched Catullus, cease being a fool and what you see to have perished consider it lost. Once suns glittered brilliant for you, when you kept on coming where the girl was leading, loved by me as much as no girl will be loved. There, when those many mirthful things were done which you wanted and the girl did not *not* want, truly suns glittered brilliant for you. Now she is no longer willing; you, powerless one, be unwilling too. Do not pursue her who flees, nor live wretchedly, but with stubborn mind persist. Be firm. Farewell, girl. Now Catullus is firm. Neither will he seek you nor will he ask an unwilling you. But you will grieve when you will not be asked. Wretch, woe on you! What life is left for you? Who will come to you now? To whom will you seem pretty? Whom will you love now? Whose will you be said to be? Whom will you kiss? Whose tiny lips will you nibble? But you, Catullus, resolved, be firm.

Catullus 12

Asinius Marrucinus, you do not use your left hand prettily; in tipsy jest you take away the napkins of the more careless. Do you think that this is witty? It escapes you, fool: the act is ever so filthy and uncharming. You do not believe me? Believe Pollio, your brother, who would wish that your thefts be exchanged for even a talent. For he is a boy stuffed with charms and wit. Therefore, either expect three hundred hendecasyllables or return to me my napkin that moves me not because of its value but because it is a souvenir of my friend. For Fabullus and Veranius sent Saetaban napkins from Spain to me for a gift. I must love these things as I love Fabullus and my little Veranius.

Catullus 13

You will dine well at my house, my Fabullus, in a few days, if the gods favor you, if you bring with you a good and plentiful meal along with a fair girl and wine and wit and all [kinds of] laughters. If, I say, you bring these things, my charming one, you will dine well; for your Catullus' wallet is full of cobwebs. But in return you will receive pure love or what is more attractive and more elegant; for I will give a perfume that the Venuses and Cupids gave my girl. When you smell it, you will ask the gods that they make you, Fabullus, all nose.

Catullus 22

That Suffenus whom you know well, Varus, is charming and witty and urbane, and the same man makes very, very many verses. I think a thousand or ten thousand or more have been written by him. These things have not been recorded, as is usual, on a palimpsest. The sheets are royal, the rolls are new, the knobs are new, the straps on the jacket are red, all things have been ruled with lead and smoothed with pumice. When you read these things, that pretty and sophisticated Suffenus seems again only a goatherd or ditch digger. He is so greatly different and changed. Why are we to think this is? He who was just now a wit—or if anything seems more skillful than this—, the same one is less clever than the unclever country bumpkin, as soon as he has touched poems. And the same man is never as happy as when he writes poems. He so rejoices in himself and so marvels at himself. Of course, we all are deceived in the same way, nor is there any one whom you are not able to see as a Suffenus in some situation. One's own fault is assigned to each. But we do not see the part of the wallet that is on the back.

Catullus 43

Hello, girl with neither the littlest nose nor pretty foot, nor black eyes nor long fingers nor dry lips nor, to be sure, with too elegant a tongue. She is the girlfriend of the rake of Formiae. Does the province say you are pretty? Is my Lesbia compared with you? O tasteless and witless age!

Catullus 46

Now spring brings back the chilly warmths. Now the rage of the equinoctial sky becomes silent with the pleasant airs of Zephyr. Let the Phrygian fields be abandoned, Catullus, and the rich territory of hot Nicaea. Let us fly to the famous cities of Asia. Already my mind trembling in anticipation wants to wander, my feet happy in their eagerness begin to become alive. Farewell, O sweet company of friends, who came far from home at the same time but whom different roads carry back variously.

Catullus 49

O most eloquent of the grandsons of Romulus, however many there are, however many there have been, however many there will be hereafter in other years, Marcus Tullius. Catullus the worst poet of all gives you the greatest thanks. He is as much the worst poet of all as you are the best patron of all.

Catullus 51

That one seems to me to be equal to a god. That one, if it is right, seems to surpass the gods, who, sitting opposite, repeatedly looks at and hears you sweetly laughing. This situation rips all senses from wretched me. For as soon as I have looked at you, Lesbia, nothing remains for me. But my tongue grows numb, a fine flame drips down my joints, my ears ring with their very sound, my eyes are covered by twin nights. Leisure, Catullus, is an annoyance to you. You rejoice in leisure and you carry on too much. Leisure has destroyed kings and wealthy cities before.

Catullus 53

I laughed just now at someone from the crowd who, when my Calvus had explained marvelously the charges against Vatinius, raising up his arms, said these words in admiration, "Great Gods, what an eloquent little squirt!"

Catullus 70

My woman says she prefers not to marry anyone except me, not if Jupiter himself should seek her. So she says. But it is necessary to write what a woman says to a lusting lover on wind and swift water.

Catullus 72

You said once that you knew only Catullus, Lesbia, and that you did not want to hold Jupiter instead of me. I loved you then not only as the crowd loves its girlfriend but as a father loves his sons and sons-in-law. Now I know you. Therefore, although I burn more grievously, you are nevertheless much cheaper and more contemptible to me. How is this possible, you say? Because such an injury forces a lover to love more but to like less.

Catullus 73

Cease to want to deserve well anything from anyone or to think that anyone can be made dutiful. All things are unappreciated. It is of no advantage to have done anything kindly. Rather it is even boring and gets in the way more, as it does for me whom no one presses more heavily or more bitterly than he who lately had me as his one and only friend.

Catullus 75
My mind has been brought down to here by your fault, Lesbia, and has so destroyed itself because of its own duty, that no longer can it be fond of you, if you should do the best things, or cease to love, if you should do all things.

Catullus 76
If there is any pleasure for a man remembering earlier good deeds when he thinks that he is dutiful and has not violated any trust and has not misused any divine agreement with the gods for the purpose of deceiving men, then many joys, Catullus, remain prepared in a long life for you from this ungrateful love. For whatsoever things men can say or do well for anyone, these things have been said and done by you. All these things entrusted to an ungrateful mind have perished. Therefore, why do you torture yourself any more? Why do you not grow strong in your mind and from there bring yourself back and cease to be wretched even if the gods are unwilling? It is difficult to lay aside a long love suddenly. It is difficult. But do this in some way. This alone is salvation. This must be accomplished by you. Do this whether it is not possible or whether it is. O gods, if yours is to show mercy or, if ever you have brought a last bit of help to any at the moment of death itself, look at wretched me and, if I have lived life purely, take this plague and destruction from me, which, creeping like a numbness into the deepest joints, drives out joys from all my soul. I no longer seek this, that she love me in return or, what is not possible, that she want to be chaste. I myself wish to be healthy and to put aside this foul sickness. O gods, render me this for my dutifulness.

Catullus 83
Lesbia curses me much while her husband is present. This is the greatest joy for that fool. Mule, do you feel nothing? If she, forgetful of me, were silent, she would be uninfected [by love]. Now because she snarls and curses, she not only remembers but, what is a much more pointed circumstance, she is angered. That is, she burns and she speaks.

Catullus 84
Arrius used to say "hadvantages" if ever he wanted to say advantages, and "hambushes" for ambushes. And then he expected that he had spoken marvelously when, as much as he was able, he had said "hambushes." His mother, his free uncle, and his maternal grandmother and grandfather had spoken this way. When he was sent into Syria, everybody's ears rested. They heard these same words gently and lightly and did not fear such words for themselves afterwards, when suddenly frightful news was brought that the Ionian Sea, after Arrius had gone there, was no longer the Ionian but the "Hionian" Sea.

Catullus 85
I hate and I love. Why I do this, perhaps you ask? I don't know. But I feel it is happening and I am tortured.

Catullus 86
Quintia is gorgeous to many. To me she is fair, tall, upright: I do agree on these individual points. I deny that she is totally beautiful, for no charm, no spark of wit is in her whole body. Lesbia is gorgeous: she is completely beautiful; she alone steals all loves away from all.

Catullus 87
No woman can truly say that she has been loved as much as my Lesbia has been loved by me. No trust so great has ever existed in any agreement as was found in love of you on my part.

Catullus 92
Lesbia is always cursing me and is never silent about me. Let me perish, unless Lesbia loves me. By what proof [do I say this]? Because my circumstances are just the same. I constantly complain about her. But let me perish unless I love her.

Catullus 96
If anything pleasing or acceptable can happen to mute tombs from our grief, Calvus, with which longing we make new our friendships once let go, then an untimely death is not so great a grief for Quintilia as the joy she takes in your love.

Catullus 101
Carried through many peoples and through many seas, I reach these wretched last rites, brother, to present you with death's due and address mute ash in vain, since fortune has wrenched you yourself from me. Alas, wretched brother unworthily taken away from me, now, nevertheless, for the moment these things which by ancient ancestral custom have been handed down in sad duty at the last rites, take them much dripping with a brother's tears. And now and forever, hail and farewell.

Catullus 109
You promise, my life, that this love of ours will be pleasant and perpetual between us. Great gods, make it that she promises truly and speaks this sincerely and from the heart so that it is allowed

for us in our whole life to draw out this eternal compact of alliance.

Horace I.3

So let the powerful goddess of Cyprus, let Helen's brothers, the gleaming constellations, and, let the king of the winds, while the other [winds] are shut in except for Iapyx, rule you, o ship, you who owe up the one entrusted to you—Vergil. May you deliver him safe to Attic boundaries, I pray, and save half my soul. He had oak and triple bronze around his chest, who was first to entrust a breakable craft to the crushing sea and was the first not to fear the South Wind fighting headlong with the North Wind, nor the sad Hyades nor the madness of Notus, than which there is no greater judge of the Adriatic, whether he wants to raise or to settle the seas. What approach of Death did he fear, who saw with dry eyes floating wonders, who saw the swollen seas and the notorious rock of Acroceraunia? In vain did god wisely cut apart the lands with incompatible ocean if nevertheless the wicked boats leap across the waters, which ought not be touched. Bold to endure all things, the human race has rushed through forbidden crime. The bold race of Iapetus with evil deceit brought fire to the nations. After the removal of fire from its heavenly home, famine and a new battalion of fevers lay upon the lands. The previously slow inevitability of distant death picked up its pace. Daedalus tried the empty air, although feathers had not been given to man. The Herculean labor broke through Acheron. There is nothing too difficult for mortals. We seek heaven itself because of foolishness and through our crime we do not allow Jupiter to lay aside his angry thunderbolts.

Horace I.5

What slender boy amid many a rose, drenched in fluid fragrances, presses you, Pyrrha, below in the pleasing grotto? For whom do you tie back your yellow hair, plain in your ornaments? Alas! How often will he lament your trust and the changed gods and in his inexperience will he wonder at the seas, harsh because of the black winds. He now trustingly enjoys you, who are golden. Unaware of the deceitful breeze, he expects that you will be always free, always lovable. Wretched are those for whom you glitter untried. The sacred wall with votive tablet shows that I have hung wet garments for the powerful god of the sea.

Horace I.9

You see how Mt. Soracte stands brilliant in deep snow and how no longer the laboring woods support their burden and how the rivers stand with sharp ice. Placing logs abundantly upon the hearth, break up the cold and more kindly pour out four-year-old wine, Thaliarchus, from the Sabine jar. Leave the rest to the gods; as soon as they have calmed the winds battling on the feverish sea, neither the ancient cypresses nor the ash trees are shaken. Avoid learning what tomorrow will be, and, what days soever Fate gives, count for gain. And do not, while a boy, scorn sweet loves or dances, while morose hoariness is absent from you in the bloom of youth. Now let both field and public squares and the gentle whispers beneath the night and now the pleasing laughter, the betrayer of the hiding girl from the inner corner, and the pledge ripped from her arms or ineptly grasping finger be sought again at the established time.

Horace I.11

Do not ask—it is wrong to know—what end to me, what end to you, the gods have given, Leuconoe, and do not try the Babylonian numbers. How [much] better [it is] to endure, whatever will be, whether Jupiter allots more winters or [this] last, which wears out the Etruscan seas upon the opposing rocks. Be wise, strain wines, from brief space cut away long expectation. While we were speaking, jealous age will have fled. Pluck the day, believing as little as possible in the time to come.

Horace I.14

O ship, new waves will bring you back onto the sea. Oh, what are you doing? Bravely seize the port. Do you not see that your side is bare of oars and that your mast has been wounded by the quick South Wind and that your yardarm groans and that without ropes the craft can hardly endure the more commanding sea? You do not have whole sails. You do not have gods whom you may call when pressed again by evil. Although you are a Pontic pine, a daughter of a noble forest, you boast a useless race and name, and the frightened sailor does not trust your painted sterns. You, unless you owe sport to the winds, beware. You, who were an anxious annoyance to me a while ago but are now a desire and a not inconsiderable concern, avoid the waters poured amid the shining Cyclades.

Horace I.22

He who is blameless in life and free from crime does not need Moorish darts nor bow nor quiver heavy with poisoned arrows, Fuscus, whether he is about to make his way through the hot Syrtes, the inhospitable Causcasus or the places which the storied Hydaspes laps. For a wolf in a Sabine wood fled me defenseless, while I was singing my Lalage and was wandering beyond the boundary with my cares put aside. Such a monster military Daunias in the wide oak forests does not nourish nor does Juba's land, barren nurse of lions, give birth to. Place me in inactive fields where no tree is brought to life again by summer breeze, a side of the world which clouds and an evil sky press. Place me beneath the chariot of too close a sun in a land denied to homes; I shall love Lalage, sweetly laughing, sweetly speaking.

Horace I.23

Chloe, you avoid me like a fawn seeking its mother on the roadless mountains, frightened with empty fear of winds and forest. For whether the arrival of spring has shivered in the shaking leaves or the green lizards have moved the bush, she trembles in heart and knees. And yet I do not follow as a fierce tiger or a Gaetulian lion to break you. Finally cease to follow your mother, you who are ready for a man.

Horace I.37

Now there must be drinking, now the earth must be struck with a free foot, now it was time to decorate the couch of the gods for Salian feasts, friends. Before it was wrong to bring out the Caecuban wine from ancestral cellars while a queen was preparing mad ruin for the Capitol and a funeral for the empire along with a tainted herd of men foul with sickness, a queen mad to hope for anything and drunk with sweet fortune. But a single ship, barely saved from the fires, diminished her rage, and Caesar drove back her mind, maddened with Mareotic wine, to true fears, pressing toward her flying from Italy with oars, as a hawk presses on soft doves or the quick hunter presses on the rabbit on the plains of snowy Thessaly, in order that he might give the deadly monstrosity to chains. Seeking to die more nobly, she did not dread the sword like a woman nor seek obscure shores with a quick fleet. Daring to gaze with a serene countenance upon her palace lying in ruin, and brave to fondle harsh serpents so that she might drink in black poison with her body, [she was] fiercer because death had been resolved upon, of course, begrudging the wild Librunian ships that she as a private citizen be led away—no humble woman—in a haughty triumph.

Horace I.38

I hate Persian falderal, boy. Crowns woven with lime bark are not pleasing. Do not search in what places the late rose may linger. Do not add anything to the plain myrtle, you [who are] fussy with concern. The myrtle does indeed suit you, a servant, and me who am drinking beneath the dense vine.

Horace II.3

Remember to keep a level head in difficult circumstances just as, in good circumstances, you keep your head unaffected by unusual happiness, you, Dellius, who will die, whether you live mournfully at every moment or make yourself happy lying on distant grass through festive days with a choice brand of Falernian. To what end do the large pine and white poplar love to ally with branches their friendly shade? Why does the fleeing water toil against the sloping stream? Order [someone] to bring wines and perfumes and the too brief bloom of the pleasant rose here, while circumstances and summer and the black thread of the three sisters allow. You will depart from the groves and home and estate that you bought, which the yellow Tiber washes. You will depart and your heir will have control over the wealth piled up high. It does not matter whether you linger [in life] as a rich son from old Inachus or a poor man from the lowliest family under heaven, you [will be] a victim of Orcus who has no mercy. We are all driven to the same place. Sooner or later, the lot of all is turned by the urn, about to come forth [from the urn] and to place us into the eternal exile of [Charon's] craft.

Horace II.14

Alas, Postumus, Postumus, the fleeing years slip by and dutifulness will not bring delay to wrinkles or pressing old age and unconquerable death not if, however many days pass by, you please tearless Pluto with three hundred bulls, [Pluto] who confines triple-bodied Geryon and Tityon with sad water that must be sailed, of course, by all of us who feed on earth's product, whether we will be kings or poor farmers. In vain we will avoid bloody war and the broken waves of the noisy Adriatic. In vain we will fear the South Wind harmful to our bodies throughout the autumn. The black Cocytos wandering with sluggish stream and the notorious race of Danaus and Sisyphus, son of Aeolus, damned to long labor, must be seen. The earth must be abandoned, and home and pleasing wife. And, of those trees that you are cultivating, none will follow you, their master for a brief time, except the hated cypresses. A more worthy heir will consume your Caecuban wine kept with a hundred keys and will stain the pavement with proud, pure wine, better than the feasts of pontifices.

Horace III.13

O spring of Bandusia, more lustrous than glass, worthy of sweet wine, not without flowers, you will be presented tomorrow with a kid whose forehead, swollen with his first horns, marks him both for love and for battles—in vain. For the offspring of the wanton herd will stain the cold streams with red blood for you. The fierce hour of the burning dog star does not know how to touch you. You offer lovable cold to the bulls weary because of the plow and to the wandering herd. You will become one of the noble springs while I sing that an oak has been placed on hollow rocks from which leap forth your babbling waters.

Horace III.30

I have raised a monument more lasting than bronze, higher than the royal site of the pyramids, which consuming rain and the raging North Wind cannot destroy, nor the uncountable sequence of the years and the flight of time. I shall not die altogether, and a great part of me will avoid Libitina. I shall constantly grow fresh with later praise so long as the priest with silent maiden climbs the Capitoline. Influential from a lowly station, I shall be called the first, where the forceful Aufidus roars and where Daunus, poor in water, ruled over a rural people, to have fit Aeolic song to Italian meters. Take pride earned by achievements and willingly crown my hair with Delphic laurel, Melpomene.

Horace IV.7

The snows have fled; the grass returns to the plains and the leaves to the trees. The earth changes and the subsiding rivers cease to overflow their banks. With the nymphs and her twin sisters, Grace dares naked to lead a chorus. The year and the hour which seize the kind day advise that you not hope for deathless things. Coldness becomes soft because of the West Wind and summer tramples on spring, [summer] about to perish as soon as fruit-bearing fall pours forth fruit, and lifeless winter soon returns. Nevertheless, quick moons repair heavenly losses, but when we go down to where dutiful Aeneas, to where rich Tullus and Ancus [have gone], we are dust and shadow. Who knows whether the gods above place tomorrow next to today? All things that you give to your own soul will escape the greedy hands of your heir. When once you die and Minos makes splendid judgments about you, not your race, not your eloquence, not your dutifulness will restore you. For Diana does not free virtuous Hippolytus from the lower shadows, nor does Theseus prevail to break apart the chains of Lethe for dear Pirithous.

*   *   *

BIBLIOGRAPHY

Editions of Catullus and Horace

Catulli Carmina I–XI, by G. Lawall. Longman Inc., White Plains, NY, 1983.
Catullus, by C. J. Fordyce. Oxford University Press, Oxford and New York, NY, 1961.
Catullus: A Critical Edition, by D. F. S. Thomson. University of North Carolina Press, Chapel Hill, NC, 1978.
Catullus: The Poems, by K. Quinn. St. Martin's Press, New York, NY, 1970.
The Poems of Catullus: A Teaching Text, by P. Y. Forsyth. University Press of America, Lanham, MD, 1986.
A Commentary on Horace's Odes: Book 1, by R. G. M. Nisbet and M. Hubbard. Oxford University Press, Oxford and New York, NY, 1970.
A Commentary on Horace's Odes: Book 2, by R. G. M. Nisbet and M. Hubbard. Oxford University Press, Oxford and New York, NY, 1978.
Horace: Odes and Epodes, by C. E. Bennett and J. C. Rolfe. Aristide D. Caratzas, Publisher, New Rochelle, NY, 1977.
Horace: The Odes, by K. Quinn. St. Martin's Press, New York, NY, 1982.
Horatius: Opera, ed. by F. Klingner. Teubner, Leipzig, 1970.

Studies on Catullus

Catullus, by J. Ferguson. Coronado Press, Lawrence, KS, 1985. A series of essays on individual poems. Although repeating much from other sources, this book provides valuable observations about Catullus' use of sound.
Catullus and His Influence, by K. P. Harrington. Cooper Square; Littlefield, Adams and Co., Totowa, NJ, 1930. A dated but still valuable study of how later poets received Catullus' work into their own writings.
Catullus and the Traditions of Ancient Poetry, by A. L. Wheeler. University of California Press, Berkeley, CA, 1934. Places the poems of Catullus in the context of Hellenistic poetry and offers valuable insights on particular poems.
Catullus: An Interpretation, by K. Quinn. Harper and Row, London, 1973. A thorough study of the entire Catullian corpus and a consideration of major problems connected with the text. This book should be used in conjunction with Quinn's commentary (Catullus: The Poems, for which, see above).

Catullus: A Reader's Guide, by S. G. P. Small. University Press of America, Lanham, MD, 1983.

Gaius Valerius Catullus: A Systematic Bibliography, by J. P. Holoka. Garland Publishing, Inc., New York, NY, 1985. The latest and most complete bibliography on Catullus. It lists works both by topic and by poem.

Sexuality in Catullus, by B. Arkins. Georg Olms Verlag, Hildesheim, Zurich, and New York, NY, 1982. An intelligent treatment of a difficult problem in Catullian criticism, which every reader, and every teacher even more, must consider.

The Catullan Revolution, by K. Quinn. Melbourne University Press, Melbourne, 1959; revised edition W. Heffer and Sons, Ltd., London, 1969. Contends that Catullus introduced many of the techniques, themes, and ideas that became central to the Roman lyric tradition.

The Lyric Genius of Catullus, by E. Havelock. Basil Blackwell, Oxford, 1939. A brilliant consideration of the historicity of Lesbia and a discussion of the biographical fallacy that so often plagues criticism of Catullus.

Three Classical Poets: Sappho, Catullus, and Juvenal, by R. Jenkyns. Harvard University Press, Cambridge, MA, 1982. An interesting essay on Catullus' poetry that casts light on the poet's erotic and satiric elements by comparison with two of antiquity's masters.

Studies on Horace

Horace, ed. by C. D. N. Costa. Routledge and Kegan Paul, London, 1973. A series of essays of varying usefulness. See particularly M. Hubbard's "The Odes" and D. West's "Horace's Poetic Technique in the Odes."

Horace, by E. Fraenkel. Oxford University Press, Oxford and New York, NY, 1957. A magisterial study of the entire Horatian corpus and of the vītae Horātiī. Abundant bibliography appears on nearly every page. Individual works are analyzed in such detail that this book can often function as a commentary.

Horace, by J. Perret (translated by B. Humez). New York University Press, New York, NY, 1964. A readable critical overview of Horace's life and works.

The Odes of Horace: A Critical Study, by S. Commager. Yale University Press, New Haven, CT, 1962. An investigation of major images, themes, and structural elements in the odes; a ground-breaking book for the study of Horace's poetry.

The Structure of Horace's Odes, by N. E. Collinge. Oxford University Press, Oxford and New York, NY, 1961. A discussion of various ways to approach the structure of individual odes and groups of odes. Still valuable despite the advances found in Commager (above) and Santirocco (below).

Unity and Design in Horace's Odes, by M. S. Santirocco. The University of North Carolina Press, Chapel Hill, NC, 1986. An important study, which demonstrates that Horace arranged the odes in each book carefully and that this organization influences the reading and understanding of the individual poems.

Word, Sound, and Image in the Odes of Horace, by M. O. Lee. The University of Michigan Press, Ann Arbor, MI, 1969. Shows how sound—the music of the odes—relates to, reinforces, and indeed shapes the meaning of the poetry.

Additional Works Useful in the Study of Latin Lyric

Critical Essays on Roman Literature: Elegy and Lyric, ed. by J. P. Sullivan. Routledge and Kegan Paul, London, 1961. See particularly K. Quinn's "Docte Catulle" and R. G. M. Nisbet's "Romanae Fidicen Lyrae: The Odes of Horace."

Golden Latin Artistry, by L. P. Wilkinson. Cambridge University Press, Cambridge and New York, NY, 1963.

Intellectual Life in the Late Roman Republic, by E. Rawson. The Johns Hopkins University Press, Baltimore, MD, 1985.

Love in Ancient Rome, by P. Grimal (translated by A. Train, Jr.). University of Oklahoma Press, Norman, OK, 1986.

The Latin Love Elegy, by Georg Luck. Methuen and Co., London, 1959.

The Latin Love Poets from Catullus to Horace, by R. O. A. M. Lyne. Oxford University Press, Oxford and New York, NY, 1980.

The Latin Sexual Vocabulary, by J. N. Adams. The Johns Hopkins University Press, Baltimore, MD, 1982.

The Meters of Greek and Latin Poetry, by J. W. Halporn, M. Ostwald, and T. G. Rosenmeyer. University of Oklahoma Press, Norman, OK, revised ed., 1980.

The Pronunciation and Reading of Classical Latin: A Practical Guide, by Stephen G. Daitz. Jeffrey Norton Publishers, Inc., Guilford, CT, 1984.